Canadian Special Publication of Fisheries and Aquatic Sciences 80

The Atlantic Salmon in the History of North America

R. W. Dunfield

Department of Fisheries and Oceans
Freshwater and Anadromous Division
Scotia–Fundy Region
Halifax, N.S. B3J 2S7

DEPARTMENT OF FISHERIES AND OCEANS
Ottawa 1985

Published by   Publié par

 Fisheries   Pêches
and Oceans   et Océans

Scientific Information   Direction de l'information
and Publications Branch   et des publications scientifiques

Ottawa K1A 0E6

Canada: $11.95   Cat. No. Fs 41-31/80E
Other countries: $14.35   ISBN 0-660-11923-4
ISSN 0706-6481

Price subject to change without notice

Director and Editor-in-Chief: J. Watson, Ph.D.
Publication Production Coordinator: Diane P. Basso
Typesetter: Graph Comp Design, Ottawa, Ont.
Printer: National Printers (Ottawa) Inc., Ottawa, Ont.
Cover Design and Chapter Graphics: André, Gordon and Laundreth Inc., Ottawa, Ont.

Correct citation for this publication:

DUNFIELD, R. W. 1985. The Atlantic salmon in the history of North
America. Can. Spec. Publ. Fish. Aquat. Sci. 80: 181 p.

Table of Contents

Abstract

Dunfield, R. W. 1985. The Atlantic salmon in the history of North America. Can. Spec. Publ. Fish. Aquat. Sci. 80: 181 p.

The Atlantic salmon (*Salmo salar*) has occupied a salient position in the history of eastern North America for at least the past 1000 years. Initially the species occupied a prominent niche in the prolific web of life that existed throughout its former occurrence area; millions of pounds of salmon were produced annually from the freshwater streams between New York and Ungava — a resource that was a principal food source for the Amerindian cultures which shared its range. In a chronological and cumulative way, the salmon became an increasingly important factor in both the domestic and commercial life of the developing colonies; it provided a recreational outlet for the sportsman, and evolved as a principal object of intellectual and scientific investigation. The documented specifics of the salmon's history, however, are largely comprised of repetitive instances of overexploitation, careless destruction of stocks and their environment, and ineffectual conservation actions. Despite the species' former importance, its more recent history is one of declining presence, and its destiny appears to be extinction. By documenting this story of discovery, exploitation, and decline, the urgent need for the employment of sound resource management practices to preserve the salmon is emphasized.

Résumé

Dunfield, R. W. 1985. The Atlantic salmon in the history of North America. Can. Spec. Publ. Fish. Aquat. Sci. 80: 181 p.

Le saumon de l'Atlantique (*Salmo salar*) joue un rôle prépondérant dans l'histoire de l'est de l'Amérique du Nord depuis au moins 1 000 ans. Au début, l'espèce occupait une niche écologique importante parmi les multiples formes de vie qui peuplaient son aire de répartition; les cours d'eau douce situés entre New York et l'Ungava produisaient chaque année des milliers de livres de saumon, lequel constituait alors la principale source alimentaire des communautés amérindiennes qui vivaient sur ce territoire. Par la suite et progressivement, le saumon est devenu de plus en plus important dans les activités familiales et commerciales des colonies en expansion; enfin, le saumon, qui constitue une prise de choix pour les pêcheurs sportifs, a fait, et continue de faire, l'objet de nombreuses études scientifiques. L'histoire du saumon est cependant marquée par de nombreux cas de surexploitation, par la destruction inconsidérée des stocks et de leur habitat ainsi que par des mesures de conservation inefficaces. Malgré l'importance qu'a eue jadis cette espèce, des données récentes nous indiquent qu'elle régresse et qu'elle semble vouée à l'extinction. En traitant de la découverte, de l'exploitation et du déclin du saumon, l'auteur fait ressortir le besoin urgent qu'il y a d'utiliser des méthodes de gestion des ressources efficaces afin de préserver l'espèce.

Preface

The following work describes the history of man's contact and experience with the Atlantic salmon in North America from aboriginal times to 1867, and is based principally on the revelations of primary archival documents and other historical material respecting the discovery, observation, exploitation, and management of the salmon resource.

Although history may be of academic interest alone, with an exploration of it undertaken because of a natural desire to discover and understand the events and conditions of the past, its examination may also precipitate more practical benefits: with regard to the Atlantic salmon, which is presently suffering severe declines throughout much of its range, a knowledge and study of the past may reveal the reasons for the species' present situation, and evince the options for its future. A knowledge and understanding of our past associations with the salmon also reveal our successes and failures in conserving and managing the resource; this knowledge can be used to support or caution our actions in applying certain development techniques, in formulating resource control policy, or in generally managing both present and future stocks of salmon. A knowledge of history, therefore, becomes fundamental to those concerned about the Atlantic salmon; it is intended that this report may be of particular value to those individuals.

Although this report is designed to provide a chronological account of man's association with, and impact upon, the salmon throughout the history of North America to 1867, it was also considered essential to provide some early history and background of the species in Europe. Such an inclusion assists in explaining what was known about the salmon in pre-Columbian times, what was its appreciation and value, and how this knowledge and understanding affected subsequent contacts with the species in North America. The initial chapter of the report, therefore, deals mainly with this background to the North American story.

It was also considered necessary to describe in some detail throughout the report the general developments which took place in the overall western North Atlantic fishery; the salmon fishery was initially a part of the whole, affected by general fishing trends and eventually emerging as a pursuit of individual importance and consideration. Even in the late 19th century, factors which affected the general Atlantic fishery also had repercussive effects on the salmon-fishing operation. Repeated references to the general fishery and related subjects, although at times appearing to deviate from the main topic of salmon, are nevertheless deemed appropriate for a better understanding of the situation.

In researching information for this historical report, a great amount of information was encountered — more, in fact, than was anticipated or hoped for when research was begun. Much of the original material was not only detailed, but also of a nature that presented some placement difficulty within the planned report format. Statistical material, for example, was voluminous and could not be adequately presented in the main body of the report without considerable encumbrance for both the writer and the reader. Such information was, therefore, assigned to a series of appendices included in a separately issued Manuscript Report.

To portray the true temper of the periods covered in this report, and to facilitate individual investigation and appraisal of original source material, a considerable amount of directly quoted contemporary comment is included; supplemental notes and comments are also provided, and a complete bibliography is appended.

Writing an historical report is rarely a completely original exercise, since one has to rely on the observations and opinions of others — biased or otherwise — to reveal the subject. In consequence, the writer can claim little credit for the work, except for that which pertains to the search-and-find aspects of the task and to the physical assembly of the information. In submitting this report on the history of the Atlantic salmon, the writer fully acknowledges his reliance on the efforts of many persons who contributed to the final work. Without the diaries of colonial sportsmen, the journals of early explorers and adventurers, and the reports of innumerable public servants and private individuals, there would be no basis upon which to construct the history of the salmon. Without the assistance and knowledge of colleagues and persons in charge of the various repositories of historical material, much valuable information would not have been obtained; in this respect, the writer is particularly indebted to Miss Shirley Elliott and the staff of the Nova Scotia Legislative Library. The assistance and cooperation of the librarians, archivists, and staffs of the New Brunswick Legislative Library; the Provincial Archives of New Brunswick; the Public Archives of Nova Scotia, Prince Edward Island, and Canada; and the many other Maritime museums and archives consulted are gratefully acknowledged. The willing help and continued assistance of Mrs. Ann Bruce and Mrs. Claire McPherson of the Fisheries Regional Library in Halifax are especially appreciated. Particular acknowledgment must also be given to Mr. Ken Smith, whose editorial skills were invaluable, and to Dr. Larry Marshall and Mr. Wesley White who reviewed portions of the draft and provided valuable suggestions for improvement. The professionalism and expertise of Mrs. Lois Kernaghan are especially appreciated; her skills in reviewing, editing, and arranging the final manuscript from the historical standpoint have significantly enhanced the results of the author's efforts. The author, however, accepts full responsibility for any errors which may occur in the final work.

Finally, without the encouragement provided to the writer by Mr. C. P. Ruggles, Mr. N. E. MacEachern, and Dr. J. E. Stewart, this pleasant and personally satisfying exploration of history would not have been possible.

Bob Dunfield
Halifax, N.S.

I

Salmo Rex

Ecce Salar

It has been said that anyone who has not seen a salmon has not seen what a fish should be — a statement which perhaps encompasses more pure and simple truth about the species than any other description. The Atlantic salmon's design is hydrodynamically perfect, streamlined, and expertly proportioned, not only to portend a functional involvement with its environment, but also to satisfy acutely the aesthetic values of man — qualities alone which make it more than just another fish. The salmon's deep, marine-blue back, its silvery profile, and its white undersides blend together to create an impression of freshness, spirit, and visual harmony which adds to the attraction of the species; these superficial qualities, however, are also complemented by the physical endowments of speed, agility, and endurance.

Apart from the feeling that we may have for the salmon as a sublime example of creation, the species has also served to satisfy two of our more basic appetites: those of food and recreation. To many gourmets, nothing can surpass the culinary delights provided by a freshly smoked, baked, or planked salmon; and to the sportsman, little can compare to the sing of the reel as the angler tests his skill with this agile and spirited opponent. It seems appropriate, however, that the first recorded remark about the salmon, made in the 1st century A.D., appears to refer to the fish's physical and aesthetic qualities rather than to its more elemental values: "The River Salmon surpasseth all the fishes of the sea,"[1] wrote Pliny; and few are prepared to challenge his unadorned but profound statement, even after the accumulated knowledge of 19 subsequent centuries has revealed to us all the fishes which are, in fact, "of the sea."

Little was known of the salmon in Pliny's time, except that it was a marvelous, leaping fish, which seemed to appear and disappear in the northern European rivers like a wanton spirit. Thousands of these sometimes elusive creatures were seen at certain periods of the year relentlessly swimming upstream and jumping over real or imaginary barriers. This remarkable ability to jump — sometimes as high as ten or twelve feet — resulted in its being called "the leaping fish," a title eventually recognized in its scientific name, *Salmo salar* — salmon the leaper.[2]

The species often took on a mystical or magical quality in ancient times, because it was believed that no fish could possibly leap so high without some supernatural assistance or power. The scientific sages of the day, however, dispelled this belief and explained the dynamics of the leap by saying that the salmon took its tail in its mouth and, by rotating its body like a wheel, was able to convolute over the most difficult waterfall.[3] Today we have considerably more knowledge about the salmon than did Pliny or his contemporaries. Its life history and habits have been studied intensely for over a century, and recent studies in archaeology and ichthyology have revealed some possible answers to the salmon's prehistory as well.

Some scientists believe that the salmon's recognizable ancestor evolved with the group of higher bony fishes which appeared in the Cretaceous Period, 70 million years ago, when a particularly significant explosion in fish adaptation was evident.[4] At this time in the earth's history, continental drift would not yet have separated the land masses of Europe, Greenland, and North America; therefore, the subsequent distribution of the species would have been facilitated both by the normal tendency of the growing population to enlarge and extend its range, and by the drifting apart of the land masses. If the species was basically marine, its principal saltwater feeding and assembly ground — in a global sense — may have remained relatively stationary, with the migration routes to and from this ground becoming more extended as the species continued to expand its range and as the continents continued to drift apart. This theory may explain the present use of common marine feeding and assembly grounds (e.g. west Greenland) by various stocks of salmon whose nuptial and coastal "home waters" are now distantly removed both from each other and from the common assembly area.

In the late 1880s, R. W. Shufeldt concluded that the present Salmonidae family had its beginnings at least as far back in time as 2 million years, during the great age of glaciation. Since a fundamental theory in biology states that the evolution of a species is reflected in the life cycle of the individual in that species, many scientists accept that the salmon was originally a freshwater fish which was forced into the marine environment by the massive terrestrial ice sheets that advanced over its range.[5] Others believe, however, that the species was basically marine and, strangely enough, developed its anadromous habits during this same period of glaciation.[6]

Whether originally a fresh- or saltwater fish, there is no doubt that the four most recent periods of ice advance and retreat forced the salmon to change and adjust its habits. It is known, for example, that Pacific salmon once ranged as far south as Mexico[7] and, although the total impact of continental glaciation on the salmon is not known, it is a salient observation that the postglacial, southerly limits of Pacific and Atlantic salmon occurrence in North America coincide remarkably with the southerly limit of terrestrial glaciation. It is also generally accepted that the barriers of ice and temperature caused the establishment of landlocked salmon varieties,[8] and that the creation of the Alaska–Siberia land bridge resulted in the separation of what are now the Atlantic and Pacific stocks.[9]

Regardless of its distant history, the Atlantic salmon was, by the advent of recorded history, an anadromous, cold-water species, distributed around the North Atlantic coastline from New York to Portugal. Shakespeare makes mention of salmon in the Mediterranean (*King Henry V*, IV, vii, 28–33), but this observation was prompted, no doubt, by poetic — rather than a fishing —

license, and there is little evidence supporting the onetime existence of the species east of the Gates of Gibraltar. Salmon were found in those rivers of France and Spain that flowed into the Bay of Biscay; they were also plentiful throughout the British Isles and in the continental rivers that empty into the English Channel and the North Sea; and they were encountered in the Baltic, Barents, and White seas, and the rivers tributary thereto. On this northern coast, they extended as far eastward as the Pechora River in Russia. They were found in Iceland and off the west coast of Greenland, although only one river in Greenland — the Kapisigdlit — was known to produce salmon.[10]

From earliest times, the people of northern and western Europe utilized the salmon resource, the first evidence of this coming from caves in France and Spain, which were inhabited 10 000 years before the birth of Christ and where well-defined drawings of trout and salmon were found on walls and bone weapons. That the salmon were meticulously drawn and readily identifiable suggests more than just a cursory acknowledgment of the species by early man. Artists, both ancient and modern, usually interpret best what they know best, and the carvings on walls, bone, and reindeer antler show a knowledge of the subject exceeding that required merely to depict the creature pictorially. The implication is that the salmon was appreciated for its aesthetic merit as well as for its value as a food source; after all, you do not need to study the fish visually if all you are going to do is consume it. Perhaps one can also better appreciate the enduring qualities of the species when one considers that this graceful leaping fish is still seen in some French rivers — while the reindeer is not.

During Caesar's occupation of Europe, the salmon was looked upon as a creature of considerable esteem and importance, and we are told that the Romans stocked the rivers of their realm to improve the fishing and replenish depleted reserves.[11] With the rise of the feudal system, the species became the prerogative of the nobility and clergy, and was classed as a "regal fish." In the 1700s, it was estimated that as many as 10 000 salmon were taken from about 50 Spanish rivers each day during the spawning runs,[12] with even higher yields probably being taken in France. By the 1840s, stocks of salmon had decreased alarmingly throughout the southern section of their range in Europe; although France in particular initiated and supported a considerable rehabilitation program throughout the 1850s,[13] the decline continued.

Salmon were mentioned in a poem about the Rhine in the 4th century,[14] and they were known to have ascended this river at least as far as Basel until the early 19th century. Rhine salmon, some weighing as much as 50 pounds, were still being sold on the London market in 1889,[15] but the increase in industrial pollution was soon to remove the runs completely. Rivers such as the Oder,

Weser, and Elbe were other German streams in which salmon were formerly taken.[16]

When the Romans left Britain in 410 B.C., Anglo-Saxon invaders soon arrived from northern Europe and brought with them some of the terms by which the salmon is known today in the English-speaking world, words such as parr, smolt, and grilse.[17] Salmon were plentiful in England at this time, and by the 11th century were receiving considerable attention as an economic and commercial product; this is borne out by the fact that salmon fishing stands and ponds were enumerated in the Doomsday Book, compiled in 1086.[18] Although Wales was noted for its fine trout streams, salmon could be found in abundance there as well. Up to 70 000 fish a year were estimated to have frequented Irish rivers such as the Shannon, Bann, Lee, Foyle, Blackwater, and Moy.[19] It was in Scotland, however, that the salmon ruled supreme.

C. F. Hickling mentions in his recent book that fish in general were never cheap in the British Isles during the Middle Ages, because demand was great and the fish were difficult to capture and keep in a marketable condition for any length of time. Fishing methods were not particularly efficient, and inadequate means were available for curing, preserving, and transporting the product. This latter drawback led to the practice of retaining captured fish in ponds until they were required; such a method was described in documents dating from as early as the Norman conquest.[20] One of the easiest species to capture was the salmon, because it normally congregated in schools and entered the shallow, fresh waters to spawn. As a result, salmon became one of the more frequently consumed fish of the realm — so common that it sometimes was an unwelcome sight at mealtimes.

Britannia Waves the Rules

It seems unlikely that fishery regulation or legislation would be enacted as a result of fish being plentiful; indeed, it is more often enacted because of the resource being scarce. Although fish were not scarce in Britain, laws did appear, and at a very early date. In Scotland, for example, a rule was enacted in 1030 by Malcolm II, who established a closed salmon fishing season from Assumption Day (30 August) to Martinmas Day (11 November).[21] Conservation, apparently, is not a modern concept.

When the Magna Carta was signed by King John in 1215, public right to the fishery was assured in general,[22] and with regard to salmon, certain formerly exclusive fishing rights were given up by the monarchy. The king's weirs, for example, were removed from certain areas, in order to allow exploitation by others and possibly to insure the perpetuation of the species for the public good. Further legislation throughout the 13th century

culminated in the Statute of Westminster, 1285, which among other provisions, established seasonal salmon fishing prohibitions, protection of stock from poachers during restricted periods, and punishment for offenders.[23] Along with the Magna Carta, this statute formed the basis of English fishing law as it pertained to the salmon, and provided a legal foundation that could be expanded and revised as the need arose.

Fish inspection service began in Britain during the reign of Edward IV (1461–1483), when a statute was passed concerning the packing and barreling of salmon. The size of the containers into which the fish were put was also regulated: the "butt" was to contain 84 wine gallons, or approximately 600 pounds; the "barrel," 42 gallons or 300 pounds. This latter container was usually termed a "tierce."[24] A statute enacted in the reign of Henry VII (1485–1509) recited the previous act and assigned a payment to the inspectors who were required to search the barrels and enforce the general terms of the law.[25]

English rivers such as the Tamar, Plym, Exe, Tyne, and Trent were particularly well known for their salmon runs; even the Thames, 209 miles long, possessed a run over its lower 65 miles.[26] Thames salmon had declined by the early 1800s, but not before Britain's record specimen was taken from its waters: the fish was reported to have weighed 83 pounds, and was taken in 1821.[27] Around 1860, the last salmon was fished from the river.[28] The Thames subsequently continued to accept increasing amounts of industrial and domestic pollution until the mid-1960s, from which time a cleanup campaign has restored it to the point where some of the more tolerant species of fish are now reestablishing themselves.[29]

Of all the British Isles, however, Scotland was the region where the salmon was best known. The Scottish parliament was particularly attuned to the necessity of regulating its valuable salmon resource at an early date, and during the Middle Ages it is unlikely that any other kingdom or state in Europe which possessed a salmon fishery enacted as many laws to preserve and protect this fish. As early as 1318, an act of parliament provided for the free passage of smolts through milldams, by requiring the owners of these structures to provide an opening in the top of the barrier "two thumbs in length and three thumbs in breadth"; the penalty for not complying was a heavy fine and 40 days in prison.[30] The Scots enacted a great number of regulations in the 15th century, at which time important river and estuarial fisheries were being carried out on streams such as the Tweed, weirs being the most common fishing device.[31]

Thus, before the discovery of the New World, the Scots had a comprehensive set of salmon fishing regulations. They had passed fishway laws, had established salmon fishing seasons, had forbidden the taking of smolts and spent salmon, and had instituted a system of fish inspection.[32] It is also clear from the old statutes and commercial records that the Scots had built up a considerable salmon trade as early as the 13th century, with barrels and kitts of pickled fish being shipped to the continent and throughout the British Isles.[33] This sale and export of salmon out of Scotland was carefully regulated — particularly to "Inglis men." The continuing trade and its potential for further expansion prompted a Scottish laird, Demster of Dunnichen, to develop a method whereby salmon could be successfully preserved and shipped in ice; this process began about 1780,[34] and provided a product that was often preferred over the brine-packed article.

Fantastic numbers of salmon were reported to have visited Scottish rivers in former times. The 100-mile-long Tweed, for example, was supposed to have possessed an annual run of 150 000 adult fish,[35] and it was on the Tweed that the record Scottish salmon was angled by the Earl of Home around 1732; the fish weighed almost 70 pounds.[36] In Scotland, as in England, the salmon was a common and valuable food source. Servants and retainers were usually expected or compelled to eat the fish,[37] and the lairds and Scottish chieftains considered themselves fortunate if they owned or had access to a salmon fishery. The story is told of one Scottish chieftain who did not possess a good salmon stream. In order to feed the many workers he had hired to build a new castle on his estate, he entered into a signed agreement with a neighboring laird who did possess a good salmon fishery, whereby the first chief might have access to the latter's fishery until such time as the new castle was completed. The craftiness of the first Scottish chief eventually came to light, for he never put the last stone in his castle, kept a number of workers and servants, and consequently retained perpetual title to a portion of the other man's fishery.[38]

Fischying from a Different Angle

Although Izaak Walton (1593–1683) is recognized as the father of the modern art of angling, the sport was actually known and practiced in more ancient times. The word *angle*, in its original sense, did not necessarily imply the use of a rod, but meant simply to fish with a hook or angle. Angling was well established in Biblical times: "They take up all of them [fish] with the angle, they catch them in their net, and gather them in their drag: Therefore they rejoice and are glad" (Habakkuk 1:15).

When the rod or pole was first used as an attachment to the line and hook is not known, but the first visual proof of its occurrence and use comes from a 20th century B.C. Egyptian temple drawing.[39] It is known that the fishing rod was used in China from around the 11th century B.C.[40] It is not supposed that angling with a rod began as a means of recreation, but rather as a method of extending the hand-line fisherman's reach. At first, a short, stout pole was used, the whole apparatus not being far removed from a simple hand-line with a wooden grip.[41] It is obvious from early drawings, however, that angling soon evolved into a diversionary activity as well as one of practical necessity.

The Egyptians certainly fished for pleasure, and the story is told that Cleopatra was apparently rather unorthodox in her approach to the sport, for it is said that she had divers place the live fish on her hook in order to insure the success to which a queen was entitled.[42] The first record of fly-fishing also comes from Egypt, where an early 14th century B.C. temple drawing shows a man of obvious omnipotence fishing in an aquarium; in his hand he holds a short rod to which is affixed seven individual lines, each with a flying insect attached.[43]

Angling appeared to maintain a low profile as a sporting activity until the 1st century A.D. Around 130 A.D., Aelien described fly-fishing in Macedonia; at this time, the rod and line were both approximately 6 feet in length, and the fly was artificial rather than real. In 1496, the first informative sportfishing report was made; it described a 20-foot fishing pole, hooped with iron, equipped with a horsehair line and several varieties of artificial flies.[44] It was not, however, until the 17th century that a proliferation occurred in sportfishing and in the literature describing it.

During this period, Thomas Barker wrote the *Art of Angling* (1651); Izaak Walton, *The Compleat Angler* (1653); Robert Venables, *The Experienc'd Angler* (1662); and other men, such as Charles Cotton, described the sport in considerable detail. Walton, in particular, glorified the sport and showed more than a passing interest in the species being angled: "God never did make a more calm, quiet, innocent recreation," he wrote, thus beginning the campaign to set both angler and salmon apart from common man and common fish.[45]

The fishing pole became more sophisticated at this time, being equipped with an end ring and a reel which was sometimes fixed to the rod. By 1655, a Londoner, Charles Kirby, had developed an improved fishhook, which is still one of the basic designs used today. It was not until the end of the 18th century that a jointed rod, with eyes, line, and reel, was in common use.[46]

The first recreational anglers were principally those of noble status, but the excitement and pleasure of the sport gradually filtered down through the class system, and by the middle 1700s, it had infected the commissioned ranks of the military. It was largely this latter group who were responsible for perpetuating and spreading the art around the imperial globe. Being able and eager to angle became almost a prerequisite for becoming a British army officer, and especially in the North American colonies, salmon angling was necessarily undertaken to avoid the boredom of garrison life in such uncivilized surroundings. The navy also had its followers of the sport, with no less a personage than Lord Nelson being a *devoté*. It was reported that when he lost his arm in the battle of Tenerife in 1797, a similar misfortune had also befallen one of his young boatswains; in visiting his injured subordinate after the battle, Nelson's chief regret over their shared loss was that "Jack, we're spoilt for fly-fishing."[47]

Salmon angling thus became akin to religion, and developed into an intense faith of fanatical proportions. Clubs were formed, setting specific rules and procedures for angling conduct, each member rising through the ranks as his skill and esteem increased. In Scotland, a man was not a man for "a' that" unless he had angled a salmon, and in England, the great theologian William Paley (1745–1805), who produced such intellectually involved works as the *Principles of Moral and Political Philosophy* was never prepared to undertake any research or writing "until the fly-fishing season was quite over."[48]

Pisciculture

The practices of fish farming, management and culture were well known in China before the time of Christ. By the 19th century, it was reported that in the Orient,

> The fishermen collect with care on the margin and surface of waters, all those gelatinous masses which contain the spawn of fish. After they have found a sufficient quantity they fill with it a shell of a fresh hen egg, which they have previously emptied, stop up the hole, and put it under a setting fowl. At the expiration of a certain number of days they break the shell in water warmed by the sun. The young fish are presently hatched and are kept in pure fresh water until they are large enough to be put into the ponds with the old fish.

This account was published in Belcher's *Farmer's Almanac* in 1825, and one wonders how many country lads rushed to the henhouse and thence to the nearest freshwater pond to try their hand at fish culture. At least we know that they were either unsuccessful or terribly secretive in their experiments, since no record — except one questionable document[49] — has been left from such an early date to suggest any North American developments in this scientific field. It is probably safe to say, however, that no fowl was ever the mother of a North American salmonid. Furthermore, although we may question the literal truth of the almanac's filler, there is no doubt that the Chinese were particularly adept at pond farming fish and in raising the spawn of various species for distribution to depleted lakes, streams, and rivers; the sale of spawn, in fact, formed an important branch of internal trade from earlier times.[50] It also appears probable that some form of artificial fecundation was known and practiced, considering the extent to which fish farming was carried out in that country.[51]

Fish farming was also practiced in Egypt and probably in other Mediterranean countries in Biblical times.[52] Although some modern writers question whether the Romans practiced fish culture,[53] it is generally agreed that they engaged in it to a large degree, stocking rivers, lakes, and streams as a public service and utility. The Romans possibly believed that fish culture could be practiced on the same scale as agriculture, and they apparently carried out breeding and rearing experiments to prove this point. One treatise on the subject stated that "The early Romans … knew and cultivated the art extensively; and not being contented with merely breeding fish, they studied also how to impart new flavours to the flesh, and were particularly zealous in fattening them to the largest possible size."[54] For all practical purposes, the widespread practice of fish culture in Europe faded with the fall of the Roman Empire. It was not to be revived until the 18th century, except in China, and perhaps in a few European enclaves where monks, savants, and a few scientific minds continued to breed fish and to stock the aquaria and ponds used by kings and bishops for their private pleasure and use.[55]

In the mid-1730s, a German naturalist named Jacobi became interested in the possibility of breeding fish artificially. As a keen observer of nature, he had attentively watched the spawning activity of salmon in a river near his home. Discovering that fertilization of the eggs was entirely an external process, he decided to collect both eggs and sperm separately, combine them in his laboratory and thus hopefully produce living embryos. It is interesting to note, from the standpoint of this history of the Atlantic salmon, that the foundation of modern fish culture, as discovered by Jacobi, had its basis in the study of the salmon. For more than 30 years, he continued his work in artificial pisciculture, eventually publishing the results of his research in 1763. He received the acclaim of the scientific community of his day, and was awarded a government pension in recognition of his efforts; his accomplishments, however, were viewed as a purely academic discovery and, as a result, little consideration was given to the practical implications of the work — viz., the possibility of using artificial culture to develop and manage his country's fishery.[56]

In general, political barriers, war, class indifference, and language tended to curb, or at least hinder, the spread of scientific knowledge in Europe. It was not until the 1840s that interest and activity again emerged in the field of pisciculture, and by that time, the resurgence was prompted by a widespread decline in many wild stocks of European fish.

Scotland was the first country in which the study was reborn. In the 1830s, John Shaw, Andrew Young, and a Dr. Knox were studying the natural history and development of the salmon; by 1840, Shaw had artificially raised specimens from ova, had followed their progress through the various stages of development, and had established that parr and smolts were the younger stages of the Atlantic salmon.[57] In 1841, Gottlieb Boccius, a British civil engineer, duplicated Shaw's studies on trout. Boccius was probably the first individual to recognize the practical and commercial advantages of fish culture, and he encouraged various groups to replenish and develop fish stocks throughout the country; he later wrote a book which widely publicized the value of the new art throughout Britain.[58]

Developments in fish culture were also being made by this time in continental Europe. A few German scientists were again taking up the work of Jacobi, while Louis Agassiz was studying the reproduction of a salmon-like species in the Swiss lakes.[59] The most important advances, however, were being made in France where, by 1852, a state fish hatchery was established on the Rhine River at Humingue, near Basel, largely due to the pioneering work of two commercial fishermen, Antoine Gehin and Joseph Rémy. The hatchery covered 25 acres and was devoted to the artificial propagation of salmon, carp, tench, and several other species which were popular at that time. New developments came quickly, improved techniques were devised, and programs were initiated to restock various watercourses throughout the country, particularly in the more economically depressed areas. These efforts soon placed France in the forefront of those countries involved in the practice of fish culture, and the expertise developed in the French hatcheries set the basis for the development of the art in other regions.[60]

Encouraged by the results in France and the efforts of Boccius in Britain, two English gentlemen of "capital and enterprise" wondered if the declining salmon fisheries of the British Isles could be brought back to their former levels of commercial production by using artificial culture and restocking techniques. The two interested gentlemen, (the Messrs. Ashworth) chose a former salmon stream in Ireland upon which to test their ideas. Their field superintendent, Mr. Ramsbottom, selected a small brook and diverted its course through a series of 6-foot wooden boxes, which were set in the bed of the stream and filled with a layer of gravel. In this hatching channel he placed fertilized salmon eggs which, in due time, hatched into thousands of fry. A great increase over the natural rearing potential of the stream resulted, and the successes of this artificial rill encouraged the supporters of the project to continue and extend their work elsewhere in the United Kingdom.

Ramsbottom's major fish culture program in Scotland was the restocking of the River Tay, which he undertook in 1853 from an estate at Stormontfield, near Perth. Here, 300 hatching boxes were used to house 300 000 salmon ova, which were collected in December 1853. Ramsbottom reported that the eggs hatched in April and May 1854, and that by June 1855, after special care and feeding, the parr had become smolts, the largest of which measured 7½ inches. The adipose fin was clipped and the fish were liberated. In August 1855, supposedly after an absence of 2 months, they were reported to have returned to the river again, showing phenomenal growth — the largest weighing 9½ pounds. With apparent results like this, who could deny the value of the science of pisciculture?[61]

End of the Beginning?

As food for man and gods, as an object of artistic interpretation for the cave dwellers, as the property of kings and princes, and as a diversion for the naturalist, the clergy, and the sportsman, the salmon was well established as a creature of special significance and notoriety in Europe even before Columbus made his historic voyage. It was to become no less illustrious in North America, being the first fish of any species to be documented in the New World. It was viewed by the Indians as the creation of the great god-spirit, a symbol of life, and insurance for a successful marriage. It encouraged territorial expansion, enhanced the prosperity of maritime communities, maintained the sanity and cultural values of military men, affected the life and death of fishermen and commercial fishing enterprises, and contributed silver to the colonial coffers. At one point in time, the North American salmon was even seen as the means of eliminating the £800 million national debt of Great Britain. As a renewable resource, its value in the past foretold a promising future.

However, as the history of the salmon progresses in the following chapters, an unattractive underlying statement on human nature and on man's association with the species will be revealed: in many instances, the incongruous fact is evident that the salmon has been observed with intensity, regulated to extremity, and driven to extinction.

NOTES

[1]*The Fisheries and Fishing Industries of the United States*, ed. G. Browne Goode (Washington: U.S. Commission of Fish and Fisheries, 1884), I, 468.

[2]The name *Salmo* was given to the Atlantic salmon by the Romans; Anthony Netboy, *The Atlantic Salmon, A Vanishing Species?* (London: Faber and Faber, 1968), p. 21. Linnaeus gave the fish its scientific name, *Salmo salar*, in 1758; John R. Dymond, "Family Salmonidae," in *Fishes of the Western North Atlantic*, ed. John Tee-Van (New Haven: Yale University Press, 1963), p. 459.

[3]W. C. Watson, "The Salmon of Lake Champlain and its Tributaries," *Report* of the United States Commission of Fish and Fisheries, 1873–74 and 1874–75 (Washington: Government Printing Office, 1876), p. 538.

[4]F. D. Ommanney, *The Fishes* (New York: Time-Life, 1963), pp. 66, 69.

[5]Charles Hallock, *The Salmon Fisher* (New York: Harris, 1890), pp. 31, 32.

[6]Edward LeDanois, *Fishes of the World* (Woodstock, Vermont: Countryman Press, n.d.), p. 32. *Anadromous* describes a fish which spawns in fresh water but which spends most of its adult life in salt water. Shad and alewives are other anadromous species.

[7]John Bardach, *Downstream* (New York: Grosset and Dunlop, 1964), pp. 225–226.

[8]G. Power, "The Evolution of the Freshwater Races of the Atlantic Salmon (*Salmo salar*) in Eastern North America," *Arctic*, II (1958), 86–92.

[9]Anthony Netboy, *The Salmon, Their Fight for Survival* (Boston: Houghton Mifflin, 1974), pp. 7–8. Not all salmon are Atlantic salmon (*Salmo salar*). Atlantic salmon are found on both sides of the North Atlantic. Landlocked salmon, sometimes referred to as Sebago salmon or ouananiche, are also *Salmo salar*. There are seven species of Pacific salmon: Chinook (*Oncorhynchus tshawytscha*), Sockeye (*O. nerka*), Pink (*O. gorbuscha*), Coho (*O. kisutch*), Chum (*O. keta*), Biwa (*O. biwa*), and Masou (*O. masou*). The first five are common to both sides of the Pacific, but the Biwa and Masou are found only on the Asian side.

[10]Netboy, *Vanishing Species*, p. 118. See also Sv. Ad. Horsted, *The Greenland Salmon Fishery and Debate Around it Biologically Illuminated*, Fisheries Research Board Translation Series, No. 2016, p. 3.

[11]Theodatus Garlick, *A Treatise on the Artificial Propagation of Certain Kinds of Fish* (Cleveland: Thomas Brown, 1857), p. 28.

[12]Netboy, *Vanishing Species*, pp. 50, 54.

[13]Richard Nettle, *The Salmon Fisheries of the St. Lawrence* (Montreal: John Lovell, 1857), pp. 96–97.

[14]Anthony Netboy, "History as a Focus for Fishery Conservation, "*Atlantic Salmon Association Centennial Award Fund* (Montreal, n.d.), p. 6.

[15]Edward Prince, "The Maximum Size of Fishes and its Causes," *Annual Report* of the Department of Marine and Fisheries, 1902, App. II, lxii.

[16]Netboy, *Vanishing Species*, p. 26.

[17]Goode, *Fisheries of the United States*, I, 468.

[18]C. F. Hickling, *The Farming of Fish* (London: Pergamon Press, 1968), p. 24.

[19]Nettle, *Salmon Fisheries*, p. 9.

[20]Hickling, *Fish Farming*, p. 24.

[21]Anthony Netboy, *Salmon: The World's Most Harassed Fish* (London: André Deutsch, 1980), p. 73.

[22]Netboy, *Vanishing Species*, p. 165.

[23]A. H. Chaytor, *Letters to a Salmon Fisher's Son* (London: John Murray, 1910), p. 271.

[24]22 Edward IV, c. 2.

[25]Chaytor, *Letters*, p. 271.

[26]Netboy, *Vanishing Species*, pp. 158, 161.

[27]*Woodbine Angling Yearbook*, ed. Colin Graham (London: The Queen Anne Press, 1973), p. 300. Officially, the world's record Atlantic salmon was taken in the Tana River, Norway, in 1928, and weighed 79 pounds, 2 ounces (*ibid.*, p. 16).

[28]Netboy, *Vanishing Species*, p. 180.

[29]A salmon was caught in the Thames, in 1974, and at least three more between 1975 and 1978. See Hugh R. MacCrimmon and Barra L. Gots, "World Distribution of Atlantic Salmon" in *Journal* of the Fisheries Research Board of Canada, Vol. 36, (1979) p. 440.

[30]Chaytor, *Letters*, p. 263. Seventeen parliamentary acts dealing with salmon were passed in Scotland prior to 1504.

[31]Dorothy Burwash, *English Merchant Shipping, 1460–1540* (Toronto: University of Toronto Press), p. 138.

[32]Chaytor, *Letters*, pp. 264–270.

[33]Derik Mills, *Salmon and Trout: A Resource, its Ecology, Conservation and Management* (Edinburgh: Oliver and Boyd, 1971), p. 3.

[34]Alex Russel, *The Salmon* (Edinburgh: Edmonston and Douglas, 1864), p. 4.

[35]Nettle, *Salmon Fisheries*, p. 9.

[36]*Woodbine Angling Yearbook* (1973), p. 311. Netboy, *Salmon*, p. 36, states that the record salmon was taken in the Devron River, Scotland; it weighed 103 pounds.

[37]Nettle, *Salmon Fisheries*, p. 7.

[38]Charles St. John, *Sketches of the Wild Sports and Natural History of the Highlands* (London, 1878), p. 67.

[39]T. B. Thomas, "Fishing from Early Times," *The Atlantic Salmon Journal*, Vol. 13, No. 1 (March 1964), p. 5.

[40]Charles Chenevix Trench, *A History of Angling* (Chicago: Follett, 1974), p. 22.

[41]Thomas, "Fishing from Early Times," p. 5.

[42]Russel, *The Salmon*, p. 29.

[43]Trench, *History of Angling*, p. 15.

[44]Thomas, "Fishing from Early Times," pp. 5–6.

[45]Trench, *History of Angling*, pp. 15, 285. Edwin C. Guillet, *Early Life in Upper Canada* (Toronto: Ontario Publishing, 1933), p. 263.

[46]Thomas, "Fishing from Early Times," p. 6.

[47]Russel, *The Salmon*, p. 28.

[48]*Ibid.*

[49]Garlick, *Treatise*, pp. 135–142 discusses the Rev. John Bachman's efforts at fish culture, 1804.

[50]*Ibid.*, p. 28.

[51]Hickling, *Fish Farming*, p. 23. Fish culture paralleled silkworm culture in China, with the pupae of the silkworm apparently used as fish food.

[52]Thomas F. Knight, *The River Fisheries of Nova Scotia* (Halifax: A. Grant, 1867), p. 46. See Werner Keller, *The Bible as History* (New York: Bantam, 1974), p. 116 for mention of fresh fish obtained from artificial ponds in Egypt, ca. 1300 B.C.

[53]Hickling, *Fish Farming*, p. 24.

[54]Nettle, *Salmon Fisheries*, pp. 95–96.

[55]Genio C. Scott, *Fishing in American Waters* (New York: Harper, 1875), pp. 350–352.

[56]Nettle, *Salmon Fisheries*, p. 95.

[57]*Ibid.*, p. 97.

[58]Garlick, *Treatise*, p. 44.

[59]*Ibid.*, p. 41. The species being studied was the palee (*Coregonus nasus*), once thought to be a species of salmon.

[60]*Ibid.*, pp. 17, 35–36, 55; Nettle, *Salmon Fisheries*, pp. 95–96.

[61]Nettle, *Salmon Fisheries*, pp. 97–103. The growth of a smolt to a nine-pound grilse in two months is hardly credible, despite the tagging experiments described by Ramsbottom in the 1850s. It was not until some years later that, by planting smolts in virgin waters, it was discovered that smolts returned as grilse the year following the smolt run. See Scott, *Fishing in American Waters*. pp. 369–370.

II
The Primeval Condition

Streams of Silver

Historical records show that Atlantic salmon populations in aboriginal times could be found in most of the accessible watercourses of eastern North America from Ungava Bay to Long Island Sound. Although this represents a longitudinal geographic distribution of approximately 1300 statute miles, the actual length of coastline along which the salmon could be found exceeded 10 000 miles. The southern limit of the salmon's aboriginal range is still somewhat contested by biologists and historians alike, and although they were once reported as far south as the Delaware River,[1] there is no definitive evidence to support the occurrence of regular or sustained runs in any river south of the state of Connecticut.

In 1609, Henry Hudson explored the eastern American coast, and reported salmon in "great store" in the river which now bears his name.[2] Apart from this record, however, no other early documentation which mentions the existence of salmon in the river can be located. Some individuals thus believe that the Hudson was not a natural salmon stream, and that its discoverer must have mistaken some other species for the salmon. This conclusion stems perhaps from the fact that natural barriers rendered a large segment of the river's potential spawning ground inaccessible, as well as from the unsuccessful attempts made in the late 1800s to establish a salmon run in the river by using transplanted stock.[3]

Nevertheless, considering that the only known species of the region that Hudson might have confused with the salmon were the speckled trout, striped bass, sturgeon, shad, and pike, one might conclude that the explorer was either correct in his observations, terribly unknowledgeable about fish, or deliberately misinforming his readers. Coming from a salmon country, being a sailor, and probably a Londoner, Hudson would have undoubtedly known and recognized the salmon had he seen it in the New World; and since the honesty of his general observations about North America is beyond question, there would appear to be little doubt that he did, in fact, see salmon in the Hudson River. The species was, indeed, observed there on occasion in the mid-nineteenth century;[4] if no regular runs of salmon were supported by the river, it must be supposed that these fish were strays from streams further north along the coast. It may be observed, however, that such strays or unestablished populations of any species rarely occur in Hudson's "great store."

Although a question mark may still hang over the Hudson with respect to its status as an early salmon river, there is no doubt that the Housatonic River, flowing into the Atlantic several miles to the northeastward, supported a run which was known to have ascended at least to Falls Village, 60 miles from the sea.[5] Fifty miles northeastward lies the estuary of the Connecticut River, undoubtedly one of the best salmon streams in America, supporting a run for over 250 miles of its course. Apart from the main stream, one of the principal tributaries is the Farmington River, where great numbers of salmon were formerly encountered.[6] Specimens weighing up to

40 pounds were once reported, and 20–30 pound fish were said to be not uncommon;[7] it is little wonder that the local Indians referred to the Connecticut as "the smile of God."[8]

Although salmon were known to have entered many of the smaller coastal streams in Connecticut, the territory between the Connecticut and Merrimack rivers was not a noted salmon-producing area. The Merrimack, entering the ocean just northeast of Boston, supported salmon runs for 150 miles of its length, with the fish penetrating as far as the White Mountains.[9] Entering the main river near Franklin is the Winnesquam, or "salmon fishing waters,"[10] a title attesting to the tributary's importance to the natives of Massachusetts.

Between the Merrimack and the St. Croix rivers, there was hardly a single coastal stream which did not possess a salmon run. The Piscataqua, or Salmon Falls River, drains approximately 550 square miles of Maine and New Hampshire and supported one of the greatest salmon runs on the continent, if one can believe the early reports about the catches of the region.[11] Next to the Piscataqua, the 25-mile long Mousom River supported "plenty" of salmon. Although the Saco River possessed a considerably larger drainage area than the Mousom, it was accessible only to the 80-foot falls located 45 miles above the river's mouth; salmon frequented the Great and Little Ossipee branches of the river, where it was said that they found the best spawning ground.

The Presumpscot River drains Sebago Lake and enters the sea at Portland; although a good salmon stream, its fame was — and still is — in the landlocked salmon which inhabit the lake.[12] It was from this lake, in August 1907, that the world's record sebago salmon was taken weighing 22½ pounds.[13] There is still the occasional argument presented that at the time of European contact the salmon in Sebago Lake were not established as a landlocked variety, becoming so sometime after 1800 when dams had forced their isolation. Just northeast of Portland, the Royal River also supported a small run.[14]

The Androscoggin River drains approximately 3600 square miles of western Maine and supported a salmon population as far as Rumford, 100 miles inland. Adjacent to this river is the Kennebec — "the long water land" — in which salmon ascended almost to Moosehead Lake, 150 miles from the sea, and into the numerous tributary streams. Between the Kennebec and the Penobscot, small streams such as the Eastern, Damariscotta, Medomak, Quantabacook, and Belfast, supported considerable runs of salmon for their size. The Penobscot provided a salmon-producing area no less than that of the Kennebec, with salmon ascending to Millinocket, where two tributaries, the Salmon and Little Salmon, were not misnamed. Nearer the international boundary, small streams such as the Union, Nar-

raguagus, Pleasant, Machias, East Machias, Orange, and Dennys, were said to have abounded in salmon.[15]

Along the present international boundary, the St. Croix River once provided a favored salmon fishery for both the white settler and the Indian, particularly at Scoodic Falls, where many hundred were taken daily.[16] Between Passamaquoddy Bay and Saint John Harbour, only the Lepreau and Magaguadavic rivers were impassable to salmon due to natural barriers; all the rest were largely unobstructed. The mighty Saint John River — the Rhine of America — provided excellent salmon habitat in all its lower tributaries and on the main river from the Mouth of Keswick to Grand Falls. Many of the remaining river systems flowing into the Bay of Fundy are relatively small, but salmon frequented most of them, with the exception of those brooks flowing down the particularly precipitous sides of North Mountain in Nova Scotia.

Along the Atlantic coast of Nova Scotia and the Gulf shore of New Brunswick and Nova Scotia, it would be easier to enumerate the few streams that did not support aboriginal salmon runs than to name the ones that did, for salmon were particularly numerous in the Maritime Provinces, and over 80 percent of inland waters supported the species.[17] The Sissiboo River in western Nova Scotia was one of the few streams almost totally inaccessible due to a natural barrier, although many of the streams on Cape Breton Island were only partly accessible, due to the rapidly inclining elevations leading to the highland plateau. The only major stream on the Gulf Coast where salmon could not be found was the Nepisiguit River, above Grand Falls; this was in marked contrast to the adjacent Miramichi and Restigouche River watersheds, which were completely free of major obstructions and unparalleled in salmon productivity. Salmon were reported in all streams of Prince Edward Island,[18] and most of the Anticosti rivers were also utilized.

The species reached its westward limit at Niagara Falls. It is still a moot question as to whether these salmon of the upper St. Lawrence drainage were of the landlocked or anadromous variety, but there is little doubt that they were once plentiful in most of the tributary streams to Lake Ontario. On the American side of the lake, the Genesse River at Rochester was probably the most prolific, even though a large part of the system was obstructed. Salmon ascended the Oswego River to some of the large, elongated lakes of that system, and at Polaski, the Salmon River was famous for its runs.[19] Salmon streams were also evident on the south bank of the St. Lawrence River proper, particularly at Massena and Malone, and early records tell of abundant stock in the Richelieu River and Lake Champlain.[20]

Canadian rivers that flowed into Lake Ontario were numerous, and most of them from Kingston to Hamilton were salmon streams; the Credit, Humber, Don, and Trent rivers were notable in this regard.[21] Although the geology of the north bank of the St. Lawrence between the outlet of Lake Ontario and Trois Rivières did not particularly favor the existence of good salmon-producing water, evidence suggests that salmon could be found in the region in aboriginal times — although probably in reduced numbers as compared either with the Lake Ontario stocks, or the Atlantic stocks east of Quebec City. Salmon were apparently scarce in the Ottawa River — if present at all — and may have entered only the lower tributaries on the eastern bank; in any case, they could not have penetrated further upriver than Chaudière Falls, just above the nation's capital. Between the mouth of the Ottawa River and Quebec City, salmon were formerly present in the St. François, St. Maurice, Ste. Anne, and Jacques Cartier rivers, while Indians traditionally fished the runs of the St. Charles River, which entered the St. Lawrence below the battlements of the Quebec Citadel. Salmon entered many of the streams on the south shore of the St. Lawrence below Quebec, with only a few streams, such as the Chaudière, Armagh, and Madeleine, being either totally or partially obstructed.[22]

Salmon rivers were numerous on the northern coast of the river and Gulf of St. Lawrence, but the massive Laurentian escarpment presented a major access problem in some areas, a noted example being observed in the spectacular falls at the mouth of the Montmorency River. Barrier falls also existed at or near the outflows of the Cochons, Manicouagan, Ste. Marguerite, Manitou, Magpie, Aguanus, Nabisipi, and Etamanu rivers. Vast salmon-productive areas, however, were still found on the Saguenay, Moisie, Mingan, and many other wild rivers of the northern coast.[23]

Salmon streams could also be found around the entire coast of Newfoundland, to a greater or lesser extent, but again, many watercourses provided only partial accessibility. One of the more famous streams was the Exploits River, which provided good catches for the natives despite the fact that only about 20% or no more than 850 square miles, of its watershed was accessible.[24]

The segment of Labrador from Hamilton Inlet to the Strait of Belle Isle possessed many fine salmon areas. In former years, Sandwich Bay and its tributaries were the gem in the salmon resources of these northern latitudes, with thousands of fish weighing from 15 to 32 pounds entering the Eagle and Paradise rivers.[25] South of Cartwright, the species were plentiful in the Hawke, Alexis, St. Lewis, and Pinware rivers. Early documents indicate that salmon were probably somewhat scarce north of Hopedale, since few of the rivers in this region exceeded 50 miles in length, and the high coastal elevations created by the Turngat Mountains limited access to all but the lower sections of the rivers. Salmon nevertheless utilized these somewhat austere and barren watercourses and were reported in such streams as the Fraser, Kogaluk,

Adlatok, Canairiktok, Kaipokok, Makkovik, Big, and Shell Bird.[26]

Of the streams flowing into Ungava Bay, salmon could be found in the George, Whale, Koksoak, Leaf, Payne, and other smaller rivers as far west as Stupart Bay. The principal salmon river of this region was the Koksoak,[27] a system that drained over 4000 square miles of northern Quebec. It is believed that early salmon populations were small in the Ungava region, due to limited access on many rivers, scarcity of spawning ground, cold temperatures, short growing season, and low food productivity.[28] Nevertheless, runs of salmon into these northern rivers occurred in August and September, and the average weight of adult fish was only marginally less than that of the more southerly stocks. In the 1960s, Ungava salmon averaged around 11½ pounds, although the Koksoak River fish tended to be slightly larger than those in the Whale or George.[29]

Landlocked salmon were also common in the interior of Labrador and Quebec. They were found, for example, in Lake St. Jean and tributaries of the Saguenay, in the upper waters of the Manicouagan, above Grand Falls on the Churchill River, in the Naskaupi, as well as the upper watercourses of the Koksoak and George rivers. The greatest weight achieved by these landlocked specimens appears to be approximately 10 pounds,[30] while mature adults south of the St. Lawrence frequently weighed 15 pounds.[31]

Apart from the freshwater distribution of the Atlantic salmon in the western North Atlantic, various recorders have noted their existence as far north as Lancaster Sound and as far west as Hudson Bay.[32] It would complete the distribution map appropriately if one could link the salmon's limits with the two major topographic features named for Henry Hudson; such, however, is not the case, for the rare, supposed sightings of salmon in Hudson Bay are actually suspected to have been Hearne's salmon, otherwise known as Arctic char (*Salvelinus alpinus*). Because of recent publicity, we are well aware that some Canadian Atlantic salmon migrate to the Labrador Sea and the west coast of Greenland; and whether the fish's aboriginal migration patterns formerly took it as far north as it is found today is not known. There are some grounds for believing that its presence on the midwestern coast of Greenland is a recent trend, perhaps associated with changes in sea temperatures.[33] The lack of recorded observation and activity in the area until the 20th century, however, may be a more acceptable reason for ignorance of the salmon's past presence in these most northerly latitudes.

New World Shangri-La

The total accessible watershed area over which salmon were distributed in aboriginal times comprised no less than a quarter of a million square miles of primeval territory,[34] untouched by human influences, except for the Amerindian who lived in harmony with it. It is difficult to envisage today what this vast region of virgin land was truly like, as most of our present wilderness area is only wild in a relative way, and has been affected to some degree by civilization, encroachment, and pollution. We are unable, therefore, to sense the impact of total wilderness, to marvel at its productivity, to feel its isolation and power, to savor its purity, or to be awed by its overpowering magnificence. It is impossible to imagine, for example, that the early emigrants from Europe knew of their nearness to the North American continent when they could smell the fragrance of its pine forests while still 200 miles at sea.[35] Francis Parkman, the famed American historian of the late 19th century, described the primeval eastern American wilderness as:

> One vast, continuous forest shadowing the fertile soil, covering the land as the grass covers a garden lawn, sweeping over hill and hollow in endless undulation, burying mountains in verdure, and mantling brooks and rivers from the light of day.[36]

For many of those who left the cultivated and civilized shores of Europe, such vastness was awesome — a "panorama of distance" where

> the seasons come and go; grass grows and flowers die; … the snow lies still and quiet over hill and lake; the rivers rise and fall, but the rigid features of wilderness rest unchanged. Lonely, silent, and impassive; heedless of man, season or time, and the weight of the infinite seems to brood over it.[37]

Its condition almost defied description, leading one observer to note, "nothing under heaven can be compared to its effulgent grandeur,"[38] while another, who once made a journey through the interior of one of the still unspoiled eastern colonies, stated:

> It is impossible to describe the grandeur and richness of scenery…Primitiveness, omnipotence, and tranquility were stamped upon everything so forcibly, that the mind is hurled back thousands of years, and the man left denuded of the mental fabric which a knowledge of ages of human experience and of time may have reared within him.[39]

The land was prolific. Nature filled her storehouse to the extremities. Stories are told of passenger pigeons darkening the skies for days during their migrations; one nesting area in Michigan covered approximately 300 square miles, and the population was estimated not in millions, but in billions.[40] Other bird species were found in abundance as well, and even with the primitive firearms of the day, Champlain, for example, found no difficulty in killing more than two thousand "larks, plovers, snipes and curlews" in an afternoon's shoot.[41] "No one spot exceeding a few superficial yards…is not bounded on all sides by deer paths," wrote another man;[42] "moose, and caribou abounded, and between 50 and 70 million buffalo were estimated to exist on the continental plains at the height of their numerical strength."[43]

An integral part of this veritable preserve of nature were the rivers and streams that flowed in their unspoiled freedom to an equally unspoiled sea. Jonathan Carver, in his travels through the "interior parts of North America" in 1767, was mesmerized by the purity and appeal of the St. Lawrence River:

> The water…was as pure and transparent as air; and my canoe seemed as if to hang suspended in that element. It was impossible to look attentively through this limpid medium at the rocks below, without finding, before many minutes were elapsed, your head swim, and your eyes no longer able to behold the dazzling scene.[44]

In this pristine environment, salmon and other fish lived and reproduced in phenomenal numbers. In the early 1600s, the governor of Acadia remarked that the sea was "paved with salmon" and other species;[45] at times, fish were so plentiful that they impeded the passage of ships;[46] and according to John Cabot, cod could be captured by simply lowering wicker baskets over the side of a boat.[47] It was once said of the Kennebecasis, a tributary of the Saint John River in New Brunswick, that the salmon were so plentiful, you could virtually cross the river from one side to the other on their backs and not get wet.[48]

Today we tend to view such comments with disbelief, or at least suspicion, but an examination of old documents and statistical records tends to weaken these doubts, if not dispel them altogether. Quantitative estimates of fish and, in particular, of salmon abundance in aboriginal times have been made, and although estimates vary, they all reveal results of astonishing magnitude. Rostlund, for example, calculated the aboriginal production of Atlantic salmon in the United States to be between 14 and 15 million pounds a year, or an average of 580 pounds per square mile in the occurrence area.[49] Applying Rostlund's base calculation to the total area of salmon occurrence in eastern North America, an estimated 145 million pounds per year is obtained — between 10 to 12 million salmon. Elson estimated, by comparison, that the average adult salmon production of the Maritimes region in 1957 was 1 million fish, or approximately 11 million pounds;[50] since this territory comprises only 20% of the total production area on the continent, 55 million pounds would be the estimated available stock of the entire occurrence region in recent times. A third study concludes that no less than 60 to 70 million pounds might be considered the maximum annual production in aboriginal times.[51]

The Amerindian Environmentalists

The areas of the continent that were frequented by the Atlantic salmon were also occupied by various

Indian and Eskimo tribes. It has been generally accepted that Palaeolithic hunters crossed the Alaska–Siberia land bridge to America approximately 26 000 years ago, during the last occurrence of continental glaciation, but a suspected 50 000-year-old human skull recently unearthed in California may suggest an earlier emigration. Archaeological discoveries in coal pits reveal man's age in eastern North America at between 14 000 and 15 000 years.[52]

With regard to the Atlantic Provinces, the earliest palaeo-Indian occupation is identified as the Clovis Culture, which was occupying locations in the Debert, Annapolis, and possibly the Medway river basins around 8600 B.C. Fishing appears to have been an important activity in their subsistence economy. Around 4000 B.C., the Archaic (Laurentian) Culture made its appearance, one of their principal campsites in Nova Scotia being located a short distance above the present White Rock fishway on the Gaspereau River, Kings County. Artifacts reveal that they relied heavily on the salmon and gaspereau resources of the region.[53]

Even in Labrador, an early culture can be traced to around 5000 B.C., with a related culture being found in Newfoundland by at least 2000 B.C. All traces of this "Maritime Archaic Tradition," which was once common from Labrador to Maine, disappeared around 1000 B.C., except, perhaps for the related Beothicks, and were replaced by the Shellfish Culture from the south and the Dorset Culture from the north. Between 100 and 700 A.D., the Algonquin Culture, represented by the Micmacs, arrived in eastern Canada, while the Dorset Culture in Labrador and northern Newfoundland was replaced by the more modern Eskimo, so that by the time of European contact (1000 A.D.), the Dorset had either disappeared or was within a century or two of extermination.[54]

Prior to European contact, the existing native populations within the salmon's northern range basically followed a summer-fishing and winter-hunting style of sustenance living. In the more southerly regions, the Indians were more numerous and agriculture was more ardently undertaken;[55] furthermore, since agriculture required at least a seasonal permanence at one location, a less transitory existence prevailed among these tribes than with those to the north. Maine, New Brunswick, and the St. Lawrence valley provided the transitional zone between the semiagricultural and nonagricultural segments of the native population.

Although a number of more or less permanent settlements existed in this zone — such as Pentegoet in Maine, St. Ann's in Nova Scotia, Meductic in New Brunswick, Tadoussac in Quebec, and Markham in Ontario — these habitations were frequently vacated in the winter, as various parties participated in the hunt for game.[56] In summer as well, periodically vacating these

major settlements for seasonal fishing camps was a regular practice. Whether permanent, semipermanent, or transitory, Indian and Eskimo encampments were generally situated along the shores of some main waterway and were frequently located to take advantage of a particular fishery.

It has been claimed that fishing was the predominant industry of the Canadian Indian, surpassing in importance the pursuit of game, and in some localities, the cultivation of the soil.[57] Although generally regarded as a spring, summer, and autumn occupation, fishing often extended into the winter months, when it was resorted to on a limited scale if the winter quest for terrestrial game was not particularly productive. The Indians were not selective in their catch; practically anything that came from either fresh or salt water was taken and consumed, frequently raw and in its entirety. Cartier related that the St. Lawrence Indians ate both their meat and fish uncooked, sometimes only smoking it a little.[58] Salmon, eels, and catfish were highly prized. These fish, strangely enough, have the highest caloric count of any North American fish species, leading one observer to comment that "Evidently the Indians chose their delicacies with nutritional wisdom. In some manner they found and learned to like what they really needed, and without any advertisements."[59]

Beach fishing was carried on when the tide was out; lobsters were taken from tidewater pools, and accumulations of clam shells at ancient Indian sites throughout the Maritimes attest to the exploitation of this particular mollusk. Crabs, preferably roasted, were another delicacy.[60] The natives were not only shallow-water fishermen, but they also went to sea in their canoes to hunt for porpoise and seal, and early European fishermen encountered these resourceful natives many miles from land. Beothuck Indians were known to have canoed even to Funk Island, 45 miles off the east coast of Newfoundland, their incentive in this case being the eggs of the now-extinct Great Auk.[61] One might accept that the traditional Eskimo kayak was capable of performing this type of voyage successfully, but the Beothucks used open birch canoes,[62] as did the southern tribes, and these Maritime groups performed considerable feats of seafaring in them.

Although the natives relied heavily on the fish resource, they did not overexploit it, since their relatively small numbers along the vast eastern seaboard guaranteed only periodic, insignificant, and rapidly recoverable depressions in the total resource. It is estimated, for example, that the Indian population in all of eastern Canada at the time of the early French explorations did not exceed 8000.[63] Beamish Murdoch estimated that the Indian population of Acadia was somewhere between 3000 and 3500 in 1610, which would indicate a maximum density of 1 individual in 15 square miles.[64] At densities such as this in regions of plentiful fish and game, no severe impact was likely to be felt on any one of the food resources.

Generally it was not in the Indian nature to store up great quantities of food for a rainy day, since the regimen of life was based on a subsistence economy linked to the nomadic habit. The storage of food was quite unnecessary when one resided in nature's inexhaustible, living warehouse. Nonetheless, small quantities of food were preserved, at least by some of the less transitory tribes, and such preservation was usually achieved by smoking or drying:

In summer these Indian women [of New England], when lobsters be in their plenty and prime, dry them to keep for winter, erecting scaffolds in the hot sunshine, making fires likewise underneath them, by whose smoke the flies are expelled, till the substance remain hard and dry. On this manner, they dry bass and other fishes without salt, cutting them very thin to dry suddenly before the flies spoil them or the rain moist them, having a special care to hang them in their smoky houses in the night and dankish weather.[65]

Cartier noted that the Indians of Hochelaga "have in their houses large vessels like puncheons in which they place their fish such as eels and others that are smoked during the summer and on these they live during the winter."[66]

The Newfoundland Indians apparently dried their salmon similarly to the way the Europeans at first dried cod; no salt was used, the salmon simply being split and spread out flat, with small sticks to hold the carcass flat.[67] Some reports indicate that a sort of fish meal was sometimes produced by taking the dried or smoked fish, pulverizing it and storing it in baskets or skin bags; such a commodity could then be used as a constituent of broth or soup.[68] Indians and Eskimos in the extreme north undoubtedly preserved some of their fish by freezing.

There is some evidence to show that certain coastal and river tribes carried on a trade of fish products with the interior, agricultural bands,[69] but fish were so plentiful throughout the Atlantic slope that few tribes could be considered as having no immediate access to a local resource. In general, therefore, the fishing Indians did not look upon their commodity as a commercial product until after the arrival of the Europeans, at which time certain tribes engaged in a considerable fish trade with the white men. It is known, for example, that the Indians of the Restigouche region traded salmon with the French vessels that entered Chaleur Bay.[70] Simeon Perkins, one of the founders of Liverpool, Noval Scotia, carried on a salmon trade with the Micmacs along the Atlantic coast in the late 1700s, employing a schooner specifically for this purpose.[71] And of the Montagnais of Labrador, it was reported that "Their chief occupation is hunting, though in early summer they catch salmon and trout, which they trade with dealers on the coast."[72]

Especially Salmon

How important was the salmon in particular as a food resource? In Newfoundland, a traveler/fisherman who visited the island in 1583 commented:

For the most part their [the natives'] food is fish rather than anything else, and especially salmon, of which they have great abundance; and although there are many kinds of birds and fruits there, yet they make no account of anything but fishes.[73]

So significant was the salmon to the Beothucks of Newfoundland that dried or smoked carcasses were traditionally buried with the dead, for use while passing through the valley of darkness to the next life.[74] The Beothucks apparently had to change their preference for salmon rather abruptly after the arrival of the British fishermen, who drove them from the coast to the interior, where salmon were absent or more difficult to procure.[75] It is also on record that the Dorset Eskimos spent the early part of each season fishing seals on the coast and then retired to the rivers in the early summer where they could engage in salmon fishing.[76] In Quebec and Ontario, early observers such as Cartier and Father Louis Hennepin noted that salmon was an important staple in the native catalogue of fish.[77]

Numerous documents tell of the migrations of Indians to important, traditional, and sometimes distant salmon fishing areas, thus indicating that a principal segment of the Gulf Indian population depended heavily on the salmon. Bands from the St. Lawrence region frequently traveled to Chaleur Bay during the salmon runs to compete with local tribes who depended heavily on that resource. So significant was the salmon to the Restigouche people that they utilized its image as a tribal symbol, painting it on their canoes, weaving it into their clothing with porcupine quills, and tatooing it on their persons.[78] A story was told of a group of Indians at Nepisiguit who arrived at their fishery too late in the season to take advantage of the salmon; caught by an early winter freeze-up they were quickly reduced to a condition of starvation.[79]

Further south, the salmon also played an important role in the seasonal activities of other tribes. Indians from the Bras d'Or Lakes in Cape Breton traveled regularly to the Margaree Forks, where they were assured of an abundance of salmon in season; they fished for 5 or 6 weeks, returning in the fall to the milder and more protected region of Bras d'Or.[80] Many places along the Saint John River in New Brunswick were known as aboriginal salmon fishing sites, the major encampment in the valley in the 17th century being at Meductic, a location just below the present town of Woodstock and now flooded for hydroelectric purposes. From here the inhabitants traveled to the falls on the Eel River to obtain their salmon, since the main river opposite the village was not particularly suited to taking large numbers easily at any one time.[81]

When an outbreak of disease occurred at Meductic, the settlement was moved to the Mouth of Keswick, a point chosen because of the large congregations of salmon that occurred at the head of the tide.[82] The islands and flats below the present Mactaquac Dam also provided excellent bases from which to conduct the fishery, as evidenced in the name Savage Island and by the fact that aboriginal artifacts were unearthed there when wells were being drilled for the Mactaquac fish hatchery.

The natives were well aware that salmon congregated at the head of the various coastal streams and below either partial or total barriers; locations of known Indian encampments attest to this fact: Scoodic Falls on the St. Croix, Bellow Falls on the Connecticut, Amoskeag Falls on the Merrimack, and Kochs Falls on the LaHave, to cite a few.[83] Perhaps the crowning example of the use of a natural barrier as a fishing location was described by Louis La Hontan when he visited Niagara Falls in 1703: "The Beasts and Fish that are thus killed by the prodigious Fall serve for food for 50 Iroquois who are settled about two leagues off, and take 'em out of the water with their Canoes."[84]

The absence of natural barriers in certain regions generally led to the use of secondary fishing sites, usually at the confluence of two streams, or at the inlets and outlets of lakes and ponds. Indians of the Lake Champlain region, for example, fished salmon where the Big Chazy River entered the lake; the confluence of the Concord and Merrimack rivers was a favored salmon fishing spot of the Indians in New Hampshire, as were the mouths of many of the tributaries to the Saint John, Miramichi, and Restigouche rivers in New Brunswick.[85] The Indians were willing to let nature assist as much as possible when it came to salmon fishing, but they were not completely averse to enhancing her providence by devising methods by which they could take a more successful advantage of the resource.

Indian-uity

The early explorers' records show that the natives of North America had little to learn from their European contemporaries when it came to fishing; indeed, aboriginal methods and expertise were in many ways superior to those of the European fishermen. Since cod was the species that dominated the early European fishing enterprise in America, it was cod fishing that these voyagers knew best — an exercise that basically involved a knowledge of handline use, cleaning, and dry and wet curing.

The native was not so limited in his pursuit of the fishery; to him, cod was not the only fish nor handline the only method. William Wood reported in 1634 that the natives were "expert" at all types of fishing, "fitting sundry baits for several fishes, and divers seasons ; being not ignorant likewise of the removal of fishes,

knowing when to fish in rivers, and when at rocks, when in bays, and when at sea."[86] The Amerindian carried out an extensive weir fishery, constructed nets of various types, built traps, hand nets, and scoop nets, speared his fish, and developed a primitive form of angling, and also discovered that certain natural toxins could be used to stun fish temporarily.[87]

When it came to the salmon fishery, however, the Indian's most prominent device was the spear. Apart from the use of the club, stone, or bare hands, the spear was probably the most ancient and primitive method of killing game; it was the most universally used weapon, in terms of its distribution and the variety of game upon which it could be used. The northern natives' style of living favored the spear; since they were nomadic, the tools that were preferred by them were those that could be easily transported or quickly constructed on the spot. Since the native effort was also directed chiefly toward satisfying individual or family needs, rather than those of the tribe in general, the individual fishing method was the only one necessary on most occasions; the spear was a one-man fishing implement which provided the best catch per unit of effort. Even where more elaborate pieces of gear, such as impoundments and traps, were constructed, the spear was still the major implement for retrieving the fish from these devices.

Although the native fishery was influenced considerably by the introduction of European equipment, the Indian spear continued to dominate the salmon fishery for several hundred years after European contact — even becoming the chief method used by the first white settlers in America to catch the larger river fish. Although several types of spear have been identified in the Amerindian culture, the typical salmon spear, which appears to have been used universally throughout the salmon occurrence area, was the trident. This device consisted of a relatively long, light, wooden shaft with pincerlike prongs at one end flanking a sharp point.

Descriptions of this trident-type spear prove that it was sometimes formed by splitting the end of a shaft into three pieces; but more commonly, the piercing point of the spear was made of a separate piece of wood, bone or — after the arrival of the Europeans — iron, which was lashed to the main shaft. Indians of the St. Lawrence were said to have fished for salmon with "harping-irons,"[88] French-made spearheads or "harpoons," shaped like an old-fashioned lyre or harp. There is also the possibility that the iron referred to was nothing more than a simple iron spike which was merely forced into or tied on the end of a wooden shaft.

Although spearing sometimes took place in extremely shallow water and at various times of the day, a common practice was to employ it in deeper water at night, using canoes and torches:

> It is a pretty sight to see these little barks [canoes] stealing from some cover of the dark pine-clad shores,

15

and manouvering among the islands...rendered visible in the darkness by the blaze of light cast in the water by the jack...fixed to a long pole at the bows of the skiff or canoe. The jack is made of a very combustible substance called fat-pine, which burns with a fierce and rapid flame, or else with rolls of birch bark, which is also very easily ignited. The light from above renders objects distinctly visible below the surface of the water. One person stands up in the middle of the boat with his fish spear...ready to strike at the fish that he may chance to see sliding in the still waters while another with the paddle steers the canoe cautiously along.

The writer went on to explain that such a mode of fishing "...requires a quick eye, a steady hand, and great caution in those that pursue it."[89]

Although the spear was the most commonly used instrument to catch and retrieve salmon, another important device was the fish barrier or weir. The first weirs were undoubtedly natural formations such as waterfalls, barachois, and beaver dams. Observing that fish were held up by such obstructions, the native began to construct his own barriers, frequently at more convenient places than where they existed naturally. The ability that the native displayed in building weirs and traps often amazed the first European visitors, who eventually adopted the Indian's methods. Early descriptions and old prints testify that massive river and estuarial weirs, containing several heart-shaped compartments, were being employed by the Indians of Virginia;[90] the Eskimos were also using large, funnel-shaped stone fences in the northern rivers; and nearly all tribes between these two groups were using some type of coastal, estuarial or river weir to facilitate the capture of fish.

Most of the aboriginal river weirs were designed to seal off the entire width of a stream. Numbers of migrating fish collected against the barrier and were easily speared; some weirs were provided with openings which led smaller species into wicker-type baskets or traps, shaped like cones, and fitted with the large end at the orifice of the weir.

Possibly the earliest notation of river weirs along the northeastern seaboard was made in 1593 by Richard Fisher, who observed that "...passing somewhat more into the land, wee founde certaine round pondes artificially made by the Savages to keepe fish in, with certaine weares in them made to take fish."[91] The location of these weirs is believed to have been on the Margaree River. Nicolas Denys, who established several trading posts in Acadia during the middle 1600s, wrote that:

At the narrowest place of the river where there is the least water they make a fence of wood clear across the river to hinder the passage of fish. In the middle of it they leave an opening in which they place a bag net like those used in France, so arranged that it is inevitable the fish should run into them. These bag nets are much longer than ours they raise two or three times a day and they always find

fish therein, it is in the spring that the fish ascend and they descend in autumn and return to the sea. At that time they place the opening of the bag in the other direction.[92]

Apart from river weirs, the Micmacs of Nova Scotia were particularly involved in constructing shore and estuarial weirs along the Bay of Fundy coast. Marc Lescarbot, writing in the early 1600s, described similar structures and the extent of the catch as follows:

The savages make a hurdle or weir across a brook which they place almost erect, propped up by wooden bars, like buttresses, and leave a space therein for the fish to pass, which find themselves caught at the fall of the tide in such numbers that the savages allow them to rot.[93]

The Sieur de Dièreville provided another description from Port-Royal in 1701:

...stakes are driven side by side at the mouth of streams and rivers into which the sea raises, the fish pass over it at high tide on their way to fatten on the ooze of the marshes. When the sea has run quite far out and the fish begin to lack water, they follow the ebb or reflux and being no longer able to pass over the stakes because the water is too low they are arrested and can be taken.[94]

Where the word "weir" — as applied to the aboriginal fishery — means a fixed barrier made of relatively heavy materials such as wood, stone, or brush, the word "net" is used to indicate an impounding, trapping, snaring or gilling device, fabricated from light, filamentous, or strandlike material which is knotted or twisted together to form an area of open meshes. Such a device, because of its relatively light construction, could be used as either a fixed or movable piece of fishing gear.

Unfortunately, the records that make reference to early aboriginal fish nets do not specifically describe their actual construction and use, and by the time that detailed information was forthcoming on native nets, the aboriginal fishery had been largely influenced by European equipment and methods. It is known, however, that the Indians possessed a type of seine-net fishing device, and may have developed a simple type of gill net as well, constructed of strands of bark or root, small branches or saplings, strips of hide, or sinews of animals. Although this device may be too crude to be technically classified as a net, there is further evidence to suggest that more sophisticated nets were made. Erhart Rostlund's research indicates that the Indians were familiar with the universal netting knot prior to European contact,[95] and archaeologists at Indian fishing sites have unearthed small grooved and notched stones, which are believed to have been used as sinkers on relatively light, netlike pieces of fishing gear. These weights are almost identical to the carved sandstone sinkers used in modern times by some of the northern New Brunswick fishermen on their salmon nets.[96] Among the aboriginal tools which John Cabot brought back to England from Newfoundland was "a needle for making nets,"[97] a device that would not be required in the construction of weirs or other crude barriers; such needles may have been similar to those recently unearthed from an ancient Indian site at Port au Choix, Newfoundland, which were fine splinters of bird bone, pierced with eyes less than one-half a millimetre wide.[98]

The first written record of a fish net of any kind was made by Jacques Cartier, when he described the Indian fishery of Gaspé Bay in 1534: "...we found a great quantity of mackerel which they had caught near the shore with nets which they have for fishing, which are of hemp that grows in their country where they ordinarily abide."[99] The actual type or design of net is not identified, but the mention of hemp may suggest a relatively refined and delicate piece of gear. The use of fibrous hemp or hemplike material also adds considerable weight to the possibility that a gilling or enmeshing net of some sort was commonly used by the natives of the Atlantic seaboard. Champlain as well mentioned the use of native hemp and likened it to that which grew in France;[100] another observer described the material as "so soft and smooth that it looks more like silk than hemp."[101] It has also been noted that in other instances, "hemp" may have been, in actuality, the bark of moose wood (*Acer pensylvanicum*), nettle, basswood, or dogbane.[102]

Another early observation of net use by Indians was made in 1634 by William Wood, who noted that the Massachusetts natives "...make very strong sturgeon nets, thirty or forty foote long; they set long seanes or Basse nets which stop the fish."[103] Apparently these nets were set and fished in such a manner as not to require constant attention, since they were only visited at periodic intervals. In the same year, Roger Williams referred to the use of sturgeon nets by the Narragansett tribes as well. The first Jesuit missionaries to the Montagnais Indians on the lower St. Lawrence reported the use of both native and French-made nets, a casual comparison that may suggest different origins but similarities in construction.[104] It thus seems safe to conclude with Erhart Rostlund's remark that "not only various small hand nets but also large seines, gill nets and towed nets were known to the Indians in aboriginal time; however, some forms were not used everywhere but had restricted distribution."[105]

Although one might doubt that the native North American was accustomed to the artful pursuit of angling, certain documents tend to imply that he may have practiced a crude form of that occupation. When John Guy founded his Newfoundland Colony in 1612, he reported finding an Indian "fishing reele" at an aboriginal campsite near his settlement.[106] This device was probably a piece of wood or bone around which a line was wound, and used in the process of gorge fishing. Gorge fishing was practiced universally in ancient times, and may be considered the primitive form of angling which, no doubt, fathered the more modern sport in Europe.

In America, gorge fishing involved the use of a small oblong piece of wood or bone which was pointed at both ends and through which a small hole was drilled slightly off center; a line was passed through the hole, tied, and the device was dropped into the water to be retrieved when the fish swallowed the gorge.[107] More conventional types of fishhooks were also developed by the native, some equipped with rudimentary barbs. Champlain described one of these hooks which was used by the Nova Scotian Indians to catch cod:

> These they catch with hooks made of a piece of wood, to which they attach a bone in the shape of a spear, and fasten it very securely. The whole has a fang-shape, and the line attached to it is made out of the bark of a tree. They gave me one of their hooks, which I took as a curiosity. In it the bone was fastened on by hemp.[108]

Gorge fishing was the only way devised by the Indian for deep water fishing. Although not an important salmon fishing device, research has shown that salmon and trout were occasionally taken in this way.[109]

From Need to Greed

Although at least one researcher, Gordon W. Hewes, has claimed that the Amerindian salmon fishery was intense enough in some locations to depress the original stock of fish,[110] it is generally believed that the native North American had no deleterious impact on the resource as a whole. There is even the suggestion that he may have enhanced it by inadvertently and unconsciously practicing good fishery management. His spearing activities, for example, may have actually prevented the destruction of salmon redds and eggs by reducing overcrowding on the spawning grounds. In any case, the Indian was neither apathetic toward his environment nor ravenous in its use. This was to change, however, with the arrival of the Europeans, who supplanted the subsistence economy by a commercial economy. The result was that the former moderation, which fed the wigwam, gave way to an avarice that fed the cities of Europe and America.

NOTES

[1]Charles Hallock, *The Fishing Tourist* (New York: Harper, 1873), p. 231.

[2]G. Brown Goode, ed., *The Fisheries and Fishing Industries of the United States* (Washington: U.S. Commission of Fish and Fisheries, 1884), I, 469.

[3]Attempts were made as early as 1770 to stock — or restock the Hudson with Atlantic salmon; see Anthony Netboy, *The Atlantic Salmon, A Vanishing Species?* (London: Faber, 1968), p. 336. Hallock believed that subsequent to Hudson's exploration of the river, certain geological changes had

occurred, barring the salmon from their major spawning ground; see Charles Hallock, *The Salmon Fisher* (New York: Harris, 1890), pp. 16–17.

[4]Charles B. Wood III, "Salmon as 19th Century Millworker's Food," *The Atlantic Salmon Journal*, II (1975), 35. Erhard Rostlund, *Freshwater Fish and Fishing in Native North America*, University of California Publications in Geography, Vol. 9 (Berkeley and Los Angeles: University of California, 1952), p. 258.

[5]Rostlund, *Freshwater Fish*, p. 258.

[6]Marshall MacDonald, "The Connecticut and Housatonic Rivers and Minor Tributaries of Long Island Sound," in Goode, *Fisheries and Fishing Industries*, p. 659.

[7]*Ibid.*, pp. 661–662.

[8]Charles McCarry, "Yesterday Lingers along the Connecticut," *National Geographic*, 142, iii (September 1972), p. 338.

[9]W. A. Wilcox, "The Rivers of Massachusetts and New Hampshire," in Goode, *Fisheries and Fishing Industries*, p. 673.

[10]Stephanie Cooper Schulsinger, "What's in a Place Name," *Yankee* (June 1972), p. 50.

[11]"...you may take 1000 tons here," "MacPhaedris' Letter Book," (1717) excerpted in John C. Pearson, ed., *The Fish and Fisheries of Colonial North America* (Washington: Department of the Interior, 1972), p. 250.

[12]C. G. Atkins, "The River Fisheries of Maine," in Goode, *Fisheries and Fishing Industries*, pp. 724–725.

[13]Colin Graham, ed., *Woodbine Angling Yearbook* (1973) (London: Queen Anne Press, 1973), p. 16.

[14]Goode, *Fisheries and Fishing Industries*, p. 470. Atkins, in *ibid.*, pp. 723–724.

[15]*Ibid.*, pp. 705–717, 723, 769.

[16]Moses Perley, *The Sea and River Fisheries of New Brunswick* (Fredericton: J. Simpson, 1852), p. 124.

[17]Approximately 4000 square miles of Nova Scotia's total watershed area of 20 500 square miles were inaccessible to anadromous fish due to natural stream barriers. These calculations may be derived by examination of topographical maps and early geographic records.

[18]John Stewart, *An Account of Prince Edward Island in the Gulph of St. Lawrence, North America* (London: W. Winchester, 1806), p. 84.

[19]Goode, *Fisheries and Fishing Industries*, pp. 473–474.

[20]John W. Parsons, *History of Salmon in the Great Lakes, 1850–1970*. United States Department of the Interior, Technical Paper No. 68 (Washington: Government Printing Office, 1973), pp. 6–8.

[21]*Ibid.*

[22]Richard Nettle, *The Salmon Fisheries of the St. Lawrence* (Montreal: John Lovell, 1857), pp. 50–51, 80–86.

[23]*The Canadian Handbook and Tourist Guide* (Montreal, 1867; reprinted Toronto: Coles, 1971), pp. 45–46.

[24]J. D. Pratt, in *Annual Report* (1971), Environment Canada, Fisheries Service, Resource Development Branch, Newfoundland Region, p. 3.

[25]Wilfred T. Grenfell, *Labrador: The Country and the People* (New York: MacMillan, 1922), pp. 334–336.

[26]G. C. Sollows, J. A. Dalziel et al., *Preliminary Survey of the Rivers and Commercial Fishery of Northern Labrador*, Manuscript Report #54-1, Resource Development Branch, Maritimes Region, Vol. II, pp. 1–22.

[27]A. P. Low, "Report on the Explorations in the Labrador Peninsula...1892–1895," in *Annual Report* of the Geological Survey of Canada (1896), Series 2, Vol. 8, p. 330L.

[28]G. Power, "The Evolution of the Freshwater Races of Atlantic Salmon in Eastern North America," *Arctic*, II, ii, pp. 89–91.

[29]G. Power, *The Salmon of Ungava Bay*, Arctic Institute of North America, Technical Paper No. 22, p. 42, Table II. Power states that the larger weights of the Koksoak River fish are not significant; *ibid.*, p. 41.

[30]Low, "Report on the Explorations," p. 330L.

[31]Power, "Evolution of Freshwater Races," p. 86.

[32]"Hudson Bay Expedition of 1897," *Annual Report* of the Department of Marine and Fisheries, 1897, p. 77. Low, "Report on the Explorations," p. 330L.

[33]Studies have shown that when the Vikings came to America the climate was warmer than at present by an average of 5°F. After a lowering of the temperature following the Middle Ages, the climate again reached warmer levels in the 1890–1940 period. The overall world temperature has again dropped 1°F, since 1940. See C. P. Gilmore, "The Famine of 1974" and Robert Wallace, "A Viking Village in America," both in *Nature-Science Annual* (New York: Time-Life Books, 1974), pp. 24, 140–141. The significance of these climatic fluctuations on the distribution and movement of salmon in the last one thousand years is not known.

[34]See R. W. Dunfield, *The Atlantic Salmon in the History of North America*. Manuscript Report Appendices A & B.

[35]Rev. Andrew Burnaby, *Travells through the Middle Settlements in North America...1759–1760* (Ithaca, New York: Cornell University Press, 1968), p. 70.

[36]Francis Parkman, *The Conspiracy of Pontiac*, 10th edition (London: Collier-MacMillan, 1966), p. 129.

[37]William Francis Butler, *The Wild North Land* (1873; reprinted Edmonton: Hurtig, 1968), p. 22.

[38]Alexander Monro, *New Brunswick, with a Brief Outline of Nova Scotia and Prince Edward Island* (Halifax: Richard Nugent, 1855), p. 8.

[39]Quoted in James P. Howley, *The Beothucks or Red Indians* (Cambridge: Cambridge University Press, 1915; reprinted Toronto: Coles, 1974), pp. 139–140.

[40]Richard Carrington, *Mermaids and Mastodons* (London: Arrow Books, 1960), pp. 210, 215.

[41]N. E. Dionne, *Champlain*, Vol. I, The Makers of Canada Series (Toronto: Morang, 1906), p. 206.

[42]Howley, *The Beothucks*, p. 140.

[43]Georges Blond, *The Great Migration of Animals* (New York: Collier, 1962), p. 94.

[44]Jonathan Carver, *Travels Through the Interior Parts of North America in the Years 1766, 1767 and 1768* (London: Walter and Crowder, 1778; reprinted Toronto: Coles, 1974), p. 133.

[45]Ruth E. Kaulback, *Historic Saga of Lehève (LaHave)* (Halifax: n.p., 1970), p. 30. At a somewhat later date in Acadia's history, some of her people credited this "pavement" or quantity of fish with causing the almost perpetual fogs in the region: the steamy breath of all the fish and sea mammals being a hazard to navigation; John Knox, *The Siege of Quebec*, ed. Brian Connell (Mississauga: Pendragon, 1980), p. 111.

[46]H. P. Biggar, *The Precursors of Jacques Cartier*, Publications of the Canadian Archives, No. 5 (Ottawa: Government Printing Bureau, 1911), p. xiv.

[47]Pearson, *Fish and Fisheries*, p. 3.

[48]Grace Aiton, *The Story of Sussex and Vicinity* (Kings County Historical Society, 1967), p. vii.

[49]Rostlund, *Freshwater Fish*, p. 52.

[50]P. F. Elson, "The Role of Hatcheries in Assuring Maritime Stocks of Atlantic Salmon," *The Canadian Fish Culturist*, No. 31 (December 1957), p. 29.

[51]See Dunfield Manuscript Report Appendix B, Table 13. One interesting speculation concerning salmon populations in aboriginal times is that they may have been held in check — as compared to the strict biological and mathematical possibilities of production — by the presence of the beaver or, more accurately, by the presence of beaver dams. In Richard Brown's *History of the Island of Cape Breton*, p. 156, for example, it is stated that beavers were found in every stream in Acadia. This fact must have hindered or checked salmon accessibility to a considerable amount of potentially good salmon spawning and rearing ground in the region. As the fur trade eliminated the beaver and killed off some of the other salmon predators, it is not unreasonable to conclude that a higher salmon production was probable in the post-contact period than before the arrival of French and English fur traders.

[52]*Nature-Science Annual*, 1975, p. 167.

[53]J. S. Erskine, "Early Cultures in Nova Scotia," *Journal of Education*, 18, ii (May–June, 1969), 19–25; 19, i (December, 1969), 18–26.

[54]*Ibid.*, *passim*. The Maritime Archaic Tradition is defined as a culture which was chiefly dependent upon the sea for its means of subsistence (Maritime), one which practiced no agriculture (Archaic), and one which persisted for several thousand years (Tradition). A major cultural site was recently discovered in Newfoundland; see *Port au Choix National Historical Park*, Department of Indian Affairs and Northern Development, publication #AQ-T034-000-BB-A2.

[55]The Malecites at Meductic, in the transitional zone, grew corn; Andrew Hill Clark, *Acadia: The Geography of Early Nova Scotia to 1760* (Madison: University of Wisconsin, 1968), p. 41.

[56]For location of Indian settlements, see "Letter from Father Biard, January 31, 1612," *The Native Peoples of Atlantic Canada*, ed. H. F. McGee, pp. 35–36, (Penobscot River, Maine); see also, W. S. MacNutt, *New Brunswick, A History 1784-1867*, p. 2, (New Brunswick and Nova Scotia); also, *Handbook of Indians of Canada*, p. 443 (Quebec). One prehistoric Indian settlement has been located at Markham, Ontario, where salmon bones were found among other archaeological material. The nearby Rouge River was a noted salmon stream at the time of colonial settlement; see W. Sherwood Fox, "The Literature of Salmo Salar in Lake Ontario and Tributary Streams," *Proceedings and Transactions of the Royal Society of Canada*, Vol. 24, p. 45.

[57]Bernard G. Hoffman, *Cabot to Cartier: Sources for Historical Ethnography of Northeastern North America, 1497–1550* (Toronto: University of Toronto, 1961), p. 210. Archaeological work in New Brunswick shows that most Indian campsites were handy to good salmon pools and at the beginning or end of rapids. On a good salmon river like the Tobique, practically every intervale showed evidences of Indian

occupation; George Frederick Clarke, *Someone Before Us* (Fredericton: Brunswick, 1968), pp. 24, 202.

[58]Biggar, *Precursors of Cartier*, p. 158. Clarke, *Someone Before Us*, p. 170, however, mentions that the Indians of New Brunswick were not adverse to cooking their fish, frequently roasting it on split sticks which served as a grille, or even by directly placing the fish in a bed of coals.

[59]Rostlund, *Freshwater Fish*, p. 4.

[60]John H. Maloney, "The First Century," in W. P. Bolger, *Canada's Smallest Province* (Prince Edward Island Centennial Commission, 1973), p. 3. "The Relation of Captain Gosnold's Voyage to the North Part of Virginia, 1602," excerpted in Pearson, *Fish and Fisheries*, p. 181.

[61]Howley, *The Beothucks*, p. 268.

[62]*Hand Book of Indians of Canada*, Sessional Paper #21A (Ottawa: Geographical Board, 1913), p. 61.

[63]Fairfax Downey, *Louisbourg: Key to a Continent* (New Jersey: Prentice Hall, 1965), p. 11.

[64]Beamish Murdoch, *A History of Nova-Scotia or Acadie*, (Halifax: John Barnes, 1895), Vol. 1, p. 43.

[65]William Wood, "New England's Prospect," in Pearson, *Fish and Fisheries*, p. 234.

[66]Hoffman, *Cabot to Cartier*, p. 158.

[67]Howley, *The Beothucks*, p. 246.

[68]Rostlund, *Freshwater Fish*, pp. 140–142.

[69]Parkman, *The Conspiracy of Pontiac*, p. 50.

[70]Philip K. Bock, *The Micmac Indians of Restigouche*, Bulletin 213 (Ottawa: National Museum, 1966), p. 11.

[71]Simeon Perkins, *The Diary of Simeon Perkins*, Vol. 1, Harold Innis, ed. (Toronto: Champlain Society, 1948), p. 8.

[72]George Waldo Browne, *The St. Lawrence River* (New York: Weathervane, 1905), p. 31.

[73]"Letter of Stephen Parmenius," 1583, in Pearson, *Fish and Fisheries*, p. 10.

[74]Howley, *The Beothucks*, p. 331.

[75]*Ibid.*, p. 62

[76]Farley Mowat, *West Viking* (Boston: Little Brown, 1965), pp. 245, 381.

[77]Hoffman, *Cabot to Cartier*, p. 207; Louis Hennepin, *A New Discovery of a Vast Country in America* (1698; reprinted Toronto: Coles, 1974), p. 524.

[78]Bock, *Micmac Indians*, p. 4.

[79]Banthelemey Vimont, "Relation de ce qui s'est passé en La Nouvelle France e's années 1644 & 1645" in Reuben G. Thwaites, ed., *Jesuit Relations and Allied Documents*, Vol. XXVIII; Document LV, p. 21. (Cleveland: Burrows, 1898), p. 25.

[80]Public Archives of Canada, Colonial Office (C.O.) Papers, 5, Vol. 68, "Samuel Holland's Survey of Cape Breton, 1766–1767."

[81]Stuart Trueman, *The Ordeal of John Gyles* (Toronto: McClelland and Stewart, 1966), p. 46.

[82]Esther Clark Wright, *The St. John River and Its Tributaries* (n.p., 1966), p. 152.

[83]*Scoodic* was the Indian word for salmon; *The Diary of Captain William Owens, 1766–1771*, *Bulletin* of the New York Public Library, 1931, p. 286. Netboy, *The Atlantic Salmon*, p. 319. Kaulback, *Saga of LeHève*, p. 10.

[84]Edwin C. Guillet, *Early Life in Upper Canada* (Toronto: Ontario Publishing Company, 1933), p. 267.

[85]Netboy, *The Atlantic Salmon*, p. 319.

[86]Wood, "New England's Prospect," in Pearson, *Fish and Fisheries*, p. 233.

[87]Rostlund, *Freshwater Fish*, pp. 162–194.

[88]Hennepin, *A New Discovery*, p. 562. Archaeologists have unearthed iron spear points of European manufacture at Indian campsites in New Brunswick, the points being barbed only on one side; Clarke, *Someone Before Us*, pp. 93, 146.

[89]*The Backwoods of Canada: Letters from the Wife of an Emigrant Officer* (London: Charles Knight, 1836), pp. 159–160.

[90]Ernst and Johanna Lehnes, *How They Saw the New World* (New York: Tudor, 1966), pp. 86, 127.

[91]Richard Fisher, "The Voyage of the Ship Called the 'Marigold,'" 1593 in Richard Haklyut, *The Principal Navigations of the English Nation*, Everyman's Library, Vol. 6 (London: J. M. Dent, 1962), p. 94.

[92]Nicholas Denys, *The Description and Natural History of the Coasts of North America (Acadia)*, William Francis Ganong, trans. and ed. (Toronto: Champlain Society, 1908), p. 437. Denys may have been in error when he stated that Indian weirs were placed at the narrowest spot where there was the least water — least, meaning depth or width? The narrowest place usually has the greatest depth and fastest flow, making weir construction more difficult.

[93]Marc Lescarbot, *The History of New France*, W. L. Grant, ed., Vol. III (Toronto: Champlain Society, 1914), p. 236.

[94]Sieur de Dièreville, *A Relation of a Voyage to Port Royal in Acadia or New France*, ed. J. C. Webster, (Toronto: Champlain Society, 1933), p. 113.

[95]Rostlund, *Freshwater Fish*, pp. 85, 86, 99, 291.

[96]*Ibid.*, p. 291. Examples of these aboriginal notched stones can be seen in the DesBrisay Museum, Bridgewater, Nova Scotia.

[97]Howley, *The Beothucks*, p. 1.

[98]*Port au Choix National Historic Park*, Department of Indian Affairs and Northern Development, Publication No. QS-T034-000-BB-A2.

[99]"The First Relation of Jacques Cartier," excerpted in Pearson, *Fish and Fisheries*, p. 6.

[100]W. D. Grant, ed., "The Voyage of Samuel de Champlain," excerpted in *ibid.*, p. 34.

[101]Wood, "New England's Prospect," in Pearson, *Fish and Fisheries*, p. 234.

[102]Carver, *Travels Through the Interior Parts*, p. 507, and Rostlund, *Freshwater Fish*, pp. 168–169. Moosewood, a maple, generally reaches a height of 10–20 feet, but sometimes grows to 40 feet under excellent conditions. It has no commercial importance at present, but the buds and twigs provide winter browse for deer and moose — hence the name.

[103]Rostlund, *Freshwater Fish*, p. 163.

[104]*Ibid.*

[105]*Ibid.*, p. 84.

[106]Howley, *The Beothucks*, p. 16.

[107]Wilson D. Wallis and Ruth Sawtell Wallis, *The Micmac Indians of Eastern Canada* (Minneapolis: University of Minnesota, 1955), p. 27.

[108]Grant, "The Voyage of Samuel de Champlain," excerpted in Pearson, *Fish and Fisheries*, p. 34.

[109]Wallis and Wallis, *Micmac Indians*, p. 27; also, Rostlund, *Freshwater Fish*, pp. 113–117.

[110]Rostlund, *Freshwater Fish*, p. 17.

CHAPTER

III

The Precolonial Fishery

Runic Salmon

Notwithstanding some evidence from Newfoundland and Quebec which suggests that Irish Druids or even the ancient Phoenicians were the first people to cross the Atlantic and touch the shores of the New World,[1] it is now established that the Vikings discovered and attempted to colonize the seaboard of northeastern North America late in the 10th century A.D.[2] The warring Norse adventurers in their westward migration from Scandinavia reached Iceland by 874 A.D., Greenland by 930 A.D., and Newfoundland by 995 A.D.[3] They were unexcelled at fishing and had previously captured salmon in the fjords of their native country — an activity which they carried to Iceland and on to Newfoundland, where stocks of the same species were found in abundance.

The story of these Viking discoveries comes to us from a modern translation of ancient runic stones, upon which Norse scribes imprinted the records of the Viking adventures, collectively known as "the sagas." Upon these stones is recorded the first evidence of the existence of both the North American continent and the North American salmon. As early as about 995 A.D., it was noted in one saga that "There was no shortage of salmon in the river or in the lake and these were larger salmon than they had ever seen before."[4] One contemporary writer places the likely location for this comment at Trickle Cove, Trinity Bay,[5] but there are innumerable other possible locations throughout Newfoundland, Labrador, and the Maritimes in general. Although a principal Viking settlement has been discovered at L'Anse aux Meadows, on the tip of Newfoundland's Great Northern Peninsula,[6] another was possibly established at St. Paul's Bay, where salmon were also known to be abundant.[7] Evidence indicates that the Norsemen ventured along the coast of Labrador as well and knew such areas as Sandwich Bay, where several salmon rivers provided considerable financial benefits to commercial fishermen in later years.[8]

How far southward the Vikings ventured along the coast of North America is not precisely known. Scattered evidence supports their landfall at various points in Nova Scotia and New England; a stone supposedly inscribed with runic script has been found near Yarmouth, Nova Scotia,[9] and what was believed to have been a Norse axe-head was once unearthed near Country Harbour, Guysborough County.[10] The Vikings could hardly avoid the salmon in any of these areas at that time, but to what extent they exploited or depended upon the species in America is another matter. It would appear likely, however, that with their fishing experience, they relied to a considerable degree on this readily available food resource; indeed, the fact that the salmon is singled out in the sagas implies a specific attention to the species. Viking methods of fishing are also somewhat obscure, but the use of nets is suggested by some writers,[11] and since the Norse undoubtedly knew the art of weaving

21

with filamentous material,[12] various types of seines or nets were no doubt possible; spear fishing was also likely.

Viking settlements in America could hardly be considered permanent; they were vacated by 1014 A.D.,[13] and several centuries were to pass before the existence of the great western continent was again reported. In the 12th century, Madog, a pretender to the Welsh throne, supposedly ventured across the Atlantic to land southward of any salmon area,[14] and in 1398, Henry Sinclair, Earl of the Orkneys, was reported to have made an unexpected landfall in Nova Scotia. He left no record with respect to the fish species that he encountered, but his biographer credits him with a landfall within sight of Salmon Hill, Guysborough County.[15]

First Tangible Wealth

Shortly after Sinclair's reputed visit to America, Basque fishermen discovered the great cod banks off Newfoundland. The Basques were known to have been fishing in the Labrador Sea off southwestern Greenland from 1400 to 1420, and probably reached within sight of Newfoundland by 1430[16] — at least half a century before Columbus made his discoveries. The Basques, like many other discoverers of new and valuable resources, were apparently not inclined to talk about what they had found, wishing instead to reserve the valuable cod banks for themselves for as long as possible.

The story of the richness of the seas around Newfoundland and the Maritime Provinces was left for John Cabot to publicize when he returned from his New World voyage in 1497. He reported that the sea was covered with fish; so plentiful were they that they could be captured in baskets lowered over the side of his ship.[17] John's son, Sebastian, stated in later years that at times the numbers of fish were so great that they slowed the passage of his vessels,[18] and on a map which the younger Cabot had made of the fishing grounds, he inscribed the following comment: "It yields plenty of fish, and those very great, as seals, and those which we commonly call salmon."[19]

In 1500, Gaspar Corte-Real, on behalf of Portugal, explored Newfoundland's northern coast, reporting "Massimenti di salmoni" — plenty of salmon.[20] His explorations established Portugal's Newfoundland fishery,[21] and by 1506, the Portuguese government began to levy taxes on the important new commodity arriving from the west.[22] At about the same time, the English began fishing the Grand Banks for cod, and in 1510, Henry VIII forbade the buying of fish from other nations, in order to further encourage the Newfoundland fishery.[23]

At first, fishermen rarely touched land except to seek shelter during storms or to replenish their water supplies. The cod fishery was initially conducted as a "wet fishery" and did not require the accommodation of a land base, the fish being simply caught and salted down in barrels after being cleaned. Lack of good curing salt, however, soon necessitated the development of a "dry fishery," in which the cod were dried rather than being immediately salted down in brine barrels. Since the deck of a ship provided insufficient space for drying large quantities, small, temporary fish-drying stations were established at convenient places along the coast. The cod could be laid out to air on the rocks or on specially constructed scaffolds called fish flakes.

The establishment of shore drying stations, frequently close to the outlet of some coastal stream where freshwater supplies could also be replenished, brought the fishermen into closer proximity to the concentrations of migrating salmon — a fortuitous coincidence which undoubtedly encouraged the fishermen to consider at least the incidental worth of the species. Salmon were a valuable commodity in Great Britain at this time, both for the common man and the gentry. In the early 16th century, for example, the servants of large British estates were fed on salmon, and £5 from an earl's money-pouch could purchase enough to keep his household supplied for a full year.[24] Quantities of salmon were, therefore, cured each season at the various Newfoundland shore stations for shipment back to England with the cod, and the salmon fishery increased yearly as a side benefit to the general cod fishery of the "New-Found-Land."

When Jacques Cartier began his voyages of discovery in 1534, the presence of salmon in other areas of North America was established. Upon entering Chaleur Bay, he noted that "there are many fair meadows and good herbs and ponds where there are plenty of salmon."[25] It would have been virtually impossible for Cartier not to sight salmon in the Bay, since he entered it in mid-July when substantial runs would be encountered; from that day, Chaleur Bay was recognized as one of the most prolific salmon areas on the continent. Indeed, the vast quantities of the species which regularly entered the region had resulted in the Indians giving it the title, *Ecketaun Nemaachi*, or "sea of fish."[26] After sailing around Gaspé, Cartier entered the St. Lawrence River, where he again documented the presence of salmon and mentioned their considerable use by the natives.[27]

Following Cartier's voyages, there was little in the way of major descriptive narrative about North America and its fish for several decades, although occasional reports on the country and its resources — particularly those of Newfoundland — filtered back to Europe. It was thought to be a cold and inhospitable New World; to the European fishermen, however, its waters were both famous and familiar.

Anthony Parkhurst, among others, reported on the commodities of Newfoundland in 1578 and listed the salmon as an important consideration.[28] With France making its presence known on the St. Lawrence and around the Gulf, Great Britain decided to express her sovereignty over the Island of Newfoundland, and to this end Sir Humphrey Gilbert was sent out in 1583 to take possession of the lands for the Crown and to advance religion in the "Paganish Regions."[29] Sailing into St. John's, which he found "very populous and much frequented," Gilbert established his authority and began extracting taxes from foreign fishing vessels. In exercising this duty as prescribed by the Crown, he explained, "Insomuch as we were presented above our allowance with wines, marmalades, most fine ruske or bisket, sweet oyles and sundry delicacies. Also we wanted not of fresh salmons, trouts, lobsters and other fresh fish brought daily unto us."[30]

After making his presence felt in Newfoundland, it was Gilbert's intention to explore south along the coast of mainland America. Leaving Cape Race, his ships first headed southwest in order to sail between Cape Breton and Sable Island; within sight of the former, however, a violent storm resulted in the loss of one of his ships. After drifting northward for 6 days in an open boat, a number of the crew from the stricken vessel managed to row back to Newfoundland, where they landed at the mouth of a river on the south coast:

> We rested there three dayes and three nights and lived very well with pease and berries, wee named the place Saint Lawrence, because it was a very goodly river like the river of St. Lawrence in Canada, and we found it very full of Salmons.[31]

They were more fortunate than Gilbert, for he lost his life in another storm while returning to Britain.

There is little doubt that some salmon fishing for commercial profit was being carried out at several places in Newfoundland at this time.[32] In 1583, one may assume that the environment for the species was still unspoiled, but in that year the first case of intentional pollution was reported in Newfoundland, the effects of which were rather devastating in more ways than one:

> We moved our Admiral to set the woods afire so that we might have space and entrance to take view of the country. Which notion did not displease him, were it not for the fear of great inconvenience that might ensue thereof. For it was reported and confirmed by very credible persons that when the like happened by chance in another part the fish never came to the place about it for the space of seven whole years after by reason of the waters made bitter by the turpentine, and rosin of the trees, which ran into the rivers upon the firing of them.[33]

British fishing activity was also spreading to the Gulf of St. Lawrence and along the Nova Scotia coast; for example, Stephen Bellinger cruised the waters of Passamaquoddy Bay in 1583 and named Grand Manan Island;[34] an English ship, the *Marigold*, while at Margaree Harbour in 1593 to fill water casks, discovered Indians there fishing for salmon with weirs.[35]

Strange Nature, Marvelous Greatness

During the precolonial period in North America, some connection with the salmon of the New World could be claimed by practically every coastal nation in Europe, either as a result of fishing it, selling it, or buying it; salted salmon were showing up in markets as far away as the Mediterranean. It is unlikely that many of the early explorers or adventurers possessed any scientific knowledge of the fish, for their contact with the species was largely peripheral.

Certain individuals, such as Henry Hudson, may have been fortunate enough to have grown up beside a salmon stream, and to have observed the periodic presence of the fish. However, unless one read Latin, and had access to Hector Boethius' *History of Scotland*, published in 1517, one would probably remain unaware of the truly "strange nature" of the fish: that the species was more plentiful in Scotland than anywhere else in the world, that it spawned in the sand of freshwater streams, that the fry would dissolve if touched, and that the young would go to sea and return in 20 days with "marvelous greatness" — but with nothing in their stomachs. At any rate, these so-called "facts" were doubtlessly unimportant to the commercial or adventuring mind; as long as the fish could be easily taken at the mouth of freshwater brooks to feed the mouths of men, the question of natural history — where the salmon came from, and where it went — was purely academic.

NOTES

[1]C.B.C. Television News, 13 April 1975.
[2]Robert Wallace, "A Viking Village in America," *Nature-Science Annual* (New York: Time-Life Books, 1974), p. 18.
[3]Alex Stephenson, "Ships West," *North*, Vol. XVII, No. 2, March–April 1971, pp. 14–19.
[4]Farley Mowat, *West Viking* (Boston: Little, Brown, 1965), pp. 117–118.
[5]*Ibid.*
[6]Wallace, "A Viking Village," p. 18.
[7]Mowat, *West Viking*, p. 239.
[8]This was the location of George Cartwright's large commercial salmon fishing operation in the late 1700s; see George Cartwright, *Captain George Cartwright and His Labrador Journal, 1770–1786*, ed. C. W. Townsend (Boston: D. Estes, 1911).
[9]Moses H. Nickerson, "A Short Note on the Yarmouth 'Runic Stone,'" *Collections* of the Nova Scotia Historical Society, XVII (19/2), 51.
[10]A. C. Jost, *Guysborough Sketches and Essays* (Kentville: Kentville Publishing, 1950), pp. 18–19.
[11]Mowat, *West Viking*, p. 78.
[12]Wallace, "A Viking Village," p. 24.
[13]Although the principal Norse settlements in America were vacated by the first decade of the 11th century, occasional

Norse adventurers were still reaching Vinland at a later date; see Samuel Eliot Morison, *The European Discovery of America* (Oxford Univesity Press, New York, 1971), pp. 57–58.

[14]Ellen Pugh, *Brave His Soul* (New York: Dodd, Mead, 1970), p. xvi.

[15]According to one theory, Sinclair landed on the Gulf coast of the province, at a point south or southeast of Pictou Island, and mistook the smoke from a burning coalfield in the interior for the emissions from a distant smoking mountain. The mountain is supposed to be Salmon Hill, Guysborough County, an 820-foot knob of ground southwest of the present town of Guysborough. See Frederick Jullins Pohl, "Land of the Smoking Hill," *Dalhousie Review*, XXXI (Autumn 1951), p. 163.

[16]Mowat, *West Viking*, p. 455. Mowat credits a Basque knowedge of the Isle de Stokfixa (Newfoundland) on the basis of a chart called the Andrea Del Bianca map. This map, however, was proven to be a fake; Wallace, "A Viking Village," p. 24.

[17]"Letter from Raimondo de Soncino to the Duke of Milan," (18 December 1497) in John C. Pearson, ed., *The Fish and Fisheries of Colonial North America* (Washington: Department of the Interior, 1972), p. 3.

[18]Peter Martyr, "The Decades of the New World," excerpted in *ibid.*, p. 3.

[19]Clement Adams, "An Extract Taken out of a Map of Sebastian Cabot," excerpted in *ibid.*, p. 4.

[20]Quoted in Anthony Netboy, *The Atlantic Salmon, A Vanishing Species?* (London: Faber, 1968), p. 315.

[21]C. J. Harris, ed., *Quick Canadian Facts*, 23rd edition (Toronto: Thorn, 1967), p. 11.

[22]Pearson, *Fish and Fisheries*, p. 116.

[23]D. W. Prowse, *A History of Newfoundland* (London: MacMillan, 1895; reprinted Belleville, Ont.: Mika, 1972), p. 33.

[24]*Ibid.*, p. 19.

[25]H. P. Biggar, "The Voyages of Jacques Cartier," excerpted in Pearson, *Fish and Fisheries*, p. 5.

[26]Moses Perley, *The Sea and River Fisheries of New Brunswick* (Fredericton: J. Simpson, 1852), p. 10.

[27]Biggar, "The Voyages of Jacques Cartier," p. 158.

[28]"Anthony Parkhurst's Letter," (1578) in Richard Haklyut, *The Principal Navigations of the English Nation*, Everyman's Library, Vol. 6 (London: J. M. Dent, 1962), p. 16.

[29]Edward Hoie, "A Report on the Voyage of Sir Humphrey Gilbert," (1583) in *ibid.*, p. 16.

[30]*Ibid.*, p. 17.

[31]Richard Clarke, "A Relation of Richard Clarke of Weymouth," (1583) in *ibid.*, p. 41.

[32]George Peckham, "A True Report of the Late Discoveries ... by Sir Humphrey Gilbert," in *ibid.*, p. 62.

[33]"Letter of Stephen Parmenius," (6 August 1583) in *ibid.*, p. 62. Gilbert had enforced a "Lords of the Harbour" or "Admiral" system, whereby the first vessel — and its captain — to enter a harbor during the season possessed the exclusive right both to govern further fisheries of that region and to fish that harbor in that year.

[34]J. Clarence Webster, *An Historical Guide to New Brunswick* (New Brunswick: Bureau of Information and Tourist Travel, 1947), p. 64.

[35]Richard Fisher, "The Voyage of the Ship Called the 'Marigold,'" (1593) in Haklyut, *Principal Navigations*, Vol. 6, p. 94.

IV
The Early Colonial Fishery 1604-1713

Arcadian Acadia

On a summer's day in 1604, a ship bearing the heraldic arms of France sailed along the coast of the Baie Français (Bay of Fundy) and into Passamaquoddy Bay. This was the expedition of Pierre du Gua, the Sieur de Monts, who, with the blessing of the King, was in search of a location upon which to build a permanent habitation in the New World. Accompanying de Monts were two men, Samuel de Champlain and Jean de Biencourt, the Sieur de Poutrincourt, both of whom have left detailed descriptions of these first efforts to establish a permanent settlement, and of the resources that the country had to offer.

Champlain, then on his third voyage to America, was impressed by the beauty, advantage, and prospect of the large body of water into which he had just sailed, and noted that "There are many good places capable of containing any number of vessels and abounding in fish in the season, such as codfish, salmon, bass, herring, halibut, and other kinds in great numbers."[1] Poutrincourt later stated that they had found so many herrings within the bay that a city could be fed on them alone,[2] although other fish were just as abundant in their proper season.

De Monts decided to erect his settlement on the shores of this bay, and to this purpose he made a landing on Ile Sainte-Croix (Dochet Island), a small mole of land rising out of the St. Croix estuary about 5 miles upstream from the present town of St. Andrew's. The first winter

spent on the island was one of misery and privation for the 79 inhabitants; although historians generally agree that the winter of 1604–05 was particularly severe in the region, the plight of de Monts and his men would have improved very little even had the season been more moderate, for they were ill-prepared for the great difference between surviving in primitive Canada and living in civilized France. By the time spring had arrived, 39 men had died — half the white population of America.[3]

The seasonal reduction in manpower due to "winter sickness" was to plague pioneering settlements in the New World for many years to come. It is rather ironic to note that fish — the principal reason for establishing many of the new settlements and the basic hope for their survival and prosperity — was considered to be largely responsible for the untimely demise of so many of the new inhabitants. Lescarbot wrote that:

> To always eat fish unless it is good and firm or shellfish without bread is dangerous and causes dysentery, as we have observed above in regard to certain savages who died of it. We can prove this also by Sieur de Monts' men who died to the number of twenty the first year they wintered at Kebec, both on account of their change in dwelling and because they ate too many eels and other fish.[4]

Of course, it was not necessarily the consumption of eels, salmon, or other fish that caused such a high mortality among Champlain's or de Monts' men, nor even the consumption of tainted fish. Poor nutrition and the lack of Vitamin C were more often the cause of sickness and subsequent death among the early Europeans in America — not what was eaten, but what was not eaten.

In the spring of 1605, de Monts removed his prefabricated settlement, and what was left of his manpower, across the Bay of Fundy to establish the Habitation at Port-Royal, on the shores of the Annapolis Basin, where the colony eventually grew and prospered. Champlain spent much of his time in North America exploring the coasts in detail, from New England to the upper St. Lawrence, and his writings contain numerous references to the presence and abundance of fish.[5] He undoubtedly tasted the salmon of the St. Croix region during his uncomfortable stay there and, afterwards, explored the Penobscot and Saint John rivers, where he suggested that many vessels could easily load a vast variety and number of fish.[6] On these rivers, he also met with Indians who for 5 or 6 weeks during the fishing season were fully engaged in taking fish. Champlain's interest in the fisheries appears to have been more than casual, as revealed in the following statement, which suggests that perhaps he may be credited with developing the first fish culture station in America:

> I, for the sake of occupying my time, made one [a garden], which was surrounded with ditches full of water in which I placed some fine trout and into which flowed three brooks of very fine running water....I made there, also, a little reservoir for holding salt water fish, which we took out as we wanted them.[7]

At Port-Royal, the French began to barter with the natives, to practice a bit of agriculture, and to fish. The oldest social club in Canada, "The Order of Good Cheer," was founded at the Habitation by Champlain, and took advantage of the great variety of fish found there by serving salmon, bass, shad, and other piscatorial delights at regular gatherings. Encouraged by reports from Port-Royal of the considerable fishery resources of the region, other commercially minded fishermen soon organized establishments in Acadia. In 1610, a party of traders and fishermen from St. Malo established a port on Caton's Island in what is now Long Reach, on the Saint John River.[8]

Although Port-Royal was ravaged by a force from Jamestown, Virginia, in 1613, which somewhat curbed French activity in the area, this hostility did not discourage the development of French fishing activity in the Gulf of St. Lawrence; in 1619, two associations of merchants were organized in France to exploit the resources of that area. One company obtained the right to establish a shore fishery — the *Compagnie de la Pêche sédentaire de l'Acadie* — while the other gained permission from the Crown to trade with the Indians. The main base of the shore fishery was established at Miscou Island.[9]

The French influence and the French fishery continued to grow throughout the coastal areas of Acadia, and even in Lescarbot's time, European fishermen were so well known among the Indians of the region that the Indian language was reported to be half Basque.[10] The English tried to follow up their capture of Port-Royal by some sporadic settlement financed by selling knight-baronet titles, but these efforts were unsuccessful, due to the return of Acadia to France in 1632. French interests once again devoted themselves to the development and extension of the fishery.

Five years earlier, in 1627, several individuals, including Champlain, Cardinal Richelieu, and Isaac de Razilly, had formed the *Compagnie des Cent-Associés*, otherwise known as the *Compagnie de la Nouvelle-France*, in an attempt to monopolize trade in French-controlled North America. In Acadia, their principal effort in the early years was to outfit Charles de Saint-Etiènne de La Tour at Cap de Sable (Cape Sable). In 1632, Isaac de Razilly formed a subsidiary company, based at La Hève (LaHave), and became governor of the colony.[11] Like Champlain, Razilly was deeply impressed with the fishing potential all along the coast, and wrote to Lescarbot that "There the lakes are filled with all kinds of fresh water fish. The sea is paved with turbot, sturgeon and salmon."[12]

Under Razilly's direction, more interest was paid to the salmon and salmon-producing areas. The species was reported at "Rivière aux Ours" (Salmon River, Digby County), and at the "Isles of Tousquet" (Tusket), where the "fishery abounds in trout and salmon."[13] At LaHave itself, a great number of the fish were being captured by Razilly's men and presumably shipped back to France as an article of export. He also established outposts at Port-Rossignol (Liverpool), Petite-Rivière, and Canseau (Canso), where he either attempted to colonize, or to establish fishing stations under his lieutenant, Nicolas Denys.[14] Under Razilly's general direction, harmony existed among the French factions in Acadia, and progress, although not rapid, was unhampered and steady. He had shown that Acadia offered more to Europe than the codfish, and during the short period of his tenure, the fishery for species other than cod expanded, the fur trade reached considerable proportions, and settlement of the land for agricultural purposes increased.

After Razilly's death in 1635, conditions deteriorated, the various operations which he supervised broke apart, and the participants fenced with one another for control over various portions of the coast. In 1640, for example, Acadia had three governors — Denys, La Tour, and Charles de Menou d'Aulnay — all of whom were in fierce competition over resources and power in the region. This internal bickering, accompanied with frequent open hostility and destruction, continued until 1654, when Britain again captured Acadia.[15]

French fishing activity, however, was not entirely curtailed as a result of this brief English occupation. It was still in evidence, particularly in the Gulf region, and on the Rivière Saint-Marie (St. Mary's River) where, about 1655, a trader named La Giraudière established himself, becoming the first to take commercial advantage of the salmon fishery there. By 1658, he had also expanded to Chedabouctou (Guysborough).[16]

Acadia was once again returned to France by the Treaty of Breda in 1667, but it did not figure largely in subsequent French plans for territorial consolidation and development. It was allowed to languish, progress being made primarily through the efforts of private enterprise of the small but permanent population, which dated from the 1630s.[17] These inhabitants — the Acadians — were primarily subsistence farmers, dispersed over a wide area in a loosely organized seigneurial system. The conditions under which they lived and worked were often harsh and unrelenting, and initially there were few markets for their produce. One governor went so far as to encourage English fishermen to the coast, since he considered that this would enhance trade and provide a ready outlet for regional products.[18]

The Acadians engaged in the river fisheries for their own needs; they were particularly attracted to salmon, shad, gaspereaux, and eels, all of which made annual migrations to and from the various streams. The Acadians' impact upon the resource, however, was slight, for their total number in 1671 did not exceed 700, and reached only 855 when the first official census was taken in 1686.[19] Along with those colonists who operated trading posts and coastal fishery stations, however, the Acadians utilized most of the important salmon rivers, notable of which were the Penobscot, Saint John, Petitcodiac, Maccan, Salmon (Truro), Shubenacadie, Avon, Gaspereau, Cornwallis, Annapolis, LaHave, Musquodoboit, St. Mary's, Guysborough, Inhabitants, Margaree, French (Colchester County), Miramichi, and Restigouche.

One of the more significant fishing operations in Acadia was that carried out by Nicolas Denys. Denys came to the colony with Razilly in 1632 and spent some time at LaHave developing a trade with France in fish and lumber. During the unsettled period following Razilly's death, Denys expanded his fishing interests to other parts of Acadia, principally in the Gulf of St. Lawrence, constructing posts at Miscou (1645), Saint-Pierre (St. Peter's, Cape Breton) (1650), Nepisiguit (Bathurst) (1652), and Chedabouctou (Guysborough) (1659). In 1653, Denys purchased from the Company of New France the rights to the coast and islands of the Gulf of St. Lawrence — a vast territory stretching from Cape Canso to the Gaspé, and including Ile Royale (Cape Breton), the Iles de la Madeleine (Magdalen Islands), and Ile Saint-Jean (Prince Edward Island).[20]

During the 1650s, Denys' domain was principally Ile Royale, where he reported that salmon fishing was being carried out at several locations around its perimeter. At St. Ann, where a small French settlement and Jesuit mission had existed since about 1635,[21] he noted that "There is fishing for Salmon in the harbour, but the Mackerel there is [especially] abundant." At another location on the island, probably at Margaree or Mabou, he commented that "one enters into a little river for boats where great numbers of Salmon are caught."[22] Of his St. Peter's station, Denys wrote: "The land... extends for more than ten leagues with nothing but Furs upon it, and with land of no value as far as a little river where good land is found, and in which Salmon are caught."[23] The "little river" was probably the Inhabitants, although some good agricultural land and some salmon were also available at Grand River.

Denys was probably one of the first individuals to take notable commercial advantage of salmon in Acadia. He frequently mentioned the species in his writings, and provided some fascinating details about his contact with them. On a planned fishing excursion to a river at the head of Chedabucto Bay, for example, Denys wrote:

> ...I made a cast of the seine at its entrance where it took so great a quantity of Salmon that ten men could not haul it to land, and although it was new, had it not broken the Salmon would have carried it off. We had still a boat full of them. The Salmon there are large; the smallest are three feet long. On another occasion I went to fish four leagues up the river, as high as boats could go. There are two pools into which I had the seine cast: in one I took enough Salmon Trout to fill a barrel, and in the other a hundred and twenty Salmon.[24]

The river was probably the Guysborough, where Denys established a fishing station about 1659; it remained a popular fishing location after he left the area. The river still possesses salmon, but not in quantity — 52 fish were angled from the river in 1972, weighing an average of about 6 pounds each, and measuring considerably less than 3 feet in length.[25]

In time, troubles with other French interests in the region and fire that destroyed his St. Peter's station in 1668, prompted Denys to move his principal interests to the Nepisiguit post. If he had been impressed by the amount of salmon in Cape Breton, he was no less than amazed at the quantity and size of the same species on this northern coast of New Brunswick, noting that in the Nigadoo River alone, there were "Salmon of an extraordinary length; some have been taken of six feet."[26] At Nepisiguit, Denys found that three of the four rivers entering the harbor had "an abundance of salmon," and as he further explored the coast, more phenomenal salmon streams came to his attention. When he journeyed south, he noted the species in the Cocagne River, and when he traveled north to Gaspé and Mal Baie, he reported that salmon ascended there "in great plenty"; but nowhere did he discover as many fish as on the Miramichi. When he arrived there, he had considerable difficulty in contending with passenger pigeons, but

> If the Pigeons plagued us by their abundance, the Salmon gave us even more trouble. So large a quantity of

them enters into this river that at night one is unable to sleep, so great is the noise they make in falling upon the water after having thrown or darted themselves into the air.[27]

Records do not indicate to what quantitative extent Denys actually made use of the salmon resources of his domain. He was principally involved in the fur trade, the cod fishery, and trade with the Indians, but it is likely that a considerable number of salmon were also taken by his men and shipped back to France each year — although no direct mention is made in his writing, however, of any such export.

In order to satisfy the terms of his huge grant held from the Company of New France, Denys was required to provide his territorial concessions with colonists, a duty apparently accomplished with moderate success; the census of 1688 shows five families settled at Percé, three in the upper Chaleur Bay, three at Nepisiguit, and three at Miramichi.[28] The principal resident at Miramichi was Richard Denys, Nicolas' son, who, after his father's death in 1688, took over the management of the senior Denys' affairs.

Richard constructed a small fortified post on the north shore of the Miramichi, immediately opposite the junction of the river's two main branches.[29] Little information is available concerning his activities, but it appears from one of his letters that he may have been largely involved in the salmon fishery. The letter in question, written in 1689, was in the form of a request to the French Court for persmission to engage an Irish crew for use in one of his ships, as a safety measure for his trade during the war between France and England, which had begun that year. The letter cited "the advantages and profits which can be made in the fishery for salmon," and suggested that an Irish crew would be able to fly the British flag for safety; presumably the vessel would be loaded with the benefits accruing from the said fishery.[30] After Richard's death in 1691, the settlements on the Gulf shore languished and were eventually abandoned; of the 102 inhabitants which the elder Denys listed in his census of 1688, only two were found on the coast by 1725 — one settler at Pabos, and a single French trader at Miramichi.[31]

Another of Nicolas Denys' trade contemporaries in Acadia was Charles de La Tour, whose trials and tribulations are well known in colonial history; not so well known, however, is the fact that, after 1631, La Tour was actively engaged in the fishery from his Saint John harbor location, constructing on the mud flats south of Navy Island one of the first weirs ever used by white men in the region.[32] Gaspereaux were sought principally, but shad, salmon, and bass were also taken. Subsequently, a French sea captain who made frequent trips to Port-Royal early in the 18th century, compared the Saint John fishery with that of the former by stating that: "Trout and salmon are also found in abundance in some places but I

never saw a slice broiling at Port Royal. In a journey I made to the Saint John River I ate so much that I lost my taste for it."[33]

By 1686, there were only five families remaining on the Saint John River. La Tour's earlier settlement at Fort Sainte-Marie had been the victim of conflict between the British and French during the 1650s. Nevertheless, the failure of the area to prosper was surprising to some French explorers, who found both the agricultural and fishery potential there the best in Acadia. Antoine de Lamothe Cadillac, for example, traveled the length of the river in 1691, reporting that "It is the richest because it has the best soil, and because the fishery for salmon there is incomparable, and can be made for 80 leagues in its length."[34] Although Cadillac may have literally stretched the salmon fishery out somewhat by extending its potential to a few leagues above Grand Falls, there was no doubt that the Saint John possessed a great number of salmon, perhaps even an abundance comparable to that of the Miramichi or Restigouche rivers.

Although the fishery operations of both La Tour and Denys are particularly noteworthy examples of the interest attached to the Acadian fishery at this time, other operations were being carried out — or were soon to be initiated — all around the coast, with increasing attention being placed on the valuable river fisheries. It has already been noted that Nicolas Denys was not able to exercise absolute control over his domain. He was frequently harassed by interlopers and competitors — various fishing interests who jostled for the King's favor, requesting their own fishing rights and grants, and protesting Denys' huge geographic monopoly. A prime example was the competition offered after 1682 by the *Compagnie de la Pêche sédentaire de l'Acadie* — the Acadia Company. Sanctioned by a royal grant permitting access to the coast of Acadia and the Saint John River, the company first attempted to make use of the latter locaion, but eventually chose the head of Chedabucto Bay — Denys' old location — as its principal base of operation. The post contained 150 people by 1687, more than half of whom were fishermen,[35] and some of whom undoubtedly packed salmon from the Guysborough and Salmon rivers for export to France.

The monopoly of this company was, in turn, contested by other fishing interests, and adjustments were required regarding fishing grants and rights. Nicolas Denys apparently retained sole possession of the Gulf coast until 1686, when Gabriel Gautier, a member of the Acadia Company, acquired the fishing rights to Ile Saint-Jean and the Iles de la Madeleine; Gautier's efforts to establish a sedentary fishery, however, failed. Denys' original grant from the Company of New France was revoked, and in 1687, rights to the Ile Royale fishery were granted to one Bergier, a principal of the Acadia Company; in recompense, Denys was given a large seigneury in the Miramichi area.[36]

By the late 17th century, therefore, French interest in the coastal salmon resource throughout Acadia was well delineated. The St. Mary's River was being fished regularly, and further westward, "Mouscoudabouet" (Musquodoboit) Harbour was described as a fit place for small fishing craft, as well as being "an excellent country for hunting and there is salmon fishing."[37] The settlements of LaHave, Port-Rossignol, Port La Tour, and Port-Royal have been previously mentioned with regard to their likely association with the salmon; another area frequently noted was Passamaquoddy Bay, about which one Frenchman remarked: "The fishery for cod is made there at a pistol shot from the land, and salmon are taken eight leagues higher on the rivière Ste. Croix."[38]

Ile Royale was also being publicized for its salmon. When Joseph Robinau, the Sieur de Villebon, became governor of Acadia in 1691, he kept himself well informed with regard to the enterprises of the colony. In his catalogue of information on the fishery, he could not provide exact descriptions of Ile Royale, but he was aware of the more important harbors where the French came to fish, such as Baie des Espanols (Sydney), Hâvre à la Baleine (Baleine Cove), Hâvre à l'Anglois (Louisbourg), and Neiganiche (Ingonish). He also noted that "There are, moreover, in [Ile Royale] many rivers teeming with fish, especially salmon."[39] Writing in 1699 to the Comte de Pontchartrain, secretary of state for maritime affairs, Villebon noted of the general fishery potential of Acadia that:

It appears to me, Sir, that we might derive from the fisheries of this country, cod, salmon, herring, mackerel, sardines, shad, gaspereau, sturgeon, bass, haddock, fish which are all suitable for salting, either for Europe or the Islands.[40]

Development of the fishery, in fact, was growing rapidly, but sole French control over it was beginning to weaken. The presence of New England fishermen had been encouraged, in the hope that they would supply a market for local produce, thus keeping the Acadian settlers on the land. The New Englanders, however, had shown little interest in this trade, but instead were reaping good harvests of their own in the waters of Acadia. When war broke out between France and England in 1689, hostilities between the two factions in Acadia had already existed for several years, with New England dominating the local fishery and often plundering Acadian vessels. The French, however, soon retaliated, and in the first year of the war alone, France was credited with confiscating 54 of Salem's 60 fishing ketches.[41]

Even after peace returned to Europe with the signing of the Treaty of Ryswick in 1697, peace did not return to the Acadian fishery. Villebon wrote to the governor of Massachusetts, suggesting with respect to the fishery, that a state of neutrality be maintained between the two colonies; this might have been accomplished, had Villebon not also stipulated in his letter that the New Eng-

landers should not fish within sight of the Acadian coast until the whole matter of rights was clarified by London and Paris.[42] The New Englanders would not agree to this, and Villebon eventually received Royal Instructions from France to seize every English vessel found fishing east of the Kennebec River.[43] Despite the new policy, fishermen from the British colonies continued to fish within sight of the Acadian settlements and forts, and they had no less than 300 vessels so employed in the region by 1700.[44]

With regard to the Acadians, it is evident that they were not very eager to engage in the valuable enterprise of commercial fishing. Villebon stated in 1699 that the potential for an excellent fishery in the Minas Basin was considerable, but mentioned that it was of little use to the people, since there were still no markets.[45] Another enduring difficulty was that "Hitherto, all the people of Acadia... have paid more attention to the beaver trade and to the sale of brandy than to the establishment of fisheries, which, nevertheless, afford the most certain and most durable profit...."[46] In addition, the Sieur de Gargas, writing from Port-Royal in the late 1600s, described an official inspection he had made of the local fishery:

My instructions also included a brief inspection of the fishing. This order was not difficult to execute, for in all of Acadia there are only four or five inhabitants who fish for cod and mackerel. In fact, they greatly neglect fishing.... In the first place there is no one to buy their fish... [and secondly] they have not the necessary supplies.... It is no use that the river [at Port-Royal] is full of fish, for there are not three settlers who own nets... [there being] no more than six nets in Acadia.[47]

Although nets were scarce, a few individuals around Port-Royal and in the Chignecto area used brush weirs. Seine nets were sometimes used to capture salmon, as Denys' reports indicate, but these devices were not generally made available to the inhabitants, being limited instead to the more enterprising commercial fishing interests. When the Acadian settler engaged upon his limited fishery, he used the spear — a device considered superior to any other piece of equipment.

Despite the fact that the social and economic history of Acadia was still in its infancy at the close of the 17th century, the knowledge of many of its natural resources was extremely complete. With respect to the Atlantic salmon at this time, if one could assemble all the known contemporary data concerning the species and its distribution, there would be but few coastal streams where its presence was not known, or its numbers not exploited. Nevertheless, in a colony dependent upon subsistence farming, salmon remained of peripheral economic importance to a commercial fishery which stressed cod, and which was the domain of a few French companies — and many New England interlopers.

River of Canada

Both Cartier and Champlain chronicled the existence of salmon in the St. Lawrence and some of its tributary streams in the late 16th and early 17th centuries, and subsequent explorations during the middle 1600s revealed a great wealth of fish in both the coastal and inland waters of what are now the provinces of Quebec and Ontario. Champlain spent considerable time and energy in trying to interest the Court of France in the fishery. Immediately before his death in 1635, his last letter to Cardinal Richelieu, for example, told of the large variety, great wealth, and extraordinary magnitude of Canada's inland fish resource.[48] The Canadian fisheries, however, remained little attended, largely because of the rapid development of the fur trade — "the life blood of New France," which left few men and little effort for any other pursuit. The French reported early aboriginal salmon fisheries from the Saguenay River in Quebec to the Credit River in Ontario, and as far south as Lake Champlain, but most of these valuable areas were to remain as Indian fishing regions, only minimally exploited by the French for almost a century.

Some of the first detailed reports of salmon and the salmon fishery in Canada come from the writings of the Jesuit missionaries, who first came to New France in 1625, establishing at Québec and carrying their faith to the Indian villages throughout the St. Lawrence basin. The missionaries soon learned from the Indians the value of the region's fish resource, and they began exploiting the fishery for their own subsistence. In their "relation" of 1646, mention is made of the order's salmon fishery on the shores of the St. Lawrence. They reported that their fishery at Quebec City usually began about the middle of May, but in 1646 the salmon did not appear until June, with the first being taken on 11 June. By the end of July, 200 fish had been captured and salted down in kegs for use by the priests throughout the winter. In their storehouses they reported two kegs of salmon sent to them from one fishery, "besides four from our own fishery; and one from monsieur the Governor, from Isle aux Oyes."[49] The first salmon in 1647 was taken on 10 May, and in the following year, on 18 May; by the time their 1648 season had ended, which was in the third week of July, they had salted down 18 kegs of salmon — perhaps 900 fish.[50]

The Jesuits' missionary travels took them over a wide area of the St. Lawrence drainage basin, and they frequently described in detail their contacts with the wildlife of the region. They reported, for example, that the Chicoutimi River, a tributary of the Saguenay, was frequented by the Indians for salmon fishing, the river being deep and "very full of fish."[51] One group of Jesuits, on a mission to the Onondaga Indians at Oswego River in 1656, suffered greatly from lack of food, until

He [God] filled the River anew with fish expressly for us; for that very night one of our men caught 20 large salmon, and some catfish. And, on the 10th of the same month of July, while passing a rapid five leagues in length, — the longest that we met — our people killed on the way 34 other salmon with spears and paddles; there were so many of them, that they were struck without difficulty.[52]

In the paternal attitude of the day, another Jesuit described the fishery of the natives, noting that

Our savages... [construct] their dams and sluices so well, that they catch at the same time the Eels that descend, and the Salmon, that always ascend.... The fish most commonly found in them [rivers of Canada] are Eels and Salmon, which are caught there from the Spring to the end of Autumn.[53]

With such a wealth of fish around the St. Lawrence, the opportunity for commercial profit in a fish trade with France was considerable. The French who came to live in Canada, however, were either tillers of the soil or adventurers in the fur trade, and as in Acadia, the fishery resource remained largely unexploited except for local needs. Although Brisay de Denonville, governor of Canada, said that the inhabitants paid more attention to beaver and brandy than to fish, Jean Talon, the intendant at Quebec, put it even more bluntly: "Confronted with such riches [in fish] they behave as if they were paralytic."[54]

This apathy could not be understood at the French Court, so in 1672 the King forwarded special instructions to the then colonial governor, the Comte de Frontenac, directing him to exert his power to promote and establish a fishery among the inhabitants. Frontenac, however, did little to encourage such enterprise, and 16 years later another letter from Court reiterated the feeling expressed earlier, emphasizing that the inactive state of the fishery could not be tolerated.[55] "That which is most remarkable," wrote Father Louis Hennepin,

[is] that those who are Masters of these Countries may [and] could keep in awe above a thousand Vessels which go every year to fish, and who bring back Whale-oil, and a great quantity of Salmon, and Poor-Jack [hake], enough to furnish whole Kingdoms.[56]

The fishery was not entirely inactive, however, for a few small stations had been — and were being — erected for commercial profit on the lower St. Lawrence. François Byssot, for example, who had been fishing in the Tadoussac region since 1650, applied for a grant on the North Shore in 1661; this covered the territory from Ile aux Oeufs to Sept Iles. Later, Byssot established a post at Mingan to oversee concessions there, and by 1671 he was fishing cod and seals in that region. It is not recorded that Byssot engaged specifically in a salmon fishery; indeed, his concession did not stipulate this species. Nevertheless, the Mingan River was one of the best salmon streams on this segment of the North Shore. Byssot's daughter later married Louis Jolliet, the Quebec-born scholar and explorer, and this merger may have sparked Jolliet's involvement in the Gulf holdings of his father-in-law. At any rate, Jolliet was granted the Mingan Islands in 1679 and Anticosti Island in 1680.[57] On Anticosti, he established a base at Rivière à l'Huile and began supplying the troops and inhabitants of Quebec City with fish; it is reported that his men captured as many as 5000 salmon in one season in the rivers of Anticosti Island.[58]

In 1685, a salmon-fishing station was established at Matane by Denis Riverin, secretary to the intendant at Québec. Riverin had secured the seigneury at Matane, as well as those of Sainte-Anne-du-Monts, Rivière Madeleine, and Anse à l'Etang, and had been granted a royal subsidy to aid him in his development of the general fishery. In the early years, he was quite successful in this venture, and by 1693 was shipping a considerable quantity of fish to France. Subsidiary stations were established at such places as Marsoui, Cap Chat, and Petite Madeleine, where cod fishing also became an important pursuit of the Riverin firm.[59]

The New Englanders had not yet extended their fishing activity into New France from Acadia, and consequently, the St. Lawrence River and Gulf fishery witnessed little encroachment in this regard. In 1670, however, Prince Rupert granted a charter to a group of London merchants who called themselves "The Governor and Company of Adventurers Trading into Hudson Bay." It was clear from this charter, which gave them sole trading access to all the Canadian watershed which drained into Hudson Bay that their intent was to have a large portion of North America's commercial resources shipped to Great Britain and Europe. The company did not immediately take advantage of the fishery since, like the French their initial and prime interest was in the fur trade. The control that the Hudson's Bay Company exercised over such a vast area of the continent, however, placed it in an excellent position to monopolize a large segment of the salmon fishery in Labrador and Quebec in later years.

The New Found Land

Newfoundland continued to be dominated by the cod fishery throughout the 17th century, but during the second decade of that period, some new interests began to emerge, both with respect to fishing diversity and in attention to pursuits other than those connected with the fishery. Until 1610, permanent colonization was not considered in Newfoundland; to this point in time, any building that had been constructed on the island was erected only for use during the seasonal fishery. Many of these small habitations and storerooms had been erected, principally around the Avalon Peninsula, but they were vacant of any human occupation from September to May.[60]

In 1610, however, John Guy, sherriff of Bristol, began a colony at Cupids, a location where a small salmon stream, the South River, enters Conception Bay. Guy does not indicate in his writings whether he took advantage of the salmon fishery at this location, but it is quite probable that he at least attempted to utilize the resource, since he was known to be an exceptionally enterprising individual. Indeed, John Mason, who later became governor of Guy's colony, commented in 1620 that June was the month when salmon first frequented the shore, and that "in some parts," they were in "pretty store."[61] By 1626, Sir William Vaughn, in his book, *Golden Fleece*, indicated that in Newfoundland an independent salmon fishery had been established, which for the first time was not subsidiary to the cod fishery: "Experience of the fishery sheweth that it yearly maintains 8,000 people for six months in Newfoundland.... products of the colony [include] tar, pitch, etc., codfish, salmon, mackerel, [and] herring...."[62]

American fishermen were taking salmon in Newfoundland waters by the middle of the 17th century, as evidenced by a crew member of a New England vessel; he wrote from Renews in 1663 that

> The harbour we were in was very much esteemed for a good fishing place — the Barnstable men prefer it above any — yet we had poor fishing and made not above 130 quintalls per boat, and £3,5s a share. At the head of this river [Renews River] are many salmon; we caught abundance and our master saved several hogsheads and dried abundance in the smoke.[63]

The Americans, however, were as yet neither persistent nor numerous in this activity, for around 1680, Charles Talbot wrote: "Those of New England fish little upon the coast, but theyr fisheinge upon theyr owne Coast increases as they can steale fishermen from hence, wch they do yearly."[64]

The value of Newfoundland as Britain's great fishing base in the western Atlantic was now well established, and to maintain her interests there, the home government encouraged fishermen to engage in the fishery in every-increasing numbers — a policy which gained added importance, given that a large section of the island was not free to English fishermen. The French were also actively engaged in fishing on the coast, and in 1662, they constructed a land base with fortifications at Placentia.[65] This base was close enough to St. John's to encourage continual hostility between the two settlements, and both groups of inhabitants persisted in harassing each other.

The French were also primarily interested in cod, but they did not overlook salmon; a plan of Placentia, contained in La Hontan's *Nouveaux Voyages* of 1703, gives the name "rivière ou les saumons se pechant" for what is now the Southeast River. French fishermen were also engaged in the cod fishery of Trinity Bay on the other flank of the English, and salmon were known to them there; a map of 1720 shows one of their fishing stations listed as "Port aux Saumons," and includes another Rivière aux Saumons on the southern coast of Labrador.[66] With respect to the latter, it was reported that from the early 1600s, the French carried on an extensive fishery in the vicinity of the Strait of Belle Isle, having erected the town of Brest at the mouth of Bradore Bay, near the Rivière aux Saumons; the community was said to contain as many as 1000 individuals and some 200 dwellings.[67]

In the late 1600s and early 1700s, Newfoundland in general was wrought with turmoil in the fishery. Not only were the French and English in constant contention over it, but the permanent inhabitants of the island were also molested and subjugated by seasonal fishermen and the fishing admirals. The situation was compounded by the absence of a civil government and any religious authority; one convoy captain commented in 1684 that if the people assembled, it certainly was not for divine worship:[68] they were more likely to be fighting, converging on the codfish — or assaulting a spawning run of salmon. Under such chaotic circumstances, in a colony where life was difficult at best, little positive progress was possible in the fishery at this time.

New English Canaan

While the French were exploring the coastline of Acadia and attempting settlement, the English were also showing considerable interest in the coast of America south of the present state of Maine; Champlain's settlement at Port-Royal predated an English community in Virginia by only 2 years. Virginia's founder, Captain John Smith, had been employed by a group of Plymouth and Bristol merchants, who soon saw an opportunity for defraying the cost of colonization and increasing their commercial wealth without difficulty — they petitioned the King for permission to carry out fishing ventures in the New World and were rewarded in 1620 by a grant from James I which allowed them a monopoly in the fishery.[69]

There were no salmon in Virginian waters. Further north, however, they were encountered by some of the first English adventurers, and in 1605, Captain George Waymouth, exploring the coast of Maine, noted: "Here we saw great store of fish, some great leaping above water, which we judged to be salmon."[70] A Captain Popham found an abundance of "leaping fish" in the Kennebec River in 1607, and some records state that a small fishing settlement was established there about this time, but soon abandoned;[71] 16 years later, Christopher Leavett ventured to what is believed to have been the same river and reported: "There I found one river wherein the savages say there is much salmon and other good fish."[72]

Evidently, occasional voyages were subsequently made to the Kennebec specifically to fish for salmon; documents of the Plymouth Colony, for example, refer to a Mr. Winslow who engaged in a fishery there in 1629, and perhaps in subsequent years as well.[73] It was not for a considerable time, however, that permanent settlement was again attempted on the Kennebec and the regions north of it; most of Maine remained a frontier of frontiers — a buffer zone and no-man's-land, which separated English and French interests in America, but was claimed by both. When Nicolas Denys explored the region in the 1630s, he found it vacant; of the Penobscot River, he wrote:

> In the upper part of this river, there is a great deal of Salmon, Trout and many other sea-fish; but as for those of the fresh water, I have never heard tell that they have been fished for.[74]

Further south, Francis Higginson reported great numbers of salmon in Massachusetts Bay in 1630.[75] The Pilgrim Fathers had founded their Cape Cod Colony in 1620, in order to fish and please God in their own way; although the records of the colony make no mention of local salmon fishing, the settlers were, in fact, wedged between two noted salmon streams, the Connecticut and Merrimack rivers. One might conjecture that had the Pilgrims landed at either of these latter locations, instead of at Plymouth Rock, salmon might then have become the traditional Thanksgiving dish, instead of turkey. The Pilgrims' fishery was principally for shad and bass, however, and they quickly acquired a knowledge of the use of the spear and the weir from the Indians, as a means of capturing these species in fresh water.[76]

New Amsterdam was founded by the Dutch in 1621; if the early reports of Henry Hudson are true, this settlement on the Hudson River was the first community in New England to be founded on what may have been a salmon stream. Two years after New Amsterdam was founded, a settlement was begun at Dover, New Hampshire, a site well chosen to take advantage of the magnificent salmon runs in the Piscataqua River. Another contemporary settlement was begun at the mouth of the Saco River in Maine, yet another important salmon stream. The first settlement in what is now Connecticut was Windsor, which, being situated on the Connecticut River, also received important sustenance from the salmon fishery. Although there is no record of salmon entering the Seekonk River — the location of the first Rhode Island community — the list of first settlements in each of the New England states shows that five out of seven were located on what were later reported as salmon streams.[77]

New England settlements were springing up at a rapid rate by 1650. There were now several small villages along the Merrimack, and the Salmon resource was used to a considerable extent by the inhabitants of such towns as Newbury and Concord.[78] Settlement was also spreading up the Connecticut River, and a town was soon established at the falls at South Hadley in Massachusetts. The natives had always fished salmon there, and when the boundary between the townships of Northampton and Springfield was surveyed north of the falls in 1685, Northampton men were still allowed fishing rights at the falls because of its great value as a salmon location. The fish were principally caught in dip nets at first, and old records state that specimens weighing 20–30 pounds were frequently taken, although the general run normally contained salmon of between 6 and 10 pounds. The captured fish were chiefly used for home consumption, but they were occasionally sold for less than a penny a pound to nearby nonfishing communities. Shad were practically valueless on the Connecticut; although they ran in greater numbers than the salmon, they were frowned upon as a food fish because they were a common staple of the Indian, supposedly signifying one's poor taste and poverty.[79]

New England had an approximate population of 50 000 people in 1685, while Acadia could boast no more than 1000, and only 3215 individuals had been reported in the Quebec census of 1667.[80] New England's fishing population and activity were growing so rapidly by the middle 1680s, that encroachment on the French fishing banks and widespread expansion of American trade in fish were inevitable. As early as 1624, the coasts of New England had a considerable number of shore-based fisheries, while New France had none; Gloucester alone in that year had no fewer than 50 boats engaged in a local cod fishery.[81] The Plymouth colony began exporting fish in 1625, and by 1628 they were selling fish to the Dutch at New York. Prowse reports that New Englanders had come to Newfoundland as early as 1645 to fish and trade.[82]

The salmon that were taken were principally kept for home consumption on local markets, but it is evident that before the end of the 17th century, salmon exports to other colonies and other nations had begun. In a letter-book of Samuel Sewall, a Boston merchant, the following entry was made for the year 1686:

To Nathaniel Dwight — Am in hopes that you will sell that pickled bass well for understand it[']s much enquired after in the West Indies; don't know but it may go off in the lieu of salmon.[83]

A report to the British Board of Trade and Plantations in 1700 stated that the colonies possessed 315 fishing vessels of their own, and before 1705, that number alone was venturing to the Acadian fishing grounds.[84] New Englanders at this time were selling fish to France, Spain, and the Canary Islands, with the "refuse cod" going to the Leeward Islands, Barbados, and Antigua. It is reasonable to conclude that salmon in some numbers figured in these fish exports.

Because of its fishery, New England became an area of great promise; Thomas Morton referred to it as the "New English Canaan," and of the salmon he noted that "there is great abundance, and these may be allowed for a commodity."[85] Unrestricted freedom to fish was given to all inhabitants in these colonies, a prime example of Britain's efforts to encourage settlement, and of her liberal attitude toward the prosecution of the fishery at this time. This policy, however, did little to preserve or conserve fish species, particularly in the river fishery, which in some areas was to suffer rapid declines in certain species even before 1700. It was not initially considered necessary to regulate the fishery in any way, for the population was relatively sparse, and the fish plentiful. When the need for regulation arose, it concerned the handling of fish after they were caught — in other words, the product, not the resource, was being protected.

Such a regulation was enacted by Massachusetts in 1641, when it set about to standardize the containers in which pickled fish were exported and to appoint gaugers to ensure that the proper amount of fish went into each standard barrel.[86] The governor issued a further proclamation 10 years later for "preventing the deceit of any person in the packing of fish" by reinstating the previous act and stipulating that all pickled fish packed for sale had to possess a gauger's mark. The gaugers' duties were now broadened to include the inspection of fish for spoilage, to ensure that each species was packed separately, and to see that the product was sound and well salted; such a measure of inspection became necessary due to complaints from various markets about spoiled fish. "Discreet and honest" persons were appointed in each fishing town as inspectors and gaugers and were generally referred to as "fish viewers"; at this time, they were paid at the rate of a penny a quintal (100–112 lb), half of their fee coming from the seller, and the other half from the buyer. This was the start of the fish inspection service in America.[87]

The type of fishing apparatus most commonly used in the river fishery at this time was the weir or wooden trap. One of the first descriptions of such a device in New England waters came from a French visitor to the Plymouth Colony around 1628:

At the south side of the town there flows down a small river [probably Billington Brook] of fresh water, very rapid, but shallow, which takes its rise from several lakes in the land above.... This river the English have shut in with planks and in the middle with a little door, which slides up and down, and at the sides with trellice work through which the water has its courses but which they can also close with slides. At the mouth they have constructed it with planks, like an eel-pot, with wings, where in the middle is also a sliding door and with trellice work at the sides, so that between the two dams there is a square pool into which the fish aforesaid come swimming...in order to get up above.[88]

Similar weirs were also constructed in New Hampshire rivers, where they were principally set for salmon.[89] The weirs built along the Merrimack were also important in the salmon fishery, as emphasized by the interesting will of a Newbury man, who stipulated: "I give the first salmon that is caught in my weir yearly to Mr. Noyes and the second to Mr. Rogers till my son be nineteen years of age."[90] Along with the weir, the spear and the dip net were the principal tools for taking salmon in New England's fresh and estuarial waters for many years, although nets specifically designed for the species began to appear around 1700.[91]

Enduring Enigma

Although salmon had grown more important in the economy of the North American colonies as the decades passed, there was still little growth in knowledge of the species since Beothius had described its natural history in 1517. In 1585, Konrad von Gesner, in his *Historiae Animalium*, supported Beothius' comments, adding only that the salmon could leap more than 8 feet and that England had the tastiest fish in the world. Francis Bacon discovered that salmon could hear, smell, and live up to 10 years. Even Izaak Walton had an incomplete story of the species when he wrote *The Compleat Angler* in 1653, although he did describe smolt tagging experiments which proved that these young fish went to sea and returned, with remarkable growth, to the same river.[92]

Walton, like everyone else who took an interest in such things, was not sure how many different kinds of salmon there were; salmonlike fish appeared in a multitude of shapes, colors, and sizes, and were given a multitude of names, but, the relationships among them were largely unknown. The sea-trout, for example, was thought to be one stage in the salmon's life cycle; and what we now know to be salmon fry and salmon parr were then thought to be separate species which never grew to any size other than that observed. Likewise, the smolt was thought to be the first stage of an adult salmon's life. Therefore, the words fry and parr, when applied to salmon, were synonymous with the terms smolt, salmon smelt, samlet, and burnt-tail — all of these being none other than today's salmon smolts.

All that was known — or unknown — about the salmon's life cycle in North America was valiantly summed up by John Josselyn, who made two voyages to the New World in the mid-17th century. He wrote:

> The Salmon likewise is a sea-fish, but, as the bass, comes into rivers to spawn; a salmon the first year is a salmon-smelt; the second a mort; the third a spraid; the fourth a soar; the fifth a sorrel; the sixth a forket-tail; and the seventh a salmon. There are another sort of salmon [that] frequent in those parts called white salmons.[93]

One did not require scientific knowledge about fish, however, in order to profit from their existence. Fees levied on certain species caught off Cape Cod, for example, were used toward the expense of operating public schools in 1673; school masters and ministers were sometimes paid in fish; and, in 1660, the rents from oyster beds in New Haven supported the beginnings of Yale University.[94] If knowledge of fish and their life cycles was not expanding as rapidly as the fishery itself, at least the resource was contributing, in a round-about way, to the general enlightenment, and even the academic progress, of the colonists.

NOTES

[1]W. L. Grant, "Voyages of Samuel de Champlain," excerpted in John C. Pearson, ed., *The Fish and Fisheries of Colonial North America* (Washington: Department of the Interior, 1972), p. 186.

[2]Marc Lescarbot, "Last Relation of what took place in the Voyages made by Sieur de Poutrincourt to New France" (1612), in Reuben G. Thwaites, ed., *Jesuit Relations and Allied Documents*, II (Cleveland: Burrows, 1896), 133.

[3]J. Clarence Webster, *An Historical Guide to New Brunswick* (New Brunswick: Bureau of Information and Tourist Travel, 1947), pp. 52–53.

[4]Thwaites, *Jesuit Relations*, II, 167.

[5]Edward Gaylord Bourne, ed., *The Voyages and Explorations of Samuel de Champlain* (Toronto: Courier, 1911), I, 6, 23, 37, 62, etc.

[6]Bourne, "The Voyages and Explorations of Samuel de Champlain," excerpted in Pearson, *Fish and Fisheries*, p. 186.

[7]*Ibid.*, p. 33.

[8]Webster, *Historical Guide*, pp. 24–25.

[9]Beamish Murdoch, *History of Nova-Scotia or Acadie*, (Halifax: Barnes, 1895), I, 64.

[10]Marc Lescarbot, *The History of New France*, ed. W. L. Grant (Toronto: Champlain Society, 1911), II, 24.

[11]George MacBeath, "Isaac de Razilly," in *Dictionary of Canadian Biography [hereafter DCB]* (Toronto: University of Toronto, 1967), I, 567–568.

[12]Quoted in Ruth E. Kaulback, *Historic Saga of Lahève (LaHave)* (Halifax: n.p., 1970), p. 30.

[13]Nicolas Denys, *The Description and Natural History of the Coasts of North America (Acadia)*, trans. and ed. William Francis Ganong (Toronto: Champlain Society, 1908), pp. 127–129.

[14]*Ibid.*, pp. 17, 129; MacBeath, "Isaac de Razilly," pp. 567–568. Nicolas Denys established a fishery at Port-Rossignol during the 1630s, involving his brother Simon in an export trade; see Jean Lunn, "Simon Denys de La Trinité," in *DCB*, I, 261.

[15]George MacBeath, "The Atlantic Region," in *DCB*, I, 21; A. C. Jost, *Guysborough Sketches and Essays* (Kentville: Kentville Publishing, 1950), pp. 31–33.

[16]John N. Grant, *The Development of Sherbrooke Village to 1880* (Halifax: Nova Scotia Museum, 1972), p. 1.

[17]MacBeath, "The Atlantic Region," p. 25.

[18]This was La Vallière, the seigneur of Chignecto, who sold fishing licences to New Englanders, a practice often criticized; C. Bruce Fergusson, "Bergier," in *DCB*, I, 90.

[19]Webster, *Historical Guide*, pp. 123–124.

[20]Unless otherwise noted, all information on Denys

comes from George MacBeath, "Nicolas Denys," in *DCB*, I, 256–259.

[21]N. E. Dionne, *Champlain*, The Makers of Canada Series (Toronto: Morang, 1906), I, 234.

[22]Denys, *Description and Natural History*, pp. 184, 186.

[23]*Ibid.*, p. 178.

[24]*Ibid.*, p. 166.

[25]Jost, *Guysborough Sketches*, p. 34; R. W. Dunfield, *1972 Atlantic Salmon Sport Catch Statistics, Maritimes Region* (Halifax: Resource Development Branch, Fisheries Service, 1973), p. 25.

[26]Denys, *Description and Natural History*, p. 214.

[27]*Ibid.*, pp. 193, 199, 213, 226.

[28]William Francis Ganong, ed., "Historical-Geographical Documents relating to New Brunswick," in *Collections* of the New Brunswick Historical Society, VII (1891), 32–36.

[29]Webster, *Historical Guide*, p. 87. This post was constructed in 1689.

[30]Ganong, "Historical-Geographical Documents," pp. 42–43.

[31]Esther Clark Wright, *The Miramichi* (Sackville: Tribune Press, 1944), p. 14.

[32]Denys, *Description and Natural History*, p. 113. Navy Island no longer exists; port development, including the harbor bridge, has obliterated it.

[33]Sieur de Dièreville, *A Relation of a Voyage to Port Royal in Acadia or New France*, ed. J. C. Webster (Toronto: Champlain Society, 1933), p. 114.

[34]"The Cadillac Memoir of Acadia," in *Collections* of the New Brunswick Historical Society, XIII (1930), 91.

[35]J. C. Webster ed., *Acadia at the End of the Seventeenth Century* (Saint John: New Brunswick Museum, 1934), p. 204. In 1686 the population was no more than twenty persons. See also, Fergusson, "Bergier," in *DCB*, I, 89–90.

[36]Nicholas de Jong, "The French Regime, 1534–1748," in W. P. Bolger, ed., *Canada's Smallest Province* (Prince Edward Island Centennial Commission, 1973), pp. 12–13; Fergusson, "Bergier," pp. 89–90.

[37]Webster, *Acadia*, p. 137.

[38]"The Cadillac Memoir," p. 93.

[39]Webster, *Acadia*, p. 137.

[40]*Ibid.*, p. 126.

[41]Francis Parkman, *A Half Century of Conflict*, 3rd. edition (London: Collier-Macmillan, 1966), pp. 88–89; "Letter of John Higginson to Nathaniel Higginson" (20 June 1697), in Pearson, *Fish and Fisheries*, p. 553.

[42]Webster, *Acadia*, p. 112.

[43]Charles B. Elliott, *The United States and the Northeastern Fisheries* (Minneapolis: University of Minnesota, 1887), p. 17.

[44]Parkman, *A Half Century*, pp. 88–89.

[45]Webster, *Acadia*, p. 132.

[46]"Letter from M. de Denonville to M. de Seignelay" (January 1690), in Pearson, *Fish and Fisheries*, p. 170.

[47]William Inglis Morse, ed., *Acadiensia Nova, 1578–1779: New and Unpublished Documents and Other Data Relating to Acadia* (London: Bernard Quaritch, 1935), I, 192.

[48]Dionne, *Champlain*, I. 247.

[49]Reuben G. Thwaites, ed., *Jesuit Relations and Allied Documents*, XXVIII (Cleveland: Burrows, 1898), 121.

[50]*Ibid.*, XXXII (Cleveland: Burrows, 1898), 87, 99; XXX (Cleveland: Burrows, 1898), 173.

[51]*Ibid.*, XXXI (Cleveland: Burrows, 1898), 251.

[52]*Ibid.*, XLIII (Cleveland: Burrows, 1899), 151.

[53]*Ibid.*, p. 261.

[54]"Letter from M. de Denonville," in Pearson, *Fish and Fisheries*, p. 170; Raymond Douville and Jacques Donat Casanova, *Daily Life in Early Canada*, trans. Carola Congreve (New York: Macmillan, 1968), p. 168.

[55]"The King's Instructions to Count Frontenac, 1672," excerpted in Pearson, *Fish and Fisheries*, p. 169; "The King's Instructions to Denonville, 1688," excerpted in *ibid.*, p. 170.

[56]Louis Hennepin, *A New Discovery of a Vast Country in America* (1698; reprinted Toronto: Coles, 1974), p. 562.

[57]Regis de Roquefeuil, "Francois Byssot," in *DBC*, I, 145–146; André Vachon, "Louis Jolliet," in *ibid.*, p. 397.

[58]Gustave Lanctot, *A History of Canada* (Toronto: Clarke, Irwin, 1964), II, 220; Donald MacKay, *Anticosti: The Untamed Island* (Toronto: McGraw-Hill Ryerson, 1979), pp. 16–18.

[59]Lanctot, *History of Canada*, II, 220. The salmon trade which developed during this period was almost exclusively with the mother country; efforts at shipping salmon to the West Indies in 1708, for example, were unsuccessful. See Harold Innis, *The Cod Fisheries* (Toronto: University of Toronto Press, 1954), p. 128.

[60]John Reeves, *History of the Government of the Island of Newfoundland* (1793; reprinted New York: Johnson, 1967), p. 16.

[61]D. W. Prowse, *A History of Newfoundland* (London: Macmillan, 1895), p. 106.

[62]*Ibid.*, p. 135.

[63]F. L. N. Paynter, "The Journal of James Young, 1663," excerpted in Peter Neary and Patrick O'Flaherty, eds., *By Great Waters* (Toronto: University of Toronto, 1974), p. 29. Prowse states that New Englanders were fishing in Newfoundland as early as 1645; *History of Newfoundland*, p. 90.

[64]Public Archives of Canada, Colonial Office Papers 5, Vol. 43, No. 121, "Report of Charles Talbot on Newfoundland, 1679–1680."

[65]Prowse, *History of Newfoundland*, p. 178.

[66]*Ibid.*, pp. 184, 279.

[67]P. W. Browne, *Where the Fishers Go* (New York: Cochrane, 1909), p. 48.

[68]Prowse, *History of Newfoundland*, p. 204.

[69]Benjamin Trumbull, *A Complete History of Connecticut* (New Haven, 1818), I, 546.

[70]George Waymouth, "A true relation of the most prosperous voyage made in the present year, 1605," excerpted in Pearson, *Fish and Fisheries*, p. 183.

[71]Captain Popham, "A relation of a voyage to New England...1607," excerpted in *ibid.*, p. 185; *ibid.*, p. 276. The settlement was founded in 1607 at Sagadahoc.

[72]"A Voyage to New England, 1623–1624," excerpted in *ibid.*, p. 308. Meister reports that a Christopher Lawson [Leavett?] was believed to be the first settler on the Kennebec River. This man had been in the employ of Thomas Purchase, who had settled at Pejebscot Falls on the Androscoggin River in 1628 to trade and fish for salmon; see A. L. Meister, "A Look Back at the Atlantic Salmon Fishing in Maine," in *The Atlantic Salmon Journal*, (Winter, 1964–65), 14.

[73]William Bradford, "The History of Plymouth Plantation," excerpted in Pearson, *Fish and Fisheries*, p. 304.

[74]Denys, *Description and Natural History*, p. 110.

35

[75]Francis Higginson, "New England's Plantation," in Peter Force, ed., *Tracts and Other Papers* (1630; reprinted Washington, 1836), I, 8.

[76]William Bradford and Edward Winslow, "Relation or Journal of the beginning and proceedings of the english Plantation settled at Plymouth in New England" (1624), excerpted in Pearson, *Fish and Fisheries*, p. 624. Although the Pilgrims had initially intended to engage in a considerable fishery, they were not, in fact, very successful at this endeavor until they followed the methods and expertise of the Indians: "During the first month in Plymouth, the Pilgrims caught only one cod.... Their first fish was a live herring that had washed up on shore. At this point, the Pilgrims seemed likely to go down in history not as Founding Fathers but as the world's worst fishermen"; see John C. Miller, *The First Frontier: Life in Colonial America* (New York: Dell, 1974), p. 32.

[77]*Book of Knowledge*, 1944 edition (1944), XX, 7306, 7395, 7399, 7417, 7418, 7454, 7510.

[78]Samuel Maverick, "A Brief Description of New England and Several Towns Therein" (ca. 1660), excerpted in Pearson, *Fish and Fisheries*, p. 343.

[79]Marshall McDonald, "The Connecticut and Housatonic Rivers..." (1884), in G. Browne Goode, ed., *The Fisheries and Fishing Industries of the United States* (Washington: U.S. Commission of Fish and Fisheries, 1884), I, 660–663.

[80]George Frederick Clarke, *Someone Before Us* (Fredericton: Brunswick, 1968), p. 51; George W. Brown, *Building the Canadian Nation* (Toronto: Dent, 1849), p. 54.

[81]Albert C. Jensen, *A Brief History of the New England Offshore Fisheries*, Fishery Leaflet 594 (Washington: U.S. Bureau of Commercial Fisheries, 1967), p. 1.

[82]Prowse, *History of Newfoundland*, p. 90.

[83]"Letterbook of Samuel Sewall" (1686), excerpted in Pearson, *Fish and Fisheries*, p. 355.

[84]"Report from the Governor to the Council of Trade and Plantations" (28 November 1700), excerpted in *ibid.*, p. 360; Parkman, *A Half Century*, pp. 88–89.

[85]Thomas Morton, "New English Canaan," in Force, *Tracts and Other Papers*, II, 57.

[86]"The Colonial Laws of Massachusetts Colony" (1641), excerpted in Pearson, *Fish and Fisheries*, pp. 443–444.

[87]"Records of the Governor and Company of Massachusetts Bay" (1651), excerpted in *ibid.*, p. 456.

[88]"Letter of Isaac de Pasières to Samuel Bloomaert" (1628), excerpted in *ibid.*, pp. 227–228.

[89]McDonald, "The Connecticut and Housatonic Rivers," p. 661.

[90]Joshua Coffin, "A Sketch of Newbury...." (1845), excerpted in Pearson, *Fish and Fisheries*, p. 631.

[91]McDonald, "The Connecticut and Housatonic Rivers," p. 661.

[92]Anthony Netboy, *Salmon: The World's Most Harassed Fish* (London: André Deutsch, 1980), pp. 20–21; Izaak Walton, *The Compleat Angler* (1653; reprinted New York: Weathervane, 1975), pp. 128–130, 132.

[93]John Josselyn, "An Account of Two Voyages to New England" (1675), excerpted in Pearson, *Fish and Fisheries*, p. 205.

[94]"The Compact with the Charter and Laws of the Colony of New Plymouth" (1673), excerpted in *ibid.*, pp. 484–485; "John Davenport's Resignation of Governor Hopkins' Donation to the General Court of New Haven" (4 May 1660), excerpted in *ibid.*, p. 461.

V

Challenge and Conflict 1713-1760

The Cod Wars

In 1701, the War of the Spanish Succession erupted in Europe and formal declarations of war were made between France and Great Britain. Any formal or traditional announcement of hostile intent in America was pointless, because active animosity had never actually subsided between New France and New England since the war of 1689. New Englanders had persisted in fishing the coastal waters of New France and, in particular, Acadia; the French authorities in these regions were determined to keep them out. In consequence, the musket and the powderhorn were as much a part of the fishery as the hook and line. Both English and French fishermen never knew when the opportunity might arise to capture an opponent's fishing boat with a full cargo of cod, salmon, or other valuable commodities; conversely, the defence of one's own fishing vessel might also be necessary.

The aggressive competition which both factions had exercised in the western North Atlantic since the middle 1600s was not easily quelled, even in times of peace, and a more or less continuous state of nefarious and open hostility was always present. In 1713, however, peace was restored in Europe by the Treaty of Utrecht, and significant changes in the colonial fishery of both nations resulted. The Hudson Bay territory, Newfoundland, and the peninsular part of Acadia (Nova Scotia) were awarded to Britain, which also retained its

New England colonies; France retained Ile Royale (Cape Breton Island), Ile Saint-Jean (Prince Edward Island), and the St. Lawrence region; the territory between Chignecto and the Penobscot River, however, remained disputed ground as a result of certain ambiguities in the treaty respecting the boundary between Acadia and New England.[1]

Acadia Smells of Fish

Initial attempts to establish a sedentary fishery on the shores of Ile Saint-Jean in the 1600s had failed, and for the most part, France neglected the area until the loss of much of her former Acadian possessions in 1713 made it necessary for her to consider the island's potential and wealth. In 1719, Louis-Hyacinthe Castel, the Comte de Saint-Pierre, was named proprietor of Ile Saint-Jean and was given exclusive rights to the fishery. He settled some three hundred colonists at Port La Joie (near present-day Charlottetown) in 1720, but after spending 1.2 million *livres* for their support, without any remuneration, his proprietorship was revoked in 1725, and his fishing rights in 1726. The latter had been contested by competitors, and the entire settlement project had been overshadowed by the rapid development in Ile Royale. As the emerging principal French base in the Gulf, it was attracting most of the money and many individuals, making it difficult to establish a viable fishing enterprise on Ile Saint-Jean, despite its favorable location for that purpose. Some of the Comte de Saint-Pierre's people, however, remained after their benefactor withdrew his support and, despite their difficulties, developed a small fishery.[2]

Cascumpeque and Havre Saint-Pierre (St. Peter's Harbour) both on the north shore, were small fishing communities by 1727, and in 1728 it was estimated that at least 125 persons within the island colony were engaged in fishing cod, salmon, and a few other anadromous or marine species. By 1730, when Ile Saint-Jean reverted to a royal domain under the jurisdiction of Ile Royale, the census revealed that out of a population of 325, there were 140 resident fishermen on the island, employing 4 schooners and 23 shallops.[3] Fish were plentiful along the shores and in the numerous small creeks and streams; it was only the shortage of salt that curbed the real potential in the fishery, and it was said that if salt were available in quantity at St. Peter's Harbour, over 300 quintals of fish could be easily taken and preserved for each shallop engaged in the fishery. Although Port La Joie was considered the center of the colony, St. Peter's Harbour contained the greatest number of inhabitants and was the principal fishing port.[4]

The *Compagnie de l'Est de l'Ile Saint-Jean* was formed in France in 1731 to engage in both settlement and the commercial fishery on the southeastern side of the island. A grant of approximately 200 square miles was given by the Crown, and in 1732 the director of the company, Jean-Pierre Roma, came to Trois Rivières (near present-day Brudenell Point) to establish the colony. In the following years, he was allowed to construct fish-drying stations on the northeast coast, where grants were secured in proportion to the number of boats employed in the fishery. Roma's influence gradually extended to St. Peter's Harbour — the most valuable fishing region — and his interests there became of such importance that a direct road was cut across the island to that point from his main base at Trois Rivières. By 1735, the fishing population had risen to 172. Roma became sole proprietor of the enterprise in 1737, but in 1745 he was obliged to leave, his properties having been put to the torch by New Englanders at the time of the first destruction of Louisbourg.[5]

Although the principal interest of Roma and the rest of the fishing community on Ile Saint-Jean was the coastal fishery for cod, there is evidence that a salmon fishery also grew up after 1730. Old records indicate that the species was present in all island streams, being seen frequently in June on the north coast, but not until September on the south coast, where they were observed ascending rivers such as the present-day Dunk and Hillsborough. Undoubtedly they were taken at Cascumpeque, but nowhere else on the island did they appear to be more plentiful than in the vicinity of St. Peter's Bay:

The old French people on the Island say that salmon were formerly in much greater plenty than they have been for many years past as a proof of which, they relate that two brigs of considerable burthen use[d] to load annually with salmon, caught in the Harbour of St. Peter's, for Rochelle in France.[6]

Besides this export trade, both the Indians and the white inhabitants made local use of the resource; the streams were generally short, narrow, and shallow, and it was hardly necessary to operate weirs and large nets, the spear being just as effective under such conditions.

The prosperity — and even the existence — of the colony on Ile Saint-Jean was principally tied to that of Ile Royale, and its prosperity, in turn, was based on the cod fishery. Here, after the Treaty of Utrecht, France had begun to erect the fortress of Louisbourg, which was designed in all respects to meet the requirements of the fishery. Plenty of open space was provided for drying fish, and numerous quays and stages were built to facilitate this operation. The relatively wide streets and low profile of the town were designed not only to reduce the threat of devastation during a possible siege, but also to provide the best ventilation possible for a town that was required to suffer the stench of the fishery.[7]

The population of Cape Breton hovered around Louisbourg and the cod; however, at least seasonal salmon fisheries were carried out at various points along the shore, principally at Mira, St. Ann's, Ingonish, Mabou, Margaree, River Inhabitants, and Grand River. In later years, Captain Samuel Holland stated that the northwest coast of Cape Breton abounded with salmon, and implied that the French had carried on a considerable trade in that commodity around the Margaree and Mabou rivers.[8]

To the British, the acquisition of Acadia in 1713 meant that a good base was now secured from which the eastern and Gulf cod fishery could be carried out, and from which all French activity could be observed. Captain Cyprian Southack wrote to the Lords of Trade late in 1713, informing them that cod was not the sole value of the waters around Acadia: "A great many others of consequence might be added as Herring, Mackerel, Bass, Salmon, and Whales in great plenty in the Season of the Year";[9] nevertheless, cod was still king. It was important enough for France to construct the fortress of Louisbourg to protect it, and it is clear from period documents that the rival New England fishing base at Canso meant more to London and Boston than any other part of the colony[10] — although the community did not possess a stable permanent population, and had only three resident English families in 1729.[11]

Scattered attempts were made to encourage permanent English settlement in Nova Scotia for reasons other than fishing, but these efforts produced nothing. For many years, the colony was to remain largely uninhabited except by Acadians, Indians, and the small military garrison at Annapolis. Settlement was, indeed, discouraged, with official stimulus being given only to the fishery, as indicated by the Royal Instructions issued to the colonial governor in 1730:

It being His Majesty's intention to give all possible encouragement to the trade of all his subjects, you are to use your best endeavours that the fishery on the coast of Nova Scotia be encouraged and protected; and in order thereunto you shall not allow any settlements to be made on the coast but what shall be at least two hundred yards distance from the sea or harbour, that there may be sufficient room left for beaches, flakes, stages, cook-rooms and other necessary conveniences... .[12]

Although towns were not prevented from being established, it was clear that there was little reason for their existence, other than to facilitate the fishery, since to the government, there was no trade but the fish trade. Nearly half a century was to pass after the peace of 1713 before the British took an interest in settlement of the colony and in any pursuit other than the fishery.

Until the mid-1700s, the principal segment of the Nova Scotian population was still French. There were more New Englanders coming to the coast to fish each year, but they were not inclined to build permanent shore establishments, and their principal contact with the established communities was restricted to a brisk commodity trade conducted for the most part by local intermediaries. Although it had previously been contended that the Acadian French had little interest in the commercial fishery, it was reported that as early as 1715 — 5 years after the British capture of mainland Nova Scotia — there were between 30 and 40 Acadian boats engaged in the Minas Basin fishery for shad, gaspereau, and salmon, in addition to the weir fishery.[13] Acadian participation in the estuarial and coastal fishery increased in subsequent years, with the product presumably finding its way to Ile Royale and New England.[14]

Tensions increased as both the French and the British shared the rich fishing grounds off Ile Royale and in the Gulf. The New Englanders in particular wanted a greater share of the Gulf fishery for themselves, and some of the principal business concerns of the American colonies were thus pressing for an attack on Louisbourg. When this course of action was finally accepted, New England fishermen made up a fair portion of the attacking force and played an important role in the subsequent capture of the island stronghold. The commander of the New England forces, William Pepperrell, was himself the son of a prominent fish trade merchant from Kittery Point, Maine.[15]

It was obvious to New England's colonial troops, when they reached Louisbourg, that the economy of the town was based on the fishery; before effective bombardment of the West Gate could commence, the gunners had to shoot down the massive assembly of fish stages that obstructed their view of the enemy's walls.[16] It did not take the conquering forces long to discover the local occurrence of salmon: a French salmon-fishing estab-

lishment on the Mira River was soon destroyed by the English.[17] The documents of this first Louisbourg affair also provide one of the earliest recorded instances of angling in Acadia; Benjamin Cleaves, a gunner with the New England forces, noted in his diary that, while encamped near the fortress, "Some men went fishing, two miles off, caught six Troutts."[18]

Although Louisbourg had been taken, it was soon returned to France by treaty, much to the vexation of the New Englanders. The British government subsequently decided that a permanent English settlement should be established on the southeast shore of Nova Scotia, as a buffer to the great French fortress, and as a base for prosecuting and protecting the British fishery. Edward Cornwallis was given the responsibility of establishing such a settlement, and on the south side of Chebucto Bay he began to lay out the town of Halifax in 1749.

Apart from building a new town, Cornwallis encouraged immediate participation in the fishery, and his initial efforts met with considerable success; in 1751, he reported to the Lords of Trade in Great Britain that "The fishery has done well for the first year, better in proportion than New England or Newfoundland, it having failed greatly everywhere."[19] To further establish and encourage the shore fishery, Cornwallis initiated a fishing bounty, made possible by a tax on the liquor sold in the new town. He also issued permits to erect wharves and buildings along the beaches at various places for the fishing population's use.[20] Itinerant fishing communities had long been established in the Chebucto area, but now small centers quickly sprang up at Cornwallis (McNab's Island), Sambro, Ketch Harbour, Cross Island just east of Lunenburg, and in St. Margaret's Bay; the latter area, in particular, was discovered to abound in fish, and several families settled there to take advantage of the salmon and cod.[21]

The years preceding and during the Seven Years War (1756–1763) brought confusion and upheaval to the colony, with the explusion of the Acadian population in 1755, the resettlement of their lands by New England Planters after 1759, and the final capitulation of Louisbourg in 1758. During the war, officers of various regiments serving in the region wrote a number of interesting accounts about the state of the colony and its resources. Captain John Knox, for example, writing of the local fishery from his station at Annapolis, noted:

The principal inhabitants of the town have parcelled out the shore or beach and enclosed it, at low water mark, to a certain height with stakes and wickered hurdles in such a manner as to confine any fish that may come in with the tide of flood; and these are called fish ponds.[22]

Weir fishing in Knox's time had changed very little since Champlain had been in the area. The first documented incident of poaching in Nova Scotia was also recorded by Knox at Annapolis, when he mentioned that the alarm was given one night at the Hog Island blockhouse as a result of "Some fellows of the town going to rob the fish ponds within the precincts of the blockhouse."[23]

Knox frequently mentioned the consumption of fresh fish by the troops in order to maintain their health; before they left Halifax for the attack upon Quebec in 1759, each soldier was issued hooks and handlines for his personal use, and it was not uncommon for detachments of men to be assigned the job of fishing in order to supply the regimental larder.[24]

Knox also took part in destroying Acadian settlements along the Gulf shore at the time of the explusion; he reported that at Gaspé and Grand River, stocks of cured fish were destroyed, along with great numbers of "netts, hooks, and fishing lines."[25] That a large quantity of salmon was being exported by the French from the Restigouche area of Chaleur Bay prior to 1760 is beyond question;[26] this commerce ended abruptly, however, with the arrival of the British expedition of which Knox was a part. Little was said of the Miramichi region at this time. If, however, one is to believe an English captive who was detained on the river in 1757, it appears that the salmon fishery there was not actively pursued: "Here is a fine river in this place for fishen sammon [sic]...trout and what not. But the people are lazey [sic], and lay up nothing for a rainy day."[27]

Other colonial officers, such as Colonel John Winslow, were in charge of expelling the French inhabitants from Cobequid (Truro), Tatamagouche, Chignecto (Amherst), and Petitcodiac; they could not fail but notice the extent to which the people of these communities relied on the local fishery.[28] In making the Saint John River secure to the British, Lieutenant Colonel Robert Monckton led an expedition up that waterway to clear the reaches of Acadian settlements. Monckton took little note of the river or its fishery, although Captain William Pote, captured by Indians and taken upriver in 1745, had observed that "on one occasion they [the Indians] caught in a small cove, a few miles below the mouth of the Tobique, fifty-four salmon in the course of a few hours."[29] Monckton constructed Fort Frederick at the mouth of the Saint John, and in subsequent years the troops who garrisoned this post soon discovered the benefits of their location: the mouth of the Nerepis was an excellent salmon fishing area.

New France

Although La Hontan had described, in 1703, the valuable potential in the salmon fisheries of New France, and had named — or at least marked — *Rivière du saumon* a number of times on his map of Canada,[30] there still appeared to be little concentrated commercial interest in the species. Although Chaleur Bay stood out as a principal resource area, exploited periodically for its salmon, and although the species must have enjoyed at least domestic importance elsewhere, contemporary references to the fish in Quebec are scarce; only a few names, such as Jolliet and Riverin, are specifically linked to the resource.

One of the reasons for this lack of more precise information may be that the Quebec fishery was basically a mixed or diversified one, with no single species — save for cod — taking precedence. The eel, for example, was as important as the salmon, and as much attention was paid to sea mammals as to fish, the catching of the former being considered fishing. This diversification was epitomized in the region to the east of Mingan — the Labrador. A Labrador journal of 1715–16 stated:

> But that which merits more attention is that the fishery which can be carried on of salmon, codfish, seals, walrus, whales, on this four hundred leagues of coast is able to produce greater riches than the richest gold-mine in Peru.[31]

The Courtemanche post, erected around 1704 at Baye de Phélypeaux (Brador Bay), was one of the first fixed stations in Quebec's Labrador to take advantage of these mixed resources. It is said that Augustin Le Gardeur de Courtemanche had peas, beans, herbs, barley, and oats in his garden; horses, cows, pigs, and sheep in his fields; whales, seals, and codfish in his excellent harbor; meat, eggs, eider-down and timber in his forests; and, "near the house...a little river [Brador] containing quantities of salmon and trout."[32] Who could ask for anything more?

This region had been fished by transient French vessels before 1700, but a rapid expansion in fixed establishments took place after Courtemanche's success. Seigneurial fishing rights were granted, for example, on the Etanamu River (1733), the Little Mecatina River (1740), the Great Mecatina River (1749), and the St. Paul, St. Augustin, and Forteau rivers by 1750. Although the long coastline northeast of the Strait of Belle Isle was somewhat of a no-man's-land between the French and British during this period, French fishing rights were granted on the Chateau Bay streams (1736) and the Alexis and St. Lewis rivers (1743); by 1743, the French had even come in contact with salmon as far north as Hamilton Inlet.[33] Although the Treaty of Utrecht had given France shoreline fishing rights along the western and northern coasts of Newfoundland, the Gulf fishery nevertheless remained centered on the Labrador and Mingan shores.

In Cod We Trust

The Treaty of Utrecht ushered in a new era of British expansion and development with regard to the Newfoundland fishery. France surrendered all her territorial claims to the colony, abandoned her major fishing base at Placentia, and transferred her sedentary fishing operations to Ile Royale. She also relinquished her rights to the fishery on the southern coast of Newfoundland, from Cape Ray to Cape St. Mary's. The treaty, however, did concede to France the right to fish on the western and northern coasts, leading down from the Strait of Belle Isle, and to erect such installations as were necessary for the prosecution of the fishery there.

The English fishery was concentrated around St. John's at the time of the treaty, with perhaps forty or fifty other locations being seasonally occupied around the Avalon Peninsula.[34] The fishery was principally engaged in for cod, and the laws and statutes which the British government passed from time to time discouraged all other ventures, favoring instead the monopoly in the fishing trade which was exercised by merchants from the western counties of England. Regulations were extant, for example, which forbade British fishermen from staying in the colony beyond the fishing season, for fear that they might be subsequently unavailable to further the interests of the English cod merchants and supply houses, or because they might eventually provide some independent competition for them. Another statute of long standing was that which forbade the permanent occupation of any section of the island which lay within six miles of the coast; this six-mile band was the preserve of the fishing admirals, who used the shore to dry their cod, and the timber thereon to construct fish stages.

Settlement was not entirely forbidden, but it was severely hindered by such policies. Nonetheless, more people were staying in Newfoundland, and some were expanding into other branches of business, such as the salmon and seal fisheries and the fur trade, despite the criticism and opposition of the West Country interests. Settlements were also appearing on outlying bays, mostly northward from the Avalon Peninsula. In these new areas, the planters and "live-heres" or "livers" were not only using the timber and wood which were found within the reserved six-mile zone, but also were burning, as firewood during the winter, the seasonally abandoned fish flakes of the "foreign" cod fishermen.[35]

In the wake of this gradual expansion northward, relaxation of previous government policy was inevitable. This new attitude of accommodation, plus the new breed of settler, are well illustrated by the career of George Skeffington, who appears to have been the first individual in Newfoundland to engage in salmon fishing as a principal operation. He had established himself as a trader at Bonavista around 1700, and apparently received financial backing from a St. John's merchant, James Campbell, to begin a fishery north of his post around 1705.[36] Although he had considerable trouble with the Indians, he continued to expand his enterprise northward, taking care not to overfish any one stream. In 1718, he set up joint fisheries with another St. John's merchant, William Keen, and in 1720, he petitioned the government for the rights to the salmon fishery between Cape Bonavista and Cape St. John for a period of 21 years. In

1723, he received the rights to Freshwater Bay, Ragged Harbour, Gander Bay, and Dog Creek.[37] In 1 year, Skeffington was reported to have employed 30 men in the fishery and to have taken 530 tierces of salmon, valued at 30 shillings per tierce. He retired from the business in 1729.[38]

Skeffington's proprietary title to the salmon fishery was one of the first major diversions in government policy with respect to the Newfoundland fishery — perhaps because the region over which he was granted sole use was not noted as a cod fishing area; nonetheless, his grant stipulated that he could cut wood and timber no closer than the regulation 6 miles from shore. By the early 1720s, salmon fisheries had also been undertaken by Samuel Shamler at Gander River, and by Philip Watson at Great Salmonier, Colinet, and Biscay Bay rivers; fisheries were also begun on the Exploits River at this time. The number of men entering the fishery led to considerable conflict over the rights to streams, and as early as 1719, one group of salmoniers suggested the following regulation be imposed:

> That if any man stops a River so yt the salmon can not get up he may not be molested by any person wt so ever in drawing with nets or otherwise takeing of salmon in any part of ye River for they may be as lawfully termed his as the cod fish under water at the hooke & line.[39]

Although the West Country merchants protested this type of expansion and officially continued to oppose settlement in Newfoundland, by 1728 they were themselves sponsoring planters to the region in return for trade and fishing commitments. In this way, expansion northward accelerated, largely encouraged by Poole and other West Country interests. By midcentury, for example, John Slade, one of 30 Poole merchants operating in Newfoundland, was firmly entrenched in the salmon and fur trade of the east coast, even reaching to Labrador by 1760.[40] Expansion along the southern coast of Newfoundland was less rapid, due no doubt to a forbidding topography and few apparent natural resources. Immediately after the peace of 1713, the British government despatched naval vessels to patrol and protect this newly acquired area to the south. In addition, they assigned William Taverner the task of surveying the coastline and reporting on its resources; Taverner's report to his superiors hinted of a potential which, nevertheless, took time to develop: "I am informed there's abundance of Salmon on this Coast. I shall Indeavour [sic] to know the truth thereof. It is certainly the best place for Fishing in Newfoundland."[41]

The colonial governors regularly reported fisheries progress to Great Britain, and between 1723 and 1763, their "Schemes of the fishery" indicated an increased participation in the salmon fishery, with more locations being added to the list each season. Between 1723 and 1727, the average production was reported to be 684 tierces a year, and between 1736 and 1739, an average of 1000 tierces were being exported each year from Newfoundland (300 000 lb pickled); by 1743, that amount was shipped to Italy and Spain alone. The total salmon export from the island reached 4848 tierces (1 454 400 lb pickled) in 1757.[42] At this time, there was little if any export to other North American colonies, as well as little local consumption. Newfoundland was a colony in name, but the economy still did not encourage rapid settlement and the island was said to be principally a British ship anchored near the Grand Banks for the benefit of the cod fishery.[43]

North of the Strait of Belle Isle, the long Labrador coastline now forming part of the province of Newfoundland, remained an area of vague contention between the French and the English, with both nationalities making incursions into the area. The potential of the Labrador salmon fishery was still largely unknown and unexploited for the first 50 years following peace. In 1729, Captain Henry Atkins made a voyage along the Labrador coast as far as Davis Strait in his ship, *Whale*; several years later, he repeated his voyage, reporting that salmon were very abundant in those waters. At Salmon River, he and his men caught specimens with their bare hands while wading in the river and took all they could salt and cure; one fish was just under 5 feet in length. His descriptions of the prolific salmon streams which he had discovered, however, stirred little immediate interest when he returned to New England.[44] Occasional other voyages, however, resulted in further reports on the great numbers of fish encountered along that coast, and commercial interest in the area eventually began to increase.

In 1752, a group of London merchants petitioned for permission to fish and trade in Labrador, but action on this request was delayed when the Board of Trade realized that such permission might conflict with the charter given to the Hudson's Bay Company in 1670. In an unusual show of commercial compassion, however, the latter Company informed the Board that by the strict terms of their charter they had no control over eastern Labrador, though a new monopoly on the coast would jeopardize their interests; on these grounds, the Board refused the merchants' request.[45] By this action, the development of the Labrador fishery was curtailed for another decade, except for the most southerly sections of the coast, to the westward of the Strait of Belle Isle, where the fishery had already been well established by Quebec interests.

Salmon in Great Plenty

In New England, both the tremendous growth in population, and the attendant proliferation of sawmill and gristmill dams along the various river systems, were wreaking havoc on the local fishery resource during the first half of the 18th century. As early as the late 1600s,

the river fisheries were being pursued with such vigor and attention that it became necessary to enact legislation to control the increased activity and to protect spawning stocks of fish; the unrestricted freedom to fish, granted a century earlier, was now causing severe problems in many areas. Massachusetts, the most populous of the colonies, found it necessary as early as 1668 to legislate a proper season for taking cod, haddock, and mackerel along the coast.[46] Initial protection for the inland fisheries, however, was left to the various townships, and they were not inclined to introduce any restriction which might be to their own detriment and to the benefit of adjacent townships. In 1687, however, the council of the town of Haverhill, Massachusetts, in answer to "the universal desire of the people," found it necessary to pass a regulation which insisted on the free passage of fish through several man-made barriers on the Merrimack River and its tributaries,

> in all suitable seasons of the year for their getting up to the Pond to spawn, and in special in the night-time, and to that end do order that no man shall make a dam, or suffer his dam so to stop any passage the fish used to have to the Ponds or Pond, without leaving his dam or weir or other device open in the night-time for the fish.[47]

The problem continued to worsen, despite this first regulation to protect the migration of fish in Massachusetts rivers. There appeared to be little compromise between fish and the structures that stopped their movement; milldams, fishing devices, and other obstructions sprung up at a rapid rate and soon became so numerous that the Massachusetts Legislature was forced to take further action. In 1709, the colony enacted the first of a series of laws designed to protect the river fisheries: "An act to prevent nuisances by hedges, weirs, and other encumbrances obstructing the passage of fish in rivers."[48] This forbade the construction of fishing devices, milldams, and other obstructions which completely barred fish from passing up the rivers, and delegated the authority to police this act to the Sessions of the various counties, stipulating that no fishing activity could be carried out unless permission was so granted by the county authority. Unauthorized fishing equipment was subject to destruction.

The act, however, was relatively ineffectual, since it did not apply to milldams that were already in existence, and new owners found it objectionable to be singled out in the legislation. The transfer of enforcement powers to the counties was another shortcoming, for these municipal courts had few resources to devote to fisheries protection. No overseers were appointed for many years — Haverhill had no fishery wardens until 1722[49] — and when appointments were made, the number of overseers were too few to do an effective job. When the towns finally, through pressure, had to provide some protection for the fishery, they began to demand some sort of remuneration from the fishermen in order to finance this protection. As a result, when the town of Newbury granted one Moses Chase the right to fish a certain stretch of river, he was obliged to pay two salmon to each of the community's fisheries officials; and in 1738, a local committee of authority for Amoskeag Falls was taxing fishermen a penny per salmon to help pay for the regulation and the protection of the local fishery.[50]

Ever since the founding of Boston in 1630, its inhabitants had acquired a particular taste for salmon. Wagonloads of the fish were brought to the Boston market each week from the Merrimack River fishery.[51] Apart from being regularly served at the table of the ordinary man, the salmon also held a high position as a culinary delicacy of the gentry: a Colonel Hutchinson, for example, was delighted to accept an invitation from the governor of the colony of Massachusetts to share a fine breakfast of salmon with him on election day, 1712.[52] The reaping of the salmon harvest each year reached such proportions, however, that periodic declines in stock occurred which, combined with the continued obstruction of the spawning runs by the increasing number of milldams, began to threaten seriously the future of the species. Good runs were more or less annually assured until the end of the century; by the late 1720s, seasonal failures were the rule. In 1728, one Boston resident found it necessary to resort to a bit of intrigue to ensure at least a taste of the Merrimack salmon in that year; in a letter to a friend, he wrote:

This is to desire the favor of you to get me one, two, or three or more of the first salmon if it can be had this year. I am willing to give a good price and a great price rather than not have it and will pay a man and horse for bringing it to content [me] but observe he don't bring for anybody else at the same time. If there be but a single salmon, send [it] away forthwith.[53]

Salmon, however, were still relatively plentiful over the balance of their former aboriginal range. William Douglas wrote in 1747 that

Salmon are plenty in all the British North America rivers from Newfoundland to about N. lat. 41 D [the Connecticut River]. They set in to Massachusetts Bay about the middle of April; they do not choose warm weather, therefore do not continue there long after having spawned; farther north they continue many months. This salmon is not of a good quality...and is not so good for a market as the salmon of Great Britain and Ireland.[54]

Not everyone shared Douglas' opinion about the quality of salmon in Massachusetts, however. In 1740, a Mr. Bennet of Boston said of the local market:

Salmon they have, too, in great plenty, which is as fine as any I ever eat of anywhere in my life; and those they will sell for about a shilling a piece, which will weigh fourteen or fifteen pounds.[55]

This "great plenty," however, was not all coming from the Merrimack River or immediate vicinity, as supplies were being brought in from Maine and the northern colonies. In fact, the Merrimack fishery was showing a considerable decline by the 1750s,[56] and the noted Swedish traveler, Peter Kalm, remarked in 1753 of the general New England fishery that, "Many old people said that the difference in the quantity of fish in their youth in comparison with that of today is as great as between day and night."[57] A huge image of the codfish, painted in gold leaf, hung for many years above the door of the Massachusetts State House council chamber as a constant reminder of its importance to the colony; by 1746, the golden fish's existence was almost inappropriate, because even the cod was now scarce on the immediate coast of New England.[58]

Further evidence of the salmon fishery decline in the 1750s may be found in reference to the Piscataqua, or Salmon Falls River in New Hampshire. It was reported in 1717 that the Piscataqua was so full of salmon "that in the season you may take 1,000 tons here. They are sold for 20 shillings a barrel but they do not understand the curing of them."[59] A thousand tons represents over 2 million pounds of fresh, round fish, and if we can accept that such a phenomenal figure was actually representative of the yield, then the Piscataqua would rate as one of the foremost New England salmon-producing streams. By 1750, however, it was said of this same river that

Formerly this river...was well stored with salmon which they took in plenty, but of late they [the salmon] have quite forsaken this river, occasioned, it is believed, from the number of saw mills on the different branches of P. [Piscataqua] river, the weirs of which, running, crop the same.[60]

At the rate of 1000 tons a year, it appears as though the salmon may have declined somewhat by overfishing as well.

The Connecticut River seemed to be holding out better than others with respect to the salmon fishery, partly because it was free from the obstructions that were common in other New England streams. Nonetheless, the fishery was actively engaged upon, with the yield fluctuating more than in former years. South Hadley was still one of the principal salmon fishing areas on the river, but Stoney Brook, Farmington River, and Northampton, at the mouth of the Mill River, were also excellent locations. In 1730, the price of salmon at Northampton was 1 penny a pound; by 1742, it had risen to 1½ pence a pound, and by 1750, 2 pence per pound. Nets and seines were gradually replacing the spear and dip net and, as these more efficient methods became widespread, the stocks declined.[61]

These decreases in the shore and river fisheries of the southern and central New England colonies during the first half of the 18th century did much to force fishing interests northward to Maine and beyond, and permanent fishing communities thus began to appear more regularly along the coast from Saco to the frontiers of

Acadia. A Dr. Noyes had established a sturgeon fishery on the Kennebec as early as 1712, where he could not avoid encountering the salmon as well.[62] Venturing into these Indian regions was frequently more hazardous than taking chances on the French fishing grounds, since the natives periodically raided and destroyed fishing establishments, stealing boats and murdering occupants.

Actually, it may be argued that Indian raids on New England fishery stations were only in reply to initial New England exploitation of the native fishery. One of the reasons which the Indians gave for the "long and bloody war" which began on the coast in 1689 was

> Because they were Invaded in their Fishery at Saco-River, by certain Gentlemen, who stopp'd the Fish from coming up the River with their Nets and Sains [sic]. This they were greatly affronted at, saying, They thought (though the English had got away their Lands as they had, yet) the Fishery of the Rivers had been a Privilege reserved Entire unto themselves.[63]

In retaliation, fishermen were encouraged to wreak havoc on the natives, with the incentive of a £100 reward for each scalp of a male Indian over twelve years of age.[64] Slowly but decisively, the New Englanders made headway against the natives, eventually driving them further into the interior. A military force ascended the Kennebec in 1754, and encountered the Indians with fresh salmon at their Norridgewock fishing station near Skowhegan, Maine.[65] By this time, salmon fishing was well established by the white populace on the lower river, with the Indians restricted to competing for their share of the resource in the upper area. So entrenched were the coastal fishermen that a considerable trade had grown up in pickled salmon between the Kennebec and Boston, and other coastal areas in Maine were also trading their salmon to New York and points further south.[66]

Casting Away Sin

Two of the more striking aspects in the evolution of sport fishing have been its numerous and varied interactions with theology, and its kinship to religion in operation, infrastructure and spiritual intensity. This correlation, to some extent, still prevails today, manifested in the dogmatic and almost liturgical approach to artificial fly-fishing, and in the overpowering attraction of the sport, which allure seems to be strongest on Sundays and certain other religious holidays.

One of the earliest examples of this liaison between angling and religion is the story which this writer once heard, concerning Adam, the first angler: Adam was so engrossed in the sport that he was away on the fateful day that Eve was tempted with the apple; had he been home at the time, the entire course of Biblical history might have been different. It has also been suggested that Adam took a rather philosophical approach to this first human

catastrophe, for inside the apple he discovered the bait for his next fishing trip.

The early Japanese considered angling a religious or spiritual experience, and most serious anglers still view sport fishing essentially as food for the soul rather than for the body. However, to flip the coin, many religious authorities have considered angling a device of the devil, and have raised moral issues concerning the infliction of pain on God's finny subjects, and the tendency of angling to draw man away from the work ethic and into the sinful pursuit of pleasure.

Angling, apart from that practiced by the Indians during aboriginal times, came to the New World with the first explorers and colonists. John Smith, for example, noted in 1614:

> What pleasure can be more than to recreate themselves [the colonists of new England] before their owne doors, in their owne boates, upon the sea, where man, woman, and childe, with a small hooke and line by angling, may take by diverse sorts of excellent fish, at their pleasure?[67]

The moral issues, however, also came with these early settlers, and as early as 1721, Cotton Mather was rebuking certain ministers of the Gospel for taking up the sport.[68] Apparently the clergy could not agree on the point that angling was wrong: other ministers, such as the Reverend Secomb in 1739, went on record as saying that angling for sport was sinless in the sight of God.[69] Although the issue remained confused as a result of these opposing attitudes, angling continued to be practiced, largely by those to whom the moral issues were clear — the fishing clergy — or by those to whom the moral issues were largely unimportant — the military.

Mention has already been made of the fishing exploits at Louisbourg by the New England besiegers and, later, by Captain William Owen of the Royal Navy. The first indication of angling for salmon in British North America comes from an old print which depicts officers of the garrison at Fort Frederick, intently engaged with the rod and line on the waters of Saint John Harbour, in 1758.[70]

Nature's Bounty — Man's Wisdom

John C. Pearson once commented that it was the kind bounty of nature rather than the wisdom of man that provided the never-ending wealth of fish to the New World.[71] However, nature's kindness and patience appeared to be waning in New England in the mid-18th century, as far as the salmon were concerned. The New Englanders were constructing more dams, clearing more land, polluting more water and netting more salmon than all of the other colonies combined, and the results were showing: in the rivers south of the Penobscot in Maine, salmon were disappearing.

North of this river, nature's bounty remained relatively undiminished. The Acadians and the Indians fished salmon principally for personal, rather than commercial, purposes, and incursions into the region by New Englanders had not yet severely affected freshwater resources. Quebec's salmon fishery was loitering, the economy of the colony being principally incited by the beaver. Even in Newfoundland, where some expansion was being witnessed in the salmon fishery, trade in the commodity was relatively insignificant — there were still more tierces of rum entering the colony than tierces of salmon leaving it.[72]

Peace finally came to North America in 1763, but France had lost half a continent and was now confined to the islands of St. Pierre and Miquelon, off the coast of Newfoundland. Although the English were not yet entirely aware of what they had won, the French were well aware of what they had lost: "The fishery, sir, is the real loss in Canada...without the fishery, Canada is nothing."[73]

It is somewhat ironic that man's impact on the species in North America at this time was as significant as it was, for more than 90 percent of the salmon's actual freshwater habitat and rearing ground was still unknown and unexploited by midcentury; and it would be some considerable time — if ever — before the migratory limits and the extent of productive salmon water were determined. Unfortunately, however, salmon had to pass through the estuaries of rivers in order to reach this freshwater habitat and propagate the species — and it was at these river mouths that man invariably placed his primary settlements. Unlike the farmer who had to swing the scythe over his entire grainfield to complete his harvest, the freshwater salmon fisherman merely had to place his net at the river's gate.

NOTES

[1]George W. Brown, *Building the Canadian Nation* (Toronto: Dent, 1849), pp. 77–78.

[2]Nicholas de Jong, "The French Regime, 1534–1578," in W. P. Bolger, ed., *Canada's Smallest Province* (Prince Edward Island Centennial Commission, 1973), pp. 14–16; Mary Maude, "Jacques d'Espiet de Pensens," in *Dictionary of Canadian Biography* [hereafter *DCB*] (Toronto: University of Toronto Press, 1969), II, 218–220; Mary Maude, "Robert-David Gotteville de Belile," in *ibid*, pp. 254–255.

[3]de Jong, "The French Regime," pp. 17–21.

[4]Margaret Coleman, "The Roma Settlement at Brudenell Point, Prince Edward Island," *Occasional Papers in Archaeology and History*, No. 1 (Ottawa: Department of Indian Affairs and Northern Development, 1970), pp. 92–96.

[5]*Ibid.*, pp. 92, 95. See also, Margaret Coleman, "Jean-Pierre Roma," in *Dictionary of Canadian Biography* (Toronto: University of Toronto Press, 1974), III, 566–567; and D. C. Harvey, *The French Regime in Prince Edward Island* (New Haven: Yale University Press, 1926), p. 73.

[6]John Stewart, *An Account of Prince Edward Island in the Gulph of St. Lawrence, North America* (London: W. Winchester, 1806), p. 84.

[7]Fairfax Downey, *Louisbourg: Key to a Continent* (New Jersey: Prentice Hall, 1965), p. 30: "No house was more than two stories high by fiat of Verrier, who believed that taller buildings would impede the free circulation of air in summer when all the ventilation possible was needed against the prevading stench of split cod drying."

[8]Public Archives of Canada, Colonial Office Papers, 5, Vol. 68, "Samuel Holland's Survey of Cape Breton, 1766–1767."

[9]*Ibid.*, Colonial Office Papers, Supplementary I, Miscellaneous Vol. 18, "Letter of Captain Cyprian Southack to Lords of Trade" (9 December 1713).

[10]Andrew Hill Clark, *Acadia: The Geography of Early Nova Scotia to 1760* (Madison: University of Wisconsin, 1968), p. 248.

[11]Harold A. Innis, *Select Documents in Canadian Economic History, 1497–1783* (Toronto: University of Toronto Press, 1929), p. 155.

[12]Leonard Woods Labarce, ed., "Royal Instructions to British Colonial Governors, 1670–1776," excerpted in John C. Pearson, ed., *The Fish and Fisheries of Colonial North America* (Washington: Department of the Interior, 1972), p. 131.

[13]Clark, *Acadia*, p. 246. By this time, the Acadian fishery was important enough for the British to use it as a bargaining point with the French inhabitants still remaining in mainland Nova Scotia. In 1718, for example, the British administration threatened to ban their fishing in the Minas Basin and its tributaries if they (the Acadians) refused to take the oath of allegiance. See Bona Arsenault, *History of the Acadians* (Ottawa: Leméac, 1978), p. 81.

[14]W. C. Milner, "The Basin of Minas," unpublished manuscript, Public Archives of Nova Scotia, p. 14. A clandestine but healthy trade existed between peninsular Nova Scotia and Ile Royale.

[15]Byron Fairchild, "William Pepperrell," in *DCB*, II, 516.

[16]Francis Parkman, *A Half Century of Conflict*, 3rd. edition (London: Collier-Macmillan, 1966), p. 322.

[17]Richard Brown, *History of the Island of Cape Breton* (London: Sampson Low, 1869), p. 222.

[18]Parkman, *A Half Century of Conflict*, p. 324.

[19]T. B. Akins, ed., *Nova Scotia Archives: Selections from the Public Documents of the Province of Nova Scotia* (Halifax: PANS, 1889), p. 632.

[20]T. B. Akins, "History of Halifax City," in *Collections* of the Nova Scotia Historical Society, VIII (1895), 25.

[21]Akins, *Nova Scotia Archives I*, p. 644; Charles Morris, "Description and State of the New Settlements in Nova Scotia in 1761," in *Report* of the Canadian Archives, Sessional Paper 18 (1905), p. 291–292.

[22]John Knox, *The Journals of Captain John Knox*, ed. A. G. Doughty (Toronto: Champlain Society, 1914), I, 130.

[23]*Ibid.*

[24]*Ibid.*, p. 305

[25]*Ibid.*, p. 278

[26]Philip K. Bock, *The Micmac Indians of Restigouche*, Bulletin 213 (Ottawa: National Museum, 1966), p. 16: "It is said that when they [the Indians] first began to trade with the whites, the youth armed with spears and harpoons, filled in

three or four days a vessel of 50 or 60 tons, and often the vessel could not contain all the fish caught in this short time."

[27]"John Witherspoon's Journal of the Siege of Quebec," in *Collections* of the Nova Scotia Historical Society, II (1881), 33. [28]Public Archives of Canada, Map Section, "Plan of the River Chibenacadie [Shubenacadie], 1754," shows that the Acadians maintained huts as far inland as Grand Lake for the prosecution of the local gaspereau fishery.

[29]W. O. Raymond, *The River St. John*, 2nd edition (Sackville: Tribune Press, 1950), p. 93.

[30]E. D. T. Chambers, *The Fisheries of the Province of Quebec* (Quebec: Department of Colonization, Mines and Fisheries, 1912), I, 56.

[31]*Ibid.*, p. 65

[32]*Ibid.*, p. 67

[33]*Ibid.*, pp. 56–96, *passim*.

[34]John Reeves, *A History of the Government of the Island of Newfoundland* (London, 1793; reprinted New York: Johnson Reprint, 1967), p. 18.

[35]*Ibid.*, p. 35. Planter: one who cultivates — a farmer; one who settles or founds a place and especially a new colony; a permanent settler as opposed to a transient fisherman.

[36]Anthony Netboy, *The Atlantic Salmon, A Vanishing Species?* (London: Faber, 1968), p. 348.

[37]Harold A. Innis, *The Cod Fisheries* (Toronto: University of Toronto Press, 1954), p. 149; D.W. Prowse, *A History of Newfoundland* (London: Macmillan, 1895), p. 283.

[38]Unless otherwise noted, details of Skeffington's activities are taken from Carson I. A. Ritchie, "George Skeffington," in *DCB*, II, 609.

[39]James P. Howley, *The Beothucks or Red Indians* (Cambridge: Cambridge University Press, 1915; reprinted Toronto: Coles, 1974), p. 283. See also C. Grant Head, *Eighteenth Century Newfoundland*, Carleton Library No. 99 (Toronto: McClelland and Stewart, 1976), pp. 75–85.

[40]W. Gordon Handcock, "John Slade," in *DCB*, (Toronto: University of Toronto Press, 1979), IV, 711–714.

[41]Public Archives of Canada, Colonial Office Papers, Supplementary I, Miscellaneous Vol. 18, "Papers Relating to the North Atlantic Fisheries."

[42]Innis, *The Cod Fisheries*, pp. 148–149. During the early years of the salmon fishery and trade, salt pickling was the principal means of preserving the product. After being caught, the fish were cut down the back, cleaned, put into puncheons, salted, and then repacked into small casks. When the pickling process was complete, the salmon had been reduced to an average of 63½ per cent of their original fresh, round weight; in other words, it took 1000 pounds of fresh salmon to produce 600 pounds — or two tierces — of pickled salmon.

[43]W. S. MacNutt, *The Atlantic Provinces* (Toronto: McClelland and Stewart, 1972), p. 103. Another author described Newfoundland more "as a naval and fishing station off the west coast of Ireland than a colony in British North America"; William Menzies Whitelaw, *The Maritimes and Canada Before Confederation* (Toronto: Oxford University Press, 1966), p. 30.

[44]Lorenzo Sabine, *Report on the Principal Fisheries of the American Seas* (Washington: Robert Armstrong, 1853), p. 88.

[45]Public Archives of Canada, Colonial Office Papers, 5, Vol. 6, "Report of the Board of Trade on the Memorial from the London Merchants, 1752."

[46]"The Charter and General Laws of the Colony and Province of Massachusetts Bay," excerpted in Pearson, *Fish and Fisheries*, p. 466.

[47]George Chase, "A History of Haverhill," excerpted in *ibid.*, p. 498.

[48]*Ibid.*, p. 505.

[49]*Ibid.*, p. 499.

[50]Joshua Coffin, "A Sketch of Newbury, Newburyport, and West Newbury," excerpted in *ibid.*, p. 631; "Journals of the House of Representatives of Massachusetts, 1738–1739," Vol. 16, p. 234, cited in *ibid.*, p. 512.

[51]Anthony Netboy, "History as a Focus for Fishery Conservation," Atlantic Salmon Association Centennial Award Fund Lecture Series (Montreal: n.d.), p. 7.

[52]"Diary of Samuel Sewall," excerpted in Pearson, *Fish and Fisheries*, p. 632.

[53]Coffin, "A Sketch of Newbury," in *ibid.*, p. 631.

[54]William Douglas, "A Summary, Historical and Political, of the First Settlement...of the British Settlements in North America," excerpted in Pearson, *Fish and Fisheries*, p. 256.

[55]"Notes of Mr. Bennet," excerpted in *ibid.*, p. 642.

[56]W. A. Wilcox, "The Rivers of Massachusetts and New Hampshire," in G. Brown Goode, ed., *The Fisheries and Fishing Industries of the United States* (Washington: U.S. Commission of Fish and Fisheries, 1884), I, 669.

[57]Peter Kalm, "Travels into North America," excerpted in Pearson, *Fish and Fisheries*, p. 211.

[58]Charles B. Elliott, *The United States and the Northeastern Fisheries* (Minneapolis: University of Minnesota, 1887), p. 21.

[59]"MacPhaedris Letterbook" (1717), excerpted in Pearson, *Fish and Fisheries*, p. 250.

[60]"Some cursory remarks made by James Birket in his voyage to North America, 1750–1751," excerpted in *ibid.*, p. 208.

[61]Marshall McDonald, "The Connecticut and Housatonic Rivers and Minor Tributaries of Long Island Sound," in Goode, *Fisheries and Fishing Industries*, pp. 659–663, *passim*.

[62]Parkman, *A Half Century*, p. 159.

[63]Quoted in George Rawlyk, *Nova Scotia's Massachusetts* (Montreal: McGill–Queens University Press, 1973), p. 56.

[64]"Letter from William Dummer to Captain Cornwall, May 24, 1725," excerpted in Pearson, *Fish and Fisheries*, p. 569.

[65]C. G. Atkins, "The River Fisheries of Maine," in Goode, *Fisheries and Fishing Industries*, p. 717.

[66]*Ibid.*, p. 709.

[67]Larry Koller, *The Treasury of Angling* (New York: Golden Press, 1963), p. 23.

[68]Charles F. Waterman, *Fishing in America* (New York: Hold, Rinehart and Winston, 1975), p. 60.

[69]*Ibid.*

[70]*A Century of Colonial Painting*, National Gallery of Canada, Catalogue N.G. 31-1964-3 (Ottawa: Queen's Printer, 1964), p. 15.

[71]Pearson, *Fish and Fisheries*, p. 179.

[72]Innis, *The Cod Fisheries*, pp. 146, 148, 149; Prowse, *A History of Newfoundland*, pp. 694–695, 719.

[73]"Choiseul's Speech to the Council at Versailles, August 1, 1761," excerpted in Pearson, *Fish and Fisheries*, p. 153.

CHAPTER

VI

Colonization and Cognition 1760-1784

The Peace of Paris

The Peace of Paris, signed in February 1763, changed many things in the New World: France ceded all her North American territory north and east of the Mississippi River to Great Britain, with the exception of the two small islands, St. Pierre and Miquelon. She still retained the right to fish in the Gulf of St. Lawrence, but was restricted in this operation to an area beyond 15 leagues from Cape Breton and 3 leagues from the rest of the territory that she had formerly possessed in America. She also retained the right to dry her catch on the southern and western shores of Newfoundland.[1] These treaty provisions supposedly excluded France from any participation in the fishery for anadromous species such as gaspereau, shad, and salmon, since the immediate coastal areas, estuaries, and inland waters were the only regions where these fish could be taken in commercial quantities at that time — a fact reflecting, perhaps, the ineffectuality of the existing deep-sea, or saltwater fishing methods on these species, rather than the scarcity of the fish. Peace, moreover, opened the door to a relatively rapid colonization of the region and a more intense exploitation of the valuable shore and river fisheries by the English subjects. The period between 1763 and 1773 was a time when salmon became more valuable as a separate commercial fact in the fishery, and as an increasingly important commodity in the daily lives of the noncommercial, public segment of the populace.

The New Acadia

During the war years, Nova Scotia's commercial development was curtailed to such an extent that by 1760 her economy was in a state of decay. Most of her agricultural land lay uninhabited and unproductive following the expulsion of the Acadian settlers in 1755. The colony's principal outports of Cumberland (Amherst-Sackville), Pisiquid (Windsor), Annapolis, Louisbourg, and Saint John were maintained almost exclusively for military rather than commercial reasons, and commerce and trade were virtually nonexistent. The only major center in the entire region from the St. Lawrence River to Massachusetts Bay was Halifax, but even this military and naval town did not project the image of progress that Cornwallis had envisioned for it in 1749; in fact, its population had declined from 6000 to around 1300,[2] and it had became little more than a parasite on the British treasury. The sorry economic state of the colony was clearly evidenced in its fishery. The small fishing villages adjacent to Halifax had languished; the boat fishery in St. Margaret's Bay for cod and salmon, which had rapidly developed after Halifax was founded, was now forsaken; and the German settlers at Lunenburg, although advantageously situated for the fishery, were initially concerned only with their small plots of agricultural ground.[3] Along the Bay of Fundy, with the exception of a few crude weirs at Annapolis, the Indian spear was virtually the only device exploiting the fish that migrated to the local rivers.

A 1760 letter written by a Haligonian to a friend in New England clearly shows the feeling of decay and disinterest: "We have upward to 100 licensed houses, and perhaps as many more which retail spiritous liquors without license; so that the business of one half the town is to sell rum, and the other half to drink it." Pointing out the obvious effects that such a mode of living had on the potential development of the colony, the writer found no reason why the liquor trade and the British navy had to be the only sources of subsistence for the local inhabitants, commenting that exploiting the fishery was one of the more logical alternatives: "Between here [Halifax] and Cape Sable are many fine harbours commodiously situated for the cod fishery; and the rivers furnish great abundance of salmon."[4]

Other visitors of the day were astounded at the wealth that remained unharvested in the rivers and coves around the colony. Thomas Jeffreys, for example, itemized the many varieties of fish found in Nova Scotia, citing the salmon first, and noting that the fishery was "capable of adding to the wealth, convenience, and commerce of this colony as well as of the mother country."[5]

At the same time as these comments were being made, Charles Lawrence, governor of Nova Scotia, was becoming aware that the time was right to encourage the development of the colony in a positive way. With the end of the war in sight and practically all of the continent under British control, a new period of peace, security, stability, and destiny could be foreseen. Lawrence, therefore, set about energetically to entice colonists to Nova Scotia, offering free grants of land to any New Englander who might come and settle in the colony. Agents that he invited to the region returned to Massachusetts and the other middle colonies, encouraged by the prospects; consequently, from 1760 to 1764, New Englanders founded such towns as Yarmouth, Liverpool, New Dublin, Chester, Truro, Onslow, and Londonderry. New Englanders also took up the lands vacated by the Acadians along the Annapolis, Cornwallis, and Avon rivers, establishing new townships such as Newport, Falmouth, Horton, Cornwallis, and Granville. A settlement was begun at the mouth of the Saint John River in 1762, and at Maugerville the following year. By 1765, new settlements had also been founded on the Miramichi and the Petitcodiac rivers.[6]

When the Peace of Paris was signed in 1763, a reorganization of the old colony took place, with Cape Breton and Prince Edward Island coming under the jurisdiction of Nova Scotia. At first these islands were held in reserve for large colonization projects based on the landlord system, but such a policy was largely unsuccessful, and development of these areas was curtailed for many years. Prince Edward Island, for example, probably contained no more than 700 inhabitants in 1767, many of whom were displaced or returned Acadians.[7]

Many former French settlers also returned to mainland Acadia after the deportation, but finding their former lands occupied by English settlers, they established new settlements in previously undeveloped areas; Cocagne was founded in this way, as were several villages between Digby and Pubnico.[8]

This new influx of people to the colony necessitated renewed consideration of the laws governing them and new regulations respecting their day-to-day activities. In 1762, the colonial council enacted an initial law to regulate the fish trade; it imposed certain standards respecting the quality of fish to be exported, and it established the legal size of containers to be used in the trade.[9] In the next year, the following regulation was made law:

> Justices annually, at their first Sessions, to regulate the river fishery; persons transgressing regulations to forfeit £10, one half to the poor, and the other to the informer, to be recovered in the Court of Record. Act to continue two years.[10]

The only other fisheries statute enacted before the Revolutionary War was one dealing with pollution: in 1770, it was made illegal to throw fish offal into the sea within 3 leagues of the shore, although it was still permissible to throw offal in the "land wash," or beach, where presumably winged scavangers would clean it up.[11] It was not until 1775 that the Legislative Assembly gave the justices authority to appoint fishery overseers, although a few had been appointed by one or two county Sessions previous to the implementation of this general act.[12] These statutes were amended periodically, with special emphasis on rivers frequented by spawning fish.

By 1767, 27 townships had been established in Nova Scotia, which by then contained a population of approximately 13 000[13] — a figure that did not greatly exceed the colony's size prior to the Acadian expulsion, but did represent a greater human diffusion throughout the territory and a greater diversity of commercial interest. Most of the new settlements were located along the coast and at the mouths of some of the major river systems, a situation that allowed the most advantageous use of both the shore and inland resources; the salmon fishery was not a small part of the industry of many of these early settlements.

The *Journal* of the House of Assembly for 1767 supplied one of the first official records of fish production in the colony, showing that 10 667 barrels of "Salmon, Mackerel, etc." had been produced in 1766.[14] Supplementary records of the day indicate that the return was incomplete, for some areas that were known to possess a salmon fishery at this time have no numerical values opposite their names in the *Journal*'s return. The omission in this regard was largely the result of poor communication and an unrefined system of data collection, exemplified by the fact that Halifax and the areas immediately adjacent provided the greatest return.

Although this fact undoubtedly shows the importance of the catch in those areas because of the concentrated local fishery, the figures do not represent an absolute picture; what they do reflect is the proximity of these fishing areas to the principal recording station. The other localities for which figures are available were generally those where communications to and from Halifax were either more or less regular, or at least easily facilitated.

SOUTH SHORE (HALIFAX TO YARMOUTH)

Late in 1759, Governor Lawrence wrote:

The people that take up the lands at La Heve and Port Senia [Liverpool] are fishermen from Plymouth in New England...Those for Cape Sable are fishermen likewise, so that in a few years it may be hoped from the natural advantages we have in point of situation for carrying on the fishery, that all the fishermen to the westward will flock to the [this] country.[15]

Fully one-half of the one hundred families settled between Yarmouth and Liverpool in 1763 were fishermen,[16] and the ratio of fishermen to the east of Liverpool was probably no less.

Liverpool itself was founded at its particular location on the coast in 1760, principally because of the magnificent salmon runs which entered the Mersey River; within a few years, the inhabitants were reported to be exporting upwards of 1000 barrels of pickled salmon each year.[17] It is quite possible, however, that a portion of this figure represents trans-shipments from the fisheries of other areas, such an assumption being deduced from the diaries of Simeon Perkins, Liverpool's chief fish dealer. In 1766, for example, he noted that his schooner, the *Liverpool Packet*, was engaged chiefly in trade with the Indians along the coast, bartering goods for salmon; in later years, he sent vessels on fishing excursions to the Bay of Fundy, Cape Breton, Chaleur Bay, Gaspé, Newfoundland, and even to the shores of Labrador. In August 1775, he reported that Captain Ford had returned from Newfoundland with 215 barrels of salmon. In the following year, at least 270 barrels arrived from the Newfoundland and Labrador fishery; Captain Drew, he reported, "found them very plenty at Labrador Shore."[18]

Large numbers of salmon were also taken in the Liverpool (Mersey) River, where fish lots had been assigned shortly after the founding of the town. Each year the Sessions Court, of which Perkins was a member, issued orders and directions for participation in the river fishery; net fishing in the area usually began in early April and lasted until the end of the salmon run. Perkins himself occasionally participated as a diversion from his mercantile duties, and on at least one occasion took enough interest in the sport to record: "Caught a Salmon 25-½ lbs., in a small net of Lathrop Freeman's."[19]

German settlers at Lunenburg continued to be interested principally in agriculture, but the people at LaHave, Dublin, and Petite Rivière were fishermen as well as farmers. At the latter location, one of the best salmon fisheries on the coast was reported in 1761; the salmon were said to have begun running in the Petite Rivière by the end of April and continued to mid-June, with the best run being in May.[20] Even the Chester grantees were not without their salmon, as the diary of the Rev. John Seccombe testifies:

August 6th, p.m., 1759 — Went to view the country lots, and had a most pleasant time and prospect. A fine spring up Middle River. Salmon jumped out of water....
August 7th, 1759 — Two Indian squaws brought in a birch canoe five salmon and eighty salmon trout. One of the salmon weighed twenty two pounds, and one dozen of the trout weighed fourteen pounds....
September 7th, 1759 — Mr. Melvin and Mr. Houghton caught a salmon in Middle River with their hands.[21]

The boat fishery for salmon and cod in St. Margaret's Bay had not been pursued, and not a single fisherman inhabited the area in 1762. The Halifax fishery was prosecuted principally in the harbor, where an abundant supply was always available. The community provided a good rendezvous for transient fishermen, and Patrick McRobert reported seeing thirty schooners in the harbor in 1774, the majority of which were fishing boats engaged in the coastal fishery and carrying their produce to New York, Philadelphia, and the West Indies.[22] Only two families were settled in Dartmouth — not to fish, but to supply the town of Halifax with firewood.[23]

SOUTHERN BAY OF FUNDY (ANNAPOLIS TO ONSLOW)

Weirs were still the most visible evidence that the fishery played a part in the economy around the old capital, Annapolis Royal. Various individuals and groups had petitioned the governor for fish lots and the right to engage in the fishery, and weirs were subsequently built on these by some of the "principal inhabitants" of the towns of Annapolis and Granville.[24] By 1760, weirs could be found at least as far below the towns as "Hog Island" (Goat Island). With the arrival during the 1760s and 1770s of more settlers interested in participating in such a fishery, the Court of General Sessions found it necessary to provide some means of regulating the industry, that it might be equitably prosecuted. In the April 1772 session, the court assigned public fishing areas further down the Annapolis Basin at The Joggins and Bear River, appointed several overseers or directors, and issued notices that anyone wishing to engage in the fishery must apply to the directors before a specified date, that they might be assigned a share in the operation.[25]

Weir fishing was not usually an individual under-taking; groups of people banded together to share in the building of the weir and divide the profits from it. This system usually prevailed regardless of whether the weir was erected on a public or private fish lot. The rights of the various groups were jealously guarded, sometimes to the chagrin of others who were not fortunate enough to have been able to engage in the operation. There are many complaints on record, referring to the miserable way in which some groups operated their weir fishery by letting fish rot in the pounds when they could otherwise have been used by local inhabitants, or demanding such high prices for their fish that no townsman or farmer could afford to buy them.[26]

Fisheries officers, apparently, were regularly ap-pointed in Annapolis County after the year 1772; they were nominated by the Grand Jury and appointed to the office for one year by the Sessions Court. In 1797, there were seven such appointments in the fishery: one culler of fish (John Burkett), one inspector of smoked herrings (Isaac Bonnett), one inspector of pickled fish (William Robertson), one gauger (Andrew Ritchie), and three overseers of the fishery (Israel Potter, John Reid, John Gates).[27]

Further eastward, the lands in the Annapolis Valley and around the Minas Basin were occupied by New England Planters, to whom fishing was second only to farming. Salmon were being speared along the Annap-olis River, and the Avon became so well known for its fishery in June, July, and August that it was commonly called "Salmon River," and was so referred to on the official charts of the day.[28] Also inside Cape "Blow Me Down," or Blomidon, were numerous other streams which the new settlers discovered were great sources of wealth; for example, salmon were found to be so plen-tiful at the head of Minas Basin that there was no choice but to name its most easterly tributary the Salmon River.

Since aboriginal times, the Shubenacadie River had provided the main route of communication across the central interior of Nova Scotia, and a major Indian settle-ment was located on its banks. At times, parties of Indians, French, and English had fished along the river, and as early as 1770, one sports-minded navy captain journeyed through the Dartmouth Lakes, "Lake Supe-rior" (Grand Lake), "Wabaniah" (Nine Mile River), and the main Shubenacadie with rod and line.[29] Stewiacke was one of the first agricultural communities to be estab-lished on this waterway, and when touring this area in 1774, Patrick McRobert stated: "I came to a new settle-ment on Suiack [sic] river; here is some very good land, a fine river with plenty of salmon."[30] Salmon fishing became a regular pursuit for families living along these rivers, and an early history of Colchester County tells the story of a 16-year-old boy who drowned at Stewiacke while salmon fishing in 1788.[31]

THE GULF SHORE

The Gulf Shore, that area of Nova Scotia fronting on Northumberland Strait, remained largely uninhabited until a later period, with the exception of settlements at Tatamagouche and Pictou. Fish were abundant, par-ticularly salmon, which, from an early date, were caught both for local consumption and for export. During this early period, their numbers must have been prodigious, since even in the first years of the 19th century, they were described as "coming in such numbers into the West River, that at a narrow place they would seem almost jammed together, so that one would think he could walk upon them."[32]

CAPE BRETON

During this period, the northwestern half of Cape Breton Island was still largely uninhabited. The local salmon rivers, such as the Margaree, Mabou and — to a lesser extent — the Cheticamp, were chiefly the seasonal resort of the Indians, who undertook summer fishing excursions to these areas from their permanently occupied settlements at St. Ann's and along the shores of the Bras d'Or Lakes. Captain Samuel Holland, who sur-veyed the Margaree coast for the Admiralty in 1768, reported that

Salmon River [Margaree River] is fresh water down to its entrance. At some distance up are fine meadow lands very proper for improvement. This river has its source — by the description of the Indians — from a lake at a great distance in the country and where there is a carrying place to another lake from which a river ascends to Bidec [Baddeck] on St. Patrick's Lake Channel by which the Indians come in their birch canoes with emmence [sic] difficulty to Salmon River to fish for salmon which is here so abundant that they every season resort here with their families....[33]

Occasional fishing voyages were also made to this north-western region by white inhabitants settled at Louisbourg and elsewhere along the Atlantic coast — principal of which were the employees of the Charles Robin firm, which had established on the island follow-ing the French surrender.

There was, however, more general fishing activity on the south coast of Cape Breton and, although the most striking example of a salmon river in all the island may have been the Margaree, there were many brooks and streams in the southerly division which were just as prolific for their size. Salmon were seasonally plentiful, for example, at North River in St. Ann's Bay, where they were taken by the Indians and the French settlers. Hol-land reported that St. Patrick's Channel abounded with the species, an indication that this particular arm of the Bras d'Or contained quantities of salmon destined for such streams as Lewis Brook and the Washabuck, Skye, Hume, Middle, and Baddeck rivers. Louisbourg was now being utilized as a fishing base by New Englanders, as well as by fishermen from Jersey Island firms.[34] Near Louisbourg was the Mira River, with two important tributaries, the Salmon and Gaspereau rivers; even closer to the community, streams such as Gerratt Brook were noted for their easily procurable trout and salmon.[35]

A census taken in 1774 listed 502 French, 230 Indians, and 509 English as residents of Cape Breton Island; the fishing segment of this population owned 136 vessels, mainly small shallops.[36] The remoteness of Cape Breton, however, and the varied cultural, ethnic, and national mixture of those groups of people who for one reason or another found themselves residents or transients on the coast, created considerable discomfort and trouble for the Nova Scotian colonial government. Even at this early point in its history, this small, detached appendage to the peninsula proper was a world — and a law — unto itself. Official control over the island and its fishery was wanting, as exemplified by Governor Francis Legge's comment that the island's people were "a lawless rabble, and often disrupted the chief magistrate, Mr. Cottnam, in the execution of his duty[;] they had no grants, and many of them even had not fishing licenses."[37]

SOUTHEASTERN TOWNSHIPS (CANSO TO HALIFAX)

The community of Canso was still largely a transient town, with boats owned by New England and Jersey fishermen arriving during the fishing period and returning home at the end of the season. The coastline between Canso and Halifax was uninhabited except for Indians and the occasional visits of fishermen who encountered the salmon at Guysborough, St. Mary's, Musquodoboit, and other coastal locations.[38]

PRINCE EDWARD ISLAND

The British had made their conquest of Ile Saint-Jean in 1758, and the French population — with the exception of some three hundred persons who managed to escape the vigilance of the troops — were deported as a part of the general expulsion of the Acadians which had taken place on the mainland in 1755. No attempts were made for a number of years to encourage immigration to the island. In 1763, this "garden of the gulf" was still almost devoid of human population, and even by 1769, the census revealed that there were only 271 residents. In fact, the colony was not to see its former maximum of 4700 inhabitants surpassed until the early 1800s.[39]

The colony was annexed, as St. John's Island, to Nova Scotia in 1763, and a principal reason for its slow growth was the policy of the home government in Great Britain to hold the island in reserve for development under the landlord system. Free grants to individuals were not made, and the colonization projects of absentee landlords were generally doomed to failure, due to the fact that every would-be tenant preferred to own his own property. Before this policy was completely formulated, however, several grants had been made, at least one of which was to a man named Gameliel Smethurst for the specific purpose of carrying on a fishery. In a memorial forwarded to the government of Nova Scotia in 1763, Smethurst stated:

> I was the first Briton who attempted a fishery on the Island of St. John. I had raised two storehouses at St. Peter's and had employed most of the people on the Island in the fishery: I had likewise brought a crew from Marblehead in New England to cause an emulation.[40]

Smethurst's operation was conducted from the same base used by Pierre Roma 30 years earlier, and it seems likely that he would also have made use of the local salmon, as had the French before him. Samuel Holland surveyed the island in 1765, mentioning the salmon which were to be found in this area.[41] Smethurst apparently did not continue his enterprise for more than a few years, since W. S. McNutt relates that at this time, the London firm of Mills and Cathgart was the only fishing enterprise of any consequence on the entire island.[42]

In time, the home government recognized that the island was advantageously situated as a base for the Gulf of St. Lawrence fishery, and to encourage the development of fishing stations along the coast, it passed a statute in 1767 which reserved a belt around the entire colony for the sole use of the fishery. This reserve extended inland for 560 feet above the high-water mark, and up the rivers and creeks to the head of tide.[43] Such a restricted zone was not popular to the landholders, but since no great fishery development occurred, these reserve lands were gradually taken up by new settlers.

Meanwhile, although the population of the island was less than 300 in 1769, it nevertheless received its own government and was granted colonial status. Because of the continuing small population, one might believe that the island's resources were barely touched; statutes of the time, however, show that some of the anadromous species were exploited to a considerable degree. In 1780, for example, the Legislature passed an act entitled, "An act to regulate the Salmon, Salmon trout, and Eel Fishery," the preamble of which stated:

> Whereas the Great Quantity of Salmon, Salmon trout, and Eels, which have hitherto been taken by the Inhabitants of this Island, has been of the Greatest Service to them and as the quantities taken and brought to market, has of late been much reduced by their being killed and taken at improper Seasons of the year....[44]

The taking of salmon was regulated in this act to a season extending from January 15 to September 30, although the species can be considered to have been consistently fished at this time, they were still appearing in most of the colony's creeks and streams.

THE RIVER SAINT JOHN

One of the first major English commercial fishing ventures in what is now New Brunswick was begun in 1762 by the Massachusetts trading firm of Simonds, Hazen and White. James Simonds, a partner in this company, erected a post at Portland Point, Saint John Harbour, and in 1764 he received a license to establish a fishery.[45] The firm's principal interest in this fishery was directed toward gaspereau and cod, but the operation also took quantities of shad, bass, and salmon from the river. Weirs were constructed on the flats adjacent to the Portland Point property, and at least one large weir was constructed further upriver, principally for bass. The catch was exported to New England, and in 1771 included two barrels of salmon shipped out on a sloop mastered by Captain John Leavett, and valued at 36 shillings per tierce.[46]

The success of the Simonds, Hazen and White firm and the reports of the advantages of settlement on the Saint John River, encouraged others to come to the area. Maugerville, the principal community before 1784, was founded some 50 miles upriver; several new townships were also established, including Sunbury on the west side, and Newtown on the east side of the river, in what is today Sunbury County. Simonds wrote of these new townships in 1765 that "The township of Sunbury is the best in the Patent and Newtown is the next to it according to the quantity of land, it will have a good Salmon Fishery."[47] Another inhabitant of the river valley at this time assessed the fishery potential in the following terms: "The river abounds in all sorts of small fry, Trout, Salmon, Bass, Whitefish and Sturgeon....On Beaubiers Point [mouth of the Nerepis River] the salmon fishery is said to be the best on the river."[48]

"PASS MACQUODDY"

The firm of Simonds, Hazen and White was also involved in the Passamaquoddy Bay fishery during the mid-1760s, but it later forsook the area for a monopoly at the mouth of the Saint John River. The Passamaquoddy — "Pass MacQuoddy" on some early maps — was already well frequented by New Englanders. Around 1764, it was reported that several sloops and smaller vessels had sailed up the St. Croix and returned to Pemaquid with between 800 and 1000 barrels of alewives, salmon, and bass, taken at Scoodic Falls.[49]

The area soon fell under the control of one man, however. Captain William Owen, a retired Royal Navy captain, was granted Passamaquoddy Outer Island — which he renamed Campobello Island — in 1767, and in 1769 an association of some dozen partners was formed in Great Britain to develop the resources of the area. In 1770, Owen arrived with 38 indentured servants to begin the operation. His naval attitudes, training, and discipline soon acquired for him a stern authority over the entire area. He had stocks and a whipping post constructed on his property to discourage any delinquency, either by his employees or by others who might infringe upon his domain. Although principally interested in developing a coastal fishery, Owen also took advantage of the salmon on the St. Croix River, and reported the beginnings of this venture in his diary entry for July 4, 1770: "In the morning Captain Denny and I proceeded with our freshwater fishermen in a whaleboat and punt for the falls of Scoodic to fish for salmon." Nine days later, he noted: "Sent two salmon nets up to Scoodic Falls by James Cochran to fish upon shares whilst our own fishermen are daily employed in the Cod, Haddock and Pollock fishery." On July 24, some produce from the Scoodic fishery arrived at Campobello: "Received some smoked salmon and two casks of salted ones from the falls."[50] Owen was to build up a large — but short-lived — fishing empire at Passamaquoddy Bay; following his departure in 1771, the industry lapsed and, until the arrival of the Loyalists at St. Andrews and St. Stephen, the salmon fishery remained the domain of a few New Englanders and the Indians.

MIRAMICHI AND RESTIGOUCHE

The Miramichi region was largely unknown to the English in 1760, but French fishermen had used the islands at the mouth of the river for drying and curing fish from the early 16th century. Around 1672, a number of emigrants from St. Malo, France, had begun a settlement at "Baie des Vents" (Bay du Vin), and in 1688, Richard Denys established a trading post in the vicinity of present-day Newcastle. Several settlements existed in the area by 1690, but little attention was apparently paid to the salmon fishery; by 1765, the only people making use of the resource were the Indians.[51] Scattered reports had been made about the potential of the river, and even the Chief Surveyor of Nova Scotia, Charles Morris, had noted at this time that "as there are convenient ports and several rivers navigable for small vessels abounding with salmon...this part of Nova Scotia may in time be settled."[52]

It was, in fact, settled soon after. In 1765, a Scot from Aberdeenshire came to Nova Scotia with the principal intention of beginning a salmon fishery — an occupation that he had known and engaged in since his youth on the shores of Moray Firth. William Davidson spent the summer of 1765 exploring the coast of the colony with his partner, John Cort, that they might search out the best location for their enterprise. They finally chose the "River Meriamerchie" and sought permission from the governor to establish there. The request was approved, and they received a grant of approximately

150 square miles surrounding the lower stretches of both the Northwest and Southwest Miramichi rivers. The conditions under which Davidson and Cort obtained their grant were that they settle on the land, clear a certain acreage each year, and encourage colonization. The grant further stipulated that their tenure was valid only "during the occupation of the same," and that they were "To have no right or title to the fisheries on the river nor to the shore, beach or banks of the river, any longer than they continue in the occupation of catching and curing fish."[53]

Such conditions were commonly included in grants at this time and were to cause no end of trouble to Davidson in the future, principally because he was principally interested in the fishery rather than in any agricultural or colonization activities. The government, on the other hand, considered that the fishery was annexed to the soil and that the conditions of land occupation had to be met if a right to the fishery was desired.

Davidson erected dwellings, warehouses, a cooperage, and netting stands at Elm Tree, near Quarryville. The Wright and Blaskurly map of the Miramichi, made under the direction of chief surveyor Samuel Holland in 1767, shows the exact location of Davidson's fishing establishment — four buildings, identified with the words "salmon fishery," on the south bank of the river at Doyle Brook. Davidson first experimented with the traditional Scottish method of salmon fishing by "scringing," or dragging the river channel with nets, but this proved ineffectual. Eventually he developed a fixed-net method of fishing, by using what was termed a "cross net" — nets extending across the river diagonally from shore to shore. These nets were hung on poles or pickets which were driven into the river bed. The captured salmon were dressed, salted, and packed into tierces of 300 pounds each.

Davidson's interests extended to the local fur and timber trades, and by 1773, he had imported craftsmen to build his own vessels on the Miramichi, in order to carry his products to Britain and the Mediterranean. At first, progress was slow; there was considerable difficulty in obtaining enough salt with which to cure the fish, and the first boatload of pickled salmon was wrecked on the shores of Prince Edward Island while on its way to Europe. By the mid-1770s, however, Davidson was annually exporting between 660 000 and 850 000 pounds of salmon from the Miramichi.[54]

Davidson and his men were not the only people to take advantage of the Miramichi fishery at this time. The Jersey firm of Robin, Piper and Company, established a main base at Paspébiac in Chaleur Bay, but also erected a substation on the lower Miarmichi around 1763. Although not so prosperous in their fishery as Davidson, they were annually shipping small quantities of salmon to Spain, 70 tierces being exported in 1769.[55]

In 1768, Commodore George Walker came to Bathurst Harbour and built a small trading post at Alston Point; about 3 miles upstream from the mouth of the Nepisiguit, or "Big River," he also erected a fishing station from which he annually shipped a cargo of salmon. The commodore was engaged in other pursuits as well, yearly exporting scale fish and cod to the Mediterranean and West Indian markets.[56] One of his subsidiary fishing establishments was located in the upper Chaleur Bay, where two English merchants — Schoolbred and Smith — had also erected an establishment about the same time, at the head of the tide on the Restigouche River. John Schoolbred reputedly began the first permanent English settlement on that river, after obtaining a grant along some 10 miles of the lower Restigouche. There he and his son caught and packed salmon, 10 or 12 to a barrel, principally for export to the southern New England colonies. They also had a subsidiary fishing station near Bathurst, and apparently were very successful at taking commercial advantage of the salmon fishery for a number of years.[57]

The salmon fishery of the Miramichi, Nepisiguit and Restigouche was just beginning to prosper when trouble erupted between Britain and her American colonies. New England privateers began depredations upon the operations at Miramichi and other locations in the Gulf of St. Lawrence, and the precariousness of the former settlement under such conditions became unacceptable. Davidson left the area in 1777, moving to the Saint John River and leaving Cort in charge; the latter, about whom little is known, died shortly thereafter, and for the duration of the American Revolution, the Miramichi fishery again reverted to the Indians.[58]

Canada

For the first 25 years following the Peace of Paris, fishing activity in the St. Lawrence River showed little expansion. Heriot mentioned that there were no more than 12 small vessels engaged in catching fish there in 1769, in addition to a number of U-shaped river weirs in operation.[59] Salmon still received nominal domestic attention, rather than concerted commercial interest; even by 1783, when the first trade statistics appeared for the colony, only "304 smoked salmon" were reported among the exports. Even if this figure is interpreted as 304 boxes of smoked salmon, the product still does not convert to more than 12 000 pounds of fresh fish. In 1784, the export was only "221 smoked salmon."[60]

On the north shore of the Gulf of St. Lawrence, the King's Post fisheries were still being pursued as a subsidiary activity to the fur trade, and some of the seigneurial grant fisheries were also still in operation. In addition, "foreign" fishing incursions by New Englanders and Nova Scotians were occasionally reported.[61] Unfortunately for Quebec interests, the Labrador section of the colony came under Newfoundland jurisdiction after the peace, and that colony's governor apparently disregarded any and all prior fishing claims to the region by issuing licenses at St. John's only to British and Newfoundland interests who wished to fish there. Sir Guy Carleton, governor of Quebec, protested this action as early as 1766 and 1767, and his representations were largely responsible for restoring Labrador to Lower Canada when the Quebec Act was finalized in 1774.[62]

In 1786, exports of salmon from Lower Canada were reported to be more than 1100 tierces.[63] It is suspected, however, that this figure did not include exports from the north shore and Labrador, and only showed a remarkable increase over previous records because of the inclusion of the Chaleur Bay production; there, an independent report stated that around 1000 tierces were taken annually at that time.[64] The singular, most important and influential fishing interest in the Chaleur area was the firm of Charles Robin, who came to Paspébiac from Jersey in 1764. His principal export was cod, but he was also involved peripherally in the salmon trade.[65]

Newfoundland

The statistical records for the colony of Newfoundland from 1760 to 1769 show that between 1000 and 2000 tierces of salmon (300 000 to 600 000 lb pickled) were exported annually from the island, with the total reaching 3000 tierces (900 000 lb pickled) by the advent of the Revolutionary War.[66] The reliability of these export figures is somewhat in question, however, since there was only the fishing admiral's reports until 1762, at which time the first customs house was established at St. John's;[67] even after that date, export records were far from being either absolute or accurate.

The principal responsibility of a customs house was to collect the duty on colonial imports and exports; in consequence, it was also the principal agency that collected and recorded the quantitative data on external commerce and trade. Needless to say, these customs houses were not the most popular departments of government, nor were the customs officers the most popular or respected of government officials; avoiding, outwitting, or harassing the civil authorities was universally in vogue in North America during the 1770s — witness the Boston Tea Party incident — and in Newfoundland, "Mr. Hamilton, the first Collector, went out, but found the People and Climate so Disagreeable, and the Emoluments so inadequate to his Expectations, that he returned to England the same year, and resigned."[68]

Customs officials were confined to recording the trade of the immediate region or port in which the customs establishment was located; during this period, this meant that only the St. John's area of Newfoundland could be given adequate surveillance. It is doubtful if much of the commerce and trade of the fishing stations outside the principal city were reported regularly in the total statistical returns given for the colony. In 1763, for example, the official record stated that salmon exports from the island amounted to 694 tierces, but one writer has estimated this to be only the amount traded by Newfoundland planters — individuals confined principally to the Avalon Peninsula.[69] Add to this the combined — and perhaps the more significant — yields of the boatmen from Great Britain, the employees of the established fishing firms, the Americans and other visiting colonial fishermen, the French on the western and northern coasts, and the Indians, and the total yield from the waters of Newfoundland then might logically be two, three, or more times greater than that reported in the official returns.

An isolated statistical record for the year 1757 is, in fact, more than four times greater than the average yields reported up to that date and more than twice that of any return prior to 1772.[70] The year 1757 may have been an exceptional one for the salmon fishery, or it may have been a year when statistical returns were received from more than the usual number of fishing stations — or it may have been a year for clerical errors. Nevertheless, it is a record that serves to illustrate the danger of relying exclusively on official statistical records as unqualified indicators of the value and extent of the salmon fishery in historical times — both in Newfoundland and throughout the other North American colonies.

Although the general statistical returns are undoubtedly incomplete, they do indicate a trend toward increasing colonial yields from the mid-1760s. The peace treaty of 1763 not only opened more of the island to English fishing enterprise, but also opened a vast area of the Labrador coast, formerly French territory, to Newfoundland interests.[71] Although the treaty created an opportunity for development and expansion, it was the newly appointed governor who supplied the impetus and encouragement needed to pursue the enterprise. Hugh Palliser came to the colony in 1764, and quickly set about to ensure that both Newfoundland and its newly acquired territory would be developed for, and dominated by, Great Britain. Among other successes, his keen and particular attention to the salmon fishery resulted in the settlement of many permanent and seasonal establishments in the colony, and the creation of a salmon fishery of considerable proportion during his tenure in office.[72]

In a letter sent to the authorities in Great Britain shortly after his arrival on the island, Palliser stated:

> I am informed that the said salmon fishery is capable of being extended and improved; but that at present very few people are employed in it, because of violent and unlawful practices of some people to discourage and obstruct new adventures, by which many ship-loads of salmon yearly return from the rivers into the sea, which might be taken and carried to foreign markets, to the great benefit of His Majesty's trading subjects, and to the nation in general.[73]

Palliser set about to pursue his imperialistic ideals by informing Newfoundlanders that they now possessed the unrestricted right to enter the countryside or coastline at any point and to fish for salmon in any and all of the lakes, streams, rivers, and bays that they might choose. Although the French were still to retain certain rights to the coast, they were now excluded from the river and inland resources, and it was hoped that in time they would be restricted solely to cod fishing.

Certain Newfoundland fishing interests were at first reluctant to establish within the former French zone because such an action was apt to arouse old animosities; by 1765, however, an estimated one-third of the colony's population of 5260 was concentrated around Conception Bay, and pioneer fishermen were now venturing northward, forming settlements at Fogo and Twillingate.[74] Dwellings were being erected at the mouths of such salmon rivers as the Exploits, Gander and South Brook, and at Halls Bay, while numerous voyages were being made up the east side of the Great Northern Peninsula, and even to the shores of Labrador.

In 1768, when Lieutenant John Cartwright explored the Exploits River in search of the mysterious and elusive Red Indians, or Beothuks, he recorded the existence of a salmon-fishing station run by a man named Cousins at the mouth of Little Rattling Brook.[75] The Beothuks had resorted to this area in the past for purposes of catching salmon, but were now rarely encountered because of the encroachment of English salmoniers. Cartwright's brother, George, who accompanied him, mentioned that the English fishermen had so taken control of the fishery that they "have now only left them [the Indians] in possession of Charles and another brook." When John Cartwright again came to the Exploits region 2 years later, Charles Brook was apparently no longer in sole control of the Indians; a crew of three Newfoundland fishermen had arrived there in that year, but had had only partial success, because the Indians had made off with one fleet of their salmon nets.[76]

At this time, it was reported that in the Exploits region and in the area around the islands and shores of eastern Notre Dame Bay,

> There is no cod-fishery, and consequently there are no inhabitants within the very extreme verge of these islands; but they are often visited by boats that carry the salmon fishers…into the respective bays and rivers situated within them.[77]

The Halls Bay salmon patentee was a merchant by the name of Squire Childs, but in 1772 a family named Rousell purchased the fishery rights from him for £90. The Rousells were apparently successful in their venture, despite problems with Indians who periodically took salmon from their weirs. One member of the family attempted to live with this problem by accepting these aboriginal depredations as a matter of course, even leaving salmon for the Indians to take. His brother, however, waged war on the natives, acquired the reputation of being one of the most successful Indian killers of Notre Dame Bay, and was himself eventually killed by natives while tending his salmon weir at New Bay River.[78]

The Indians, of course, stole salmon for food, but they also took salmon nets and twine for other reasons. Salmon nets, with every other mesh cut away, were frequently used by the natives for catching seals. It was also reported that birch bark was frequently tied to short lengths of salmon twine and attached to brush fences which the natives used to direct caribou to areas where they could be easily slaughtered; the swinging birch bark spooked the deer along the fence. One writer even mentioned that salmon twine was strung among the Indians' wigwams as a sort of primitive telegraph; if one household or "tenthold" wanted to draw the attention of another, a tug on the salmon line which connected the two dwellings would serve the purpose.[79]

Salmon fishing was also pursued along the south shore of the island, the main base being Placentia. An excellent review of the local fishery there comes from the diary of Thomas Curtis, an English emigrant who came to the colonies in the mid-1770s. His introduction to the coast of North America was an eventful one, since his ship was wrecked in a storm off Hogg Island, Prince Edward Island, and he was cast ashore to spend a miserable winter at New London, a desolate little community which faced the cold and inhospitable Gulf of St. Lawrence. His views on emigration changed abruptly as a result, and he decided to return to England at the first opportunity. The opportunity, in half measure, came in the spring, when he managed to secure passage as far as Placentia. Unable to pay the remainder of his fare from there, he was forced to accept a job as a net mender with an English cod-fishing firm then based at this southern port. In June, he was asked to "go out a salmon catching," an activity which he discovered was an annual custom of the firm. With one man to navigate a small boat, and another to assist with the common labor of fishing, he set out with plenty of provisions and everything necessary," including a small skiff which was towed behind the "shallop."

> The first harbour we made and got up near the fresh water we proposed to fix our nets but with much difficulty to fasten our line on Shore the Breakers being very rough and the place rockey. Dark coming on we agreed to do it better in the morn. We hauld our Boat up and went into the Wood and made a Wigwam and slept tolerable. That night the muskatoes were Troublesome. As soon as day light appear[d] we went to our Boat and began to take in our Nets in which we found four small salmon….Here we found…very few salmon, which Obliged us to move Our Quarters. We then Sail[d] to a very noted place at the Bottom of Placentia Bay call[d] Pipers Hole whare some Years great Quantitys have been caught. We several times araged a hold cal[d] the Salmon

hole and caught very few sometimes none....After staying two weeks at this place we return^d home with only forty-five salmon.[80]

It is apparent from Curtis's narrative that a large segment of the Newfoundland fishery was still being carried out by a transient population and only on a seasonal basis. Even the major fishing port of Plancentia, second only to St. John's, was practically deserted after the fishing season was over; several hundred individuals were employed in various fishing tasks when Curtis arrived there in May, but only two were left at the port when the ships sailed to Great Britain with cargoes of cod and salmon in the fall.

With regard to Labrador, Governor Palliser wished to develop the newly acquired territory as a strictly controlled British monopoly. As a result, he initiated a set of requirements for the prosecution of the Labrador fishery, and based its regulation on the long-established fishing admiral system: the masters of the first British ship to enter a Labrador harbor in the spring had the sole right to the seal and whale fishery of that harbor for that season, while "The Master of the second arriving British Fishing Ship in any season shall besides being Vice Admiral of the Harbour have the exclusive right to all the salmon fishery in that harbour during the season."[81] The third ship had the right to trade with the Indians, and apparently all ships could fish for cod, due to the inexhaustible presence of the species. The order of arrival probably indicates the order of importance of the various operations at that time.

Palliser's regulations in no small way conflicted with the rights of established proprietors on the southwestern shore of Labrador, where the British administration of Lower Canada had already, since 1763, granted a fishing monopoly to Daniel Bayne and William Brymer, two Quebec merchants. In addition, part of the territory around Bradore Bay was claimed as the seigneury of Augustin Le Gardeur de Courtemanche, dating from the early 18th century. These political considerations led to problems that were not completely resolved until the beginning of the Revolutionary War.[82]

The general fishery became so important along the Labrador coast after Palliser had issued his instructions, that to regulate and protect it, the governor erected fortifications at Chateau Bay and garrisoned the outpost with a detachment of troops.[83] One of the first Newfoundland-based firms to fish and trade on the east coast of Labrador was that operated by Nicolas Darby who, after 1765, established posts at Chateau Bay, Cape Charles, Forteau, and Ile aux Bois. He achieved some success in the salmon, seal, and cod fisheries, but encountered difficulties with the Inuit and with his own employees. By 1770, Darby had been maneuvered out of his holdings, largely because he failed to conform to the government regulations for a monopoly fishery.[84]

Other early firms in Labrador included John Noble and Company — later Noble and Pinson — at Lance Cove, Temple Bay in 1770 and at Pitts Harbour in 1772, and John Slade, who ventured north along the coast at least as early as 1771.[85] These firms had strong ties to the West Country of England, and maintained Palliser's dream of British monopoly in Labrador. It has been estimated that as early as 1765, 117 sloops and schooners, employing 1565 men, were engaged in the general Labrador fishery; by 1767, at least 18 boats were occupied solely with the salmon fishery and had taken 45 tierces (13 500 lb pickled) during that season. By 1773, these and other firms had taken more than 265 tierces of salmon (79 500 lb pickled) from Labrador.[86]

By 1774, it was reported that many of the Labrador salmon streams, such as the Alexis, Eagle, and those of Sandwich Bay, were completely closed off by salmon nets.[87] The rivers of the latter region were under the sole control of Captain George Cartwright, whose fame is perpetuated in the modern settlement of that name. "Old Labrador," as he came to be called late in life, was a native of Nottinghamshire, England, and was described as a lover of truth, a hard worker, a good observer, and a man of honor, justice, and resourcefulness. Cartwright was the second of 10 children born into an old landed family then in straightened circumstances. He joined the army and achieved the rank of captain, but when he went on half pay at the end of the Seven Years' War, his income was, as stated, "Too small...to enable me to live in a Baronet's seat, and to keep a female companion, two servants, a couple of horses and three brace of dogs."[88]

Cartwright subsequently decided to seek his fortune in Newfoundland, where his brother John was stationed as first lieutenant on the *Guernsey*, Governor Palliser's flagship. George initially entered into partnership with an English firm from Bristol, to engage in the lucrative salmon fishery at Cape St. Francis and Point Spear. Difficulties with his partners resulted in his subsequently quitting the firm and moving to Labrador, where he established himself at the former Darby post at Cape Charles in 1770. He became dissatisfied with the latter location, however, and in 1775 moved further north to prosecute the salmon, seal, cod, and fur trades at Sandwich Bay, where he built a fine house called Caribou Castle. Cartwright was impressed with the potential of Sandwich Bay and set about to reap a valuable harvest of salmon. In July 1775, he wrote of his Eagle River fishery: "We have 140 tierce [42 000 lb] ashore, but have had to take up two nets as fish got in too fast. The big pool is so full of salmon, you could not fire a musket ball into it without injuring some."[89]

In August 1775, Cartwright captured 1230 salmon in 5 days. He had packed 214 tierces (64 200 lb pickled) at his Paradise River fishery, and mentioned that very few had escaped his 10 nets of 40 fathoms each, all tied together to stretch entirely across the river's mouth. By July 1779, he noted in his journal that

In Eagle River we are killing 750 salmon a day, or 35 tierce, and we would have killed more had we had more nets. Three hundred and fifty tierce [7,500 salmon] ashore already at Paradise. If I had had more nets, I would have killed 1,000 tierce alone at this post, the fish averaging from 15 to 32 pounds apiece. At Sandhill Cove two men have 240 tierce ashore, and would have had more, but we had no more salt.[90]

Between June 23 and July 20, 1779, 12 396 salmon were taken at Eagle River, and he commented that 32 000 could just as easily have been caught.

In the 16 years during which Cartwright participated in the general Labrador fishery, his success was mixed. There were good years, but these were balanced by years like 1782, when the salmon fishery lagged, and only 80 tierces were cured at his namesake station of Cartwright.[91] Although he had eliminated one potential problem by maintaining a good relationship with the Inuit, there were other setbacks. A terrible storm, for example, wrecked a large part of the Newfoundland and Labrador fishery in 1775, and in 1778, Cartwright lost some £14 000 when his posts were raided by American privateers. There was still rivalry between French and English on the shore, fierce competition among trading firms, and jurisdictional problems between the governments of Newfoundland and Lower Canada. The end result was that Cartwright went bankrupt, and returned to England in 1786.[92]

Generally speaking, the Labrador salmon fishery was increasing its yield during each year of this period, and was attracting fishing interests in great numbers from the lower colonies. Canadian participation, interference, and influence became so great that, regardless of Palliser's earlier intentions, a large segment of Labrador was returned to Lower Canada through a provision of the Quebec Act, which took effect in 1774.[93] This action by the British government disrupted Newfoundland's fishery on that coast, but the outbreak of war with the American colonies resulted in a far more effective curb to local development.

The collapse of the Newfoundland bank fishery (dry fish) in 1776 led to an increased demand for pickled fish from the shore fishery, and this in turn added impetus to the general Labrador fishery. American privateers, however, began to harass both the banks and coastal operations, and soon extended their raids to Labrador. On one occasion, 30 employees of one firm, along with the produce of the year's fishery, were abducted by a Yankee vessel. The situation became serious enough to warrant a letter of warning from the then-governor, Commodore Robert Duff, to his Massachusetts counterpart, in August 1776: "The great trouble and difficulty I meet with in keeping good order amongst the fishers of Labrador, is occasioned by disorderly people from your province."[94] The governor's curt note had little effect, however, because the Americans had already severed themselves from any British authority by signing the Declaration of Independence a month earlier.

Despite American incursions, however, catch returns were being reported from such areas as Rivière au Saumon, St. Modeste, Mary Harbour, St. Francis River, Black Bear Bay, Sandwich Cove, and Sandwich Bay during the period of the American Revolution. In 1784, these areas had reportedly taken 676 tierces; Sandwich Bay, with 19 salmon fishermen, was proving to be the most productive area, contributing some 400 tierces (120 000 lb) to the total Labrador catch.[95]

The American menace, moreover, might well be considered mild in relation to the general lack of social order prevalent throughout Newfoundland and Labrador at this time. Cartwright, for example, considered his employees to be uncouth and rowdy — "at night, all hands were drunk and fighting, according to custom," he wrote;[96] indeed, several of his own men abetted the Americans when depredations were being made on his establishment. Employers resorted to harsh tactics to maintain a semblance of order; the cat-o-nine-tails was frequently used on disobedient and delinquent employees and some of the more unmanageable men were no doubt left behind in the wilderness to fare for themselves when the fishery closed for the season and the boats returned to their home ports. Living conditions aboard ship and on shore were also squalid and repulsive, and in a colony where the calming influences of religion and polite society were remote indeed, it is little wonder that it was said — in an understatement — that "These early establishments were not remarkable for their observance of the Christian virtues, and sobriety was evidently not held in great esteem."[97]

New England

Although reports of the 1750s and 1760s indicated that salmon were apparently not so numerous in many of the smaller streams of central New England as they had been in former times, substantial runs continued to frequent some of the major watercourses, such as the Connecticut, Merrimack, Piscataqua, and Kennebec, until the period of the Revolution. Wagonloads of salmon were still taken out of the Connecticut at the falls at South Hadley each year, and a 90-yard net yielded as many as 100 salmon a day at Amesbury while the run was on in the Merrimack.[98]

The necessity of improving and regulating the river fisheries was recognized, in many instances, before the war, but when hostilities broke out, the regulations were either ignored, revised, or set aside due to the economic pressures of the war effort.[99] In 1761, for example, a proposal was considered for enhancing the fish runs into the Pawtucket River, Rhode Island, by providing a fish pass over Pawtucket Falls; although this was apparently not accomplished, private individuals were allowed to break down the falls in 1773 to assist the remaining runs to pass upward with greater ease. Also, the Pawcatuck River fishery in Connecticut had been regulated to prevent the use of weirs and seines in the lower river, because of their adverse effect on the fish runs; the regulation, however, was suspended in 1779.[100]

Fish from the inland waters were an important staple at this time, when external trade and fishing had been curbed by the British navy; fishing pressures on the waters within the continent continued to increase as the war progressed. On March 8, 1778, the Continental Congress let a contract for 10 000 barrels of fish to feed the army, and although shad were preferred, salmon would not be refused.[101] At least one resident of the Champlain Valley was known to have supplied annually the American army at Ticonderoga with fresh salmon from Lake Champlain, and by 1779, smoked salmon were being shipped south from the frontier outposts in Maine.[102]

The Americans, however, never lost sight of the sea fishery of the North Atlantic and its importance to their well being. Among the other restrictions placed on the rebellious colonies in 1775 by the British Parliament was one that forbade New Englanders to fish in Newfoundland and other loyal colonial waters. The restriction was made public in New England sometime after April 5, 1775, and incensed the fishing populace.[103] Fishermen at Marblehead were particularly angry at the increasing restrictions placed on their freedom, and threatened that

as soon as General Gage shall begin to execute any of his orders, that every friend of government there is [will] be immediately seized and destroyed; that neither parents nor children shall be spared.[104]

In 1778, Congress signed an agreement with their ally, France, concerning fishing rights off Newfoundland.[105] The colonists' determination to secure a place for themselves in the North Atlantic was reflected in official instructions forwarded to Benjamin Franklin, the American representative in Paris; he was advised to

constantly inculcate the certainty of ruining the British fisheries on the Banks of Newfoundland, and consequently the British marine, by reducing Halifax and Quebec; since, by that means they [the British] would be exposed to alarm and plunder, and deprived of the necessary supplies formerly drawn from America.[106]

Independence in the fishery was second only to political liberty, and the American insistence on access to the North Atlantic fishery did not bode well for the future.

Roll Out the Barrel

Between 1760 and 1784, the salmon fishery in North America expanded at a rapid rate, encompassing virtually all of the important salmon regions by the latter date. Yield and export records for the period indicate that British North American catches ranged between 3 and 8 million pounds annually, with possibly as many as 1 million salmon and grilse taken in an exceptional year, most of which was exported. The salmon trade at this time was largely in the form of pickled fish which were packed principally in barrels containing 200 pounds or in tierces containing 300 pounds. These weights, however, did not represent the true weight of the fish taken, as the cleaning and pickling process reduced the live weight by between 35 and 40 percent; a barrel of pickled salmon would therefore represent between 300 and 350 pounds of live fish. Thousands of these barrels and tierces of salmon were placed aboard sailing vessels at harbors along the Atlantic coast for shipment to foreign ports. Major centers in England were now feasting on Labrador salmon, and Newfoundland salmon could be found in the markets of France, Portugal, and the other northern European states. Quebec fish found their way to Spain, and New Brunswick rivers supplied Italy and the neighboring Mediterranean countries. Nova Scotian salmon were shipped to the West Indies, and Ontario fish appeared on the menus in the northern United States, while the rest of the American colonies received salmon from all the producing regions. If cod was the gold from the New World, salmon was rapidly becoming the silver.

NOTES

[1]George W. Brown, *Building the Canadian Nation* (Toronto: Dent, 1849), p. 111.

[2]*Ibid.*, p. 113

[3]"Description of the State of the New Settlements in Nova Scotia in 1761, by the Chief Surveyor Charles Morris," in *Report* of the Canadian Archives (1905), p. 292: "They have no inclination for the fishery though well situated for that purpose."

[4]"Letter from a Haligonian to Rev. Dr. Stiles," in Lorenzo Sabine, *The Principal Fisheries of the American Seas* (Washington: Armstrong, 1853), pp. 84, 87.

[5]Thomas Jeffreys, *A Natural and Civil History of the French Dominions in North and South America* (London: Jeffreys, 1761), p. 24.

[6]C. Bruce Fergusson, "Pre-Revolutionary Settlements in Nova Scotia," in *Collections* of the Nova Scotia Historical Society, XXXVII (1970), 15–17.

[7]Francis W. P. Bolger, ed., *Canada's Smallest Province* (Prince Edward Island: Centennial Commission, 1973), pp. 37–39.

[8]J. Clarence Webster, *An Historical Guide to New Brunswick* (New Brunswick: Bureau of Information and Tourist Travel, 1947), p. 51; see also Fergusson, "Pre-Revolutionary Settlements," p. 20.

[9]*Statutes of Nova Scotia*, 2 Geo. III, c. 2.

[10]*Ibid.*, 3 Geo. III, c. 2; this act was made perpetual in 1766.

[11]*Ibid.*, 10 Geo. III, c. 10.

[12]*Ibid.*, 15 Geo. III, c. 10.

[13]Fergusson, "Pre-Revolutionary Settlements," p. 19.

[14]See D. Allison, "Notes", in *Collections* of the Nova Scotia Historical Society, VII (1891), p. 56.

[15]C. Bruce Fergusson, "*Early Liverpool and its Diarist*, Bulletin No. 16 (Halifax: Public Archives, 1961), p. 6.

[16]*Report* of the Public Archives of Nova Scotia (1933), p. 25.

[17]John Harvey, "General Description of Nova Scotia in 1848," quoted in *Report* of the Public Archives of Nova Scotia (1947), p. 28.

[18]Simeon Perkins, *The Diary of Simeon Perkins*, ed. Harold Innis (Toronto: Champlain Society, 1948), I, 99, 128.

[19]*Ibid.*, p. 72. In 1767, the first salmon of the season was netted in the Liverpool River on 8 April; see *ibid.*, p. 20.

[20]"Description of the...New Settlements in Nova Scotia in 1761," p. 292; see also, Mather Byles DesBrisay, *History of the County of Lunenburg* (Toronto: Briggs, 1895; reprinted Belleville, Ont.: Mika, 1972), p. 360.

[21]DesBrisay, *History of Lunenburg County*, pp. 256–257.

[22]Patrick M'Robert, "Tour Through Part of the North Provinces of America, 1774," in *Pennsylvania Magazine of History and Bibliography*, 59 (1935), 153.

[23]"Description of the...New Settlements in Nova Scotia in 1761," p. 291.

[24]W. A. Calnek, *History of the County of Annapolis* (Toronto: Briggs, 1897; reprinted Belleville, Ont.: Mika, 1972), pp. 217–219.

[25]*Ibid.*, p. 175.

[26]*Ibid.*, pp. 217–219.

[27]*Ibid.*, p. 175.

[28]*Report* of the Public Archives of Nova Scotia (1933), p. 25.

[29]"Diary of Captain William Owen, 1776–1771," in *Bulletin* of the New York Public Library, February (1931), 91.

[30]M'Robert, "Tour Through Part of the North Provinces," p. 153.

[31]Thomas Miller, *Historical and Genealogical Record of the First Settlers of Colchester County* (Halifax: MacKinlay, 1873; reprinted Belleville, Ont.: Mika, 1972), p. 40.

[32]George Patterson, *A History of the County of Pictou* (Montreal: Davison, 1877; reprinted Belleville, Ont.: Mika, 1972), p. 70.

[33]"Samuel Holland's Survey of Cape Breton, 1766–1767" C.O.-5, Vol. 68, Public Archives of Canada.

[34]Jersey Island capital was prominent in the fishing industry of the Maritimes after the fall of New France, principal interest being exemplified by the Robin, Callas, Mauger, and LeBouthilier families; see E. T. D. Chambers, *The Fisheries of the Province of Quebec*, (Quebec: Department of Colonization, Mines and Fisheries, 1912), pp. 106, 107, 114.

[35]"Diary of Captain William Owen," p. 89.

[36]Richard Brown, *A History of the Island of Cape Breton* (London: Sampson Low, 1869), pp. 376–377.

[37]*Ibid.*, p. 376.

[38]Douglas B. Boylan, "Rule Britannia," in *Canada's Smallest Province*, p. 34.

[39]There were approximately 4400 inhabitants in 1797; see Bolger, *Canada's Smallest Province*, pp. 44, 70.

[40]A. B. Warburton, *A History of Prince Edward Island* (Saint John: Barnes, 1923), p. 128.

[41]*Ibid.*, p. 128.

[42]W. S. MacNutt, *The Atlantic Provinces* (Toronto: McClelland & Stewart, 1972), p. 65.

[43]Warburton, *History of Prince Edward Island*, p. 228.

[44]*Statutes of Prince Edward Island*, 20 Geo. III, c. 5.

[45]W. O. Raymond, *The River St. John* (Sackville: Tribune, 1950), pp. 143–144.

[46]MG4, Business Records, Simonds, Hazen and White, ca. 1760–1790, Public Archives of Nova Scotia.

[47]Raymond, *The River St. John*, p. 161.

[48]*Ibid.*

[49]Esther Clark Wright, *People and Places I: New Brunswick* (Windsor, N.S.: Lancelot, 1973), p. 93. Apparently fishermen representing a Boston firm had taken salmon at Scoodic Falls in the months of May and June, as early as 1764; see Harold A. Davis, *An International Community on the St. Croix (1604–1930)*, Maine Studies No. 64 (Orono: University of Maine, 1974), p. 32.

[50]"Diary of Captain William Owen," p. 124.

[51]W. H. Davidson, *William Davidson: 1740–1790, The North Shore Leader* (Newcastle: n.p., 1947), pp. 22–23. Beamish Murdoch, *History of Nova-Scotia or Acadie* (Halifax: Barnes, 1865), I, 152.

[52]"Description of the New Settlements in Nova Scotia in 1761," p. 298.

[53]Davidson, *William Davidson*, p. 24. See also, *Collections* of the New Brunswick Historical Society, IX (1914), 310. Unless otherwise cited, information on Davidson is taken from W. A. Spray, "Davidson, William" in *Dictionary of Canadian Biography* [hereafter *DCB*] (Toronto: University of Toronto, 1979), IV, 195–197.

[54]Davidson, *William Davidson*, pp. 26–27. "Wright and Blaskurly Map," Map Section, Public Archives of Canada. Robert Clooney, *A Compendious History of the Northern Part of the Province of New Brunswick and the District of Gaspé in Lower Canada* (Halifax: Howe, 1832), p. 42.

[55]Harold A. Innis, *The Cod Fisheries* (Toronto: University of Toronto Press, 1954), p. 192; Innis also notes the presence at Chaleur Bay, 1767, of the Moore, Finlay and Mackinsy firm.

[56]Clooney, *History of Northern New Brunswick*, pp. 171–172.

[57]George MacBeath and Dorothy Chamberlain, *New Brunswick: The Story of Our Province* (Toronto: Gage, 1965), pp. 135–136.

[58]Davidson, William Davidson, p. 31.

[59]George Heriot, *Travels Through the Canadas* (London, 1807; reprinted Edmonton: Hurtig, 1971), pp. 228–229. R. H. Hubbard, ed., *Thomas Davies, 1737–1812* (Ottawa: National Gallery, 1972), plate 49.

[60]Lorenzo Sabine, *Principal Fisheries*, p. 76.

[61]E. D. T. Chambers, *The Fisheries of the Province of Quebec* (Quebec City: Department of Colonization, Mines and Fisheries, 1912), II, 100–102.

[62]*Ibid.*, pp. 99–100.

[63]Sabine, *Principal Fisheries*, p. 76.

[64]Chambers, *Fisheries of Quebec*, II, 114.

[65]*Ibid.*, pp. 105–106. Innis, *The Cod Fisheries*, p. 192.

[66]See "Report of Committee Appointed to Examine the Trade and Fishery of Newfoundland, 1791," in C.O. 325, Vol. 7, Public Archives of Canada.

[67]D. W. Prowse, *A History of Newfoundland* (London:

Macmillan, 1895; reprinted Belleville, Ont.: Mika, 1972), p. 316.

[68]Colonial Office (C.O.) Papers, 325, Vol. 7, p. 211, Public Archives of Canada.

[69]Richard Brown, *A History of the Island of Cape Breton*, (London: Sampson Low, 1869), p. 394.

[70]See statistical table on Newfoundland salmon exports contained in "Report of Committee Appointed to Examine the Trade and Fishery of Newfoundland, 1791," C.O. 325, Vol. 7, Public Archives of Canada.

[71]Prowse, *History of Newfoundland*, p. 597.

[72]Rev. Charles Pedley, *A History of Newfoundland* (London: Longmans, Green, 1863), p. 108. See also, William H. Whiteley, "Palliser, Sir Hugh" in *DCB*, IV, 597-601.

[73]Pedley, *History of Newfoundland*, p. 108.

[74]Prowse, *History of Newfoundland*, pp. 277, 336. See also, Innis, *The Cod Fisheries*, p. 148.

[75]Public Archives of Canada, Map Section, "A Sketch of the River Exploits."

[76]James P. Howley, *The Beothucks or Red Indians* (Cambridge: Cambridge University Press, 1915; reprinted Toronto: Coles, 1974), pp. 29–33, 49.

[77]*Ibid.*, p. 36.

[78]*Ibid.*, pp. 267, 270, 282.

[79]*Ibid.*, p. 72, 271, 273.

[80]Thomas Curtis, "Voyage to the Island of St. John's," in D. C. Harvey, ed., *Journeys to the Island of St. John* (Toronto: Macmillan, 1955), p. 62.

[81]W. C. Gosling, *Labrador: Its Discovery, Exploration and Development* (London: Alston Rivers, 1910), p. 217.

[82]P. W. Browne, *Where the Fisheries Go* (New York: Cochrane, 1909), p. 3. William H. Whiteley, "Bayne, Daniel" in *Dictionary of Canadian Biography* (Toronto: University of Toronto Press, 1974), III, 37–38.

[83]Prowse, *History of Newfoundland*, p. 597.

[84]William H. Whiteley, "Darby, Nicholas" in *DCB*, IV, 194–195.

[85]K. Matthews, "Pinson, Andrew" in *Dictionary of Canadian Biography* (Toronto: University of Toronto Press, 1983), V, 674–675; W. Gordon Handcock, "Slade, John" in *DCB*, IV, 711–714.

[86]Gosling, *Labrador*, pp. 380–382.

[87]Wilfred T. Grenfell, *Labrador: The Country and the People* (New York: Macmillan, 1922), p. 335.

[88]Quoted in A. Copeland, "No Common Man," in *North*, Sept.–Oct. 1968, 43. Unless otherwise cited, information on Cartwright is taken from G. M. Story, "Cartwright, George" in *DCB*, V, 165–167.

[89]Quoted in Grenfell, *Labrador*, p. 335. Anthony Netboy, *The Atlantic Salmon, A Vanishing Species?* (London: Faber and Faber, 1968), p. 349. Innis, *The Cod Fisheries*, pp. 197–198.

[90]Quoted in Grenfell, *Labrador*, p. 336.

[91]*Ibid.*

[92]Cartwright's problems at Cape Charles included encroachment on his salmon fisheries by the Noble and Pinson firm in the spring of 1772. See David William Zimmerly, *Cain's Land Revisited* (St. John's: Institute of Social and Economic Research, Memorial University, 1975), p. 51.

[93]Prowse, *History of Newfoundland*, p. 597.

[94]Browne, *Where the Fishers Go*, pp. 43–44. Newfoundland authorities found it impossible to control the Labrador fishery, as the available British warships were employed elsewhere; only one naval vessel extended its surveillance to Labrador in 1773. Duff also cited the possible potential of the salmon fisheries there. See K. G. Davies, ed., *Northern Quebec and Labrador Journals and Correspondence*, *1819–1835* (London: Hudson's Bay Company Record Society, 1963), p. xxv.

[95]Gosling, *Labrador*, p. 385. See also Colonial Office Papers, Supplementary, Misc. 1, Vol. 18, "An Account of the Seal and Salmon Fishery on the Coast of Labrador." (1784) Public Archives of Canada.

[96]Quoted in Browne, *Where the Fishers Go*, p. 53.

[97]*Ibid.*

[98]Larry Koller, *The Treasury of Angling* (New York: Golden Press, 1963), p. 22. Anthony Netboy, *Salmon: The World's Most Harassed Fish* (London: Deutsch, 1980), p. 173.

[99]Charles J. Hoadly, "The Public Records of the State of Connecticut," excerpted in John C. Pearson, ed., *The Fish and Fisheries of Colonial North America* (Washington: Department of the Interior, 1972), p. 527.

[100]Clark A. Howard, "Historical References to the Fisheries of New England," excerpted in *ibid.*, p. 522. Hoadly, "Public Records of Connecticut," pp. 525–526.

[101]"Journals of the Continental Congress," excerpted in Pearson, *Fish and Fisheries*, p. 527.

[102]W. C. Watson, "The Salmon of Lake Champlain and its Tributaries," in *Report of the United States Commission of Fish and Fisheries (1873–4 and 1874–5)* (Washington: Government Printing Office, 1876), III, 532. "Letter from Timothy Parsons to Samuel P. Savage, Pownalboro, Maine, April 12, 1779," excerpted in Pearson, *Fish and Fisheries*, p. 650.

[103]"Circular to All Governors in America, London, April 5, 1775," excerpted in *ibid.*, p. 587.

[104]"The Diary of William Pynchon of Salem," quoted in *ibid.*, p. 591. Apparently the Marblehead fishermen were almost as unruly under their own government, since a number of them were put in jail for refusing to pay their own taxes in 1786; see *ibid.*

[105]"Treaty between the King of France and the United States of America; May 4, 1778," excerpted in *ibid.*, pp. 596–597.

[106]"Message from Congress to Benjamin Franklin at Paris; October 22, 1778," quoted in *ibid.*, p. 599.

CHAPTER

VII

Emulation and Exploitation 1784-1815

The Treaty of Versailles

The American Revolution ended in 1782, and with the signing of the Treaty of Versailles in 1783, the United States of America was recognized by Great Britain and the rest of the world as a separate and independent nation. This momentous event of nationhood resulted in substantial changes to the old order of things in what remained of Britian's possessions in the New World — changes which, among other things, affected the fishery resources on the eastern part of the continent in an immediate and significant way.

The war and its aftermath, for example, had compelled New England's fishermen to largely forsake the North Atlantic for a decade or more; consequently, the American fishing population turned inwards to exploit more heavily the already declining resources of its own coastal, estuarial, and inland waters. The same war that forced this introverted action upon one segment of the American population also forced another group of people, the Loyalist refugees, to seek new regions outside the old Thirteen Colonies. One immediate result of the situation which circumstances had forced upon both these groups was the rapid expansion of the salmon fishery, an expansion which for the first time in history encompassed the entire geographical range of the species in North America. The degree of exploitation was also intense, so that within a few years after peace, the fishery had been carried on to such an extent that certain salmon stocks were quickly depleted, while others were brought to the verge of extinction.

The Maritime Colonies

It has been estimated that between 70 000 and 100 000 Loyalist refugees came to the British North American colonies as a result of the Revolutionary War. Most of them took up new land in the St. Lawrence Valley above Montreal. Several hundred came to Prince Edward Island and to the Gaspé; several thousand came to Cape Breton, and over 10 000 came to the province now known as Nova Scotia. In the Maritimes, however, it was to the new colony of New Brunswick that the greatest influx of immigrants came, up to 20 000.[1] One of the principal towns established there by the Loyalists was Parrtown, now the city of Saint John. Before the war, the population at the mouth of the Saint John River had not exceeded 100 but in 1783, 14 000 people arrived to take up new lands,[2] and in a short time Parrtown contained more inhabitants than were in the entire territory east of the Penobscot prior to the war. Parrtown became an important center of trade and the focal point for subsequent development, growth and expansion on the Saint John River and for a large segment of the province of New Brunswick.

Another settlement which initially equalled the growth of Parrtown was Shelburne, Nova Scotia. For a short period, Shelburne existed as the fourth largest city

61

in North America, its population exceeded only by those of Boston, New York, and Philadelphia.[3] Other settlements, such as St. Andrews, St. Stephen, Fredericton, Sussex, Miramichi, Digby, Weymouth, Guysborough, and Sydney, rapidly came into being or expanded at this time, creating cultural, sociological, economic and commercial situations which, under normal conditions of frontier development, would have taken decades to evolve.

The massive influx of people to the Maritime colonies resulted in a great demand on the natural resources of the country to supply their needs, and it was quickly realized that the fish resources of these regions supplied a steady and reliable source of sustenance. Hollingsworth reported of Nova Scotia that

> From the middle of April when the rains which break up the frost commonly prevail, and put an end to the winter season, a constant succession of all types of fish common to the country takes place in the harbours and inlets. Of these the herrings are generally the first, and in a little time becoming gradually intermixed with the shad, [and] are succeeded by them; these are accounted almost equally [as] good as salmon for drying and salting; both the one and the other run in prodigious shoals towards the heads of the creeks and rivers, in order to deposit their spawn at the falls or rapids which stop them from proceeding further, and where they may be taken in baskets in any quantity.[4]

With the grants of land given to the new colonists came the right to all fisheries bordering each grant, and such a right was jealously guarded.[5] The salmon fishery was pursued with particularly great interest and result, and the phenomenal runs that existed in all the accessible rivers played a significant part in the choice of property and subsequent prosperity of both homesteaders and townsfolk.

The growth of the river fishery for shad, gaspereau, and salmon soon received the attention of colonial legislators, who recognized the need to regulate the fishing operation in order to ensure its perpetuation. In 1786, both Nova Scotia and New Brunswick passed legislation to this end. In fact, one of the first pieces of legislation of any type to be drafted for the newly formed colony of New Brunswick was an act to protect the fishery: entitled "An act to prevent nuisances from hedges, weirs and other encumbrances," it was outlined in the exact style and terminology of the old Massachusetts regulation.[6] Since no season was established, and no method or type of fishing gear was classified illegal, conservation of the resource was hardly guaranteed, and consequently, this first fishery act stayed in effect for only a short period of time. Subsequent legislation imposed further restrictions on an otherwise liberal fishery: a Sunday closure on all salmon fishing (1793), and a penalty of up to 30 days in jail for offences against the act (1794); a closed salmon season — August 30 to April 1 — was imposed on the Miramichi and Restigouche rivers (1799), and milldams

in all streams in the colony were required to possess fish-passes (1810).[7]

As noted previously, some initial legislation regarding the Nova Scotian fisheries was passed during the early 1760s. Between 1763 and 1786, however, very little legislation was imposed, either by the colonial administration or by the county courts, except for setting the limits of fines. Only in a few cases did the counties establish a closed season for a species or in any way illegalize any fishing device. In the first fishery act passed after the Revolutionary War, Nova Scotia carried its regulations somewhat further than did New Brunswick, by stipulating that all milldams in the province had to be provided with fishpasses:

> Mill Dams, or other obstructions, hereafter to be placed in rivers, where fish resort, are to have a proper wastegate kept open, while the season lasts, for fish to pass: where that is not the case, the Sessions, on complaint, are to give notice to the party, and to order the Sherriff to take an inquest; and, if the finding be for the complainant, the Sessions are to order a sufficient waste-gate to be fixed by the owner, who is likewise to pay a fine, not exceeding fifty pounds, nor be less than ten, with costs; to be levied by the distress; and for want thereof the party to be committed for three months.[8]

Evidence of the application of this 1786 regulation can be found in the Pictou County Sessions Court records where, in 1805, it was

> Ordered that a fish gate be placed in Archibald's Milldam, Middle River, to be only one foot high from the bottom of the river in front of the dam and 3½ feet on the back, 4 feet wide in passage — according to the frame given by David Archibald so as to allow passage at all seasons.[9]

The responsibility for imposing further regional regulations fell to the county Sessions Courts, which from time to time, and in varying degrees, carried out this task. Appointments of fishery constables or overseers were made in some regions, but the main legislative concern was directed toward fish inspection rather than protecion; consequently, cullers of dried fish, surveyors of pickled fish and gaugers of barrels outnumbered those officers appointed to oversee the general application of the fishery laws pertaining to protection and conservation.

Although the river fishery may have seemed restricted to some, the sea and coastal fishery was free to all, and a great number of new colonists participated in this aspect of the fishing operation. The valuable commercial promise inherent in this undertaking was not be denied; fish were plentiful. Furthermore, at the close of the hostilities, Great Britain had passed legislation excluding the new United States from the lucrative West Indies fish trade; consequently, in the remaining British colonies, the resource was in great export demand. Edward Winslow, who was deeply involved in Loyalist resettlement and enterprise, noted:

I shall say but little on the subject of Fish because it must occur to every man of common sense, that if the New England Traders could find a profit in sending their vessels to this coast for fish, those who inhabit its borders can carry on the business to much greater advantage. The exertions now making are very spirited and I have no doubt that the exports of fish from Shelbourne and the other new places added to the former usual exports from the old ports, will be an ample supply for the West Indies this year [1784].[10]

As the fishing enterprise grew, the colonies began to build vessels with which to supply their expanding foreign markets. Large quantities of salmon were soon being shipped from Nova Scotian ports and from the Restigouche, Miramichi, and Saint John rivers to Europe, the Mediterranean, the British West Indies, and even the occasional cargo to Boston and New York; it is estimated that before 1814, no less than 4 million pounds of salmon were exported annually from the Atlantic colonies, in addition to what was being consumed locally.[11]

By the late 18th century, however, a serious hindrance to the enterprise of the British colonies in the sea, coastal, and even estuarial fisheries had begun, in the form of American encroachment. Revolution had temporarily curbed the New Englanders' fishing activities — and indeed, it would take them several years to regroup after the end of hostilities. Nevertheless, they strongly held the belief that they still had the right to continue their traditional operations off the northern colonies, regardless of their present existence as a separate and foreign nation.

Even before the peace negotiations had commenced, Boston fishing interests openly predicted ruin for America if their vessels were banned from fishing in northern waters. The city took action to insure that their view of the situation was known to the chief American negotiators; after all, Bostonians alone had had 400 vessels in the fishery off Nova Scotia prior to the outbreak of war:

Gentlemen; the brilliant successes, which have attended the allied arms through the course of the preceding campaign, afford us the most flattering prospect that our enemies (though hitherto obstinate to a degree of infatuation) will soon sue for peace. In the consideration of that peace, your constituents…think it their duty to open to you their sentiments, on the importance of that principal branch of eastern trade, the fishery, and the necessity of confirming a right to it by an express article of the Treaty of Peace.[12]

John Adams, America's chief negotiator, was reported to have told the British commissioners that peace was not possible without an American right to the fishery, particularly to the Grand Banks of Newfoundland. The strongest objection to this demand came from America's ally, France, since any American claim to the fishery might jeopardize that of France, and to the Gallic mind, it was much more advantageous and less competitive to divide a fish into two parts than into three.[13] The British negotiators knew their fishermen would be pleased to see the Americans refused access to British colonial waters; furthermore, they recognized the energy of New England fishermen, and they acknowledged the close competition that would invariably result if the Americans were allowed to reenter the North Atlantic fishery.

The British negotiators, however, were weak in dealing with the problem: they were mainly interested in having peace — even at the cost of inciting the wrath of their colonies. They also had little apparent interest in or knowledge of the colonial fishery; when Henry Strachey, the chief British negotiator, asked another commissioner, Richard Oswald, for some background on the value and extent of the Newfoundland fishery, Oswald replied: "Agreeable to my promise I lookt out for the paper I wrote about the Newfoundland Fishery when you was [sic] here. But I have it not and must have thrown it into the fire along with other useless papers."[14]

In consequence of this antipathy and disinterest, the British colonial fishery was seriously jeopardized when the following articles were written — in precise English, it might be noted — into the peace:

(1) The people of the United States shall continue to enjoy unmolested the right to take fish of every kind on the Grand Banks, the Banks of Newfoundland, also in the Gulf of St. Lawrence, and at all other places in the sea where the inhabitants of both countries used at any time heretofor to fish.

(2) The inhabitants of the United States shall have liberty [as opposed to right] to take fish of every kind on such part of the coast of Newfoundland as British fishermen shall use, and also on the coasts, bays and creeks of all other of His Britannic Majesty's dominions in America."[15]

Except for the Island of Newfoundland, the Americans were additionally granted the right to cure their catch on any uninhabited piece of British colonial soil.

These articles of concession effectively placed the North Atlantic fishery in the hands of the enterprising Americans, thus frustrating the designs of the British colonials. The promise that the Loyalists first foresaw was now grasped by the Yankees, and Nova Scotians, New Brunswickers, and Newfoundlanders soon found that the fishery, even within a net's length of the shore, was not free from American activity. Although it took the Americans some time to regroup their fishing energies after the revolution, it was noted that

As early as 1807 the colonists appealed to the British government for protection against the 'aggressions' of their American neighbors. In their jealous interest they employed a watchman who 'sat in the fog' and counted the vessels of the Yankee fishermen as they passed through the Strait of Canso, counting in one day nine hundred and thirty-eight.[16]

By 1815, 1500 American vessels were alleged to be fishing in Labrador, and every bay and inlet from this northern area to Passamaquoddy was occupied by American boats, which either set their own nets for all species of fish, including salmon, or traded New England produce in exchange for fish. The British colonial fish trade fell sharply, except for that which was carried on with the West Indies; with the reopening of this latter market to the United States in 1822, British colonial efforts in this direction were also hampered.[17]

CHALEUR BAY

It was a few years after the close of the Revolutionary War before fishing activity was once again undertaken with ardor in Chaleur Bay. Hollingsworth reported of "Chaleum Bay" in 1787, that

on the east end of the land which forms the eastern entrance into the River St. Lawrence on the south side was once a famous settlement [Gaspé?], when the French were in possession of Canada, and carried on a considerable fishery, but has since been deserted, and is now only resorted to occasionally.[18]

Gaspé, Restigouche, and Miscou — the three points fixing the boundaries of the bay — were, however, not altogether deserted. The Robin firm, which as early as 1763 had obtained grants at various locations such as Percé, Newport, Miscou, and Grand Rivière, had apparently fished from their central depot at Paspébiac throughout the war, largely free from American interference because they displayed the French flag.[19] Just east of Paspébiac, the new settlement of Hopetown was founded by Loyalists in 1786. Villages such as New Carlisle and Matapédia were established, and Loyalists also flocked to the then-fledgling communities of Carleton, Maria, and New Richmond. A small group had even settled permanently on Bonaventure Island, for the sole purpose of maintaining possession of the fisheries.[20] On the south side of Chaleur Bay, settlement was not quite so rapid as on the north, although Commodore Walker reestablished himself at Nicolas Denys' old post on the Nepisiguit and began to ship salmon from that place to foreign markets very soon after the war.[21]

Progress, however, was slow, and as George Heriot reported in the early years of the 19th century, "Cod fish, salmon, and herrings, are the only productions of commerce derived from the Bays of Gaspé and Chaleurs." Agriculture was "uncommonly neglected," and initially fishing was sluggish to develop, due to the scarcity of salt, a shortage caused by the Revolutionary War.[22]

One of the first grantees on the upper Chaleur Bay was Peter Bonamy, who established himself near the present town of Dalhousie about 1787. Bonamy came from the Miramichi, where he had been associated previously with the Davidson fishing interests on the northwest branch of that river; in his memorial for land at Chaleur, he stated: "I have declined the former branch of the fishery and have determined to become a farmer and follow the Salmon and Herring fishery here."[23] How much farming Bonamy undertook is not recorded, but his activity in the salmon fishery was probably considerable. The industry prospered as others soon joined him in the Dalhousie area, and the extent of activity is indicated by the fact that a considerable portion of the land upon which Dalhousie now stands was originally reserved for cooperage work.[24]

Between 1790 and 1800, it was not uncommon for the Chaleur area to produce between 3000 and 4000 tierces (900 000–1 200 000 lb pickled) of salmon annually; with exports like these, it was little wonder that the bay was considered to be one big fish bowl. Robert Ferguson of Athol House, near Campbellton, annually caught and exported 1400 barrels (280 000 lb pickled) of salmon from his own fishing stations alone. Such volumes were apparently common until about 1815, at which time they began to decline, principally from overfishing, although biological factors cannot be totally excluded as the cause.[25]

Other prosperous fisheries were also carried out at the mouth of the Restigouche River, where large numbers of salmon congregated. The local Indians were particularly adept at fishing the area, and although their traditional method of capturing salmon was with the spear, they frequently borrowed nets from the white settlers to make their work a little easier. A traveler on the Restigouche in 1791 reported that the Indians frequently sealed off the outflow of a large pool at the mouth of the river with these nets and, having done so, they would

go with a number of canoes up the river sometimes 8 or 10 miles, each being provided with a boiled salmon in it; and when they get up as far as they intend, they arrange their canoes in proper order from side to side of the river, and crumble out the boiled salmon as fast as they are able till the water appears white and muddy by it. They then fall to work and beat down the fish with their poles and spear shafts, keeping pace with the crumbled fish as they go along, until they come to the large pool at the foot of which the net is set and they scringe [drag] the pool.[26]

George McGregor, a settler in the area, once reported that he had seen nine hundred salmon taken in this way on one occasion, and another inhabitant claimed that he knew of as many as "1,100 being taken on one of these expeditions."[27]

By the end of the first decade of the 19th century, fishing for salmon and cod had developed to a great extent in the Chaleur area, with one observer noting that

There are several fishing stations along the coast; those of most importance are at Percé and Chaleur Bay. The trade employs annually about a dozen square rigged vessels, besides a great many small craft. Fish to the value of £60,000 a year, including what is sent to Quebec to be reshipped for the West Indies, and elsewhere, or used in the country, are cured and sent to a market.[28]

MIRAMICHI

At the close of the American Revolution, William Davidson returned to the Miramichi. He had spent the war years developing a lucrative masting trade from his timber holdings on the Saint John River. Now he wanted to reestablish his Miramichi fishery, and to exploit further the timber potential of his vast land grant. His return coincided with the arrival of a considerable number of Loyalists who wished to start a new life in that part of the province; in fact, a large portion of Davidson's original grant was soon escheated by the government for non-development, then surveyed and parceled out into farm and fish lots for the new colonists. Davidson managed to salvage, in a new grant, some of his former property, principal of which was the land adjoining his former salmon fishing station near Quarryville.[29]

In 1784, the first year of his renewed fishing operation, he cured 500 casks of salmon, both from the Miramichi and Chaleur Bay. In the next year, it was estimated that the total yield from his Miramichi operation was in the range of 1000 tierces, equivalent to approximately 472 000 pounds of round, fresh salmon.[30]

Davidson reentered the fishery with vigor and enterprise; because his methods of operation had not changed since his former tenure in the region, however, his business was frequently criticized, and most severely by Benjamin Marston, the newly appointed Loyalist sheriff of Northumberland County, who complained in 1785 of Davidson's local operations that

> These [salmon nets] are so far extended into the river from each shore as in some places to interlock with each and are set along the banks of the river from the lowest settlement to the upper line of Davidson & Corts grant at every proper place to stop fish. At the [upper boundary] line they do worse. There they have a cross net extending quite from one side of the river to the other. The set nets from this extravagant length must undoubtedly in the narrow parts of the river turn many shoals of fish back. But the cross nets, while they are set, absolutely stop the whole body of them from getting up to their spawning places and must eventually, much lessen, if not destroy the breed.[31]

Marston had no direct involvement with the local fishery, and although his criticisms no doubt had a reasonable foundation in his efforts to preserve the resource for all, nevertheless his complaints must also be assessed in the light of general refugee rancor against the pre-Loyalist establishment. His report carried little weight in official circles, but other similar protests followed. At one point,

it was stated that the Indians on the river above Davidson's fishery were virtually on the brink of starvation from lack of salmon, while Davidson's fellow settlers — presumably Loyalists — also complained that they were not getting their fair share of the resource.[32]

Until 1786, there were no regulations respecting the salmon fishery on the Miramichi — or elsewhere in New Brunswick. In that year, however, an initial act was passed to regulate the colony's general fishery, although the Miramichi was unfortunately excluded from regulatory consideration; the following amendment to the act gave the basis for this omission: "Whereas there is no court of Sessions at present installed in the County of Northumberland, be it further enacted that nothing in this act shall extend or be construed to extend to the said county or River."[33] By this amendment, virtually half the province was still without fishery regulations, since Northumberland County at that time also included the present counties of Restigouche and Gloucester.[34]

The act disappointed some, but favored many, for it meant continued and unrestricted freedom in the regional salmon fishery. In the same year that the act was passed, the county magistrates protested to the legislature about continuing irregularities in the Northumberland salmon fishery, stating specifically that the cross nets used by Davidson "cause the peace to be broke"[35] — all to no avail, since the area remained unregulated for several more years.

An estimated 3000 tierces, or 1 416 000 pounds of fresh salmon was the annual yield from the Miramichi fishery by 1789; although the fisheries of 1790 and 1791 were slightly lower, the maximum yield in any year prior to 1800 was reported to be 3800 tierces, or 1 800 000 pounds, fresh. Davidson's operations alone, on the northwest branch of the river, accounted annually for between 1200 and 1500 tierces of this total yield.[36]

Patrick Campbell, a Scottish gentlemen who traveled to the Miramichi in 1791, remarked that each of the river's inhabitants

> has a right to fish his own property to a certain extent of nets; and few or none exercise this right without vast advantage and profit. Mr. Lee Dernier [Delesdernier] told me that 70 tierces of salmon were caught on his lot, with only one net set of about 30 fathoms to the back; and many others were nearly in that proportion; but that he was among one of the best stations on the river.[37]

A regulated fishery is implied in Campbell's comment about the right to fish a certain length of net, and indeed, by 1791 a county Sessions Court had finally been organized, and was assisting in making some general regulations in the local fishery. Ironically, William Davidson died of pneumonia that same winter. It seems appropriate that his body was laid to rest at Wilson's Point, where the two great branches of the Miramichi come together; Davidson had had fishing stations on both rivers, and at spots that have been continually fished until a total salmon fishing ban was imposed in 1972, some 180 years after his death.[38]

No sooner had regulations been applied in 1791 than measures were taken to oppose them; the county grand jury petitioned against the new rules, but to no avail.[39] The prohibitions, however, were difficult to enforce, and in many cases, disregard for the law was common; as in the other colonies, the first efforts to regulate an existing and traditional fishery met with little success, and it was common to hear the statutes referred to as worthless. The general laws of the province, however, became applicable, and the County Sessions continued to make further regulations respecting the fishery, from time to time.

Because the inadequacy of the local regulations was frequently mentioned, the Provincial Legislature found it expedient in 1799 to reconsider the statutes as they applied to the Miramichi, and to invoke a new "Act for Regulating the Fisheries in the County of Northumberland." Principally, this statute established gear limits, and a full three pages were devoted to describing the legal lengths of nets permitted for each river and bay stand. Weekly and seasonal closed times were also set down: no net could be set, no seine drawn, and no salmon speared between sunset on Saturday and sunrise on Monday; and no fishing of any kind was to take place between August 13 and April 1. The act also provided for the appointment of an overseer for each town or settlement along the river, to be chosen by the County Session and paid a fee of one shilling for each net under his charge. The act also technically included the Restigouche River, but the only provision specifically relating to this latter area was the one limiting the fishing season. The Chaleur region, therefore, was still largely a free fishing zone, particularly since these Northumberland County regulations stayed in effect without change until 1816.[40]

A close examination of the Northumberland County fishery regulations of 1799 reveals some interesting conditions regarding the salmon fishery at that time. First, fish lots were established and specific regulations were in place at all points on the Miramichi from Escuminac Point and Neguac to the Nashwaak Portage (Taxis River, Boiestown). Nets were permitted at all locations along the river east of Boiestown, provided that two-thirds of the river was left unobstructed. One of the few places in the entire area where fishing was not allowed due to its being reserved for the Admiralty was Portage Island, then known as Waltham Island, an area of much controversy in later years. Spear fishing was also actively undertaken as a legal method, although the established season largely prevented the spearing of spawning salmon. Fishery officers or overseers were not paid a government salary, but instead collected their fee from the net proprietors, a method of remuneration that was difficult to apply at the best of times. Finally, if the officer failed in any aspect of his duty, he was subject to a fine of £5 — which in some cases amounted to more than his annual income.

By 1813, it was evident that, regardless of fisheries regulation, the Miramichi continued to support a prodigious local salmon industry, with still no serious depletion of stock. Joseph Gubbins, a military official sent to inspect the local militia in that year, noted in his journal entry for 21 July that

> I proceeded in the morning with the tide up the Miramichi. Major McDownell had one of his sons with him, whom he left at the mouth of the Bartibog River, as we went past it to attend to his salmon net that he had previously placed there. In the course of our voyage I observed that every land owner had salmon nets projected into the water about a quarter of a mile in length and from thirty to forty feet in width. These are supported perpendicularly by rows of strong poles or rather young trees, and the quantity of salmon that are daily taken in them is prodigious. Indeed nothing but an ample return could cover the expense of such extensive apparatus for catching them. Such Fisheries as I have just noticed occurred within every five or six hundred yards on each side of the river during the whole of this morning's sail of five and twenty miles.[41]

RICHIBUCTO AND SHEDIAC

When Thomas Powell came to Richibucto with his father in 1787, he was only 13 years old, but he was not too young to engage in the fishery. The Powell family were the first white settlers on the Gulf coast of New Brunswick — south of the Miramichi and north of Cocagne — since the explusion of the Acadians. Although the Richibucto had been known as a good salmon and unsurpassed gaspereau river for many years, the considerable Indian population and the early French settlers took little commercial advantage of this fact.

In 1798, however, the younger Powell formed a company with Thomas Pagan, and began an extensive business in the capture and export of salmon and gaspereau. On one occasion, Powell personally caught 700 salmon in a 24-hour fishing stint on the river. The Powell and Pagan firm remained in business until 1807, when fish stocks became too low to make their enterprise profitable. Although they had reaped a considerable harvest in 10 years of operation, the decline in fish was instead attributed to increased exploitation after 1800 by other settlers who came to the area, since the inhabitants around Kouchibouguac, Kouchibouguacis, and Buctouche relied heavily on both the salmon and gaspereau runs.[42]

It is difficult to assess the true yield of the salmon fishery along the North Shore of New Brunswick, since official records are delinquent in showing the actual extent of export during this period. For example, the customs house records of 1808, 1809, and 1810 show less than 100 tierces being exported each season.[43] These low figures are partly due to the fact that the customs house was in Saint John — Miramichi being considered only an outport of the Bay of Fundy city; in truth, the separated commercial and territorial interests of these two regions placed them worlds apart. The export records do show, however, that a large portion of the Miramichi export was shipped to the West Indies. An early historian, writing in 1806, spoke of an extensive general fishery in northern New Brunswick:

> great quantities of salmon are taken in different rivers which run into the Gulph, particularly the Restigush [sic] which runs into the head of the Bay of Chaleur, and the River Miramichee.... In the former 4000 tierces of 300 pounds each has often been exported in a year.... I think I may venture to say that 10,000 tierces have frequently been exported from the Gulph in a year.[44]

The area's first historian, Robert Clooney, no doubt gave another accurate picture of the true state of the export fishery when he wrote in 1832 that during the first decade of the 19th century, the salmon fishery was very productive, "often varying in the catch or quantity cured for exportation from 3,000 barrels to 5,000 tierces.... Such may be considered the extent and character of our trade, until about the year 1813 or 1914."[45]

RIVER SAINT JOHN

Of all the areas in British North America, few were subject to such rapid and extreme change after 1783 as the Saint John River Valley. In 1782, less than 200 families were living along the river, but by 1785, more than 10 000 immigrants had settled along the main river and its tributaries.[46] The effects on the fishery were instantaneous. Before 1784, the only fishery was that carried out by the Indians, a few white settlers, and the firm of Simonds, Hazen and White, the last-named having a considerable commercial fishery at the mouth of the river.

With the arrival of the Loyalists and the subsequent founding of Parrtown (Saint John), the Simonds, Hazen and White firm had to contend with the demands of the new settlers. When the city charter was drawn up, it provided that the fishery between high and low watermark on the eastern side of the harbor was for "the sole use, profit and advantage of the freemen and inhabitants of the City."[47] The right to regulate and manage the fishery — jurisdiction over which was later extended to the western shore of the harbor as well — was vested in the city council. Both the fishing rights granted in the charter and the council's right to regulate the harbor resource were jealously guarded, to such an extent that when the first New Brunswick fishery act was drafted in 1786, the fifth article stipulated that the statute was in no way to interfere with the already-established regulations governing the Saint John fishery. The substance of this article has had application almost to the present day.[48]

The Saint John council annually disposed of the various fish lots by lottery; this procedure became known as the fishery draft and was carried out each January amid a hubbub of unruly excitement. For the price of two shillings, any freeman of the city was entitled to a ticket in the lottery; if his number was the first to be drawn, he was allowed to make his choice of the harbor fish lots. He could then utilize the lot himself or lease it to someone else, usually receiving a certain portion of the catch from the lot as payment for the lease. In 1791, for example, one of the better set-net sites was leased for 450 salmon — an indication of the value and extent of the Saint John fishery at this time.[49]

The lottery was looked upon by some — particularly the bona fide fishermen — as an inequitable way of distributing the fishing privilege, since it provided no bias in their favor. If the fishermen themselves were not successful in the lottery, they had to purchase the rights of someone who was, and this was not always possible; the lottery, therefore, had its critics from the start. Because of this, much ill will and illegality existed. In 1795, for example, one Jabez Husted, a butcher who had acquired a lot at Cedar Cove, brought Richard Bonsal, John Boggs, Godfrey Leydick, and several others to court for illegally fishing his berth. The accused were fined £10; Bonsal considered it a stiff and unwarranted penalty, particularly since the butcher himself was known to have committed similar crimes. Evidently Boggs and Leydick were not rehabilitated by this penalty, since records show that they were soon again in court, charged with "setting nets within six inches of another man's lot."[50]

The weir fishery in the harbor was operated differently from the set-net fishery; weirs were held as common property, as Patrick Campbell described in 1791: "[On the] St. John side, there is another large weir, intersected with lesser ones within, of which every inhabitant who takes the trouble of repairing and upholding it, has the right to a share." Both setnets and weirs took vast quantities of fish: "There is sometimes caught," wrote Campbell, "more than the whole town can consume, and find casks to salt and cure." Salmon nets, from 20 to 30 fathoms in length, were set with their landward end at low watermark and the other end anchored in deep water, all along the shore on both sides of the harbor, with heavy concentrations in the places where the water eddied. According to Campbell,

> When the tide makes, and these nets become afloat, the schools of fish that push up the river, strike with such amazing force, and in such numbers as to raise a considerable part of it [net] out of the water. So numerous are salmon here, that 3000 I am told, were caught in a day in this way.[51]

A single net set at the Devil's Hole, acknowledged as one of the better sets on the river, took 100 salmon in one day. The general run of salmon into the harbor at this time was said to range between 10 and 15 pounds per fish, although some of 20 and 30 pounds were encountered. The best fish, unless unusually large, sold for only a shilling in the local market.[52]

Salmon was an important food source to the early townspeople, and the opportunity to obtain a piece of good fishing property either inside or outside the council's jurisdiction was diligently sought after. The following notice, which appeared in the Saint John newspaper *Royal Gazette*, December 31, 1798, shows that the mention of a salmon privilege was considered a worthy inducement to purchase property: "For Sale: The lease and improvements of lot #3 commonly known by name of Pangburns Point, just above the Falls — its situation for the Salmon Fishery, is equal to any on the River Saint John...."[53] Merchants of the town found profit in catering to fishermen: advertisements appeared regularly in the local papers, advising of the arrival of new shipments of fishing equipment. Imported netting material was particularly desirable; in a listing of over 200 general items available at the merchandising firm of Louis Deblois, "SALMON TWINE" was the only one capitalized.[54]

The old firm of Simonds, Hazen and White soon felt the pressure of encroachment upon its fishing domain. By the conditions stipulated in their original grant, the owners of the firm understood that they possessed the exclusive right to the fishery off their property, which extended northward from Union Street; this area was commonly referred to as Portland Point or the North Shore. About 1800, fishery officers appointed by the city proceeded to lay out the North Shore into individual fish lots. The firm immediately brought its claim to this fishery to the Supreme Court, which upheld the right of the firm, on the grounds that river bank ownership was tied to the soil upon which an original grant was made; in other words, all grants of land included the unquestionable right to the fishery off that particular grant.

The firm, however, was not sure whether the Supreme Court ruling actually applied to its grant, since it had been one of the earliest concessions issued. To clarify its position, the firm sent a memorial to Governor Guy Carleton, requesting a license of occupation to the low watermark; this the governor granted in February 1802. Regardless of the Court's decision and the subsequent license in the firm's favor, however, some Saint John inhabitants continued to set their nets on the North Shore, even dismantling and destroying those of the firm and of other grantees, in order to set their own. They argued that, because of the City Charter, it was beyond the governor's power to grant specific licenses of the nature given to the Portland Point or North Shore grantees. At this point, two Saint John city aldermen proposed to both Simonds, Hazen and White and the other area tenants that the North Shore fishery problem might be solved by an agreement to set alternate nets — one

Portland net to every Saint John net. This measure the Portland people would not accept and, trusting that the Supreme Court favored their rights, they requested an official and precise interpretation of the decision handed down previously.

Late in February 1804, the Court replied that the fishery between high and low watermarks must be considered free to all. The Portland grantees and the Simonds, Hazen and White firm had lost. By the end of March, the Corporation of Saint John had moved quickly to consolidate its victory and issued the following ordinance, requesting that:

> all persons wishing to be concerned with taking of fish on the same [north side of the harbour] flats and shore, to give their names at a certain time and place by the said Overseer to be fixed on. And those persons only, who give their names, and appear when notified, to assist in repairing and making the Weirs, to be classed or considered as entitled to take fish.[55]

The Portland proprietors, however, chose to ignore the city ordinance and proceeded to set their own weirs and salmon nets. This was a red flag to the fishing inhabitants of the city, and a large party of "lawless rabble" from Saint John descended on the flats, threatened and assaulted the Portland fishermen, carried off and burnt their nets, and took over their fish lots. In the spring of the following year, 1805, these assaults were repeated when the Portland men again attempted to erect their fishing equipment. On one occasion, over one hundred Saint John men absconded with most of the fish from the Simonds, Hazen and White weirs; and in 1806, they were again in virtual control of the Portland fishery.

In frustration, some of the Portland proprietors eventually came to terms with the Saint John men, but the old firm was untiring in its efforts to have its fishing rights restored. Simonds, Hazen and White once again petitioned the government to consider their rights. This time, they were rewarded when the Legislative Assembly passed an act annexing the fishery to the soil, thus reestablishing the firm's right. The fish was now on the other hook — or in the other weir — and the irate city Corporation immediately sent a delegation to London, armed with the city charter and no less a document than the Magna Carta to support its cause. Castlereagh, the British secretary, ordered the New Brunswick government to suspend operation of the recently devised act until all proper representations could be studied, and early in 1808, the British government officially disallowed the colonial statute. The battle was over, and the old guard — Simonds, Hazen and White — had truly lost.[56]

By 1808, Saint John's salmon yield was serving more than just local needs; naval office reports for the years 1808 to 1811 show that a considerable amount of pickled salmon was being exported to various West Indian colonies: Jamaica, Tobago, Barbados, the Dominican Republic, St. Lucia, Tortola, St. Croix, Dominica, St. Vincent, and Nevis appear regularly on the register as points of destination. Exports were also made to New York, but this city seemed to prefer smoked salmon, and cargoes of 1000 to 2000 fish were shipped in this manner on a more or less regular basis. Boston also received a small amount of pickled fish annually from Saint John, and the occasional shipment was made to Halifax and other ports closer to home. The largest trade in pickled fish usually occurred in the fall and winter months, while smoked fish were more frequently shipped during the warmer season.[57]

Prosperity in the salmon fishery was also evident all along the Saint John River and its tributaries, but here the spear competed strongly with the net and the weir as the chief means of capture. Salmon were speared nightly on the Kennebecasis River, and even in the early 1800s, salmon were being speared and netted in the Sussex area and taken by barge to Saint John for sale.[58] Salmon were known to have ascended the Kennebecasis to well above Portage Vale, where as early as 1811 they, along with trout, were served to travelers crossing the portage between the Kennebecasis and Petitcodiac rivers. On the Petitcodiac side of the portage, they could also be found, although as one observer reported,

> From some unaccountable cause no salmon had been known to frequent a small river called the Poulet [Pollett], which falls into the Petitcodiac, until one of the inhabitants brought a few and put them into it, since when it has been as well supplied with them as any other.[59]

Earlier, in 1791, Patrick Campbell made the following comment about the Nashwaak River fishery:

> The salmon fishing on this river is very useful...Captain Lyman told me that he knew two Frenchmen in one canoe, in the month of July to spear in one night 96 salmon with torch light. And one of these men told him this was nothing to what he had seen, viz. that three canoes, in one of which he himself was, had speared in the same season of the year, 700 salmon in one night.[60]

It was an easy matter for the early settlers to supply their households with salmon, particularly in the fall, when the fish could be easily speared as they entered the smaller tributaries. Although the prime objective of spearing was to fill the families' larders for the winter, the activity took on the aspect of a sport, and many spearmen took pride in developing a high degree of skill and proficiency, particularly when a canoe was used. Campbell further noted that "A man fishing in a canoe, is considered a wretched fisherman, if, when he spears a salmon, he wets himself, and goes ashore with the fish."[61]

THE RIVER ST. CROIX

Following William Owen's settlement on Campobello Island in the 1770s, other settlers, traders, and fishermen came sporadically to the Passamaquoddy region. It was not until the arrival of the Loyalists, however, that a serious threat developed for the anadromous fish runs of the many productive streams of Charlotte County. The fishery was considered of great importance to many of the new settlers, with fishing reserves and public fish lots being laid out along the borders of the river for their use.[62]

Timber, however, soon competed with fish, and by the turn of the century, milldams were being erected on many streams; there were at least three such dams on the St. Croix above Scoodic Falls by 1802, facilitating the enormous timber industry that developed on the watershed. In the construction of these dams, little consideration was apparently given to the passage of fish. Some of the early structures, however, did not hinder movement, as they were built only partially across the stream bed, or were left open for certain periods of the year.[63] Gradually, however, complete obstructions were erected, fish runs began to decline, and the fishing segment of the population became fearful of the consequences brought on by the timber industry. One dam in particular seemed to pose the worst threat, and in 1793 the County Sessions saw fit to order "That Scoodic Upper Mill Dam must be opened to allow free passage or at least to assure the Fishery Overseer that an opening will be allowed during the fall and winter."[64]

The Sessions Court of Charlotte County was well advanced in its respect of fishery preservation, since it not only recognized the necessity of initiating fish passage regulations, but also took steps to protect the resource by appointing officers. In this regard, Charlotte County was well ahead of many other counties in the province, and the Provincial Legislature as well. The regulation respecting fishways on the St. Croix was to a certain degree complied with, but by 1803, further action was necessary, as indicated by the following order sent to the owners of the Scoodic Dam, Messrs. John and William Watterten of St. Stephen:

> You are hereby informed that the preceding order hath been extended by the Court of General Sessions to the year one thousand eight hundred and five, and you are served with this notice to the intent that you remove the Obstruction to the Passing of the Fish on the River St. Croix heretofor by you erected in the water herein pointed out, and in case of default you will be complained of and prosecuted as the law directs....[65]

Such prosecutions were frequent in Charlotte County, where the officers continued to exercise their duties more diligently than many others in the province, and where they were often successful in bringing breaches of the Fishery Act to court. The poor of the county must have been well cared for by the sale of confiscated fishing equipment. Nets and gear were generally sold at public auction and, in at least one case in 1805, a yoke of oxen was sold in this manner after being taken from their owner for his particular breach of the Provincial Fishery Act.[66]

Until 1820, the salmon fishery at Scoodic Falls and in the St. Croix estuary prospered, and enough salmon were taken periodically to justify a small export trade; several kitts, for example, were shipped from St. Andrews in 1811.[67] Salmon were captured in weirs and with drift nets, but the principal fishery for the species was still at Scoodic Falls, where they were taken in dip nets. William Porter, a fishery officer for the St. Croix in the early 1800s, stated that prior to 1825, "there was a great abundance of salmon, shad and gaspereau in the St. Croix ....We have known a lad, 15 years of age, take 500 salmon in one season; and we have known one man with a dip net at the salmon falls, take 90 to 100 salmon, two days in succession."[68]

Porter also mentioned that these salmon weighed about 10 pounds each and sold locally for 4 or 5 cents a pound. Another early resident, Edward Sydney Dyer, estimated that the average catch of salmon at Scoodic Falls was 200 fish each day for a full 3 months of the season. Since salmon are now a rarity on the St. Croix, it might seem that a catch of 18 000 fish (90 days × 200 fish) was inconceivable. There is no reason to doubt Dyer's assessment, however, since a number of contemporary records support his comments; with modern estimates indicating a salmon-rearing area on the St. Croix of 4 million square yards, adult populations in excess of Dyer's figures were possible.[69]

PRINCE EDWARD ISLAND

By 1800, Prince Edward Island's population had grown to 5000,[70] and this figure was to double in the following 15 years. Salmon still frequented all the rivers at the turn of the century, although they did not appear so abundant as before. A description of the island's salmon resource in 1806 stated that

on the north side of the Island, in all the harbours they [the salmon] may be seen leaping out of the water frequently in the months of June and July, particularly at St. Peter's Bay, where, in the River Morelle, which runs into it, a great many are taken: they do not come into the Hillsboro River, and other rivers on the south side of the Island, until the latter end of September, and the beginning of October.[71]

Agriculture, however, was regarded as the prime resource industry during the period fom 1785 to 1815; eighty-five percent of the island was suitable for growing crops, and already much of it was devoid of trees.[72] Little attention was paid to the general fishery by the legislators, although there had been a growing interest in its

exploitation — and a rapid destruction of its habitat — as evidenced by Walter Johnson's comment in 1820 that

Front lands have always been most prized by the first settlers; these affording them several privileges, such as conveniency for fishing, which before the production of grain, or mills to grind it, constituted a great part of the living of the inhabitants.[73]

PICTOU

The river fishery in Pictou County at the end of the 18th century was heavily relied upon by an increasing number of Scottish settlers who had come to the area. They knew the salmon and prized it highly; many had lived beside streams in Scotland possessing fine runs forbidden to them — wealthy landlords or leaseholders who owned the rights frequently took harsh measures against poachers. Grantees along the river courses of Pictou County built small weirs for capturing salmon and gradually acquired or made seines and nets for the same purpose. So active did the river fishery become that, in 1787, the County Sessions found it necessary to take action to regulate it. Initially, steps were taken to limit the length of fishing nets and weirs to two-thirds the width of the stream in which they were set — a measure devised more to allow the settlers above the obstruction to obtain their share of fish than to conserve the species. In addition, a salmon season was established: no fishing could take place each calendar year after 19 October. Spearing and sweeping with a net were also outlawed, and a fine of 20 shillings was imposed for each breach of the law.[74]

Some of the Pictou County regulations were quite specific in their content, and although they appear mild by today's standards, to the independent Scot of pioneering days, they were an unwarranted curb on freedom, criminal in application, and echoing the restrictions common to the country from which he had emigrated. A 20 shilling fine was next to extortion, for money was scarce; indeed, almost any fine was a formidable prospect. Taxes, for example, were often paid in produce, as was the cleric's salary, and more country store accounts were paid in grain, maple sugar, and fish than in silver or gold. With money being scarce, a breach of the law usually meant a stint in the local jail in lieu of the fine. Nor did Pictou County relent in its stern regulations; in fact, the county clerk often used more ink to describe the penalty than the law. In July 1797, the Sessions Court enacted the following regulation:

No settler to buy or barter salmon fish, salt or fresh from any Indian or Indians in the district from the 19th day of October, 1797 to the 19th day of May, under penalty of £10, one half to the prosecutor, the other half to the overseers of the poor.[75]

In 1798, the court forbade a weekend fishery; forbade the practice of chasing, following, or driving salmon into nets; and forbade anyone to even be seen with a spear near any river — anyone caught with a forked stick in their possession near a watercourse could be considered guilty of intent and fined £2. Furthermore, if the individual charged with such an offence saw fit to blaspheme because of his misfortune, he was subject to an additional fine of 2 shillings.[76] Profuse and strict legislation, however, did not produce the desired results. At this time, no other county in the colony had more statutes protecting its fishery — but on the other hand, there appeared to be no other county in the colony where the inland salmon resource declined so rapidly.

CAPE BRETON

Cape Breton had become a separate colony with its own governor in 1784, but could boast of little progress until the early 1800s, except that which was attributed to the fishery. Settlers were not particularly encouraged to the island, since both the coal mines and the forests were preserves of the Royal Navy,[77] and agriculture was almost unthinkable on such an inhospitable outcrop, "surrounded with many sharp pointed rocks, separated from each other by the waves, above which foam from the tops are visible, and intersected by lakes and rivers."[78] The fishery was all that was left to those few settlers of an independent bent.

The Robin firm was established at LaPointe (Chéticamp) at least as early as 1786, and cured fish was regularly exported from there to European markets. A statistical report for the island in 1785 also indicates that, besides the principal centers of Sydney, Louisbourg, and Isle Madame, fish were exported as well from outports such as Juste-au-Corps (Port Hood), Lingan, St. Anns, and several other locations familiar to fishermen since the early 1500s.[79]

Shortly after 1800, a permanent salmon fishery was established by new settlers on the Margaree, and a perusal of information relating to that region reveals a regulation, prepared by freeholders in 1813, in which is described the procedure of assigning and controlling the salmon fishery. Selected articles from the minutes include the following:

Item 3: That Salmon Berths shall be laid off by the overseers and a fair lot drawn for the berths.
Item 4: That the 10th day of Next May, providing the weather permits, the salmon berths shall be laid off and drawn up.
Item 5: That no nets more than 30 fathoms long shall be sat [sic] in this river in this present year.
Item 6: That the distance between each net shall be 50 fathoms.[80]

SOUTHWESTERN NOVA SCOTIA

The southwestern coast of Nova Scotia, from St. Margaret's Bay to Yarmouth, had been sparsely settled since the 1760s. A salmon fishery developed in a few locations as incidental to cod, but participation in river fisheries developed on a large scale only after the arrival of the American Loyalists. There were exceptions to this general statement, such as Colonel William Freeman's fishery at St. Margaret's Bay, which employed many men,[81] and the salmon fishery near New Germany, which was exploited by the early German settlers, and which was described by John Fiendel about the turn of the century:

The Indians…used to dip salmon, sometimes as many as eighty in a day, at Indian Falls. Lohnes and my father once put a net in an eddy under the falls. It sank, and they did not find it till the water fell away in the summer. Bones of salmon were left in the meshes. Salmon would try to jump over the falls, and would strike the rocks and fall down helpless, and then come to again. In dipping, three salmon would often be got at once.[82]

Benjamin Marston, who later became the sheriff at Miramichi, was assigned to survey the townsite for Shelburne immediately before the arrival of the first shipload of Loyalists in 1783. In his diary, one of the first notations concerning the new community also refers to the salmon which he had discovered in the Roseway River.[83] The settlers soon made use of this valuable resource, and it is documented that one enterprising individual in the town employed Boston King, from the Black community at Birchtown, to build three flatbottomed boats, at £1 each, exclusively for the harbor salmon fishery. This contractor also had aspirations for participation in the Chaleur Bay fishery.[84]

By 1787, it was reported that "All the country, for several miles [around Shelburne] is exceedingly populous, particularly upon Jordan River, five miles east of Port Roseway [Shelburne], noted for an extraordinary Salmon fishery…."[85]

Shelburne, for a number of reasons, proved not to be a viable community, and the inhabitants soon began to drift away. It was, nevertheless, remarkable that, within ten years some people were recognizing that the "extraordinary Salmon fishery," both in the Shelburne area, and along the coast in general, was no longer a truth. In his diary of 1795, the Reverend James Munroe reported the following about the LaHave River salmon:

[They] come on the beginning of April, for common, and run a little more than two months.…The salmon is said not to be near so plenty as they were, owing, people think, to so many sawmills upon the river. No doubt the sawdust, for one thing, and the dams, for another, prevent them getting up the river to the lake to spawn, or their catching them about the time they spawn. Whatever cause it may be owing to, the salmon are not near so plenty as they were on the rivers along the coast, and the people on general assign the above reasons for it.

Munroe went on to comment that the fish abundance was declining "not only in the rivers, but along the coast. Those that fish along the coast say they do not catch them in such plenty: this may be owing to the increase of those who catch them, who may be said yearly to increase."[86]

Further southwest, in Argyle and Yarmouth townships, the first County Sessions were assembled in 1789 to meet the legal needs of the growing population. It was not until 1791 that these Sessions recognized the need to control the fishery: in that year, regulations were formulated to govern the resource equitably in Yarmouth harbor and along the Tusket and Salmon rivers. Barrington Township had also enacted fishery regulations by this time, but there the alewife was the most important species of concern.[87]

Of all the regions along the southwestern shore and, indeed, in all of Nova Scotia, there was probably no other so deeply engaged in the salmon fishery as the Liverpool area. Shortly after the town was founded, Simeon Perkins began salmon fishing as an enterprise, not only in the river which flowed through the community, but also elsewhere in the province, at Chaleur Bay, and even on the coast of Labrador.

In succeeding years, several Liverpool fishing interests followed Perkins' example. In 1794, an ambitious new project began; banding together, they sent George Collins to Quebec City to negotiate for some part of the Labrador salmon fishery. Collins managed to secure fishing rights in the Mingan region for a period of 8 years, from May 1795 to May 1803, under the terms that one-tenth of the salmon catch would go to the seigneury agent in Quebec. The enterprise became very profitable to the Liverpool group, and they sold part-interests in the venture to their fellow townsmen. After 1803, their leases were renewed for a longer period, and in one year, it was reported that 1500 barrels of salmon came into Liverpool from this Labrador fishery.[88]

During the War of 1812, Liverpool fishermen continued their work, as well as their trade with the West Indies — but at some hazard to themselves, due to the war at sea. Nonetheless, they increased their fishing potential through their privateering activities, in which they captured enemy fishing vessels and converted them to their own use. The fishery prospered, but there was a major drawback to the West Indies trade: since the principal market for fish during and after the war was the Caribbean islands, and since money was limited, Nova Scotians had to accept West Indian goods in return. These consisted largely of rum, and it is said that as many as 4000 puncheons of the liquor could be seen on the Liverpool wharf at one time. James More, the Queens County historian, noted that everything ran on rum, and this superabundance had the effect of enticing Liverpool people to seek new markets for fish; after 1815, they also took to lumbering, in order to widen their markets and increase the variety of their imports.[89]

BAY OF FUNDY

Weirs were still the most common fishing device to be found in Digby County, and particularly in the Annapolis Basin, but net fishing was also carried out for salmon in the rivers and at the mouths of the various creeks. A county regulation passed in 1784 limited the length of nets which could be set in the Basin to 60 fathoms; no "draw" nets were allowed, and the regulation clearly favored the weir fishery by stipulating that no net could be used in the vicinity of any private structure of this type. The weir fishery for herring took precedence over all other species; even those who normally engaged in seal and porpoise killing in the Basin and off Digby were forbidden to do so by a Sessions act of 1808, since these activities were disadvantageous to the herring fishery, on the grounds that the continued presence of both these sea creatures frightened the herring into the pounds.[90]

The people of Minas Basin were still enjoying the advantage of the salmon, shad, and gaspereau of that region, each species being heavily fished in its proper season. Salmon were plentiful in the tributaries of the Avon River in June, July, and August, and Hollingsworth reported in 1787 that at least one establishment in this region was already catching and exporting salmon commercially.[91] Salmon were also being killed on the Shubenacadie River by every conceivable means — even clubs were used — and the fishery was of enough concern to the Halifax County authorities that they had appointed two constables to protect the industry along the Shubenacadie by 1808.[92]

Lower Canada

After the Revolutionary War, Lower Canada, or Quebec, was frequently looked upon as comprising three distinct geographic districts: the St. Lawrence River Valley, Labrador, and the Gaspé. In the first-mentioned district, fishing was described as not being pursued with "spirit" for some 15 years after the close of the war; this was basically due to the agricultural orientation of a large segment of the population, and to the engagement of the rest in the lucrative profits of the fur trade. Although occasional commercial fishing operations could be found at some locations such as Kamouraska, where a large brush weir was constructed between the islands and the mainland for taking porpoises, the general fishery was principally conducted on a small scale for local needs, utilizing the annual runs of fish into the rivers. Salmon and eels were the main interests of the habitants and salmon, for example, were reported to have been taken in great numbers on the Jacques Cartier River during the summer months.[93]

A slightly different situation existed on the north shore of the St. Lawrence River. Along this coast, from the Saguenay River eastward to Sept-Îles, were located the old King's Posts — small centers of semicivilization situated at such widely separated locations as Tadoussac, Chicoutimi, Lac Saint-Jean, Mistassini, Ashuapmuchuan, Îlets-Jeremie (opposite Rimouski), Sept-Îles, and Pointe-des-Monts (above Baie Trinité). These posts actually served a multitude of purposes and were customarily let by the government for a moderate fee to commercial interests, for such purposes as the fur trade and for the salmon, whale, seal, and porpoise fisheries. After 1802, these posts were let to a consortium of traders known as the North West Company, the only real commercial rival of the Hudson's Bay Company.[94]

The territory northeast of the King's Posts was the terra incognita of eastern Canada, which was beginning to be recognized for its great wealth as a salmon area. Jurisdiction over this vast region, which stretched to the Straits of Belle Isle, was vested in the government of Lower Canada by the Quebec Act (1774). By the early 1800s, both the colonial administration and the proprietors of the north shore seigneuries were leasing an increasing number of salmon rivers to commercial interests from inside and outside Lower Canada. Liverpool, Nova Scotia interests, for example, held leases on several rivers as early as 1795, and the Lymburner family had secured the Mingan seigneury in 1807 for purposes of salmon fishing.[95] This latter region was particularly valuable; Hugh Gray, for example, reported that among the islands at the mouth of the Mingan, "there is secure and good anchorage and they present an excellent situation for a cod, seal and salmon fishery."[96] The success of the Lymburner firm in the area is indicated by the following entry in the journal of James McKenzie, 1808:

> The largest river on the south of Mingan is the Natasquan [Natashquan] near half way between Napioshibou [Nabisipi] and Masquaro [Musquaro], it is about two and a half miles wide at its entrance but very shallow. Two hundred and fifty tierces of salmon [118 250 live lb] are taken in nets out of this river every year by five men.... Exclusive of the river already mentioned, there are seven more in the seigneury, into which salmon enter and which are pretty large....[97]

The growing importance of the Quebec salmon fishery at the turn of the century is illustrated in the rents received by the colony for its salmon rivers. Prior to 1800, the King's Posts were leased for £400 per annum; when the North West Company took over these posts, the yearly rents had increased to £1025. For the salmon fishery alone, the Lymburners paid £500 in 1807 for a 3-year lease; just to recover the cost of the lease alone, the firm would have had to capture over 50 000 pounds of salmon.[98]

The fish captured in these areas were either taken directly to domestic ports, where they were subsequently consumed, or they were exported to markets in the United States, the West Indies, or Europe. Despite the fact that the official export records maintained at the port of Quebec claimed to include the total exports for the entire province, it is again likely that a substantial segment of the colonial catch never found its way onto the customs house books.[99] The statistical record of 1804 shows that 597 tierces and 264 barrels of salmon were exported in that year. Hugh Gray reported that the average export of salmon for the 3-year period ending in 1805 was 610 tierces and 197 barrels, equivalent to approximately 350 000 pounds of fresh, round salmon; at this time, the species was valued at 65 shillings per tierce and 45 shillings per barrel. By 1808, 794 tierces and 61 barrels were exported (400 000 lb round).[100]

The district of Gaspé was another world, almost as remote as the coast of Labrador. The fishery there suffered during the revolution primarily because of the scarcity of salt, but several new townsites were established after the peace of 1783, principally on the Chaleur Bay side, and the fishery was activated once more. Some Gaspé salmon were sent to Quebec, but the larger portion was exported directly to the West Indies and the Mediterranean. By 1805, the district was assigned its own lieutenant-governor, and the permanent population numbered 3500, although there were a great many more people involved in the general fishery during the summer months. Hugh Gray summed up the extent of the local industry when he stated in 1809 that "There are several fishing stations along the coast; those of most importance are at Percé and Chaleur Bay. The trade employs annually about a dozen square rigged vessels, besides a great many small craft."[101]

Upper Canada

To this point in the history of the salmon, little has been said about the region west of the Ottawa River. Of the historic Ottawa waterway itself, there is little on record which points to its being a salmon stream, except for notations on several early maps of New France, which identify one of its lower tributaries as the "Rivière au Saumon,"[102] a name by which the branch is sometimes known today.

If salmon did ascend the Ottawa, they would have had a choice of three access channels after approaching the river's mouth at what is now the city of Montreal. They could ascend the Lachine Rapids on the main St. Lawrence — a possibility which some biologists consider remote, and a question which is at the center of the controversy as to whether Lake Ontario salmon could have been sea-run fish; after overcoming this barrier, they could ascend the relatively mild Ste. Anne Rapids, on the westerly outlet of the Ottawa. The other two access channels would be the Back River and the Rivière des Milles Îles, both entering the St. Lawrence below the Lachine Rapids; these two channels also possessed rapids which may have been barriers to access. If they could ascend these obstructions, however, the salmon would have had relatively free access as far upstream as Ottawa, where the Chaudière Falls would have barred further progress. An examination of the Ottawa River and its tributaries below the capital city, however, shows that much of the aquatic environment is unsuited to the propagation of salmon, particularly with respect to the quality of spawning area and the lack of suitable rearing ground. This area is the flat, sandy Ottawa Lowland, supporting streams that are relatively docile, and thus unattractive to salmon.[103] It seems unlikely, therefore, that the Ottawa River supported any notable runs of the species.

Until the founding of Montreal in 1642, little was known about the central Canadian wilderness; missionaries, fur traders, and adventurers gradually moved into the territory after midcentury, and by 1670, concentrated efforts were being made by France to take possession of the country around the Great Lakes. In that year, a traveller to the Humber River region reported seeing salmon, the behavior of which was somewhat different from that normally witnessed: "September is the season in which salmon spawn in these parts, contrary to what they do in any other place I ever knew them before."[104] If we can accept this comment as a factual observation, it becomes an interesting point for discussion, for there are no known records, either historical or contemporary, that refer to a salmon spawning in North America as early as September; obviously it was just as unusual in 1670. Even in Ungava, where one may expect the growing season to be shortened, it has been concluded that spawning was unlikely before the end of September.[105] Investigations indicate that the earliest spawning occurs in mid-October, with no known instances in September. One may conclude that this deviation from normal activity suggests a separate or isolated population of the species, perhaps landlocked — but the spawning dates of all known populations of landlocked salmon are also not recorded as early as September.

More conclusive evidence about the existence and distribution of salmon in what is now Ontario did not become prevalent until after the American Revolution. After 1783, a massive Loyalist migration to the Lake Ontario region resulted in the creation of the new colony of Upper Canada in 1792, and revealed to many the potential of the country from an agricultural and, later, a piscatorial point of view. One of these new arrivals, Isaac Weld, wrote that "Lake Ontario and all rivers that fall into it, abound with excellent salmon and many different kinds of sea fish which come up the St. Lawrence."[106] Another observer stated that the new inhabitants made considerable use of the great and relatively untapped resources, and "varied their diet by netting large numbers of whitefish, salmon, sturgeon and other species so plentiful...."[107]

One of the more astute and informative reports about Upper Canada before 1800 was written by Mrs. John Graves [Elizabeth] Simcoe, wife of the colony's first governor. Among her many observations are those pertaining to the fishery. In 1793, she was present with her husband at the founding of York, now Toronto; the Don River, which flowed beside the townsite, and the Humber, 6 miles west of the settlement, were prolific salmon streams in these early years, and while there on August 4, she wrote:

An Indian named Wable Casigo supplies us with salmon, which the rivers and creeks along this shore abound with. It is supposed they go to sea; the velocity which fish move makes it not impossible, and the very red appearance and the goodness of the salmon confirms the supposition; they are best in the month of June.[108]

The species was such a common food source to the early settlers that if one chose not to fish for them oneself, they could be procured as cheaply as the cheapest item. Robert Gourlay reported that "a salmon of ten to twenty pounds brought one shilling, a gill of whiskey, a cake of bread or the like trifle."[109] Trifling though the fish may have been, they were often considered valuable inducements in real estate transactions, as indicated by the following advertisement which appeared in the *York Gazette* in 1798:

To be sold at public auction on Monday, the second of July next at John Macdougall's hotel in the town of York, a valuable farm situated in Yonge Street, about twelve miles from York on which is a log house and seven or eight acres well improved. It affords an excellent salmon fishery, large enough to support several families.[110]

Just before the turn of the century, salmon were principally taken with the spear in Upper Canada; nets were only occasionally used, even in the general fishery, one incident being in 1793, when Mrs. Simcoe mentioned that the troops at Niagara used nets to capture whitefish and sturgeon.[111] Although the farmer was not particularly interested in spearing as a sport, there were certain boys and gentlemen in York who found the pursuit a most enjoyable pleasure and diversion; Toronto Bay was a popular area for the activity: "The Gentlemen of York also engage in field sports — hunting, fowling, hawking and fishing. Many a canoe might be seen on the Bay in the evening, its occupants intent upon the exciting sport of spearing fish by Jack light."[112] Paul Kane, the noted painter of American Indian life, recalled that "In my boyish days I have seen as many as a hundred lightjacks gliding about the Bay of Toronto and have often joined in the sport."[113]

Although salmon were plentiful in the Don and the Humber, to the extent that several people ventured to make it a commercial enterprise, trade in salmon was strictly local in these years, and no export market was practical. Salmon were sometimes salted in 200-pound barrels, which sold for thirty or fifty shillings, and most households possessed their own winter supply of the pickled product. Fresh salmon were also sold at town markets; the night's catch of Toronto Bay, for example, was brought ashore at the landing place between Princess and Caroline Streets, where a bayshore market developed.[114]

Fresh salmon were apparently available at York during the greater part of the year. Mrs. Simcoe noted that on November 1, quantities of the species were speared near her home, Castle Frank, at the mouth of the Don: "At eight this dark evening we went in a boat to see salmon speared. Large torches of whitebirch bark being carried in the boat, the blaze of light attracts the fish, when the men are dexterious in spearing." Such an excursion, however, aroused mixed emotions in the governor's lady: "The manner of destroying the fish is very disagreeable but seeing them swimming in schools around the board is a very pretty sight."[115] And Sherwood Fox reported in his article on the Lake Ontario salmon that every village along the rivers tributary to the lake feasted on salmon from May to November.[116]

To the west of the York and Don rivers, there was another stream which was reputed to be the best salmon river in Upper Canada; this was the Credit, a traditional salmon-fishing river of the local Indians. Their favorite spot was a Erindale, where they had constructed a weir and regularly took from it several hundred fish nightly. When white settlers came to the area, they profitably duplicated the Indians' successes. A Mr. McCuaig, for example, stated that during his residence in that locality around 1810, "salmon... swarmed the rivers so thickly that they were thrown out with a shovel and even with the hand.[117] Many other rivers, such as the Clarke, Darlington, Whitney, Pickering, "Tobyco" [Etobicoke] and Dufferin were mentioned as salmon streams in the early reports. Still further west, the earliest settlers discovered salmon in Burlington Bay and the river that flows into it via the Dundas Valley. It was Mrs. Simcoe who first recorded the most westerly limit of the salmon's range: in what is now the city of Hamilton, she saw large quantities of the species taken by both Indians and white settlers in 1796.[118]

After 1800, the result of unrestricted fishing was being seen in several areas of Upper Canada. The increasing use of nets and weirs had allowed a greater efficiency, and some individuals were obstructing the entire width of certain streams with these devices, causing complaints from other fishermen. This situation resulted in the Legislature formulating the colony's first fishing regulation, an act "for the Preservation of Salmon," which was made law on 10 March 1807. The act forbade the use of any net, "wear," or "other enjine" in or at the mouth of any river in the Home and Newcastle districts, the best-known salmon rivers of the colony being in these two regions; a fine of £5 or one month in jail was provided upon the first conviction.[119]

The legislation, however, was of little merit; spear fishing was still permitted anywhere and at any time while the slaughter of fish on the spawning grounds was not prevented, and consequently continued. Neither was there any provision in the act for appointing overseers, and as a result, it is doubtful if even net fishing was significantly reduced by the introduction of the statute. With a net — or even with a spear — it was not difficult for one man to capture a hundred fish in an evening, the sale of which would more than compensate for his fine — or a short stay in jail — if he ever suffered the misfortune of being caught. Robert Gourlay wrote that even a crotched stick — as unrefined as it might be — would suffice in taking salmon in any of the Upper Canadian streams; he had known of one instance where 70 had been taken in one afternoon in this manner.[120]

It soon became apparent that the legislation was inadequate; three years after it had been passed, the Legislature revoked its application and enacted a new law to take its place. This 1810 effort was thought to provide more stringent regulations for the protection of salmon, since it imposed a closed season from October 25 to January 1. Fishing within 100 yards of the foot of a dam was also outlawed, as was netting at river mouths in the Home District.[121] The only group of individuals who were completely free to follow their traditional fishing practices were the Indians, and the following description shows that their methods had changed little since the arrival of the white man, with the exception, possibly, of a more frequent use of the net:

> The savages catch the fish in the rivers and lakes either by spearing them with a long, wooden fork sharpened at the points, or shod with iron, or by placing nets where a rivulet, or spring of cold water empties itself into a river or lake. Across the mouth they plant stakes, leaving a small opening for the fish to enter, when they become entangled in the snares.... The natives procure fish in the winter season by making holes in the ice, and carrying thither at night flambeaux of birch bark, by whose light the fish are attracted to the openings, and are then taken by means of the spear, or entangled in nets.[122]

Lake Champlain

At the same time that the Atlantic seaboard salmon were rapidly diminishing, new populations of the species were being discovered and exploited in the wild interior of the Lake Champlain country. The head of one of the first pioneering families to come to that region, William Gilliland, found remuneration in supplying American troops with lake salmon during the Revolutionary War; it was reported that he had provisioned the army with as many as 1500 salmon in one year from his "salmon crib" or weir.[123]

During the early 1800s, salmon were still in great abundance in the lake's tributaries, such as the Au Sable, Bouquet, Missiquoi, Lamoille, and Winooski — so plentiful, in fact, that during the run a horseman was considered to be taking his life in his hands if he attempted to ford a stream with a horse that spooked easily. Wagons were sometimes driven into the river, and men with pitchforks hoisted out the fish until a full load was obtained; on one occasion, 500 salmon were taken from the Bouquet River in this way in one afternoon. Although Edward Oliphant reported that the Champlain salmon were small, some of these fish were nevertheless reported to have weighed as much as twenty pounds.[124]

Newfoundland and Labrador

The salmon fishery of Newfoundland expanded rapidly after the close of the American Revolution. By the end of the war, the Americans were no longer engaged in the daring and precarious adventure of fishing in Newfoundland waters, and their allies, the French, had abandoned activity on the designated French Shore (Cape Ray to Pointe Riche). In 1784, therefore, probably for the first time in colonial history, the western North Atlantic fishery was principally — but temporarily — in the hands of British subjects.[125]

Such circumstances allowed British and Newfoundland fishermen to advance and intensify their activities westward and northward without competition, and this they attempted to do with speed and energy. It was reasoned that the war had nullified any traditional rights that both the French and Americans had had to the fishery of the colony prior to the revolution; the home government in Britain, however, was not so quick to accept this interpretation, and considered foreign rights to the fishery a bargainable point in the peace negotiations that were to follow. In turn, Newfoundlanders insisted that if such was the inevitable view of the government, then at least the colonial salmon fishery should be placed solely in their hands; Great Britain accepted this principle, since it had always been intended to restrict foreign fishing to cod only. Apart from this, the salmon, being anadromous, was not competely a sea fish, and was as much a freshwater resource as a saltwater one — a fish belonging to the land. However, when the treaty was signed, the subject of specific rights to the salmon fishery was not defined.[126]

Even before the peace was signed and the full intentions of the government known, British and Newfoundland fishermen moved into the contested areas to secure their assumed rights by occupation. During and immediately after the war, British salmon fishermen, for example, established themselves on the northern section of the French Shore at White Bay, Hare Bay, and Southwest Brook; they also occupied the west coast at St. Georges Bay. These individuals and firms were warned by their government to remove their fixed establishments until the question of French fishing rights was settled;[127] but many a salmonier had already tasted the profits

gleaned from the rivers north of capes St. John and Ray, and were reluctant to be displaced.

French territorial and cod fishing rights were redefined and reinstated in 1783, to comprise principally the northern loop around Newfoundland from St. Georges Bay (Cape Ray) to White Bay (Cape St. John). To offset shore rights from Cape Bonavista to Cape St. John — an area neglected by them and encroached upon by the English — the French were conceded the right to utilize the shore from Cape Riche to Cape Ray. These fishing and shore rights were jealously guarded by the French, even to the extent of assuming rights to the salmon fishery and vehemently opposing the existence of British salmon fisheries in the area. On the west coast, for example, the contest over control of the salmon fisheries heated up in 1785 when at least two English salmon posts at St. Georges Bay were destroyed.[128]

Although intimidated by both the French fishermen and, apparently, by their own government, some British fishermen nevertheless remained on the French Shore or engaged in hit-and-run sorties to the salmon streams within the French zone. The prosperous firm of Noble and Pinson, for example, had been fishing salmon in Newfoundland since the 1760s, and had set up stations in the French zone at Hare Bay and elsewhere. In 1787, one of their vessels was captured by a French brig, presumably for encroaching on the fishery. In addition, one of their employees engaged in salmon fishing at Hare Bay was so harassed by the Frenchmen that he considered himself fortunate to have survived the ordeal, which he described in a complaint forwarded to the British Secretary of State early in 1788.[129]

Forced from the French Shore by circumstance, the salmon fishermen withdrew, to some extent, in two directions: to Notre Dame Bay and to Labrador. The firm of Payton and Miller was fishing in Notre Dame Bay by 1786, and its operation was one of the more extensive, since the Exploits River was its salmon fishing ground, the principal station being at the head of the bay, approximately 20 miles below Grand Falls. In addition, the firm of Jeffrey and Street, based in Poole and Trinity, probably had had a permanent crew in Gander Bay since 1775, and these men were also furriers in the winter.[130] Other interests engaged in the salmon fishery south of Cape St. John were Charles Rousell at Halls Bay; John Crease at Loo Bay; John Slade Jr. at Indian Arm and Dog Bay; Matthew Ward and Company at New Bay; and Lester and Company at Ragged Harbour, Freshwater Bay, and Indian Bay. Thirty-seven men were employed by these firms, and their total catch in 1786 was recorded at 1170 tierces; in 1789, the Lester firm alone exported 1183 tierces of the fish. Salmon were being taken in weirs and in nets of 4-inch mesh at all locations except Ragged Harbour and Gander Bay, where only nets were used.[131]

The second area where salmon fishing was rapidly expanding was on the Labador coast. By 1784, the yield there had increased almost threefold over that of 1773, and an increasing number of firms were engaged in the operation. Noble and Pinson bought out the interests of George Cartwright about 1785, when they had six salmon stations, employing 30 men, in Labrador: St. Modeste, Mary Harbour, St. Francis River, Black Bear Bay, Sandhill Cove, and Sandwich Bay; their total catch for that season amounted to 161 tierces.[132] By this time, the Hunt and Henley firm was also fishing Labrador rivers, as was the Jersey firm of Simon du Bois, at Rivière aux Saumons. Between 1783 and 1800, Jersey firms established at Blanc Sablon and Forteau, and other people were employed in stations at Henley Harbour, Grady Harbour, and Lance au Loop.[133] Indeed, Newfoundland interests were expanding so rapidly in the Labrador fishery and along the coast toward Quebec that the whole area north from Mingan Passage was ceded to Newfoundland in 1809 by an act of the British Parliament. Anticosti Island was also included in this transfer.[134] Newfoundland firms were not the only ones to seek the rewards of the Labrador salmon fishery, since Lower Canadians and Nova Scotians were also helping to fill the gap left by the Americans on this northern coastline.

The rapid commercial development of the Labrador and northeastern Gulf coast is clearly indicated by the export returns of the day. In 1804, Labrador catches comprised 14 percent of the combined Newfoundland–Labrador export; by 1815, it had risen to 36 percent — and even this figure was low, since a portion of the Labrador catch was not being recorded at this point, due to a failure to obtain the returns of American and Nova Scotian salmon fishermen who were also operating there. The percentage figure for Labrador becomes even more significant when one considers that Newfoundland catches were also increasing.[135]

Export records for October 1786 to October 1791 show that 97 percent of the Newfoundland–Labrador salmon trade was with Portugal, Italy, and Madeira. Although there was a great demand in the United States for fish, there was some difficulty in securing British entry to American markets, because the British government had forbidden trade with the United States except under license. Nonetheless, for anyone who could secure a fishing lease and an American trading permit, the enterprise was lucrative — particularly, according to Simeon Perkins writing in 1788, for "those that carry on the salmon and mackerell [sic] fishery[,] as Boston and other parts of the U.S. is the best market for them articles at present."[136]

Meanwhile, Americans were once again venturing to the Newfoundland and Labrador fishing grounds. By the early 1800s, John Stewart noted that "The salmon fisheries in the rivers on the coast of Labrador and the Straits of Bellisle are at present chiefly in the hands of the Americans, as is also a considerable share of the Indian trade on the coast[,] both without any other right than sufferance."[137] Simeon Perkins stated that the cod fishery was entirely monopolized by Americans, and he deplored the competition that now existed. Moreover, conditions in the salmon fishery were so bad that he concluded the industry was nearly finished by 1804 due to overfishing.[138] American participation in both the general and the salmon fishery was of concern, but no quantitative estimate of Yankee catches could be obtained. When Captain Innis of the government sloop *Childers*, on the Labrador station, was asked to report on the amount of salmon taken by Americans during the 1806 season, he intimated the impossibility of an assessment by simply replying, "Uncertain."[139]

Animosity toward American participation grew, particularly during the War of 1812, and all manner of verbal charges were heaped upon their destructive activity in the Labrador fishery. Vice Admiral Sir Richard Godwin Keats, governor of Newfoundland, complained in 1814 of the slightest encroachment and irregularity by the Americans, even noting that the fish offal thrown overboard by the Yankees in Labrador

> produced the worst effect on the neighboring Salmon Fisheries, and also on the Capelin.... The Americans claim and dispute with us the Right of the Salmon Fishery — and by setting their nets at the mouths of Rivers prevent half the fish from entering to lay their spawn.[140]

Americans continued to fish in the region despite the war, believing or contending — that their "rights" to the salmon fishery were not nullified by the current state of hostilities, and that the belligerent acts of both sides had nothing to do with the honest pursuit of the fishery. In fact, it is estimated that of all the fish caught in Newfoundland waters in 1814, 50 percent was taken by American, 15 percent by French, and 35 percent by British fishermen. Indeed, the fact that the westward approaches to Newfoundland and Labrador were free of ice before those of the east, definitely favored the American fishermen over the Europeans.[141]

Although Perkins had stated that the salmon fishery in the Gulf of St. Lawrence and Labrador was on its last legs in 1804, export records show that the catch was steadily growing, due to American activity and also to increased British interest. A bounty of 4 shillings a tierce was applied by the British government in 1807, to help offset the restricted United States market and to encourage exports to a Britain fish-starved by the Continental Blockade of the Napoleonic Wars. The bounty had a considerable effect: in 1804, only 32 percent of Newfoundland's salmon exports went to Great Britain, but in the year the bounty was applied, British markets received 66 percent of the total export. By 1812, over 90 percent of the trade went to Britain.[142]

The price of pickled salmon had also risen; for the first dozen years following the American Revolution, the highest price paid for a tierce of the pickled product was £3, with an average price around £2 being more common; by 1814, however, the price had risen to between £4 and £5 per tierce. Undoubtedly, the War of 1812 helped to effect these higher prices, plus an increased percentage export to Britain as opposed to the United States. In spite of the war, Nova Scotian and other British North American fishermen were continuing each season to sail to Newfoundland and Labrador under the protection of the British Navy, and the catches of these years made risking the hazards worthwhile. Between October 1813 and October 1814, 3425 tierces of salmon were reported taken and exported from Newfoundland; in 1812, the Labrador fishery produced 2069 tierces, followed by 2129 tierces the next year.[143]

Although the returns for 1814 show unsurpassed prosperity in the Newfoundland and Labrador fishery, the year proved to be the turning point, in many respects, from the successes of the past. Peace in Europe after the Napoleonic Wars once again opened British markets to fish products from regions other than Newfoundland, and to futher depress the fishery, the terrible winters of 1817 and 1818 brought Newfoundlanders to the brink of starvation: known as the "Winter of the Rals [Rowdies]," the 1817–18 season forced extreme hardship on the people and precipitated near social and political chaos in the colony.[144]

New England

Although by 1783 the Americans had managed to retain by treaty their former sea-fishing privileges in North American waters, these rights were of little value, due to the loss of their foreign markets, particularly those of the West Indies, which had been the mainstay of their former fishing trade. In addition, the revolution had greatly weakened the sea-going capabilities of the new states, and for almost two decades after the peace, New England's traditional fishery in British North American waters remained prostrate.[145]

Times were politically unsettled in the United States during these years, and a period of convalescence was required to heal the economic and social wounds of the recent war. There was little or no effective federal power or direction exercised; the country was financially broken; and authority had virtually reverted to government by 13 independent nations: wrote John Jay, "Congress could declare everything and do nothing."[146] Finally, a constitution was formulated in 1791, which drew the states together and created a strong federal authority. At this time, Benjamin Franklin was still influential in national affairs, and in his paper entitled, "Consolation for America," he stressed the importance of a firm agricultural and fishing base for the country; the resources of land and sea, he said, were inexhaustible: "Every man who puts a seed into the ground is recompensed forty-fold; everyone who draws a fish out of the waters draws up a piece of silver."[147]

With Franklin's vision and wisdom to encourage them, Congress attempted to assist the fishery by offering a bounty on exported fish and imposing a duty on all imported species. This helped the fishery to expand slowly, but in the meantime, the inhabitants relied heavily upon their own river fisheries, and severe inroads continued to be made on the anadromous stocks within the country. When overfishing was coupled with the increasing use of rivers for mill operation at the turn of the century, an alarming decline occurred in the fish stocks of New England.

The southern limit of the salmon's range was the Connecticut River, and in a state history written in 1783, the following comment was made:

> The shad, bass and salmon more than half support the province. From the number of seines employed to catch fish passing up the lakes one might be led to suppose that the whole must be stopped, yet in six month's time they return to the sea with such multitudes of young ones as to fill the Connecticut River for many days, and no finite being can number them.[148]

Salmon were still so plentiful in the Connecticut at that time that individuals wishing to buy shad were compelled to take a certain number of salmon as well.[149] In 1800, Edward Oliphant mentioned that salmon were still being caught along "the whole length of the Connecticut River and in most of the tributary streams," but in diminishing numbers.[150] A dam constructed at South Hadley about 1795 had considerably impeded, but did not totally obstruct passage; a few years later, however, a mill and dam at Montique practically eliminated all salmon runs above that point. With increased dam construction, very few specimens were seen in the river by 1810, and by 1815, it was rare to see them at all. The decline was reflected in the increased price paid for the fish in Connecticut: salmon taken in dip nets and seines were selling for 2 and 3 pence per pound in 1787; by 1794, they brought 4 pence a pound, and by 1798, 7 and 8 pence a pound.[151]

Salmon were fast disappearing in all their former freshwater streams, from the Connecticut to the Penobscot. Both dams and overfishing were criticized as the causes of the decline, and one New Hampshire individual offered an ominous corollary to the salmon's situation by stating in 1813 that each river possessed its own distinct salmon, and once the run was eliminated, it could not be reestablished.[152] There was little heed paid to this postulation, and the species continued its inevitable decline.

Like the Connecticut, the Merrimack River still supported good runs until the American Revolution, although it has been noted that long before 1774, salmon had stopped running past Concord.[153] As early as 1773, the people of Haverhill, Massachusetts, had noted a decline in the salmon runs past their community, and in September of that year, the General Court passed an act "to prevent the destruction of salmon in the Merrimack River," by which the practice of stretching seines and nets entirely across the stream was outlawed; seines, under the new regulation, could also be no more than 16 rods (264 feet) long.[154] Amoskeag Falls remained one of the favorite fishing spots on the river, and on June 7, 1785, one fisherman wrote, "I went to the falls towards the middle of the day and I fished at the upper setting place. I got a salmon of nine pounds, and I sold it for one-half dollar."[155] The diarist also reported a 20-pound specimen being taken by a friend. The continued construction of dams on the river escalated the decline of the fishery, however, and prompted the town of Haverhill to appoint 12 fishery wardens in 1801, and, in the following year, to revise the fishery regulations. The fish appeared to benefit little from the new limitations, however, even though the river was now kept open to its headwaters; by the time Haverhill decided to control the resource industry fully by licensing fishing stands in 1809, the runs had declined even more. Edward Oliphant had reported around 1800 that "In spring and summer considerable quantities of salmon, shad and alewives are caught which [are] either used as bait in the cod fishery or shipped, pickled, to the West Indies,"[156] but by 1817, it was obvious that the Merrimack had lost its appeal as a salmon stream. The price of the Haverhill fishing privileges bears this out: in 1815, revenues from the sale of stands totaled $91.35; the following year, $46.25; and in 1817, they had declined to $36.25.[157]

The following quote suggests that some salmon were still being taken in the Piscataqua River in 1792: "The Indian scoop-net is shaped like a pocket; the edge of which is fastened to a wooden bow, at the end of a long pole. With these are caught salmon, shad, alewives, smelt and lampreys."[158] Excessive gillnetting and the construction of dams, however, continued to reduce fish stocks as the turn of the century approached. When the bass were almost eliminated from the river by overfishing, laws were imposed, but the stocks did not recover. The salmon fishery was restricted by law to three days a week, to little avail, and Jeremy Belknap reported in 1813 that

> The salmon formerly frequented the River Piscataqua; but the numerous dams built across its branches have obstructed the course of this valuable fish, and it has, for many years, totally forsaken the river. It still ascends the Saco, Merrimack, and Connecticut.[159]

At the close of the war, the species was still abundant in the Androscoggin River, where excellent breeding grounds abounded in the gravelly beds of the upper stream and in such tributaries as the Swift River. Salmon had access up river for over 100 miles, to Rumford Falls, although they were partially hindered before this point by the falls at Lewiston. Nonetheless, specimens were still being seen at both these locations as late as 1815, although they were eliminated from the upper river

shortly afterwards by the construction of a dam at Brunswick.[160]

Until about 1800, the principal method of fishing salmon in Maine was by mesh nets, their standard length being about 40 feet; these nets were usually constructed of 7-inch mesh and were from 8 to 9 feet in depth. Obviously, with 7-inch mesh, the salmon had not yet declined to the point where consideration was being given to taking grilse. The nets employed were made of medium-weight hempen twine and were used either as stationary or drift nets. When the net was employed as a fixed one, it was set in a method that was practically universal to the whole eastern seaboard: one end was fastened at or near the shore, while the other end was secured in deep water by using a homemade anchor called a killick. Fishermen usually took advantage of islands, channels and points of land when setting their nets, and frequently the shore end of the net was actually a considerable distance from the bank, the intervening space being filled in with rock and brush. Between 1787 and 1800, the product from these nets brought Bangor area fishermen tuppence per pound, and an extra half pence per pound if the fish was pickled. The merchant who purchased this pickled product would sell it later at 4 pence per pound.

The use of these nets was generally unrestricted; in the Penobscot, however, they came under a regulation in 1814 which stipulated that they were not to extend to more than one-third the width of the stream. After 1800, these hemp nets began to be replaced by brush and stake weirs, which rapidly reached a high degree of sophistication. At first, the weirs were simple brushwood divides, consisting of three compartments or pounds. Sometime before 1815, however, an enterprising Irishman, Tristram Holliday, introduced to the inside of these structures, a netting made of two-stranded cord or marline, and also introduced wooden floors to the pounds. By this time, the side nets were being modified into traps, with configurations resembling an arrow.[161] Such advances in equipment, while initially enhancing catch returns, guaranteed depletion of stock over the long term, and were a contributing factor to the continuing decline of the New England river fisheries during this period.

Fish and Be Damned

In the late 18th and early 19th centuries, salmon were still relatively safe in the sea-life segment of their migratory cycle, suffering only the predations normally expected in the natural food chain of their saltwater environment. The principal deep sea fishery by man was still centered on other species — predominantly the cod — and this effort had no direct effect on the salmon resource. There were no commercial interceptions on the species' migratory routes at sea or upon their feeding grounds, and even the coastal fishery for such species as herring and mackerel had only minimal impact upon salmon. Offshore drift nets and trap nets had not yet made their appearance, and the limited number of tidal weirs, beach seines and shore gill nets took only random and inadvertent catches of the species. It was only when the salmon reached the river estuaries on their way to the spawning grounds that they began to run the gauntlet of man's attention.

Upon these rivers they were not only subjected to a direct and growing commercial and domestic exploitation — which, no matter how intense, would not completely eliminate the species — but also were encountering a potentially more devastating hazard in the form of dams. Where, in times past, some salmon might escape the fisherman's inefficient fishing devices, by 1815 entire watercourses were being rendered inaccessible by man-made barriers, and were thus unproductive for the salmon in their life cycle. Although fish pass legislation was enacted in several colonies — 1786 in Nova Scotia, 1810 in New Brunswick — the implementation of these regulations was rarely effected, not least because of the influence wielded by the mill owners themselves. The outlook for the future was not bright: by the beginning of the second quarter of the 19th century, the salmon appeared to be truly damned.

NOTES

[1]George W. Brown, *Building the Canadian Nation* (Toronto: Dent, 1848), pp. 135–143. New Brunswick had been separated from Nova Scotia in 1784.

[2]James Hannay, *History of New Brunswick* (Saint John: Bowes, 1909), I, 136.

[3]W. O. Raymond, "The Founding of Shelburne," in *Collections* of the New Brunswick Historical Society, VIII (1909), 207.

[4]S. Hollingsworth, *The Present State of Nova Scotia with a Brief Account of Canada and the British Islands on the Coast of North America* (Edinburgh: Creech, 1787), pp. 61–62.

[5]W. S. MacNutt, *New Brunswick: A History, 1784-1867* (Toronto: Macmillan, 1963), p. 88. Patrick Campbell, *Travels in America*, ed. H. H. Langton (Toronto: Champlain Society, 1937), p. 75, notes that the abundance of salmon was considered a drawback to early agriculture in the colony: "The great risque would be, and which has already hurt the lower settlement on the river Saint John[,] that the vast abundance of fish might induce the settlers to apply more to fishing than to the cultivation of their lands." Harold A. Innis, *The Cod Fisheries* (Toronto: University of Toronto Press, 1954), p. 263fn., notes that this salmon resource began to support a considerable trade with the West Indies.

[6]*Statutes of New Brunswick*, 26 Geo. III, c. 33.

[7]*Ibid.*, 33 Geo. III, c. 9; 34 Geo. III, c. 3; 39 Geo. III, c. 5; 50 Geo. III, c. 20.

[8]*Statutes of Nova Scotia*, 26 Geo. III, c. 7.

[9]George Patterson, *A History of the County of Pictou, Nova Scotia* (Montreal: Davison, 1877; reprinted Belleville, Ont.: Mika, 1972), p. 206.

[10]Quoted in James J. Talman, ed., *Basic Documents in Canadian History* (Princeton, New Jersey: Van Nostrand,

1959), p. 44. At the close of the war in 1783, an act was passed which forbade trade between the British colonies and the United States, except that which was carried in British vessels. Americans were also prohibited to trade fish in the British West Indies at this time; see Innis, *The Cod Fisheries*, p. 220.

[11]See statistical information on salmon exports contained in Hannay, *History of New Brunswick*, I, p. 312; Montgomery R. Martin, *History of Nova Scotia* (London: Whittaker and Co., 1837), p. 62; D.W. Prowse, *A History of Newfoundland* (London: MacMillan and Co., 1895) p. 679; and "Shipping Returns, Lower Canada" in PAC, Colonial Office Papers Supplementary Documents, I Miscellaneous 18 (Fisheries, 1712–1852).

[12]"Message of Samuel Adams" (1781), excerpted in John C. Pearson, ed., *The Fish and Fisheries of Colonial North America* (Washington: Department of the Interior, 1972), p. 604.

[13]Charles B. Elliott, *The United States and the North-eastern Fisheries* (Minneapolis: University of Minnesota, 1887), p. 26. D. H. Montgomery, ed., *Benjamin Franklin: His Life*, (Boston: Ginn, 1906), p. 285.

[14]Oswald to Strachey, 8 January 1783, in Colonial Officer [hereafter C.O.], Supplementary Papers, Misc. 1, Vol. 18, Public Archives of Canada [hereafter PAC].

[15]Wallace Graham, "The Fisheries of British North America and The United States Fishermen", in NSHS Coll, (Halifax: Wm. MacNab & Son, 1909), Vol. XIV, p. 2.

[16]Charles B. Elliott, *The United States and the North-eastern Fisheries* (Minneapolis: The University of Minnesota, 1887), p. 39.

[17]*Ibid.*, p. 58. MacNutt, *New Brunswick*, p. 176.

[18]Hollingsworth, *The Present State of Nova Scotia*, p. 193.

[19]Innis, *The Cod Fisheries*, pp. 92, 283.

[20]*Bas Saint-Laurent Gaspésie* (Québec: Ministère du Tourisme, de la chasse et de la pêche, 1972), pp. 94–97.

[21]Robert Clooney, *A Compendious History of the Northern Part of the Province of New Brunswick and the District of Gaspé in Lower Canada* (Halifax: Howe, 1832), pp. 171–172.

[22]George Heriot, *Travels Through the Canadas* (London: (1807); reprinted Edmonton: Hurtig, 1971), pp. 39–40.

[23]"Grant to Peter Bonamy, May 22, 1788," Dalhousie Museum Archives, Dalhousie, N.B.

[24]Plan of the Town of Dalhousie, (1820) Dalhousie Museum Archives, Dalhousie, N.B.

[25]John Stewart, *An Account of Prince Edward Island in the Gulph of St. Lawrence, North America* (London: Winchester, 1806), p. 299. Moses Perley, *The Sea and River Fisheries of New Brunswick* (Fredericton: Simpson, 1852), p. 76.

[26]Campbell, *Travells in Canada*, p. 76.

[27]Quoted in *ibid.*

[28]Hugh Gray, *Letters from Canada* (London: Longman, 1809; reprinted Toronto: Coles, 1971), pp. 225–226.

[29]W. H. Davidson, *William Davidson: 1740-1790, The North Shore Leader* (Newcastle, New Brunswick: n.p., 1947), p. 57. W. A. Spray, "Davidson, John" in *Dictionary of Canadian Biography* (Toronto: University of Toronto Press, 1979), IV, 195–197.

[30]W. F. Ganong, ed., "Historical-Geographical Documents Relating to New Brunswick," in *Collections* of the New Brunswick Historical Society, IX (1914), p. 335.

[31]Quoted in W. F. Ganong, "The Founding of Modern Settlement on the Miramichi," in *ibid.*, p. 335.

[32]MacNutt, *New Brunswick*, p. 88. Davidson was no doubt relieved to see his enemy leave the colony in 1787.

[33]*New Brunswick Statutes*, 26 Geo. III, c. 33.

[34]Esther Clark Wright, *The Loyalists of New Brunswick* (Fredericton: 1955) pp. 146–147.

[35]*Journals of the House of Assembly of New Brunswick*, 1791.

[36]Campbell, *Travells in Canada*, pp. 63, 66. Wright, *The Miramichi*, p. 30, notes that besides Davidson, another large salmon fishing operation had begun on the river in 1788, that of James Fraser.

[37]Campbell, *Travells in Canada*, pp. 65–66.

[38]New Brunswick Statutes, 31 Geo. III, c. 13. Davidson, *Davidson*, p. 68.

[39]*New Brunswick Journals*, 1791.

[40]*New Brunswick Statutes*, 39 Geo. III, c. 5; 56 Geo. III, c. 2.

[41]Joseph Gubbins, *Gubbins' New Brunswick Journals*, ed. Howard Temperley (Fredericton: King's Landing Corporation, 1980), p. 80.

[42]Moses Perley, *The Sea and River Fisheries of New Brunswick* (Fredericton: J. Simpson, 1852), pp. 54–56, 79–80. Gubbins, *Journals*, p. 70, 78.

[43]Exports of salmon from Miramichi were reported to be seventy-one barrels and thirty-five tierces for the period 16 July to 28 October 1808; 179 barrels in 1810. See Naval Office Records, New Brunswick Museum Archives.

[44]Stewart, *An Account of Prince Edward Island*, p. 299. Campbell, *Travells in Canada*, p. 66: "it takes only twenty to twenty-five salmon of the [Restigouche] river to make a tierce; whereas from thirty-six to forty of those of the [Miramichi] are required to make one."

[45]Clooney, *History of Northern New Brunswick*, p. 56.

[46]Wright, *The Loyalists of New Brunswick*, (Fredericton, 1955), pp. 116, 244–250.

[47]*Canada's First City*, (Saint John: Langley Printing Co. Ltd., 1962), p. 31.

[48]*New Brunswick Statutes*, 26 Geo. III, c. 33. Although subject to most of the provisions of the provincial Fisheries Act, licensing of the Saint John harbour fishery was still vested in the city council until 1919, when the National Harbours Board took over the right. In 1971, however, the harbour fishery came fully under federal jurisdiction, being licensed by the Department of Fisheries.

[49]Campbell, *Travells in Canada*, p. 27.

[50]Complaint of Jabez Husted, and Charge against Boggs and Leydick, in Jarvis Papers, New Brunswick Museum Archives. Strangely enough, Godfrey Leydick had held many appointments from the city corporation, including deputy clerk of the market and high constable, and along with Boggs, in April 1794, was appointed an overseer of the fishery. The actions of overseers in carrying out their duties were often brought into question — at times with some reason. See *Canada's First City* (St. John: Lingley, 1962), pp. 92, 139, 165.

[51]Campbell, *Travells in Canada*, pp. 26, 27.

[52]*Ibid.*, p. 28.

[53]*Royal Gazette* (Saint John), 21 December 1798.

[54]*Ibid.*, 9 March 1798.

[55]Quoted in W. O. Raymond, "The Fishery Quarrel," in *New Brunswick Magazine*, III, 2 (August 1899), 62; see also *Royal Gazette*, (Saint John) 5 March 1804, 2 April 1804.

[56]Raymond, "The Fishery Quarrel," pp. 57–66. Castlereigh to Ludlow, October 1807, in C.O., Supplementary Papers, Misc. 1, Vol. 18, PAC.

[57]Naval Office Records, 1808-1811, New Brunswick Museum Archives (C.O. 193, Vol. 1 & 2).

[58]Campbell, *Travells in Canada*, p. 28. Grace Aiton, *The Story of Sussex and Vicinity* (n.p.: Kings County Historical Society, 1967), p. 41.

[59]Gubbins, *Journals*, p. 13.

[60]Campbell, *Travells in Canada*, pp. 46–47.

[61]*Ibid.*, p. 47.

[62]George Sproule's Map of the Scoodic Shore, 1802, Map Section, PAC.

[63]*Ibid.* Such dams were still in evidence in the Maritimes in the twentieth century; the remains of such a structure could be seen on the Medway River, at Greenfield, Nova Scotia, in 1967.

[64]Orders of the General Session of Charlotte County, September 1793, in Hazen Papers, New Brunswick Museum Archives.

[65]Overseers of the Fishery to Messrs. John and William Watterten, 28 August 1803, in *ibid*.

[66]Notice of Peter McDermaid, Constable, 13 December 1805, in *ibid*.

[67]Naval Office Records, 1811, New Brunswick Museum Archives.

[68]Quoted in Perley, *The Fisheries of New Brunswick*, p. 126.

[69]*Ibid.*, pp. 123–127. Current estimates of salmon potential are from unpublished and preliminary work carried out by various members of the biological staff of Environment Canada, Fisheries and Marine Service, Maritimes Region.

[70]Edward Oliphant, *The History of North America and Its United States* (Edinburgh: Johnstone, 1800), p. 32.

[71]Stewart, *An Account of Prince Edward Island*, pp. 84–85.

[72]William Menzies Whitelaw, *The Maritimes and Canada before Confederation* (Toronto: Oxford University Press, 1966), pp. 23–28.

[73]Walter Johnstone, "Letters and Travels," in D. C. Harvey, ed., *Journey to the Island of St. John* (Toronto: Macmillan, 1955), p. 113.

[74]J. W. MacDonald, *History of Antigonish County* (1876), ed. R. A. MacLean (Antigonish, N.S.: Formac, 1975), p. 11. notes that in nearby Antigonish County, it was said that the early settlers commonly took forty or fifty salmon in a morning, even from inferior nets.

[75]Patterson, *History of Pictou County*, p. 205.

[76]*Ibid.*, p. 206.

[77]W. S. MacNutt, *The Atlantic Provinces* (Toronto: McClelland & Stewart, 1972), pp. 64, 66–67.

[78]Oliphant, *History of North America*, p. 24.

[79]Clara Dennis, *Cape Breton Over* (Toronto: Ryerson, 1942), p. 9. Richard Brown, *A History of the Island of Cape Breton* (London: Sampson Low, 1869), pp. 381, 394. Brown notes, p. 381, that Robin claimed to be the first "adventurer" on the island, 1764.

[80]John Lorne McDougall, *History of Inverness County* (Truro, N.S.: n.p., 1922; reprinted Belleville, Ont.: Mika, 1972), p. 423.

[81]James F. More, *The History of Queens County* (Halifax: Nova Scotia Printing, 1873; reprinted Belleville, Ont.: Mika, 1972), p. 82.

[82]Quoted in Mather Byles DesBrisay, *History of the County of Lunenburg* (Toronto: Briggs, 1895; reprinted Belleville, Ont.: Mika, 1972), pp. 368, 369.

[83]"The pilot wounded a fine large salmon with his musket, and afterwards caught him with his hands" (3 May 1783), quoted in W. O. Raymond, "The Founding of Shelburne," p. 210. In 1788, Shelburne exported, apart from dried cod, 4193 casks of pickled fish and 61 casks of smoked salmon; undoubtedly some of the pickled fish were also salmon; see Beckles Willson, *Nova Scotia: The Province that has been Passed By* (London: Constable, 1911), p. 122.

[84]Phyllis R. Blakely, "Boston King: A Black Loyalist," in Phyllis R. Blakely and John N. Grant, ed. *Eleven Exiles* (Toronto: Dundurn, 1982), p. 280.

[85]Quoted in George S. Brown, *Yarmouth, Nova Scotia: A Sequel to Campbell's History* (Boston: Rand Avery, 1888), p. 135.

[86]Quoted in DesBrisay, *History of Lunenburg County*. pp. 358–358.

[87]Brown, *Yarmouth*, p. 327.

[88]Simeon Perkins, *The Diary of Simeon Perkins*, ed. Harold Innis (Toronto: Champlain Society, 1948), I, 21–72, *passim*. More, *History of Queens County*, pp. 80–81. Innis, *The Cod Fisheries*, p. 239, reports that 1429 barrels of salmon were entered at the Liverpool customs house in 1803.

[89]More, *History of Queens County*, pp. 85, 116–117. Thomas F. Knight, *Report on the Fisheries of Nova Scotia* (Halifax: Grant, 1867), p. 26, states that in 1815, as many as eight hundred tierces (378 000 live lb) of salmon were being taken from one of Nova Scotia's larger rivers. This was probably the Mersey, although the Medway and LaHave rivers cannot be ruled out. It is rather difficult to accept that such a catch actually came from one river system.

[90]Isaiah W. Wilson, *The Geography and History of the County of Digby* (Halifax: Halloway, 1900), p. 104. W. A. Calnek, *History of the County of Annapolis* (Toronto: Briggs, 1897; reprinted Belleville, Ont.: Mika, 1972), p. 210.

[91]Hollingsworth, *The Present State of Nova Scotia*, p. 62.

[92]T. B. Akins, "History of Halifax City," in *Collections of the Nova Scotia Historical Society*, VIII (1895), 140.

[93]Gray, *Letters from Canada*, p. 217. Heriot, *Travels Through the Canadas*, p. 101; on pp. 228–229, Heriot mentions that prior to 1769, not more than twelve small vessels were engaged in the fisheries of the St. Lawrence River.

[94]Heriot, *Travels Through the Canadas*, p. 52.

[95]Innis, *The Cod Fisheries*, p. 283; on p. 236, Innis notes that with an associate named Crawford, Lymburner had also leased the St. Paul's River at the northeastern extremity of Quebec's territory.

[96]Gray, *Letters from Canada*, pp. 24–25.

[97]James McKenzie, "The Journal of James McKenzie" (1808), in *Les Bourgeois de la Compagnie du Nord-Ouest*, ed., L. R. Masson, (Quebec: De L'Imprimerie Générale A. Coté Cie, 1890).

[98]Heriot, *Travels Through the Canadas*, p. 52. Innis, *The Cod Fisheries*, p. 236.

[99]Gray, *Letters from Canada*, pp. 216–231. C.O. 47, Vol. 80, 81, *passim*, PAC.

[100]*Royal Gazette* (Saint John), 14 January 1805. Gray, *Letters from Canada*, pp. 171–173, 373.

[101]Gray, *Letters from Canada*, pp. 225–226.

[102]Jacques Bellin map, "Partie Orientale de la Nouvelle France ou du Canada," 1755; copy in possession of the author.

[103]Robert Legget, *Ottawa Waterway* (Toronto: University of Toronto Press, 1975), pp. 11, 17, 20, 23.

[104]Quoted in Edwin C. Guillet, *Early Life in Upper Canada* (Toronto: Ontario Publishing, 1933), p. 264. The date of this quote is given in terms of the Julian calendar, which was ten days in advance of the Gregorian calendar now in use. Depending on the actual days for which our observer saw salmon spawning in a Julian September, it is conceivable that the actual spawning season could have been as early as late August.

[105]G. Power, *The Salmon of Ungava Bay*, Technical Paper No. 22 (Montreal: Arctic Institute of North America, 1969), p. 45.

[106]Quoted in Guillet, *Early Life*, p. 267.

[107]*Ibid.*, p. 177.

[108]Mrs. John Graves Simcoe, *The Diary of Mrs. John Graves Simcoe*, ed. J. Ross Robertson (Toronto: Briggs, 1911; reprinted Toronto: Coles, 1973), p. 187.

[109]Robert Gourlay, *Statistical Account of Upper Canada* (London: Simpkin and Marshall, 1822), I, 268.

[110]*York Gazette*, May 1798, quoted in Ken Johnstone, *The Vanishing Harvest* (Montreal: Star, 1972), pp. 23–24. The description places the farm on the east branch of the Don River, near the present town of Thornhill.

[111]Simco, *Diary*, p. 139.

[112]Guillet, *Early Life*, p. 114.

[113]Paul Kane, *Wanderings of an Artist* (New York: Longman, Brown, Green, Longmans & Roberts, 1859; reprinted Edmonton: Hurtig, 1968), p. 22.

[114]W. Sherwood Fox, "The Literature of *Salmo salar* in Lake Ontario and Tributary Streams," in *Proceedings and Transactions* of the Royal Society of Canada, third series, XXIV (1930), 48. Robert S. Allen, "Mr. Secretary Jarvis," in Blakely and Grant, *Eleven Exiles*, p. 308, notes that William Jarvis, a local magistrate, attempted to encourage a trade in York salmon.

[115]Simcoe, *Diary*, pp. 209, 335, notes that while the fishing method may have been "very disagreeable," the taste of salmon was not; she claimed that salmon was excellent when cooked in a sauce made from wild gooseberries.

[116]Fox, "The Literature of *Salmo salar*," p. 47.

[117]Simcoe, *Diary*, pp. 238, 331. Fox, "The Literature of *Salmo salar*," p. 48. Quoted in Edward E. Prince, "The Maximum Size of Fishes and its Causes," in *Annual Report* of the Department of Marine and Fisheries, 1903 (Ottawa: King's Printer, 1904), Appendix II, p. 1x.

[118]Heriot, *Travels Through the Canadas*, p. 137. See also *Annual Report* of the Department of Marine and Fisheries, 1903, p. 141. Simcoe, *Diary*, pp. 222, 323.

[119]*Statutes of Upper Canada to the Time of the Union* (Toronto: Queen's Printer, 1841), 47 Geo. III, c. 12. R. M. Baldwin and J. Baldwin, *The Baldwins and the Great Experiment* (Don Mills, Ont.: Longmans, 1969), frontispiece. The colonial acts of Quebec, which were applicable to this region before the division of the colony into Upper and Lower Canada, did not contain any reference to the fishery.

[120]Gourlay, *Statistical Account*, I, 176.

[121]*Upper Canada Statutes*, 50 Geo. III, c. 3.

[122]Heriot, *Travels Through the Canadas*, pp. 518–519.

[123]W. D. Wilson, "The Salmon of Lake Champlain and its Tributaries," in *Report of the United States Commission of Fish and Fisheries* (1874-75) (Washington: Government Printing Office, 1876), III, 532.

[124]*Ibid.*, p. 533. Oliphant, *History of North America*, p. 116.

[125]D. W. Prowse, *A History of Newfoundland* (London: Macmillan, 1895; reprinted Belleville, Ont.: Mika, 1972), p. 379; see also Elliott, *The Northeastern Fisheries*, pp. 26, 40.

[126]Elliott, *The Northeastern Fisheries*, pp. 31–32. Prowse, *History of Newfoundland*, p. 336. See also note 15, this chapter.

[127]Innis, *The Cod Fisheries*, p. 215.

[128]John J. Mannion. "Settlers and Traders in Western Newfoundland," in John J. Mannion, ed., *The Peopling of Newfoundland* (Toronto: University of Toronto Press, 1977), p. 244. Innis, *The Cod Fisheries*, p. 215 reports that one man at Humber River exported seventy-six tierces of salmon to St. John's in 1787, but did not continue his efforts the following year, presumably due to French pressure. As more English settlers came to the St. Georges Bay region, they eventually overcame French opposition. By 1808, the settlers and salmoniers were reported to have taken around eight hundred tierces (equivalent to 378 400 live pounds) of salmon from the region.

[129]Memorial of John Noble and Andrew Pinson to Lord Carmarthen, and statement of Matthew Furlong, 1788, in C.O. Supplementary Papers I, Misc. Documents Vol. 18 (Fisheries 1712–1852), PAC.

[130]James P. Howley, *The Beothucks or Red Indians* (Cambridge: Cambridge University Press, 1915; reprinted Toronto: Coles, 1974), p. 59. Many of the Newfoundland fishing stations were abandoned at the close of each season, but an increasing number of individuals were beginning to winter at these posts in order to facilitate early preparation for the next year's fishery. Such arrangements also had the advantage of extending the effective fishing season at both ends. It was not always by choice, either, that people wintered over. C.O. 325, Vol. 7, p. 131, PAC, cites an incident in which two boys were left behind at a fishing station by accident, and without any payment for their year's labor, which meant that they could not get back to England. They were fortunate, however, in finding a trader who agreed to employ them for two years in the salmon fishery, leaving them on the island to prepare for each season's activities.

[131]Innis, *The Cod Fisheries*, p. 294. D. F. Beamish, "Lester, Benjamin" in *Dictionary of Canadian Biography* (Toronto: University of Toronto Press, 1983), V, 490–492.

[132]Account of the Salmon and Seal Fishery on the Coast of Labrador, 1785, in C.O. Supplementary Papers I, Misc. Documents Vol. 18 (Fisheries, 1712–1852), PAC.

[133]*Ibid.* Prowse, *History of Newfoundland*, p. 601.

[134]Joseph Bouchette, *A Topographical Dictionary of the Province of Lower Canada* (London: Longman, 1832), pp. 1–2.

[135]See statistical information in Prowse, *History of Newfoundland*, p. 697, and in W. G. Gosling, *Labrador: Its Discovery, Exploration and Development*, (London: Alston Rivers Ltd., 1910), p. 476.

[136]Quoted in Innis, *The Cod Fisheries*, p. 231. C.O. 325, Vol. 7, p. 276, PAC.

[137]Stewart, *An Account of Prince Edward Island*, p. 299.

[138]Innis, *The Cod Fisheries*, p. 238.

[139]Queries answered respecting the American Fishery on the Coast of Labrador in the season of 1806, in C.O. Supplementary Papers I, Misc. Documents Vol. 18 (Fisheries, 1712–1852), PAC.

[140]Report of Richard Keats, 27 July 1814, in *ibid.*

[141]*Ibid.*

[142]Innis, *The Cod Fisheries*, p. 241.

[143]Prowse, *History of Newfoundland*, p. 710. C.O. Supplementary Papers, Misc. 1, Vol. 18, PAC, notes that Governor Keats reported, 1813, that "the quantity of fish taken this season exceeds that of any former year."

[144]Prowse, *History of Newfoundland*, pp. 402–403.

[145]Elliott, *The Northeastern Fisheries*, pp. 26, 40.

[146]Quoted in D. M. Montgomery, *Benjamin Franklin: His Life* (Boston: Ginn, 1906), p. 298.

[147]*Ibid.*, p. 288.

[148]Elliott, *The Northeastern Fisheries*, p. 40. Quoted in Samuel A. Peters, *General History of Connecticut* (New York: Appleton, 1877), p. 44.

[149]Anthony Netboy, *The Atlantic Salmon, A Vanishing Species?* (London: Faber, 1968), p. 323.

[150]Oliphant, *History of North America*, p. 116.

[151]Marshall McDonald, "The Connecticut and Housatonic Rivers," in G. Browne Goode, ed., *The Fisheries and Fishing Industries of the United States*, (Washington: U.S. Commission of Fish and Fisheries, 1887), V, 663–669.

[152]"We shall find on examination that the fish though of the same kind in one river are much larger and fatter than in any other river in its vicinity. If these fish were suffered to intermix, the difference now so very apparent would not exist. If the fish are not directed by some laws in nature to the rivers in which they were spawned, how shall we account for the salmon being in Connecticut river, and in Merrimack, and the rivers lying between perfectly destitute of those fish? Was there not something irresistibly enchanting in the waters in which they respectively originated, we should probably find some straggling salmon in the intermediate rivers." A Letter from the Hon. General Lincoln to the Author [Jeremy Belknap], (1791), quoted in John C. Pearson, ed., *The Fish and Fisheries of Colonial North America*, U.S. Fish and Wildlife Service (Washington: Department of the Interior, 1972), p. 218. It was not difficult to form a theory of separate stocks by also observing the differences in the timing of the runs into the various rivers. As early as 1760, one historian wrote: "Salmon are a high latitude fish. They are not be be found south of New England; the farther south, the later they set in and continue a shorter time. For instance, in Connecticut River they set in the beginning of May and continue only about three weeks; in Merrimack River they set in beginning of April, to spawn, and lie in the deep cold brooks until September and October, then silently (so as not to be observed) and with dispatch, they return to the sea; in Chebucto, Cape Breton and Newfoundland, they continue the greater part of the year." See William Douglas, "A Summary, Historical and Political, of the First Planting, Progressive Improvements, and Present State of the British Settlements in North America, 1760," excerpted in Pearson, *Fish and Fisheries*, p. 215.

[153]Robert A. Gross, *The Minutemen and Their World* (New York: Hill and Wang, 1976), p. 4.

[154]George W. Chase, "The History of Haverhill," excerpted in Pearson, *Fish and Fisheries*, p. 508.

[155]"The Diary of Matthew Patten, 1785," excerpted in *ibid.*, p. 651.

[156]Chase, "The History of Haverhill," p. 508, 509. Oliphant, *History of North America*, p. 145.

[157]Chase, "The History of Haverhill," excerpted in Pearson, *Fish and Fisheries*, p. 509.

[158]Jeremy Belknap, "The History of New Hampshire," excerpted in Pearson, *Fish and Fisheries*, p. 261.

[159]*Ibid.*, p. 263.

[160]C. G. Atkins, "The River Fisheries of Maine", in G. Brown Goode, ed., *The Fish and Fishing Industries of the United States*. (Washington: U.S. Commission of Fish and Fisheries, 18) I, p. 723.

[161]*Ibid.*, pp. 679–710, *passim*. Alfred L. Meister, "A Look Back at the Atlantic Salmon Fishery in Maine," in *The Atlantic Salmon Journal*, (Winter 1964–65), 14.

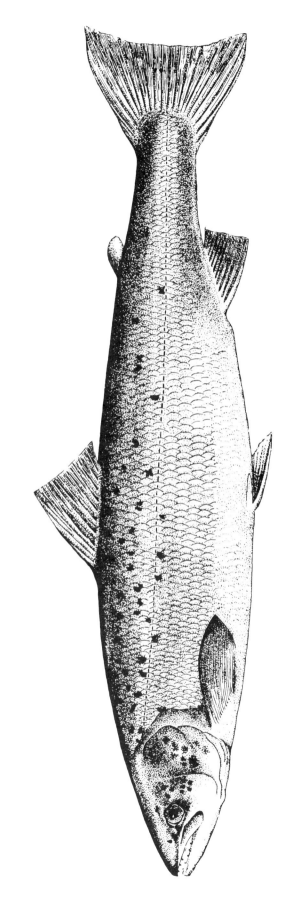

The Atlantic salmon — "What a fish should be!" *Source: A. H. Leim and W. B. Scott. Fishes of the Atlantic coast of Canada.* [1966]

An Atlantic salmon leaping approximately twelve feet at Orrin Falls, Ross-shire, Scotland. *Source: Salmon and Trout Magazine.*

Angling, in Egypt, ca. 2000 B.C. *Source: From a wall drawing reproduced in Percy Newberry's Archaeological survey in Egypt, Beni Hasan. [1893–1896]*

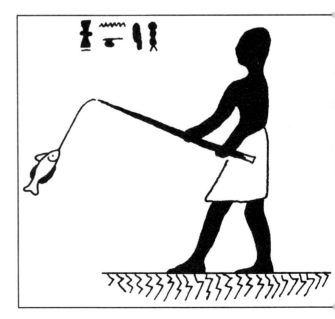

A fifteenth century angler. *Source: Dame Juliana Berners. A Treatyse of fysshynge wyth an angle. [1496]*

Angling at Fort Frederick, Saint John River, New Brunswick, 1758. *Source: A north view of Fort Frederick. w.c. 8⅞″ × 13″, 1758: An original painting by Thomas Davies (1737–1812) in the National Gallery of Canada (NGC 6269).*

Aboriginal Distribution of Atlantic Salmon in North America

Virtually all of the naturally accessible watercourses in eastern North America from Ungava Bay to Long Island Sound were historically reported to have contained salmon. Map numbers identify some of these streams and locate the upper limits of former salmon occurrence or migration. The names of the rivers are listed on the facing page and keyed to the map numbers. Bracketed information beside the name of the river identifies the specific upper limit of salmon occurrence by location name, or by number of miles from the mouth of the river. *Source: Department of Fisheries and Oceans.*

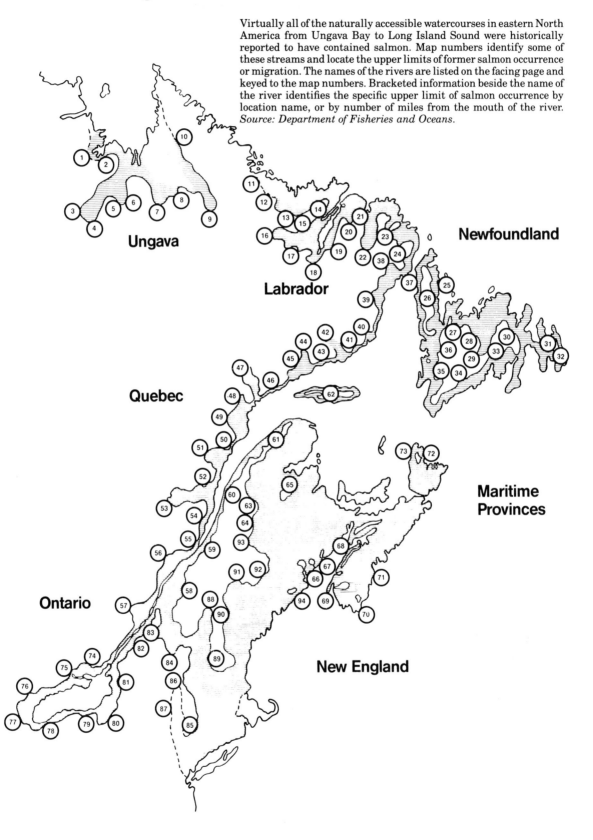

River Identification

Ungava

1 Leaf River (Leaf River Lakes)
2 (Finger Lakes Rapids)
3 (Natwak Lake)
4 (confluence of Delay River)
5 (Aigneau Lake Falls)
6 Koksoak River (Limestone Falls)
7 Wheeler River (lower reaches)
8 Whale River (mile 100)
9 George River (Helen Falls)
10 Ford River (mile 12)

Labrador

11 Siamese Lakes Brook (mile 6)
12 Hunt River
13 Kanairiktok River (barrier falls)
14 Big River
15 (Napishish Lake)
16 Naskaupi River (Maid Marion Falls)
17 Beaver River
18 Hamilton River (Muskrat Falls)
19 Kenamu River (Kenamu Rapids)
20 North River
21 Eagle River (mile 4)
22 Paradise River (headwaters)
23 Alexis River (mile 33)
24 Pinware River (mile 15)

Newfoundland

25 Cloud River (mile 5)
26 Cat Arm River (Cat Arm Falls)
27 Hampden River (headwaters)
28 Exploits River (Grand Falls)
29 Gander River (headwaters)
30 Southwest Brook (mile 4)
31 Northeast River (Quigley Falls)
32 Salmonier River (Murphys Falls)
33 North Bay River (Smokey Falls)
34 White Bear River (mile 12)
35 Serpentine River (mile 8)
36 Humber River
37 East River (mile 20)

Quebec

38 St Paul River (mile 40)
39 St Augustin River (mile 25)
40 Little Mecatina River (mouth)
41 Washeecootai River (mile 18)
42 Natashquan River
43 Nabisipi River (mouth)
44 Romaine River
45 St Jean River (mile 25)
46 Pigou River (mile 4)
47 Moisie River
48 Pentecote River

49 Godbout River
50 Manicouagan River (mile 3)
51 Betsiamites River (mile 40)
52 Portneuf River (mile 8)
53 Saguenay River (Lake St John)
54 Du Gouffre River
55 Jacques Cartier River (mile 10)
56 St Maurice River
57 Ottawa River (?) (Chaudiere Falls)
58 St Francis River (Hamming Falls)
59 Chaudiere River (Chaudiere Falls)
60 Montmagny River (Montmagny Falls)
61 St Anne River (mile 54)
62 Vaureal River (Vaureal Falls)

New Brunswick

63 Restigouche River (headwaters)
64 Saint John River (Grand Falls)
65 Nepisiguit River (Grand Falls)
66 Magaguadavic River (St George)
67 LePreau River (mouth)

Nova Scotia

68 (Cobequid and North mountains)
69 Sissiboo River (Weymouth Falls)
70 Jordan River (mile 8)
71 LaHave River (Morgan Falls)
72 Indian Brook (Big Falls)
73 Cheticamp River (mile 11)

Ontario

74 Salmon River (headwaters)
75 Trent River (Fenelon Falls)
76 Humber River (Bond Head)
77 Grindstone Creek
78 Niagara River (Niagara Falls)

New England

79 Genesee River (mile 7)
80 Oswego River (headwaters)
81 Salmon River (mile 25)
82 Salmon River
83 Big Chazy River
84 Bouquet River (mile 3)
85 Housatonic River (Falls Village)
86 Hudson River (?) (Glens Falls)
87 Mohawk River (?) (Cohoes Falls)
88 Connecticut River (Beecher Falls)
89 Merrimack River (Lincoln)
90 Androscoggin River (Rumford Falls)
91 Kennebec River (Carratunk Falls)
92 Penobscot River (Grand Falls)
93 Aroostook River (mile 100)
94 Pleasant River (Saco Falls)

Amerindian fish weir. *Source: Detail from John White's drawing of Amerindian fishing techniques. 1585. In Charles Waterman, Fishing in America. Ridge Press, New York, 1975, p. 16.*

Aboriginal stone weight used on fishing lines or nets. *Source: George MacBeath, Ph.D., and Dorothy Chamberlin, New Brunswick, the story of our province, p. 11.*

Amerindians spearing salmon. *Source: R. G. A. Levigne. Echoes from the backwoods. [1846]*

William Davidson's salmon fishery on the South-west Miramichi River, 1786. *Source: Collections of the New Brunswick Historical Society, No. 9, p. 326. [1914]*

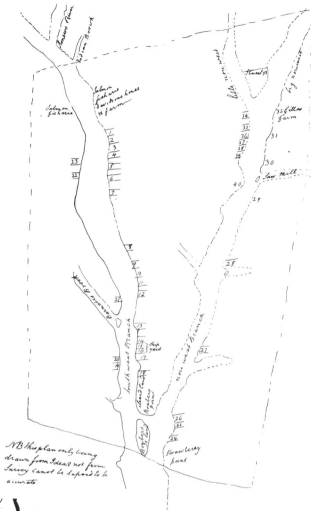

The Loyalist salmon fishery of Lake Ontario. *Source: K. M. Lizars. The Valley of the Humber, 1615–1913, p. 104, 1913, facsimile edition published in 1974 by Coles Publishing Company. The original map was drawn by D. W. Smyth in 1800 and is in the Public Archives of Canada.*

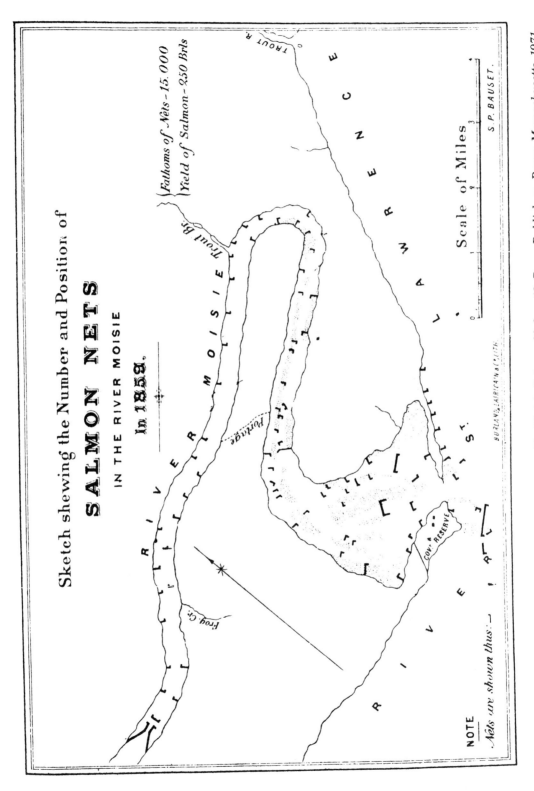

The Moisie salmon fishery, 1859. *Source: Edward Weeks. The Moisie Salmon Club, p. 13, Barre Publishers, Barre, Massachusetts, 1971.*

This "old style" float, wing, hook, or gill net was the only type of salmon trap used in Chaleur Bay prior to 1878. *Source: Annual Report of the Department of Marine and Fisheries, 1890, Part 2, Figure 1.*

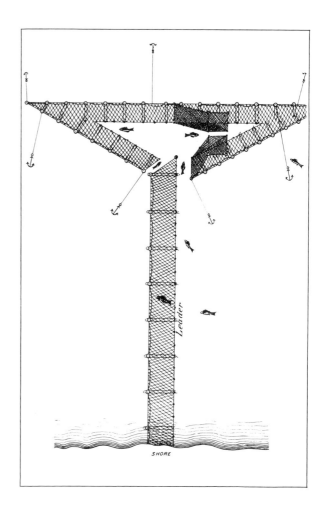

A salmon weir in Saint John Harbour, New Brunswick. *Source: Sport with Gun and Rod. Alfred M. Mayer, ed., p. 408. [1883]*

"A Canadian salmon leap": one of Canada's earliest fishways, as used in Quebec, ca. 1855. *Source: The Canadian Journal of Science, Literature, and History, No. VII, p. 2. [1857]*

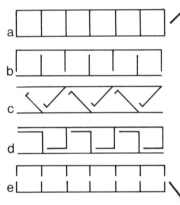

a, b.   Old fishway designs used in Canada and the United States prior to 1865.

c.   The Rogers Fishway: designed ca. 1867 by W. H. Rogers of Amherst, Nova Scotia.

d.   The Brackett Fishway: developed in Massachusetts ca. 1867 for use on New England streams.

e.   The Hockin Fishway.

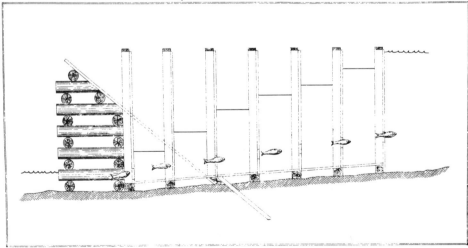

The Hockin Fishway: developed by Inspector of Fisheries Robert Hockin, ca. 1890, for use in maritime streams. *Source: Annual Report of the Department of Marine and Fisheries, 1890, Appendix A, Plate I.*

La Canadienne: Canada's first fisheries patrol vessel. *Source: Thomas E. Appleton. Usque ad Mare, Department of Transport, Ottawa, 1968.*

Salmon barrels on the beach at Gaspé. *Source: George Browne. The River St. Lawrence, p. 29.* [1905]

Dominion salmon culture station at Newcastle Creek, Ontario: (a) bird's eye view; (b) ground plan. *Source: Annual Report of the Department of Marine and Fisheries, 1877.*

The hatching building. *Source: Annual Report of the Department of Marine and Fisheries, 1877.*

The reception house. *Source: Annual Report of the Department of Marine and Fisheries, 1877.*

CHAPTER

VIII

Disregard and Destruction 1815-1845

Manifest Destiny

The 35-year period that followed the War of 1812 was one in which considerable growth was seen in the economic and social development of eastern North America. Between 1815 and 1845, approximately 8 million European immigrants landed on the Atlantic mainland of the continent[1] — a human flood which had an immediate and lasting effect on what was left of the original natural resources of the colonies. Among other things, there was a surge in exploitation of the inland, coastal, and sea fisheries, with the effect that the decline of certain anadromous stocks of fish was accelerated. With the axe and the plow, the new arrivals also began to push back the wilderness frontiers to make way for settlement and agriculture, and by the mid-1800s, large segments of eastern America were reshaped. The unbroken aboriginal forest, which had once covered the land "as the grass covers a garden lawn," was now gone; it was said that in New England alone, three-quarters of the land was under cultivation by midcentury. In British North America, there was less property development, but nonetheless, thousands upon thousands of riverfront acres were clear-cut or burned to make way for crops or livestock. What forest wilderness remained, moreover, did not stand untouched, for the early part of the century also ushered in the era of the timber trade, which denuded many river valleys of their primeval timber before 1850.

All of these progressive human intrusions had a devastating effect on the salmon resource. In clearing the land for agriculture, destruction of the species' natural environment occurred, since land clearance caused greater and more frequent fluctuations in water levels and periodically produced drought conditions in tributary streams during the summer months. Total land clearance also resulted in soil erosion, silting, hydrochemical changes, and the elevation of both soil and water temperatures. Many early reports describing the agricultural potential in the more northerly states and colonies even suggested that a moderation of the overall climate might be expected as large areas were cleared and cultivated.[2] Land clearance also reduced the forest canopy over the streams, eliminating the cover and changing the streams' productivity. Needless to say, when fire was used as a tool in clearing the land — a more than occasional method — the aquatic environment would frequently become sterile.

Of even more consequence was the development of the timber trade; besides creating many of the same survival problems as agricultural development, lumbering in many instances completely eliminated entire runs of salmon due to the construction of mill and driving dams across streams. These dams, normally built with no provision for fish passage, not only stopped the salmon from reaching their spawning grounds, but also provided effective barriers below which the fish congregated and could easily be captured. The timber industry, however, was not the only operation requiring dams: tanneries, carding mills, gristmills, etc., also required a head of water to drive machinery. It has been calculated that at least 50 percent of the aboriginal salmon habitat in eastern North America was totally eliminated as productive ground by 1850, with an additional 25 percent being appreciably reduced in production capacity — by being partially obstructed by dams or damaged by the pollutants of agricultural and industrial society.[3]

In some areas of the Maritimes and the Canadas, agriculture and the timber trade attracted the energies of a major portion of the populace, resulting in an accompanying decline in the coastal and offshore fishery. This void, however, was quickly filled by enterprising New England fishermen who, by sheer weight of their numbers, soon gained control of the fishery in the Gulf of St. Lawrence and Bay of Fundy. It was reported that by 1829, the Americans had approximately 1500 vessels engaged in the northeastern fishery. It was also said that of the 715 vessels which fished the Bay of Fundy in 1840, only 65 were owned and operated by British colonials; the rest were American.[4]

This overpowering New England influence, dating back to the late 1600s, had been fostered by the Treaty of Versailles in 1783, which had perpetuated American fishing privileges off British territory. When war broke out again in 1812, Nova Scotians saw the event as a reason to nullify the earlier fishing agreement. The fish question, however, was such a touchy political subject that Britain signed the 1814 peace treaty without considering removal of the clause pertaining to American fishing rights. A few years later, a commission was established to settle the question; the result was the Convention of 1818 which allowed American fishermen (along with British subjects) the liberty to 'take fish of every kind' along certain seacoasts, shores, bays, harbors and creeks of the British–American colonies. These coastal zones comprised all of Labrador, the northern shore of the Gulf of St. Lawrence from the Strait of Belle Isle to the St. Lawrence River opposite Mont Joli, the Magdalen Islands, and the coast of Newfoundland from its northern tip (Quirpon) southward to Cape Ray and hence eastward to the Ramea Islands. The only fishing restriction placed on the Americans was that they were not to infringe upon the exclusive fishing rights previously granted to the Hudson's Bay Company. Liberty to fish was also granted to the Americans in other waters off the British colonies beyond the 3-mile limit.

At the time of the signing of the convention, the clause 'fish of every kind' had little significance except for the cod, since the cod fishery was still the principal activity of concern for both parties. It was not forseen that the specific clause would cause considerable concern and difficulty in subsequent years as the interest in mackerel, herring, salmon, and other shore species developed

and increased. Tensions rose as the British colonial fishermen found themselves in keen competition with the Americans over fishing property and fish species which they considered their own. Even where the 3-mile limit existed the Americans were frequently accused of taking fish where they clearly had no liberty to do so, and this was complicated by the fact that the Americans and British took different views with respect to the location of the 3-mile line: the British claimed that the line extended from headland to headland while the Americans claimed that it followed the indentations of the coastline.[5] This contentious issue was to remain debated, questioned, and unresolved for many years, and resulted in frequent confrontations between fishermen on both sides of the argument. An early Canadian report on the situation stated that

> Upon the slightest pretext they [the Americans] take advantage of the humane intentions of the treaty and enter harbours, rivers and creeks to obtain wood and water. On such occasions they frequently set their nets on the shore, and anchor as near to land as safety will admit. Meanwhile their crews are actively employed in fishing.[6]

The "humane intentions" of the treaty included the right to enter the 3-mile limit for purposes of trade, protection from storms, and for the procurement of wood, water, and other necessary supplies. The Americans, however, were charged with disregard for the treaty at every opportunity, and the remarks of one bold Yankee indicate that the charges were in many cases well founded; this New Englander described the 3-mile limit as "a net set by the British to catch the Yankee; but the meshes were so large that a fishing craft to 100 tons burthen might pass through it without touching."[7]

The effect that American enterprise had on the salmon fishery outside its own territorial waters is not accurately known, but it is believed to have been considerable; the salmon fishery of the United States had declined rapidly since the turn of the century, and import records show an increasing amount of salmon being purchased and brought from the British colonies. These imports were, in turn, supplemented by catches made by American fishermen, mainly along the coasts of Newfoundland, Labrador, and Quebec.

New Brunswick

New Brunswick was on the threshold of a great economic upsurge in 1815; in that year her population was estimted at 40 000, but it would increase more than fivefold by 1845.[8] The mass immigration that occurred in these 30 years was a result of privation and disruption in Europe and the promise that the North American colonies and states afforded for a new and independent life. Many of the new arrivals settled down to a life of farming, but although the colony grew steadily in agricultural development, this pursuit was soon overshadowed by the growth of the timber industry. The increasing interest in forest resources was accompanied by a decreasing participation in the fishery. Salmon, mackerel, herring, and gaspereau resources were hardly pursued at all; cod, still considered the most valuable sea fish, was taken only at two stations — Shippegan and Miscou. The remainder of the industry was in a state of depression, as more and more individuals abandoned it for the more profitable timber trade.

The noticeable decline in fish exports from the colony as early as 1816 induced the governor, Sir Howard Douglas, to introduce several measures to encourage the fishery in his throne speech of that year, the main incentive being a bounty on fish caught and cured in the province for the Mediterranean market. In 1819, the laws governing fish inspection were also updated; these laws had been formerly obscured by being included in the statutes which regulated the timber trade, and their removal from the latter suggested an effort to establish the fishery as a separate and important branch of industry. These and other nominal actions, however, actually did little to encourage the salmon fishery or to increase salmon exports. Furthermore, there was reason to believe that the depressed state in which the resource wallowed was not entirely due to the change in the economic base of the colony. Indications were that the species was not as plentiful after 1815 as before, and it is clear from reports of those who remained in the fishery that it was becoming increasingly difficult to catch enough salmon to make the effort worthwhile.[9]

Many reasons were given for this scarcity. The exceptionally cold seasons that prevailed between 1814 and 1818 were somehow credited with poor abundance, but the cause that received the greatest acknowledgment was overfishing — the unrestricted exploitation to which the salmon resource had been subjected since the turn of the century. As this cause was recognized by the Legislature, new regulations were drafted to try to improve the situation. In 1816, the length of set nets in the Miramichi was limited to 65 fathoms, in order to provide better escapement. In 1820, the practice of drift netting was outlawed in all parts of the province, because this method was "found greatly injurious to the fisheries." Penalties for breaches of the Fishery Act were increased in 1823, and because of the severe depletion of the Petitcodiac River salmon stocks in 1826, fishing was allowed there for an unprecedented 3 days a week only. To protect the Chaleur Bay stocks, the justices of the peace for Gloucester County — which included presentday Restigouche County — were authorized in 1831 to enact whatever regulations they thought necessary, but their inaction resulted in the Legislature stepping in to pass an 1833 act which established seasonal and weekly closed times and limited the lengths of nets in the rivers.[10]

These legislative actions, however, did little to maintain or improve the salmon resource, largely because they failed to take into consideration or to regulate the destruction caused by various activities associated with the timber industry — principally, stream driving, clear cutting, and the construction of milldams. Prior to the outbreak of war in 1812, there were only a few sawmills and dams in the province, operating only to supply local needs, since the timber industry at that time was composed primarily of mast timber export, a commodity requiring no milling. It was uneconomical to ship any timber products to Britain other than masts, as most of Britain's supplies were readily available from the Baltic countries.

> "But only the scarce and correspondingly valuable sticks essential for the great masts of the navy's largest vessles could bear the costs of transatlantic shipment."[11]

After 1812, however, a market developed for lumber, laths, staves, and square timber, and the war in Europe expanded the British timber trade with B.N.A. This resulted, over the next 40 years, in the contsruction of more than 15 new mills annually, most of which were operated in conjunction with dams placed across rivers and streams at the milling site. As early as 1819, nearly 300 vessels per year were loading timber at Miramichi, and by 1824, more than 140 000 tons of timber were being shipped annually from the gulf ports of New Brunswick alone.[12]

Salmon suffered from this activity; their spawning areas were scoured by stream drives, and their former haunts were barred to them by dams, which also provided excellent locations for spearing the fish in vast numbers. Although legislation had been passed in 1810 making it necessary to provide fishways in such structures, the law was universally evaded. In addition, the government turned a blind eye to the problem by taking the attitude that if the timber industry and the fishery were incompatible, then the fishery must give way for the moment — New Brunswick's trees were far more valuable.[13] It is significant, therefore, that the statutes enacted to preserve fish stocks at this time acknowledged only one cause of the resource decline; the legislation was directed towards limiting overfishing, rather than opposing or restricting the timber interests in any way. The people who controlled the timber business were omnipotent; properly termed "lumber barons," they quickly challenged any action to restrain their efforts and profits or to divert their activity and, as a result, the already low stocks of salmon remained low until more influential parties took up the cause of restoration several decades later.

At least one individual in the 1830s, however, felt that he had a solution which could benefit both the fisherman and the lumberman. Richard McFarlan carefully outlined his ingenious program for rehabilitating the province's river fishery at a lecture in the Mechanics' Hall in Saint John in 1837. He proposed that fishways should be constructed in all milldams, using the fishway pools as slaughtering pens when salmon and other fish ascended, and allowing only enough fish to escape to perpetuate the species naturally. Since the dams and the fishways were an indispensable part of the scheme for profit, he saw no reason why lumber barons and mill-owners would object to constructing fishways in return for a reasonable portion of the proceeds from the fish kill. He concluded that the costs of construction and requirements of space would be kept to a minimum by designing the fishway like a spiral staircase, rather than a long, stepped trough.

His ideas, however, did not receive the widespread acceptance and acclaim that he had anticipated. His lecture, in fact, was poorly attended and he was out-of-pocket for the rental on the lecture hall. Part of this lack of interest may have been due to the fact that McFarlan also chose to expound upon his idea for a perpetual motion machine during the same lecture. Undaunted, he continued to air his ideas throughout the province, proposing at one point that his fishway could be constructed easily over Grand Falls on the Saint John River. He was untiring in his efforts to have his ideas accepted, and in 1847 he published a small booklet on the subject, and distributed it at his own expense — but it appears that he ended his mortal days without receiving either acceptance of, or profit from, his dream.[14]

In 1841, there appeared to be a slight general increase in the salmon catch, and the downward trend in yields seemed to have been halted.[15] Although it might appear that the legislation enacted between 1815 and 1845 had thus had some effect, in reality the legislation existed only as noble words printed and bound in elegant leather journals. Poaching was rampant, seasons were ignored and drift netting was still widely practiced; overseers appointed to police the statutes were few, and more dams than ever before completely barred the rivers. The slight increase in salmon, therefore, was perhaps partially the result of some natural cyclical pattern which had slumped after 1815, and which rose again around 1840. Perhaps part of the recovery can also be attributed to the resurgence of the great salmon-producing areas of the Miramichi, which had been devastated by fire in the 1820s. The best explanation, however, may simply be the fact that large segments of the three principal New Brunswick rivers — the Saint John, Restigouche, and Miramichi — were too wide to dam and too large to fish out completely.

MIRAMICHI

The vast exports of salmon that left the Miramichi region in the first decade of the 1800s gradually dwindled after 1815, as increasing number of men abandoned the fishery to obtain the more assured and steady profits found in the lumber woods. By 1851, it was estimated that fully 75 percent of Northumberland County's adult male population was engaged in one way or another in the timber industry.[16] The influx of immigrants into the county at this time was considerable; in 1817, for example, a great number of people took up land between the Miramichi and Nashwaak,[17] and other new inhabitants had a particular relish for similarly remote areas, partly due to the influences of the forest industry. Large segments of the population of these pioneering settlements were of Irish and Scottish descent. They were a particularly hardy breed of pioneer, naturally suited for work in the woods, and it was said that they were 50 percent Irish, 50 percent Scotch, and 100 percent rough. Collectively known as the "Rories and Anguses," a favorite expression of these hardy woodsmen at this time was: "I was born on the Miramichi. The further up you go, the tougher they get, and I was raised on the headwaters."[18]

In 1819, 297 vessels entered the Miramichi to load lumber for foreign markets.[19] The country for miles around rang with the song of the woodsman's axe, and lumbering was so profitable that large timber rafts were brought down the coast from points as far away as Shippegan.[20] The disinterest in fishing was so acute by 1824 that only 580 barrels of pickled fish — principally salmon — were exported from the Miramichi.[21] Any interest that might have resulted from the colonial administration's renewed efforts to promote the industry in 1825[22] was quickly nullified on the Miramichi by the Great Fire which broke out in the autumn of that year.

The early season had been hot and dry, and several fires had broken out in various parts of the province. In October, a massive blaze consumed the Miramichi watershed and, before burning itself out, destroyed between 6000 and 8000 square miles of central New Brunswick — nearly one-quarter of the province.[23] In the large triangle formed by the points of Fredericton, Bathurst, and Richibucto, most of the forest was burned, many of the homes were destroyed, much of the wildlife was killed, and a considerable number of human lives were lost. The only spot of land in all the great Miramichi watershed to escape disaster was a small section on Clearwater Brook, above its junction with the main river. One writer described the conflagration in the following way:

> The Hurricane raged so tremendously at some points that large bodies of burning timber, and parts of the flaming houses, were carried to the river with astonishing velocity, and so affected the water, as to occasion in the shallow places, large quantities of salmon, and other fish to spring on the shore. They were seen afterwards laying [sic] along the sand by hundreds.[24]

Undoubtedly, the salmon run of 1825 was almost completely wiped out, and the eggs already deposited were killed by the abnormal rising of the water temperature so late in the season. In addition, large segments of the progeny of all runs since 1822 were probably eliminated, and thus it would not be until the 1830s that the river resources would recuperate sufficiently for the Miramichi to be recognized as a salmon river once more.[25] Amazingly, the timber trade recovered faster on the Miramichi than the fishery, although its resurgence was again detrimental to the salmon resource; 4 years after the fire, it was reported that "The exportation of lumber [has] since superseded almost every other pursuit and the waters of the river being much disturbed by vessels, boats and rafts of timber... an extraordinary decrease in quantity has followed the salmon fishery."[26]

CHALEUR BAY

Most of the watershed area of the Restigouche River and the larger drainage area of Chaleur Bay had not been subjected to the ravages of fire which had devastated the Miramichi in 1825; consequently, the Chaleur area received an influx of population from these burnt-over regions in the late 1820s. The focus of the timber trade also moved to Chaleur Bay, and such communities as Dalhousie and Campbellton grew and expanded at this time. As early as 1826, the region was sufficiently populated to receive county status, being separated from the northern half of the former Northumberland District, and comprising what is now Gloucester and Restigouche counties.[27]

Even before 1824, the timber industry was rising to prominence on the Chaleur shore, but by 1830 it was firmly established as the principal activity. Concurrent with the incline in the timber business was, again, a corresponding decline in salmon fishing. Although part of the slump was due to the number of persons who chose to follow lumbering rather than fishing, there was also evidence that, like the Miramichi, the lower catches were partly due to a decline in stock. James McGregor reported in 1828 that:

> A profitable salmon fishery was for many years followed on the Restigouche which has for sometime been declining and the timber trade seems to be almost supplanting it altogether. I have been told by those longest settled on the river, that an extraordinary decrease in the number of salmon annually frequenting it has taken place: this may be in consequence of the water being much more disturbed than formerly.[28]

Undoubtedly, the timber industry had some deleterious effects on the salmon fishery: stream obstruction, removal of forest cover, and silting and scouring of spawning and nursery areas would all reduce production to a certain degree. However, there were other factors,

equally significant, which caused the decline in stock. Robert Ferguson, salmon fisherman, businessman, and magistrate, made perhaps the most noteworthy comment on the local fishery at this time. In a letter written in 1829 to his friend and business associate, Richard Simonds, he said:

> the fisheries in this quarter are much on the decline within these few years past — the salmon fishery on the Restigouche and its branches in particular — It would be highly necessary to repeal the acts respecting the Salmon fishery and to have some amendments thereon, to correspond as near as possible to those on the north side of the Bay viz the District of Gaspé — in order to prevent the abuse of the laws in transgressions passing from one side of the river to the other — Sweaping [sic] the river and its branches even to its source and continuing that, together with the Spear to a late season of the year will in a short time complete the total river of the Salmon Fishery — It would be highly necessary to have certain enactments passed to prevent these abuses — but the greatest difficulty is in executing the laws on such an extensive river as Restigouche and bordering on the Canada line, are by the offenders passing from one province to the other.[29]

At this time, salmon fishing was still principally confined to the rivers and their estuaries; the Restigouche, of course, was the most prominent fishing river, with the main activity being carried out from Campbellton to the headwaters. There were few salmon fishing stands in Chaleur Bay itself at this time (1830), compared with later years. From the comments of John Mowat, it can be presumed that between 30 and 40 nets were in operation below the middle ground at Campbellton and around the main settlements of Campbellton, Dalhousie, Bathurst, Janeville, Caraquet, Port Daniel, New Carlisle, New Richmond, and Schoolbred (Nouvelle). Spearing was still a favorite and popular means of taking salmon, and it is a matter of debate whether more fish were taken with the spear or with the net. Spearing was largely carried out at night with the aid of canoes and birchbark torches. It was said that the Restigouche was so littered with discarded torchsticks that they looked like windrows of hay along the banks, and that if one could walk the entire network of streams comprising the Restigouche system in one night, one would never lose sight of a burning torch.[30]

Set nets, drift nets, or sweep nets were primarily used on the lower sections of the river, and their use was not confined to the white population only; for example, a trader reported in 1824 that the Micmacs had taken away as many as 3000 salmon with nets on the Restigouche in two nights' fishing.[31] The Indians appear to have been almost continually engaged in the fishery during the salmon run, and gathered no little profit from this enterprise; their traditional rights had placed them in a somewhat better position than the white settlers to exploit the resource, their principal settlement being at Mission Point, Quebec, directly opposite the growing town of Campbellton. This Indian reserve was much coveted by the white settlers because of the good agricultural potential of the property and its proximity to the valuable middle ground salmon fishery. Recognizing this value, Lord Dalhousie had offered the Indians £600 and twice as much land elsewhere if they would resign their title to the reserve and its fishery; the Indians wisely declined.[32]

Overfishing undoubtedly contributed to the decline of the Restigouche and Chaleur salmon stocks, but despite the decline, a few individuals were hopeful that the fishery would return, and some were able to foresee great potential for the region. John McTaggert wrote in 1829:

> The small rivers which fall into the Bay of Chaleur swarm with the finest salmon fish, which are also very much neglected in this and all the other bays opening into the Gulf of St. Lawrence. The tides generally rise in Chaleur to three feet, in spring tides to six. Trapnets might[,] therefore, be fixed to some advantage in the shallows. Snow and ice are both very plentiful in their season, and proper houses might be constructed to preserve them in the summer; a small steamboat would then carry the fish while sweet to Quebec, where a ready sale could at once be obtained; or to Montreal, where they would be always very graciously received. Such things require a little cash at the onset; but, as the thing is now represented, fishermen will soon be seen there.[33]

Although salmon abundance was considered to be at a low level in the late 1820s, and the fishery relatively inactive, it was not as depressed as it was to become by the late 1830s. John Duncan, a Campbellton farmer who had followed salmon fishing since the turn of the century, noted that 3000 barrels of salmon were still being taken annually from the Restigouche in the late 1820s; this, of course, was a decline from the thousands of tierces shipped from the Restigouche when Duncan first came to the area. By the mid-1830s, however, production had dropped to a few hundred barrels; the catch reported at Dalhousie (Restigouche) in 1835 was approximately 150 000 live lb and it was further reduced to 40 000 live lb by 1839.[34]

Further down the bay at Bathurst and Caraquet, the same downward trend was observed; although the fishery had never been as substantial at these latter locations as at the mouth of the Restigouche, it had expanded along the shore to the extent that regulations were enacted in 1833 to control its operation.[35] Seventy-two barrels of salmon were reported exported in 1835, but by 1838, the number was down to only 41 barrels.[36] Fishing became so poor that many individuals ordinarily involved in the local industry, and not wanting employment in the forests, were entering the Labrador fishery instead.[37]

The Chaleur Bay salmon fishery was at its lowest ebb in 1841. Of the period between 1830 and 1840, it was stated that individual stations in the bay rarely took more than 10 or 12 barrels of fish in a season — probably representing between 125 and 175 large fish per station; if by chance a catch of twenty barrels was taken, both the station and the run were considered to be particularly good. Although the export records available for this period are probably not complete, other contemporary data indicate that in the best years, no more than 2000 barrels were taken from Chaleur Bay, the largest percentage being exported.[38] At this time, barreled salmon was sold principally to American vessels that entered the bay; occasional shipments were made to Halifax, and the rest were consumed locally. The average price paid was equivalent to $8 per barrel.[39] Although after 1841, production again rose, the increase was hardly significant when compared to the disastrous general decline since 1815.

One might believe that officialdom was completely oblivious to the situation on the Chaleur — once renowned for its important salmon fishery — but this was not entirely the case. The complaints of men like Robert Ferguson resulted in the province granting the county justices the right to regulate the fishery in 1831. Little action, however, appears to have been taken by them; consequently, in March 1833, the province passed an act to regulate more stringently the Gloucester County fisheries. Drift netting and spearing were made illegal; a closed season was established, which extended from 20 July to 31 December; and a weekly Sunday closure was imposed. It was also made illegal to seal off completely a channel with a net, and several regulations were made respecting the maximum length of nets to be used. The act was to continue in force until May 1840.[40] Like all former legislation, however, practical application of this statute did not exist; apparently if salmon were to survive on the Restigouche, it would be completely by accident or through some freak of good fortune. This, in fact, was strongly believed to be the case by such observers as John Mowat, who stated that the Restigouche River was saved by the late autumn salmon run — so emaciated were the fasting and spawning fish, that they were ignored with distaste by both Indians and whites.[41]

SAINT JOHN

The salmon fishery of Saint John continued to expand and prosper after 1815; a visitor to the town in 1816 reported: "The river is wide and has a noble fishery for salmon, shad, herrings and sturgeon which furnishes employment and wealth to several hundreds of the inhabitants....For a fine salmon I have given 2 shillings and 6 pence."[42]

In addition to a considerable local market, trade continued to grow with both the United States and the West Indies. In the 1820s and 1830s for example, the

Ward Company of Saint John was shipping salmon to Jamaica and Barbados.[43] Although this trade slackened somewhat after 1822, and particularly after 1830 as a result of the Americans being allowed entry to the British West Indies trade, the products of the Saint John fishery continued to find a ready market in the New England colonies, especially in the fresh and smoked state. In 1824, 3662 smoked salmon were exported from Saint John, but by 1835, almost 10 000 were shipped out of the port. Between 1815 and 1845, annual salmon exports from the city ranged between 100 000 and 400 000 pounds, with the average being around 200 000 pounds.[44]

Home consumption was also considerable, and salmon were in constant supply at Saint John's major fish market, which was first opened on June 20, 1838; although it was a popular source of fresh fish, it was reported to be in a despicable, filthy condition.[45] An important development in the salmon fishery, and one which eventually spread to all branches of the industry, occurred in Saint John in 1839, when Tristram Halliday began the commercial fish-canning industry in North America by preserving salmon and lobsters in tins. Adopting Halliday's techniques, U.S. Treat began the American canning business at Eastport, Maine, in the following year.[46]

It does not appear that salmon on the Saint John River suffered the drastic declines witnessed on the eastern coast of the province at this time — a peculiarity partly due to the freedom of the Saint John watershed from the disastrous effects of the Miramichi area fires. Very little decline or depression was noted, exports continued at a high level, and settlers were not conservative in their efforts at taking the species. In fact, William Corbett reported in 1829 that "in the creeks at the foot of the cascades [upon the tributary streams of the St. John] there [are] in season salmon, the finest in the world, and so abundant, and so easily taken, as to be used for manuring the land."[47]

Salmon at Saint John were, during this period, being captured in increasing numbers of drift nets, a system of fishing that was greatly encouraged by the local difficulty of obtaining fish lots along the shore. The great number of men, nets, and boats engaged in the drift netting operation in the early 1800s led many to believe that this particular mode of fishing would have disastrous effects on the salmon runs of the entire river, and this general opinion in no small way influenced the Legislature to outlaw drift netting throughout the province in 1820. The practice, however, continued in Saint John harbor in defiance of the act, and because of the free and unrestricted rights granted in the city's charter. Milldams were as yet not numerous on the river, but in a few local areas these obstructions had already eliminated some runs. The Mispec River, for example, was dammed in 1825 at the head of tide and, although salmon once ran up

this stream and into Loch Lomond, the run was obliterated after that date.[48]

ST. CROIX

By about 1825, the Charlotte County fisheries had begun a general decline which was to last for several years. Although salmon had managed to overcome the St. Croix dams for many years, because of the concern of the county Sessions Court, their days were apparently numbered, for in 1825 a massive milldam was erected, without a fishway, at Scoodic Falls.[49] Reacting in part to the general stock decline in all species, Charlotte County fishermen were leaving the local industry to take part in the more lucrative Labrador fisheries; they were, in fact, only following the crowd. John Wilson of St. Andrews succinctly summed up the local situation when he wrote in 1828 that "The British shore fishery has been gradually falling off for several years past, owing partly to the fish not being so plentiful and partly to the restriction on the supplies necessary to carry it on."[50]

Nova Scotia

The legislature meets generally in winter, and continues in Session from six to twelve weeks. The principle [sic] business consists of investigating the public accounts; in appropriating the Revenue; which, after the discharge of the civil list, is chiefly applied to the improvement of the roads and bridges, bounties for the encouragement of agriculture; and sometimes for promoting the fisheries.[51]

Such was Thomas Chandler Haliburton's 1829 assessment of the work of the Nova Scotia Legislature, and one can thus surmise that the fisheries had a relatively low priority in the business of the colony. In fact, if it had not been for the intense participation of the United States in the province's offshore fishery, causing intimidation of fishermen and insult to colonial pride, it is unlikely that much legislative attention would have been placed on the resource at all.

One of the first concerted actions that Nova Scotia took concerning the fishery, after the Convention of 1818 established the 3-mile limit, was to equip a vessel and commission it to police the fishery within the geographical bounds set by the convention. The vessel engaged for this work was the *Chebucto*, contracted from Samuel Cunard, the contract being renewed in 1823.[52] Apparently provincial vessels could do little to protect the coast from increasing American encroachment, however, for in 1839, the Legislature sent a delegation to Britain to solicit additional help. As a result, the Royal Navy admiral on the Halifax station was instructed to assist the province in its fisheries protection activites, and three armed cutters were used annually in this work in the early 1840s between April and November. One vessel

103

patrolled the Bay of Fundy, one between Cape Sable and Chedabucto Bay, and one the Gulf of St. Lawrence.[53]

Other legislative actions pertaining to the fisheries dealt mainly with regulating the trade of pickled fish and in maintaining some control over local exploitation of the sea fisheries.[54] Very little attention was paid to the inland resource, that which accounted for the major production of salmon. Instead, the regulation of the river fisheries was principally in the hands of the county Sessions Courts; but in many cases, the counties were lax in this regard, and enforcement was rarely pressed unless open conflict arose or severe criticism was expressed by people with influence. Prosecutions were few, but there is at least one anecdote on record which tells of a county court exercising its duty:

> There was a very good man once lived in Liverpool, so good, he said he hadn't sinned for seven years; well, he put a mill dam across the river, and stopped all the fish from goin' up, and the court fined him fifty pounds for it, and this good man was so wrathy, he thought he would feel better to swear a little, but conscience told him it was wicked. So he compounded with conscience, and cheated the devil, by calling it a 'dam fine business.'[55]

It is little credit to the Provincial Legislature that such a state prevailed in the inland fishery, but the legislature conducted much of its business solely for the benefit of Halifax, the heart, soul, and commercial center of the colony. Joseph Howe once stated that it was not difficult to believe that

> the whole province of Nova Scotia is bounded on the south by Miller's Wharf, north by the Dock Yard, east by [the] harbour of Halifax and west by the Town Clock; and that all the wealth, influence and intelligence of the Province aforesaid may be found every day, from one till two, in front of the Province Building.[56]

There was, of course, more to the province than Halifax; distributed throughout the colony from Yarmouth to Cape North were more than 130 000 inhabitants,[57] many of whom utilized the river fisheries for either commercial or private purposes. The value of this inland resource eventually came to the notice of the fisheries committee, which afforded the inland fishery some special mention in its report to the Legislature during the session of 1839–40. With respect to salmon, the report is interesting because of its mixture of fact and supposition concerning the natural history of the species:

> The Salmon Fishery of this Province, once of great value, but, from neglect, and want of suitable regulations, rapidly dwindling, requires also a reference to the nature of that species of Fish; it inhabits the European Coasts from Spitzburgen to France, but is never seen in the Mediterranean; on the Western Shores of the Atlantic it is found from Greenland to the Hudson, and never further south. A cold climate and clear water are congenial to its constitution — when the ice melts Salmon enter the mouths of Rivers, and almost always of those which gave them birth — they swim in immense bodies near the surface — they are timid, easily frightened, and on such occasions return to the sea — they penetrate far into the interior, surmounting rapids and cascades, etc., and deposit their spawn in the Lakes, etc., at the sources of Rivers — when the young are about a foot in length they descend to the Ocean, and the ensuing Summer follow after the old, which have ascended to spawn, and are then about eighteen inches long. At 2 years old, the Salmon weighs from 6 to 8 pounds; and at 5 or 6 years, attains the weight of 10 or 12 pounds. Wise rules for the protection of this fishery still retains it among the most important of the North of Europe, while a contrary system has destroyed the Fishery to the Southward of Maine. Formerly New York was supplied from the Connecticut River, but the erection of Mills, Mill Dams and other Obstructions, have reduced the Fish, or rather destroyed the supply, by turning the old Salmon back to the sea, where their seed is cast in unproductive waters. The salmon at full size in the Northern Seas weighs 170 pounds — they live on insects, small fish and worms — deposit their eggs in holes made in the sand, and are a prey of Seals, Porpoises and other large fish.[58]

There is an old saying, probably penned as a memorial to anglers, that goes: "By the time the tale of a salmon has travelled ten miles, its weight has often doubled." Such being the case, the description of the salmon given in the Assembly *Journal* must have traveled some distance, for the record for Atlantic salmon is just under 80 pounds.

THE GULF SHORE

The prosperity of Pictou County was expanding rapidly by 1815. John and Abraham Patterson, who began business there in that year, were primarily interested in timber, fish, and the West Indies trade, and in a short period of time, they had built up a sizable enterprise, expanding their influence throughout most of the southern Gulf of St. Lawrence. The Patterson firm set about to take advantage of all commercial fisheries likely to produce a profit, and therefore concentrated on gaspereau, herring, cod, and salmon. They outfitted small vessels with salt, gear, barrels, and all the requirements necessary to satisfy a fishing populace, then regularly sent these vessels to the fishing stations in the Gulf of St. Lawrence, dispersing the supplies and embarking barrels of pickled fish which were brought back to Pictou and transshipped for the West Indies market. Their sphere of influence in this business extended to Richibucto, Rustico, Chéticamp, and Canso. Acquiring a substantial fortune from this enterprise, they retired from the business in 1832.[59]

Although the major salmon fisheries of the Gulf areas of New Brunswick were beginning to decline rapidly in the late 1820s and through the 1830s, the northeastern rivers of Nova Scotia still maintained fairly substantial runs. The most frequently discussed stream on this coast was the River Philip, noted for trout as well as salmon. Haliburton had sung its praises, and William Moorsom knew of three men taking 180 pounds of trout there with casual effort in a short time.[60] Barney's River was also popular, Joseph Howe noting in 1830 that "A skillful handler of the 'Rod and the Line' will, at the proper season, take a good share of trout, or perhaps a brace of salmon."[61] In addition to Pictou County, all of Antigonish County, then known as the upper district of Sydney County, was known to be extremely valuable for its fishery; the Scots who settled at Arisaig in 1815, for example, took immediately to the salmon resource, while Antigonish itself was an Indian word, meaning "river of fish."[62]

CAPE BRETON

The statistical records for Cape Breton Island show that 70 barrels of salmon were exported from the ports of Sydney, Arichat, and Ship Harbour (Port Hawkesbury) in 1816, valued at 50 shillings a barrel. This meager export of approximately 14 000 pounds of pickled salmon hardly suggests an extensive fishery; and even 30 years later, only 370, 470, and 20 barrels were reported exported from all ports in 1843, 1844, and 1845, respectively.[63] As pointed out elsewhere, however, it is unlikely that the export figures indicate the true trade or even the intensity of involvement in this branch of the fishery. Throughout this period, there is little doubt that the island's principal article of export was fish,[64] and the salmon segment of this export trade was probably greater than that indicated on the record.

Apart from the commercial aspects of salmon fishery, carried on by Jersey merchants and firms like the Pattersons of Pictou, general archives information indicates that the domestic value of salmon was substantial. It is unlikely, for example, that the species did not play the major role in supplying individual and local needs in communities along such rivers as the Margaree, Mabou, North, Mira, and Inhabitants, communities which alone, in later years, would account for an annual inland fishery of upwards of 70 000 pounds of salmon.[65]

EASTERN SHORE (CHEDABUCTO BAY TO HALIFAX)

Fishing was a primary activity in Guysborough County, where it was reported that a considerable commerce was carried out with buyers and traders who came to the area in great numbers during the fishing season. Mackerel was the chief export, being sold to traders or purchased by local merchants for shipment to Halifax or the West Indies.[66] Although the timber trade was enveloping the region around the St. Mary's River, both the local and Labador fisheries remained viable resource industries. As early as 1813, Elisha Pride and Robert Dixon of Sonora had built a schooner specifically for the latter.[67]

Joseph Howe, touring the region at about the same time, spent the night at an inn on the shores of Glenelg Lake, at the junction of the two main branches of the St. Mary's River; after a hard day's journey, he commented, "A clean cloth, a slice of fine fresh salmon, caught in the lake not two hours previous, are not to be slighted by the wayfarer after a six hours' fast."[68] Indeed, salmon were considered a valuable commodity along the St. Mary's, and were sufficiently plentiful to permit a small export trade with Halifax.

SOUTHEASTERN SHORE

One of the most comprehensive descriptions of the southeastern part of Nova Scotia during the 1820s may be found in the writings of Thomas Chandler Haliburton, who frequently made close observations of the fishery. His writings clearly indicate a disastrous decline in the regional salmon resource around 1825, brought about largely by the construction of dams on the principal rivers. In discussing the Barrington River, for example, Haliburton noted that "There was formerly an excellent salmon and alewife fishery in this river, but in consequence of Mill dams and other obstructions, which have prevented the fish from getting to their usual places of spawning, the former have been almost annihilated..."[69] He noted as well that the erection of mills on the Mersey had somewhat injured the river, but that the stream still remained fairly productive with respect to the salmon fishery.

The LaHave River was reported to possess 30 sawmills on its course at this time, but despite these obstructions, it too was still fairly productive as a salmon stream; Charles Owen reported that great numbers were still being taken there in 1842.[70] The principal run along this coastline appeared in May, but some fish were taken as early as March, and it was reportedly common to take 20–30 salmon from a net in a single haul. A settler who moved to New Cornwall on Mushamush Lake in 1838 noted that alewives and salmon were plentiful at that time, and that he used to catch between fifty and seventy fish each season at the mouth of the lake.[71]

At the turn of the 19th century, salmon had been commonly taken in the New Ross area; at Lake Lawson, 22 and 23 pound specimens were reported.[72] The Gold River also continued to support a reasonable salmon fishery, since in 1842 it was said that the Indians still took advantage of its runs, skillfully using the spear as well as the hook and line.[73] The salmon resource of these areas, however, was hardly comparable to what it had been prior to 1800, and as another observer has commented, "Salmon nets were set in the rivers in late May and remained there through much of the summer. Catches varied from one to a dozen fish, with many unlucky days."[74]

The regional fishery was relied upon only for local consumption; commercial interests followed the traditional route to Labrador. By 1829, Lunenburg fishermen were entirely dependent on Labrador cruises for their commercial salmon, while the greatest amount of the species caught, handled and shipped by Liverpudlians also came from their enterprises on that northern coast.[75]

Prince Edward Island

Prince Edward Island's population had risen to 15 000 by 1820.[76] Apparently, during the period between 1806 and 1820, salmon disappeared from many island streams, due to heavy local exploitation. In 1806, John Stewart mentioned that the species, although not abundant, was found in all the island's rivers;[77] by 1821, however, Walter Johnstone reported: "There are a few salmon in some of the rivers (although I never saw any caught, except by Indians) and a smaller kind of fish called the salmon trout, are caught in several places; I thought them the finest eating of all the fish that they had."[78] In 1832, J. L. Lewellin reported that many of the settlers lived largely on fish, but in his list of species, the salmon was absent.[79]

Lower Canada

By 1820, the salmon fisheries of Lower Canada were of considerable importance to the local and export trade of the colony. Salmon from the Jacques Cartier and St. Charles rivers and those from the St. Lawrence proper — at least as far downstream as Île aux Coudres — were mainly fished for home consumption; but from the latter island through to the Gulf, large quantities of pickled and dried salmon were being exported to foreign markets, the salted fish going mainly to the West Indies and the smoked product to Europe. One report of the period stated that

> The principal salmon fishery of the colony is at the River Restigouche, at the head of the Bay des Chaleurs; there are others in the different rivers falling into the Bays des Chaleurs and Gaspé and at most of the rivers from thence up along the St. Lawence to the South River [Rivière du Sud], which empties into the St. Lawrence at St. Thomas, on the South Shore; and on the North Shore from Malbaie downwards, at every considerable river.[80]

At this time, however, numerous complaints were received by the government concerning American disregard for the Convention of 1818 and encroachment upon the colony's fishery. An agent of the Robin firm, for example, described how New England vessels were filling their holds with fish taken within the 3-mile limit in the Chaleur area, "to the great prejudice and annoyance of His Britannic Majesty's faithful and loyal subjects."[81] It was even reported in 1822 that the Americans were treating the seigneury of Mingan virtually as their own,

on one occasion taking a boatload of salmon from the Natashquan River.[82]

As a result of these and other complaints, a special Legislature committee was set up to study fishery problems within the colony. When the study was completed, the recommendations included one advocating that "the Bill for regulating the fisheries in the Inferior District of Gaspé be amended, containing regulations to prevent the wasteful and unnecessary destruction of fish, particularly of salmon."[83] The specified bill was one passed in 1807, which with respect to salmon, merely had made it illegal for any person to drift net or set nets above the first rapids on either the Restigouche or Grand Cascapedia rivers, or "to assist the Indians to do so, either diectly or indirectly." Needless to say, the bill had had little effect until the time of the 1822 inquiry.

Certain other of the committee's regulations were incorporated into legislation passed in 1824. Apart from initiating a fish inspection service for Quebec City and Montreal, and providing some general support for Canadian fishermen, the new regulations attempted to supply some additional protection for the Gaspé salmon resource. Although Indians could still spear salmon in the daytime for their own use, torchlight fishing was now outlawed, as was the use of weirs. The legislation also made it illegal to use any method for diverting or deflecting salmon into nets.[84]

Regulation of the salmon fishery for the rest of the colony, including Labrador, was apparently deemed unnecessary at this time, for these areas were not cited in the 1824 legislation. Actually, the fishing population along the north coast of the Gulf of St. Lawrence increased steadily between 1815 and 1830. The Lymburner firm, later to become the Labrador Company, had been at Mingan since 1807, and continued operations there until 1820. After this latter date, a Scot, Samuel Robertson, apparently introduced to the coast by the Lymburner firm, became preeminent in the local seal and whale fishery, which he extended to several areas beyond Mingan. Other Quebec interests followed Robertson's example, engaging in the salmon fishery as well, and annually fitting out several vessels for the Labrador fishery.

These Lower Canadian interests occupied so much of the Labrador coast, and their influence was so considerable, that the territory from Mingan to Blanc Sablon, previously administered by Newfoundland, was returned to Quebec jurisdiction in 1825. At the time of this transfer, the Hudson's Bay Company leased a large segment of the coast formerly granted to John Richardson and John and Alexander Greenshields, the cost of the lease being £500 per year. The Company had eleven establishments in the region by 1831, nine of which possessed salmon fisheries.[85] The Hudson's Bay Company also held leases to the King's Domain or King's Posts, that area of the north shore southwest of the seigneury of Mingan; the company continued to trade with the Indians and to fish for salmon.

In perusing salmon export records for the colony for the years 1820 through 1839, it is evident that the figures are basically for the city of Quebec, with occasional reports for the outports of Gaspé, New Carlisle, and St. John's. From these records, it appears that the total exported catch ranged between 200 000 and 400 000 pounds annually (live weight). Although notations indicate that no record was available for the number of boats engaged in the fishery, the catch record was taken as accurate. However, there is no indication that catches from the Labrador fishery, or from the fishery at the King's Posts, were ever considered in the export totals. The available statistics also indicate that a large percentage of the Quebec export went to the British Isles, with lesser amounts to the United States and other British American colonies.[86]

Upper Canada

By 1815, salmon were still being taken in most of the 40 enumerated rivers and streams in which the Atlantic salmon were once native and which flowed into Lake Ontario.[87] Despite the wholesale slaughter of the species which had continued since the 1790s, runs did not at first appear to diminish rapidly, and a 200-pound barrel could readily be procured for a reasonable 30–35 shillings.[88] John McCuaig, who in later years became superintendent of fisheries for Upper Canada, said of this period: "I have seen them [salmon] from 1812 to 1815, swarming the rivers so thickly, that they were thrown out with the shovel, and even with the hand."[89]

The presence of salmon was an important economic factor within the colony: the locations of homesteads and even towns were frequently considered in respect to their proximity to salmon areas. The careless and carefree manner in which the fishery was undertaken and the pertinent laws abridged incited legislative authorities to revamp the existing regulations, and in 1821 the former statutes were repealed in favor of more stringent fisheries legislation. The new act strictly forbade the practice of torchlight fishing within 100 yards of any milldam; evidently, incidences had occurred where fishermen, while fishing at night close to such dams — an action in itself illegal — had accidently burnt down several mills. Other provisions of the statute reinstated the Act of 1810, forbade fishing at the mouths of rivers, and restricted the use of nets and weirs in the Home, Gore, and Newcastle districts.[90]

The act had no application to the Indians, who were still permitted to fish when, where, and how they pleased, except by torchlight at milldams. The freedom allowed to the native population, however, soon caused some difficulty; the white inhabitants, restricted by season, area,

and method, encouraged and even paid the natives to catch salmon. An amendment to the act in 1823, however, made these solicitations illegal. Further amendments in 1823 totally forbade the use of nets and weirs in the Trent River and established a new fishing season for the province, running from January 1 to November 30. This certainly was no conservation measure, however, since it actually added 15 days to the former season.[91] In any case, there is every evidence that the fishery laws continued to be ignored, since the pioneering energy of the expanding frontier society bred independence, and an almost blatant disregard for the law and for the people who made and enforced it.

By 1822, the extreme westward range of the Atlantic salmon in Ontario was definitely known, for the settlers who reached lakes Erie, Huron and Superior found none. An occasional report mentioned the existence of the species west of Lake Ontario, but Robert Gourlay found these instances to be false, noting that "there are in Lake Superior trouts of three kinds. The same are found in Lake Ontario. They are, however, only varieties of the same species. Two of them are usually called salmon...."[92] A little later, in 1824, Edward Talbot claimed:

Salmon are taken in large quantities as high up the country as the falls of Niagara but neither salmon nor eels are found in any of the upper lakes or rivers. On account of the remoteness of Lake Ontario from the sea, the salmon which it contains are of an inferior quality.[93]

Two points in this last statement have caused some speculation as to the peculiarities of salmon in Lake Ontario. Firstly, the existence of salmon in the Niagara River appears questionable, since the river possessed no spawning ground — unless these fish were strays, merely using the rivers as a feeding area, returning to the lake and some other tributaries at spawning time. The other point is the reference of "inferior" salmon, a quality mentioned several times in the literature of this period. Talbot went on to note that the flesh of lake salmon appeared to be a little softer, with less of the pinkish tint that was common to the lower St. Lawrence fish.[94] John MacTaggart also reported that "These [lake] fish are found weighing from 20 to 60 pounds, are good to eat, although not so finely flavoured as those which live more in salt water."[95] Although these observations were not conclusive proof, they led to the belief that Upper Canadian salmon were landlocked, a theory still open to debate. Other individuals, however, found no difference between the Lake Ontario salmon and those caught in saltwater, and one homesteader wrote in 1832 that "I have taken, in the river Credit, in spring, within twenty yards of our hall door, as fine a fish [salmon] as I have ever met in Ireland, as firm and full of curd as within ten miles of the sea, instead of five hundred."[96]

Inferior though Ontario salmon may or may not have been, they were nonetheless desirable as a food fish, and the catching of them — although basically for economic rather than recreational reasons — was at times considered an enjoyable, sporting diversion. Fly-fishing was practiced on trout to a certain extent at this time, but the use of the rod to catch salmon was neither popular nor common.[97] Mrs. Simcoe once reported that "Many people carry trolling lines, or lines which run out of a small fishing wheel or pulley laying out of the stern in their boat, and catch abundance of black bass and other fish all the way up the St. Lawrence."[98] The sport in salmon fishing, however, was in the use of the spear. It did not have to be an elaborate device; Gourlay pointed out in 1822 that even the dexterous use of a crotched pole could procure enough salmon to satisfy any fisherman.[99] T. W. Magrath, who resided on the bank of the Credit River in 1833, described the mode of spearing in his day:

> If this takes place in the day time, a bright sun is preferred, and a tree having been felled, so as to fall across the river, the sportsman taking his stand on this, rests quiet, and strikes the fish as they pass up.... By observing stillness and composure, I have known a good spearsman to kill from forty to fifty salmon in a few hours.[100]

Daylight spearing, however, was not as common as nighttime, torchlight fishing, the popularity of which was reported in 1836 by a settler's wife living on the upper reaches of the Trent River: "S_____ is considered very skillful as a spearsman, and enjoys the sport so much that he seldom misses a night favourable to it. The darker the night, and the calmer the water, the better it is for the fishing."[101] William "Tiger" Dunlop reported in 1832 that spearing was a "pretty amusement," but recommended that the novice should learn the art in shallow water: "for so sure as they commence their career, they will let their zeal outrun their discretion, and upset the canoe at least twice for once they will strike a fish."[102]

There was little or no export of salmon from Upper Canada at this time, most sales consisting of fresh fish passed through local markets. The colony, in fact, had no legislation to cover the inspection and packing of pickled fish for the export trade until 1840, and it was not until this date that fishing in Lake Ontario emerged as a significant commercial export venture.[103] Some export was carried on with American cities across the lake before the colonial salmon stocks were totally depleted, but trade statistics were not maintained in Ontario for the early years. Reports available for the period 1821 to 1829 mention that the extent of trade could not be ascertained, since the colony had no designated "sea port;" thus there is no reliable way of determining the size of the salmon export at this time.[104]

On the American side of Lake Ontario, the presence of salmon was instrumental in attracting many immigrants to the region. Rochester, New York, began to expand after 1815, developing along the Genesee River, which supported a salmon run estimated at 10 000 fish in the early years; after the first dam was constructed on the river in 1817, the runs rapidly declined.[105] Seventy-five miles east of Rochester was another major system, the Oswego River, where the salmon entered in no less numbers than they did on the Genesee. The runs on the Oswego did not, however, exhibit the rapid decline witnessed on the Genesee, and instead, salmon continued to frequent the river, though in diminishing numbers, until the 1860s.[106]

Twenty miles further eastward was another salmon stream entering the lake at Port Ontario; this fairly small Salmon River was accessible to fish for only 10 miles of its length, due to a 108-foot falls. The lower section of stream, however, was one of the most productive rearing areas on the south shore of the lake, and as such, was a great source of wealth to area fishermen. Populations of salmon were sustained on this river, and also on the adjacent streams of Grindstone and Deer, until the 1840s, in spite of fishing pressures. On the Salmon River, as late as 1836, 2000 fish could be taken in one night's work, and in that year, the largest fish taken weighed 44¾ pounds. One resident, speaking of these productive years, remembered that "The salmon fisheries on the rivers brought more money to the people than all the machinery now [1881] on the river."[107]

One firm which purchased salmon in Polaski frequently had no fewer than 1500 fish in their ice houses at one time. Commercial fishermen sometimes captured as many as 25 fish per hour in their nets, and literally tons of salmon were annually speared by those residing along the streams. Dams, however, were eventually constructed on the Salmon River and on most of the adjacent streams. The dams themselves acted as weirs at which fish could be easily taken, but sawdust from lumber mills, lime from tanneries, and other pollutants and obstructions resulted in a stock decrease dating from about 1840.[108]

Lake Champlain salmon were still being taken in considerable numbers in the first decade of the 19th century, but by the 1820s, many of the tributaries to the lake were dammed, and a corresponding decline in the resource was seen. In 1819, for example, a dam was erected at the mouth of the Saranac River, a stream that had been formerly open to salmon for approximately 20 miles. Fish were accustomed to entering the river in June and July, but mainly in August and September, and they were unmercifully slaughtered as they congregated at the base of the dam. Several local residents took the millowners to court in an attempt to secure salmon passage through the barrier, but their efforts were in vain; the millowners argued that the salmon were not the sea-running variety, and were thus indigenous to the lake region, not necessarily requiring a run to the river in order to reproduce their kind. On these grounds, the millowners won their case.[109]

Although stocks rapidly declined in these rivers, occasional catches were still made, principally in the lake itself; it was reported as late as 1823 that one haul of the seine at Port Kendall produced 1500 pounds of salmon. As the species became more scarce, it was sometimes reasoned that steamboats were the cause, because their continued disturbance of the lake had frightened the fish into oblivion. As far-fetched as this theory seems, it is a remarkable coincidence that in 1838, the year the only steamer on the tributary Richelieu River burnt, salmon were again seen in the Au Sable River for the first time in years. The spear and the net, however, were unrestricted and were undoubtedly the reasons why salmon had disappeared from Lake Champlain by 1845.[110]

Newfoundland and Labrador

The prosperous fishery which Newfoundland and Labrador had experienced between 1800 and 1814 reached its peak during the War of 1812. Very few American vessels chanced the precarious activity of fishing in hostile waters, and since the British were at war with Europe as well, the only nonlocal supply of fish available to Englishmen in their homeland was that which came from the North American colonies. After the close of hostilities, Great Britain could again secure fish from northern European countries, and the United States could again safely extend its fishing activity to the coastal waters of the British colonies. In consequence, Newfoundland fish prices fell; whereas the returns of 1814 showed unequalled prosperity in the fishery, the returns of 1815 indicated a serious depression. At the same time, one of the most severe winters ever recorded gripped the island and brought a large segment of the population to the point of starvation. In addition, famine and lawlessness occurred in St. John's after the great winter fire of 1816, while the winter of 1817–18 was commonly referred to as the "Winter of the Rals [Rowdies]." It took almost 4 years for the island to recover from these setbacks, and even longer for the fishery to recuperate.[111]

Salmon fishing firms on the east coast, from Cape John to Bonavista, continued to persevere through the depressed years. John Peyton was still fishing on the Exploits River and having some problems other than those brought on by slack markets; he continued to be harassed by the dwindling tribe of Beothucks, who were not confined to the Red Indian Lake region. In June 1814, he sent out Matthew Huster and John Morris to set two new 60-fathom salmon nets, which were subsequently stolen by Indians. When, in 1818, the Indians made off with his boat and its entire cargo of salmon destined for St. John's, Peyton decided that retaliatory action was

necessary. Gathering together a group of local salmoniers and furriers, he traveled to Red Indian Lake where, apart from killing one of the natives, frightening the tribe, and driving its remnant even further inland, he managed to bring back a female captive who eventually received great notice in St. John's; many people there had never seen a Beothuck before, and Demasduwit (Mary March) was one of the last of her race to be seen in Newfoundland. Meanwhile, Bishop Charles Inglis reported in 1827 that Peyton had 12 fishing stations along a 30-mile stretch of the Exploits.[112]

Some important insights into the Newfoundland salmon fishery in the early 1820s come from William Epps Cormack, a native son who achieved a name for himself as a naturalist and authority on many aspects of Newfoundland life. In 1822, Cormack crossed the interior of Newfoundland from Bonavista to St. Georges Bay, the first white man to do so. Although he mentioned capturing salmon fry in one of the feeder streams of the upper Gander River, his more significant remarks apply to the fishery of the west coast.

Arriving in St. Georges Bay, he stated that there were approximately 100 souls residing there, natives of England and Jersey:

> Their chief occupation is salmon fishing and furring; a little cod is also cured. They catch annually three or four hundred barrels of salmon, according to the success of the fishing.... To the southward... at Barasway are... 60 souls... who annually take 150 to 200 barrels of salmon.[113]

Some 50 barrels of salmon were also caught annually by the 80 or so settlers at "Great and Little Cod Roy." The able-bodied men in St. Georges Bay, with few exceptions, took to salmon fishing in the summer; about 30 crews, with two or three men in each boat, were stationed along the shores and at the river mouths at the time of the salmon run.

As one continued northward from St. Georges Bay, a few English families could still be encountered on what was commonly acknowledged as the French Shore: six families were settled at Bay of Islands (Humber) and several others were found at Bonne Bay. The latter fishery was principally undertaken by a Mr. Bird, who had been situated there even before the peace of 1814. The French made his life rather uncomfortable on several occasions, forbidding him, for example, from carrying on his fishery in 1822. He was, however, operating there unmolested in 1826.[114] There were also a few families settled between Quirpon and Cape St. John, and Cormack wrote,

> Taking an aggregate view of the French shore, there are resident upon it upwards of fifty British families, consisting of about three hundred souls, who catch annually nearly seven hundred barrels of salmon.... The British residents on the French Shore feel very insecure in the

enjoyment of their Salmon fishery and in any extensions of their property by reason of the particular tenure in regard of the French.[115]

Concerning the south coast of Newfoundland, Cormack reported that salmon were of little importance in the area between Cape Ray and the Ramea Islands, the rivers not being "so large or numerous" as those on the [east] coast.[116] There were, however, many small ports between Ramea and Grand Bank where the inhabitants fished and traded their catch to the Nova Scotian, American, and Lower Canadian merchant vessels which annually plied the coastline. A Captain Milne reported of this region in 1841 that

> There are also Salmon fisheries in the vicinity, fished by the inhabitants and also by the Indians, there being a settlement of about 100 of them a few miles to the west, at Little Barasway, who trade with the inhabitants of the Coast, and at Burgeo Islands, exchanging Salmon, Geese, and Furs for Clothing, Spirits and Powder.

Milne went on to report of Grand Bank that "There are Salmon Fishings at this small Port, as at all others, where ever a small rivulet communicates with the sea."[117]

Further north, in Labrador, various observers noted the continuing exploitation of the vast salmon resource. Of all the locations on the eastern Labrador coast, Sandwich Bay was perhaps the most important:

> The principal and almost only fishery is salmon, taken in the Eagle and other rivers in Sandwich Bay. The salmon are cured at the rivers, which are 20 miles from Sandwich Bay, packed in tin cases, sent down to Dumplin Island, and from thence shipped to England direct. The people, who fish the rivers, are brought out from England in the spring, and return again when the salmon season is over which is the beginning or end of August.[118]

Hamilton Inlet was the farthest northern point where serious commercial salmon fishing was undertaken, but the arctic waters north of latitude 55° were also being explored and used, principally by Moravian missionaries who had established themselves at locations such as Nain and Hopedale late in the 18th century. Reports by Eskimos of the great numbers of salmon and whales which inhabited the Ungava Bay region enticed the Moravian priests to explore those areas as early as 1811. Soon to follow was the Hudson's Bay Company, which established Fort Good Hope on the Koksoak River in 1830, for purposes of trading with the natives and engaging in a whale and salmon fishery. Good Hope was a somewhat inappropriate title for their post, and the name was changed to Fort Chimo; attempts at trade and enterprise were unsuccessful, however, and the post was subsequently closed in 1843.[119]

Although the Convention of 1818 had allowed American fishing rights to the coast of Labrador and the west and south shores of Newfoundland, the British interpreted the liberty as applying to the cod fishery only and attempted to restrict American activity for other shore species such as the salmon by attempting to bar them from harbors and estuaries where the species could be taken. There is little evidence that this was a successful move.

The problem of encroachment was general, for besides the Americans, fishermen from Lower Canada and Nova Scotia continued to venture northward. This encroachment was particularly evident in southern Labrador, through the vast area from Rigolet to the Mingan Passage — an area which Newfoundlanders considered their preserve.

As early as 1816, the Newfoundland government was receiving petitions from Labrador fishermen protesting foreign influence in the regional salmon fishery. One such petition, which culminated in some legislative action, was that of Philip Beard in 1819, in which Beard stated:

> In the Month of July 1816 Your petitioner P. Beard went out to Sandwich Bay with three Vessels and about Eighty men, in order to prosecute the fishery, when he found that a Mr. McPherson had arrived from Nova Scotia, and had taken possession of a part of the Bay, and was fishing for Salmon, & preventing the salmon from taking the usual course to the Rivers, which had been, for so long a period uniformly fished by your Petitioner's predecessors.

Beard also stated that despite the fact that Captain Coakesley of the local protection vessel, the H.M.S. *Hazard*, had laid down a strict rule that strangers were not to fish within 3 miles of the boundary line drawn across the mouths of rivers, repeated encroachments occurred:

> the consequence is that instead of the annual average of 750 Tierces of Salmon as caught prior to 1817, the quantity caught last year [1818] was only 450, 250 Tierces having been caught by the said McPherson and by Vessels from the United States and from Nova Scotia.[120]

As a result of this and other complaints, the Newfoundland governor, Vice Admiral Sir Charles Hamilton, issued several regulations for the Labrador coast. Nets could not be placed closer than within 40 yards of each other, and salmon nets could not exceed 30 fathoms in length; no nets could be fished after dark; and a weekend closure was "strongly recommended" in order to provide escapement to the spawning grounds. In addition to these regulations, foreigners were not allowed to set nets within 3 miles of the river boundaries fished by Newfoundland and Labrador proprietors.[121]

These regulations did little to stem the tide of foreigners fishing for salmon and other species on the coast.

In July 1821, the captain of the British protection vessel *Clinker* reported that Canadians had established an extensive salmon fishery at Grady Harbour, and other reports indicated that the Stars and Stripes had literally replaced the Union Jack in many Labrador harbors.[122] With regard to the Americans, little could be done, for the Convention of 1818 gave them the right to almost the entire coastline from the Natashquan River to Hamilton Inlet, for purposes of fishing and drying fish. Even Lower Canadian encroachment on the Labrador coast went unchecked, and resulted, as noted previously, in a large segment of Labrador being given back to Quebec in 1825.

A particularly bad year for Newfoundland interests in Labrador was 1826; not only had their territory been recently reduced through an act of Parliament, but the fishery of that year also turned out to be poor. Furthermore, the governor had begun to levy import duties on goods entering Labrador, a move which the people vigorously protested; it is unfortunate that the governor stirred up so much indignation in this matter, for the average annual revenue from Labrador duties was less than £70. Apart from this, Newfoundland proprietors were being blatantly intimidated by an increasing number of American fishermen; civil actions on the coast more than doubled between 1826 and 1828.[123] Fishery protection was inadequate, since the one vessel appointed for this duty could not keep the whole coast under surveillance, and was frequently unsuccessful in prosecuting known irregularities.

The Labrador situation was summed up in 1832 by George Young, a Nova Scotian who was furious at both the encroachment of American fishing interests and the apparent apathy of the British government toward the whole British North American fishery. Writing a lengthy series of letters to E. G. S. Stanley, a member of the British Parliament, Young noted of Labrador that:

> The rivers of that coast are known to be as affluent in salmon as any in the world, but the inhabitants are not allowed to enjoy that branch of the fishery unmolested, for the Americans not only enter their rivers, and set their nets, but frequently draw the nets of the residents in broad light of day, and in the presence of their owners, who dare not console themselves, even with the poor satisfaction of complaint, for less resistance.[124]

How much salmon was taken in Labrador by American ships at this time is not accurately known. It was reported that 1124 tierces (337 200 lb pickled) were caught between Lance-au-Loup and Rigolet in 1825; the amount caught by British, Jersey, and Newfoundland firms was recorded as 2200 tierces (660 000 lb pickled) in 1829. It is not inconceivable that at least an additional unrecorded 1500 tierces were taken annually by Americans, since salmon was a desirable commodity in the

United States at this time, and records indicate the following amounts were imported between 1829 and 1843: 999 barrels in 1829; 2104 barrels in 1832; 3790 barrels in 1838; and 2640 barrels in 1843.[125] It is likely that a large portion of this production was taken by American fishermen on the Labrador coast.

Newfoundland continued its efforts to control the Labrador salmon industry, often to the detriment of local as well as foreign fishermen. It was a difficult life for the people in Labrador, who often felt neglected by government; on one occasion in 1836, 16 salmon fishermen refused to accept a new regulation imposed on them by the Newfoundland governor, on the grounds that Labrador, not being represented in the Newfoundland Assembly, was required to accept the laws of Great Britain, but not the laws of the island colony.[126] Many who fished in Labrador were also at the mercy of the large fishing firms, and as late as 1841, it was reported that the agent for one firm at Blanc Sablon had put most of the firm's employees in irons and fed them on bread and water, because they refused to work on the Sabbath Day.[127]

By 1842, Richard Bonnycastle noted that Newfoundland's salmon fishery was inconsiderable when compared to that of Labrador. Although the export records tend not to support this opinion, the true situation becomes more understandable when one considers that a large portion of the recorded Newfoundland export actually originated in Labrador. The Newfoundland salmon fishery, nevertheless, was prosperous in certain traditional areas, such as in Gander, White, Exploits, and Bonavista bays, plus several other stations on the southwestern shore. The cod fishery so controlled the interest of mainland Newfoundlanders, however, that salmon were almost as scarce and expensive in the markets of St. John's as they were in London, although the usual selling price of six pence — or 12 cents — a pound, hardly appears costly by today's standards.

The 1840 export records for Newfoundland show where the markets for salmon were at this time: of the 3396 tierces exported, 38 percent went to the United States; 22 percent went to foreign European markets; 19 percent to other British North American colonies; 13 percent to the British West Indies; and the remaining 8 percent to Great Britain.[128]

New England

After the War of 1812, the people of New England and, in particular, of Massachusetts, were hungry for fish; more accurately, they were hungry for the right to continue fishing in British North American waters. So intent were they upon securing this right that their chief negotiator recalled: "It is an extraordinary thing that the question of peace or war depended solely on two points... Moose Island, and the fisheries within British jurisdiction.[129]

This longing for foreign waters points clearly to the sorry state of the New England fisheries, both coastal and inland, at this time. Like British North America, the eastern states were caught up in the timber trade, resulting in the obstruction of many rivers to anadromous fish runs. By 1837, for example, 250 sawmills could be found along the Penobscot River system alone, with approximately 1300 existing in all of Maine.[130] In speaking of the sawmill menace to salmon during this period, one observer has commented that "Almost every stream... large enough to turn a saw-mill has been thus obstructed at from one to a dozen points in its course."[131]

Unlike New Brunswick, Nova Scotia, and Newfoundland, the early development of an enormous factory system in New England, largely for cotton and textile manufacture, added considerably to the many river obstructions; by 1840, 1200 such factories had been erected in the United States, 800 of which were located in New England. The Merrimack River was dammed at Lowell as early as 1822, limiting the salmon run in the main stream to about one-fifth of what it had previously been. Salmon, however, continued to ascend the river to this structure for a number of years, since in 1830 it was reported that Merrimack salmon were partially supplying the Boston market. Further north, in the Kennebec River, a dam was built at Augusta in 1837, an action which completed a chain of obstructions that limited the salmon run to about 50 miles, rather than the previous three hundred. By 1840, Kennebec River salmon were becoming scarce, and so keen were Bostonians to obtain fresh specimens, that the first one captured in the Kennebec that year was sold in Boston for 42 dollars.[132]

Military and Social Maneuvers

Salmon angling in British North America grew slowly between 1760 and 1840. It was practiced and perpetuated mainly by a small group of British army and navy officers who were posted at such locations as York (Toronto), Quebec City, Halifax, and Fredericton, and who found it desirous to escape periodically from the monotony and confinement of garrison duty.[133] Extant narratives and travelogues describe the officers' efforts in pursuing cod and mackerel for sport, and also their engaging in the pastime of spearing lobsters; nevertheless, the search for salmon with a rod and line gathered more and more appeal. In consequence, the rivers that became the first important salmon angling streams in British America were those proximate to the military posts. Near Fredericton, for example, salmon angling on the Nashwaak River was described as "serviceable, delightful and amusing" as early as 1791.[134]

The men posted at Quebec City frequented the Jacques Cartier River in the early years, and those serving at Halifax found that the Gold, Sackville and Musquodoboit rivers were ideal watercourses upon which to practice the Waltonian art; regular visits were made to these areas after 1800 to engage in the sport.[135]

Salmon angling on the Gold River, for example, was said to have begun around 1833; in 1842, one party of army officers took 114 in three weeks. And as early as 1825, the Mason family bought land around Indian River, in eastern Halifax County, for the specific purpose of catering to anglers from the Halifax garrison.[136]

In the literature of the day, Nova Scotia emerges as a place where angling was practiced as a relatively frequent sporting diversion, and where concentrated efforts were made to overcome the difficulties of the sport. In 1830, Captain William Moorsom wrote:

> I know a worthy disciple of Izaak Walton in this country, who, in proof of his devotion to the craft, and at the same time of his willingness to escape death by piecemeal, has been seen to wind his solitary way to the lakes, clad in the defensive armour of a huge pair of hedger's gloves, his face smeared with a composition of camphor and grease, his fishing-rod in one hand, and a formidable torch of birch bark in the other; the last being a sort of flaming sword, whereby a constant fumigation is maintained around the head and all access thus interdicted to the agents of evil in the shape of black flies.[137]

One of the prime trout streams, and perhaps the most popular salmon-angling river in Nova Scotia was the River Philip, of which Moorsom said, "The early part of June is the most favorable season for fishing; at that time I have known three gentlemen, without making any exertion beyond a mere day's sport, bring to land a hundred and eighty pounds weight of fine trout before evening."[138] The previous year, Thomas Chandler Haliburton also remarked that "The River Philip, though not navigable for any extent, is extremely beautiful, and remarkable for its excellent salmon fishery, and the abundance and size of its trout.[139]

Further eastward, Joseph Howe advertised the advantages of Barneys River:

> If the gentle traveller be an angler, and has had the precaution to carry his gear on the journey, he need not desire a prettier place to cast a fly than Barney's River, which flows along through a little intervale, about a hundred yards beyond Murray's tavern. A skillful handler of the 'Rod and Line' will, at the proper season, take a good fare of trout, or perhaps a brace of salmon....[140]

Apparently the anglers of Upper Canada sought the trout more than the salmon, a trend which was due to the difficulty of angling for the latter, rather than to any particular preference for the former. In 1832 "Tiger" Dunlop commented:

> The stream is no less prolific in sport than the forest and field. And if a man thinks proper, in the words of Izaak Walton, 'to be pleasant and eat trout,' he can gratify his taste to any extent in Upper Canada.... The banks being overhung with trees, fly-fishing is rarely to be had, except you station yourself on a bridge or mill-dam.[141]

A year later, T. W. Magrath reported:

> In fishing for trout, the bass frequently takes off the fly. The salmon fly is best suited to them — which is here but seldom used, as the salmon are so well fed at the bottom of the rivers, they are not, in but few instances, known to take the fly.[142]

The wife of an immigrant officer to Upper Canada in 1830 wrote, however, that "The large sorts of fish are mostly taken with the spear, few persons having time for angling in the busy country,"[143] and this, indeed, seemed to be the case with the common people of all the colonies. Angling was still the preserve of the man of means, the idle, the gentleman traveler, or the commissioned officer.

Gold and Silver, Have I Some?

If we could speak to the man best informed on Atlantic salmon in North America in 1845, and ask him to supply us with a short summary of his knowledge on the topic, his discourse would probably be somewhat as follows:

> Sirs: *Salmo* is the noblest of all freshwater fish; the prince of streams, whose title to this precedence is beyond question. He is a creature of beautiful proportions, graceful motions, speed, agility, and intellectual instinct, with a keen and lively eye. He is a source of considerable wealth to fishermen, as evidenced by the records of commerce, which show that upwards of 12 000 tierces, valued at over £45,000, are exported annually from all the British North American colonies. In addition, he provides subsistence to the farmer, the immigrant and the Indian alike; and is the legitimate object of the sportsman's loftiest aspirations — the true and ultimate test for those elevated individuals who follow the Waltonian art.
>
> "*Salmo* once ranged as far south as the Hudson River and Lake Champlain, and as far west as the magnificent falls of Niagara, but is now rarely encountered at these extremities. Its limits of occurrence in the north have not been ascertained, but scattered reports indicate that it provides food for the savage and his dogs in the frigid regions of the Eskimos. Salmon are still relatively abundant in many of the pure, clear, and unencumbered streams of the eastern colonies from New Brunswick to the Labrador, but are rapidly declining in numbers almost everywhere, as a result of the unrestricted use of the net and the negog and the erection of milldams and other engines of destruction upon their former habitats.

> "Their chief method of capture is with set nets in the river estuaries and deeper regions, and with spears on the shallower stretches.
>
> "The natural history of this member of the finny tribe is still wrapped in considerable mystery, but we are now rapidly achieving full enlightenment on the topic, as a number of scientific minds have become engaged in unraveling these piscatorial enigmas. The female salmon are the first to enter the rivers of the colonies, beginning in April; next follow the males, and lastly the half-salmon, or grilse. Although the dates at which each succeeding group enters the rivers may vary from region to region, they are all available for spawning in October or November.
>
> "They pass upward in shoals, leaping over every barrier of less than twelve to fifteen feet in perpendicular height. Spawning takes place in the gravel at the headwater lakes and rivulets, where the water is constantly agitated. Like the swallow, *Salar* shows a strong desire to return to last year's quarters to perform the act of perpetuation, and dies if he cannot reach his nuptual bed. The male digs a nest in the gravel with his snout, and the female deposits her spawn when the water temperatures are sufficiently low to accommodate their survival.
>
> "After the ova is deposited, it becomes quickened into life by some hidden and inscrutable process, and the shells burst to emit the fry. Until recently, it was thought that these fry attained a length of from four to seven inches by March or April, and descended to the sea in June, July and August, at which time they were termed parr, smelts or smolts; and many still subscribe to this contention. However, experiments by Dr. Shaw in Scotland show beyond any doubt that the parr — common in all salmon rivers and previously thought to be a separate species because of their non-silvery appearance and their different markings — are nothing more than older salmon fry.
>
> "Dr. Shaw's revelation has also opened to question the length of time salmon fry remain in freshwater before they molt to become smelts (smolts). Some observers contend that a full year intervenes between fry and smolt, while others believe that two whole seasons may elapse before the fry don their silvery coats and seek the salt water which, if they cannot attain it because of some obstruction, they will dash themselves upon the bank and perish.
>
> "Smolts which reach the ocean will return to the same river the following year as salmon peale, or grilse, weighing two to seven pounds, although again, some examiners contend that this is not the case, the peale being altogether different than the larger fish. At sea, the salmon may attain a weight of upward of one hundred pounds, although few have recently been taken whose weight exceeds fifty or sixty pounds.
>
> "Where the salmon resides in Neptune's element is a mystery as yet unsolved, since they are never encountered at any great distance from the shore. They are, however, subject to the predations of diverse sea creatures of a larger size, as fewer return to the river than leave it. Also, the depredations of man and the many engines he has devised on the waterways to stop the fish,

unless otherwise checked, will totally eliminate this noble species from its ancestral home at no distant day."

This combination of Victorian gingerbread and scientific architecture was to be an integral part of the academic salmon investigation process for several decades to come. Nevertheless, the true wisdom emerging from these studies was not lost on a rather select group of individuals who began a conservation campaign during the 1850s and 1860s, to save from complete destruction the silver fish that laid the golden eggs.

NOTES

[1]James Bingay, *A History of Canada* (Toronto: Nelson, 1947), pp. 242–250, 343.

[2]William Cattermole, *Emigration: The Advantages of Emigration to Canada* (London: Simpkin and Marshall, 1831; reprinted Toronto: Coles, 1970), p. 3.

[3]Robert Legget, *Ottawa Waterway* (Toronto: University of Toronto Press, 1975), p. 119. Edward Davis, "Opening the Way Upstream — The Fish Escalator," in The Atlantic Salmon Journal, Vol. 2, (1974), p. 14.

[4]Abraham Gesner, *New Brunswick with Notes for Emigrants* (London: Simonds and Ward, 1847), pp. 273, 283.

[5]Wallace Graham, "The Fisheries of British North America and the United States Fishermen," *Collections of the Nova Scotia Historical Society*, Vol. XIV, (Halifax: Wm. MacNab & Son, 1909), p. 6.

[6]Gesner, *New Brunswick*, p. 277.

[7]Quoted in *ibid.*, p. 278.

[8]George W. Brown, *Building the Canadian Nation* (Toronto: Dent, 1849), p. 193.

[9]W. S. MacNutt, *New Brunswick: A History, 1784–1867* (Toronto: Macmillan, 1963), p. 144, *Statutes of the Province of New Brunswick*, 59 George III, c. 13. Robert Clooney, *A Compendious History of the Northern Part of the Province of New Brunswick and the District of Gaspé in Lower Canada* (Halifax: Howe, 1832), p. 56.

[10]*New Brunswick Statutes*, 56 George III, c. 3: 60 George III, c. 21: 4 George IV, c. 23; 7 George IV, c. 22; 3 William IV, c. 27.

[11]Graeme Wynn, *Timber Colony* (Toronto: University of Toronto Press, 1981), p. 28.

[12]Clooney, *History of Northern New Brunswick*, p. 59; MacNutt, *New Brunswick*, p. 179. There were 584 sawmills in the province by 1851; see Alexander Munro, *New Brunswick, with a Brief Outline of Nova Scotia and Prince Edward Island* (Halifax: Nugent, 1855), p. 120.

[13]*New Brunswick Statutes*, 50 George III, c. 20. MacNutt, *New Brunswick*, p. 296; p. 322: "The forests, it was conceded, were exhaustible, but the fisheries were not."

[14]Richard M'Farlan, *River and Brook Fisheries* (Fredericton: Reporter's Office, 1847); *New Brunswick Courier* (Saint John, N.B.), 11 February 1837.

[15]See export statistics in Lorenzo Sabine, *The Principal Fisheries of the American Seas*, (Washington: Robert Armstrong, 1853), p. 91.

[16]Munro, *New Brunswick*, p. 203.

[17]James Hannay, *History of New Brunswick* (Saint John: Bowes, 1909), I, 354.

[18]Stewart H. Holbook, *The American Lumberjack* (New York: Collier, 1962), p. 66.

[19]MacNutt, *New Brunswick*, p. 197.

[20]William Francis Ganong, *The History of Miscou and Shippegan* (Saint John: Globe Printing Co., 1946), p. 57.

[21]Peter Fisher, *History of New Brunswick* (Saint John; Chubb, 1825; reprinted Saint John: New Brunswick Historical Society, 1921), p. 81.

[22]Hannay, *History of New Brunswick*, I. 400: Governor, Sir Howard Douglas, "expressed the opinion that the fisheries might be made much more productive, and that a trade in that article might be established with the new states of South America." *Ibid.*, p. 401, notes that an act was passed establishing bounties on fish caught and cured for the Mediterranean market.

[23]J. Clarence Webster, *An Historical Guide to New Brunswick* (n.p.: Government Bureau of Information and Tourist Travel, 1947), p. 66.

[24]John West, *The Substance of a Journal* (London: Seeley, 1827), p. 239.

[25]*Journal of the House of Assembly of New Brunswick*, 1847, "Fisheries Reports," Appendix, p. cxxxix; the average export for 1828, 1829, and 1830 was 550 barrels; for 1835, 1836, and 1837, 860 barrels; for 1838, 1839, and 1840, 1070 barrels; and for 1841, 1842, and 1843, 1630 barrels. See also Clooney, *History of Northern New Brunswick*, pp. 91–93.

[26]James McGregor, *Historical and Descriptive Sketches of the Maritime Colonies of British America* (Liverpool: Picken, 1828), pp. 162–163.

[27]MacNutt, *New Brunswick*, p. 216; see also Esther Clark Wright, *The Loyalists of New Brunswick* (Fredericton: n.p., 1955), p. 147, and Hannay, *History of New Brunswick*, I, 406.

[28]McGregor, *Sketches of the Maritime Colonies*, p. 183.

[29]Letter of Robert Ferguson to Richard Simonds, 19 January 1829, F36, New Brunswick Museum Archives.

[30]John Mowat, *Chaleur Bay* (n.p.: privately printed, ca. 1889), pp. 4, 6. *Scots Canadiensis*, "Salmon Fishing in the Restigouche," in *Maritime Monthly*, II, 6 (December 1873), 542: The statement that "Forty or forty-five years ago, when net fishing had not well begun, and the spear was also the only weapon used by the few white men and the Indians alike, the fish were more abundant in the river than now...," implies that the spear was dominant during the 1820s and 1830s.

[31]Pat Ryan, "A River Running Out of Eden," in *Sports Illustrated*, Vol. 32(21) (25 May 1970), p. 88. Apparently a considerable number of salmon from the Restigouche bore spear marks and were, consequently, suitable only for the West Indies market, where slaves did not object to less than perfect specimens. See also Harold A. Innis, *The Cod Fisheries* (Toronto: University of Toronto Press, 1954), p. 278.

[32]Philip K. Bock, *The MicMac Indians of Restigouche*, Bulletin 213 (Ottawa: National Museum, 1966), pp. 16-17. "Middle ground" is a common term used to indicate somewhat shallow, submerged fishing banks in river estuaries; deeper water is found on either side of a middle ground.

[33]John MacTaggart, *Three Years in Canada* (London: Colburn, 1829), I, 20–21.

[34]Moses Perley, *The Sea and River Fisheries of New Brunswick* (Fredericton: Simpson, 1852), p. 761. *New Brunswick Journals*, 1847, Appendix, p. cxxv.

[35]*New Brunswick Statutes*, 3 William IV, c. 27.

[36]*New Brunswick Journals*, 1847, Appendix, p. cxxxvii.

[37]Letter of Robert Ferguson, New Brunswick Museum Archives.

[38]Mowat, *Chaleur Bay*, p. 4. *New Brunswick Journals*, 1847, Appendix, p. cxxxvii. James S. Buckingham, *Canada, Nova Scotia, New Brunswick, and the Other British Provinces in North America* (London: Fisher, 1843), p. 312, states that salmon catches were up to 2000 barrels for Chaleur Bay by 1843.

[39]Mowat, *Chaleur Bay*, p. 4.

[40]*New Brunswick Statutes*, 3 William IV, c. 27.

[41]Mowat, *Chaleur Bay*, p. 4.

[42]Joshua Marsden, *The Narrative of a Mission to Nova Scotia, New Brunswick and the Somers Islands* (London: Kershaw, 1827), pp. 86, 88.

[43]Ward Papers, New Brunswick Museum Archives.

[44]Fisher, *History of New Brunswick*, p. 81. *New Brunswick Journals*, 1847, Appendix, p. cxlvii.

[45]Index Cards, New Brunswick Museum Archives.

[46]Cicely Lyons, *Salmon, Our Heritage* (Vancouver: Mitchell, 1969), pp. 140–141.

[47]William Corbett, "Advice to Young Men" (1829), quoted in Michael Collie, *New Brunswick* (Toronto: Macmillan, 1974), pp. 120–121.

[48]Perley, *The Fisheries of New Brunswick*, p. 136.

[49]*Ibid.*, p. 124. William Francis Ganong, *Ste. Croix (Dochet) Island*, Monographic Series 3 (Saint John: New Brunswick Museum, 1945), p. 102, notes that, beginning in 1826, several fishermen from Penobscot came to Ste. Croix Island annually to attend six salmon weirs in the region; for a few years, many fish were taken.

[50]Letter of John Wilson, St. Andrew's, 17 December 1828. New Brunswick Museum Archives.

[51]Thomas Chandler Haliburton, *An Historical and Statistical Account of Nova Scotia* (Halifax: 1829; reprinted Belleville, Ontario: Mika, 1973), II, 322.

[52]Military C Series, Index Cards, "Fisheries, N.S.," 1818, 1823, Public Archives of Canada (hereafter PAC).

[53]*Journals of the House of Assembly of Nova Scotia*, 1839–40, Appendix 85, "Fisheries Commission Report," p. 213.

[54]Charles Boidman Owen, *An Epitome of History, Statistics, etc., of Nova Scotia* (Halifax: English and Black-adar, 1842), pp. 84, 96.

[55]Thomas Chandler Haliburton, *The Clockmaker: or, the Sayings and Doings of Samuel Slick, of Slickville* (New Canadian Library edition, Toronto: McClelland & Stewart, 1958), p. 133.

[56]Joseph Howe, *Western and Eastern Rambles: Travel Sketches of Nova Scotia*, ed. M. G. Parks (Toronto: University of Toronto Press, 1973), p. 88.

[57]William Dunlop, *Tiger Dunlop's Upper Canada* (New Canadian Library edition, Toronto: McClelland & Stewart, 1967), p. 135.

[58]*Nova Scotia Journals*, 1839–40, Appendix 85, "Fisheries Commission Report," pp. 215–16.

[59]George Patterson, *A History of the County of Pictou, Nova Scotia* (Montreal: Davison, 1877; reprinted Belleville, Ont.: Mika, 1972), p. 305.

[60]Haliburton, *Nova Scotia*, II, 63. William Scarth Moorsom, *Letters from Nova Scotia* (London: Colburn, 1830), p. 327.

[61]Howe, *Western and Eastern Rambles*, p. 62.

[62]*Nova Scotia Tour Book*, 1971 edition (Halifax: Department of Trade and Industry, 1971), p. 93. Haliburton, *Nova Scotia*, II, 77–79.

[63]Richard Brown, *A History of the Island of Cape Breton* (London: Sampson Low, 1869), p. 433. *Nova Scotia Journals*, 1845, Appendix 87, p. 310.

[64]For example, see Haliburton, *Nova Scotia*, I, 252, and McGregor, *Sketches of the Maritime Colonies*, p. 117.

[65]See statistical records published in various *Annual Reports* of the Department of Marine and Fisheries, 1867–1899.

[66]Haliburton, *Nova Scotia*, II, 91.

[67]John N. Grant, *The Development of Sherbrooke Village to 1880* (Halifax: Nova Scotia Museum, 1972), p. 5. Moorsom, *Letters from Nova Scotia*, pp. 341, notes that two small fishing establishments had been formed locally; their principal interest appeared to be in carrying lumber to Halifax in April, and then outfitting in that port for Labrador.

[68]Howe, *Western and Eastern Rambles*, pp. 193–94.

[69]Haliburton, *Nova Scotia*, II, 190.

[70]Owen, *An Epitome of Nova Scotia*, p. 120; see also, Haliburton, *Nova Scotia*, II, 142.

[71]Mather Byles DesBrisay, *History of the County of Lunenburg* (Toronto: Briggs, 1895; reprinted Belleville, Ont.: Mika, 1972), pp. 154–55, 462–63.

[72]*Ibid.*, p. 463.

[73]Owen, *An Epitome of Nova Scotia*, p. 120.

[74]J. Lynton Martin, "Farm Life in Nova Scotia Prior to 1850," in *Collections* of the Nova Scotia Historical Society, XXXVII, (1970), 84.

[75]Haliburton, *Nova Scotia*, II, 139, 144.

[76]D. C. Harvey, ed., *Journeys to the Island of St. John* (Toronto: Macmillan, 1955), p. 77.

[77]John Stewart, *An Account of Prince Edward Island in the Gulph of St. Lawrence, North America* (London: Winchester 1806), p. 84.

[78]Quoted in A. B. Warburton, *A History of Prince Edward Island* (Saint John: Barnes, 1923), p. 360.

[79]J. L. Lewellin, "Immigration: Prince Edward Island," in Harvey, *Journeys*, p. 199.

[80]E. D. T. Chambers, *The Fisheries of the Province of Quebec* (Quebec: Department of Colonization, Mines and Fisheries, 1912), I. 126. Unless otherwise noted, the information in this section comes from *ibid.*, pp. 103, 117–142.

[81]*Ibid.*, p. 118.

[82]*Ibid.*, p. 120.

[83]*Ibid.*, p. 127.

[84]*Ibid.*, p. 133.

[85]These establishments were "Mingan, Cormorant, Nabaysepie, Musquarou, St. Johns, Great Romaine, Washisou, Natasquem, Kikaska, Washicoute and Little Romaine;" the latter seven were specifically salmon fisheries. See K. G. Davies, ed., *Northern Quebec and Labrador Journals and Correspondence, 1819–1835* (London: Hudson's Bay Company Record Society, 1963), p. 108h.

[86]Colonial Office (hereafter C.O.) Papers, 47, "Blue Books," Vol. 122–139, *passim*, "Letter of J. F. LaRocque to George Simpson," in K. G. Davies, ed., *Northern Quebec and Labrador Journals and Correspondence, 1819–1835* (London: Hudson's Bay Record Society, 1963), p. 232. The valuable Mingan fishery was "failing materially" in 1831, thus giving credence to a general decline evident into the 1830s.

[87]John W. Parsons, *History of Salmon in the Great Lakes, 1850–1970*, Technical Paper No. 68, Bureau of Sport Fisheries and Wildlife (Washington: Government Printing Office, 1973), p. 9.

[88]Robert Gourlay, *Statistical Account of Upper Canada* (London: Simpkin and Marshall, 1822), I, 271.

[89]Edward E. Prince, "The Maximum Size of Fishes and Its Causes," in *Annual Report* of the Department of Marine and Fisheries, 1903 (Ottawa: King's Printer, 1904), Appendix, II, p. lix.

[90]*Statutes of Upper Canada to the Time of the Union* (Toronto: Queen's Printer, 1841), I, 313.

[91]*Ibid.*, pp. 313–15, 371.

[92]Gourlay, *Statistical Account*, I, 176. Paul Kane, *Wanderings of an Artist* (New York: Longman, Brown, 1859; reprinted Edmonton: Hurtig, 1968), pp. 16–21. *passim.*, notes salmon in the "straits between lakes Huron and Michigan" and in other areas above Niagara as late as 1858.

[93]Edward Allen Talbot, *Five Years' Residence in the Canadas* (London: Longman, 1824), I, 268.

[94]*Ibid.*

[95]MacTaggart, *Three Years in Canada*, I, 130–31, reported salmon above Niagara Falls and claimed they were not a sea variety — the latter fact being hardly disputable. Even Lake Ontario fish, he supposed, could not overcome the rapids of the St. Lawrence. He stated that the salmon were found only in those waters which were tributary to the St. Lawrence, and not in any of the interior lakes with their "more compact floorings of ice." "We know," he wrote, "that fish are fond of air holes and breathing places."

[96]T. W. Magrath, *Authentic Letters from Upper Canada: With an Account of Canada Field Sports* (Dublin: n.p., 1833), pp. 298–99.

[97]*The Backwoods of Canada: Letters from the Wife of an Emigrant Officer* (London: Knight, 1836), p. 161: "The large sorts of fish are mostly taken with the spear, few persons having time for angling in this busy country."

[98]Mrs. John Graves Simcoe, *The Diary of Mrs. John Graves Simcoe*, ed. J. Ross Robertson (Toronto: Briggs, 1911; reprinted Toronto: Coles, 1973), p. 106.

[99]Gourlay, *Statistical Account*, I, 176.

[100]Magrath, *Letters from Upper Canada*, pp. 287–88. *Ibid.*, pp. 291–92: "Shortly after our arrival here, my brother and I speared one hundred and twenty salmon of a night; but they are now becoming less numerous, in consequence of the number of saw mills erected, the profusion of saw dust on the water... and the multitudes of oak stoves annually floating down the river."

[101]*The Backwoods of Canada* p. 159.

[102]Dunlop, *Tiger Dunlop's Upper Canada*, p. 95.

[103]*Statutes of Upper Canada at the Time of the Union*, p. 1032. Gourlay, *Statistical Account*, I, 271.

[104]C.O., 47, "Blue Books," Vol. 144–55, *passim*, PAC.

[105]Anthony Netboy, *The Atlantic Salmon, A Vanishing Species?* (London: Faber, 1968), p. 333.

[106]G. Browne Goode, "The Salmon Tribe," *The Fisheries and Fishing Industries of the United States*, ed. G. Browne Goode (Washington: Commission of Fish and Fisheries, 1884–87), I, 473.

[107]*Ibid.*, p. 474.

[108]*Ibid.*, pp. 473–74.

[109]W. C. Watson, "The Salmon of Lake Champlain and Its Tributaries," in *Report of the United States Commission of Fish and Fisheries (1873–4 and 1874–5)*, (Washington: Government Printing Office, 1876), p. 537.

[110]*Ibid.*, p. 535.

[111]D. W. Prowse, *A History of Newfoundland* (London: Macmillan, 1895; reprinted Belleville, Ont.: Mika, 1972), pp. 402–03. James P. Howley, *The Beothucks or Red Indians* (Cambridge: Cambridge University Press, 1915; reprinted Toronto: Coles, 1974), p. 177.

[112]Howley, *The Beothucks*, pp. 92, 105, 117, 295. G.M. Story, "Demasduwit," in *Dictionary of Canadian Biography* (Toronto: University of Toronto Press, 1983), V, 243–44.

[113]Quoted in Howley, *The Beothucks*, pp. 143, 159–60, 235. G.M. Story, "Cormack, William Eppes" in *Dictionary of Canadian Biography* (Toronto: University of Toronto Press, 1976), IX, 158–62. In later years, Cormack documented and wrote about the various kinds of salmon found in the Fraser River of British Columbia, and was in charge of that colony's ichthyological displays at the provincial exhibition of 1862.

[114]"Letter of Governor Hamilton to Lords of Trade." in C.O. Supplementary I, Misc. Papers, Vol. 18, "Fisheries, 1712–1852," PAC. (26 September 1827)

[115]Quoted in Howley, *The Beothucks*, p. 160.

[116]*Ibid.*, p. 166.

[117]*Nova Scotia Journals*, 1841, Appendix 62, "Captain Milne's Report," p. 168.

[118]*Ibid.*, p. 168.

[119]A. Copeland, "Ungava," in *North*, Vol. xvii (2), (March–April, 1970), 43. Davies, *Northern Quebec and Labrador Journals*, p. 143, notes that in 1818 the Hudson's Bay Company sent out one of its employees to examine the Ungava region. The Indian guide who accompanied the expedition told the group that there were "great plenty of salmon to be procured" at the mouth of he Koksoak River. *Ibid.*, p. 143, cited Hendry's journal of 1831, where he noted that near Fort Chimo, "there is also a small river where they make a weir and catch a good many salmon."

[120]"Letter of P. Beard to Prince Regent," 19 November 1819, in C.O. Supplementary I, Misc. Papers, Vol. 18, Fisheries, 1712–1852, PAC.

[121]*Ibid.*, "Regulations of the Salmon and Herring Fisheries of Sandwich Bay." 15 June, 1820.

[122]W. G. Gosling, *Labrador: Its Discovery, Exploration and Development* (London: Alston Rivers, 2910), p. 405. David William Zimmerly, *Cain's Land Revisited* (St. John's: Memorial University, 1975), p. 59: "In a letter written 24 July 1921 (1821), Captain William Martin relates that he left his ship in western Lake Melville and went up the source of the lake to a waterfall (Muskrat Falls). The Canadians, he said, had many salmon fishing establishments although 'their principal gain is the Fur Trade with the Red Indians, the fishing (cod) Establishments up the river for 40 miles were numerous, principally Americans for the Season."

[123]C.O. Supplementary I, Misc. Papers, Vol. 18, Fisheries, 1712–1852; PAC. Zimmerly, *Cain's Land*. P. 65, notes that the first Court of Justice in that part of Labrador which was administered by Newfoundland took place at Rigolet on 3 August 1826, and dealt with one case only — "a dispute with respect to a salmon fishing in the Kinnumas Brook."

[124]George R. Young, *The British North American Colonies: Letters to the Honourable E.G.S. Stanley, M.P.* (London: Ridgway, 1834), p. 56.

[125]Gosling, *Labrador*, pp. 402, 406. Perley, *The Fisheries of New Brunswick*, Appendix II, p. 283.

[126]See "Petition of Salmon Fishermen, 1836" in C.O. Supplementary I. Misc. Papers, Vol. 18, *Fisheries, 1712–1852*, PAC.

[127]*Ibid.*, "Letter of Captain Wyville, Commander of H.M. Sloop *Cleopatra*," September 1841.

[128]Sir Richard Henry Bonnycastle, *Newfoundland in 1842* (London: Colburn, 1842), pp. 189, 268.

[129]Charles B. Elliott, *The United States and the Northeastern Fisheries* (Minneapolis: University of Minnesota, 1887), pp. 52–3.

[130]Netboy, *The Atlantic Salmon*, p. 325.

[131]C. G. Atkins, "The River Fisheries of Maine," in G. Browne Goode, ed., *The Fisheries and Fishing Industries of the United States* (Washington: U.S. Commission of Fish and Fisheries, 1884–87), I, p. 678.

[132]Netboy, *The Atlantic Salmon*, pp. 322, 325, 632. Anthony Netboy, *Atlantic Salmon Association Centennial Award Fund* (Montreal: n.p., n.d.), p. 5. Atkins, "The River Fisheries…," in Goode, p. 678.

[133]For Example, see T. W. Magrath, *Authentic Letters from Upper Canada: With an Account of Canada Field Sports* (Dublin: n.p., 1833), p. 287, and *Sporting Magazine* (1843) (London: Pitman, 1843), pp. 24–5.

[134]Patrick Campbell, *Travells in America*, ed. H.H. Langton (Toronto: Champlain, 1937), p. 46.

[135]Francis Duncan, *Our Garrisons in the West* (London: Chapman and Hall), p. 75; N. E. J. MacEachern and J. R. MacDonald, "The Salmon Fishery of Nova Scotia," in *The Canadian Fish Culturist*, 31 (Oct. 1962), 46–7.

[136]Charles Boidman Owen, *An Epitome of History, Statistics, etc., of Nova Scotia* (Halifax: English and Blackadar, 1842), p. 120; MacEachern and MacDonald, "The Salmon Fishery of Nova Scotia," p. 46.

[137]William Scarth Moorsom, *Letters from Nova Scotia* (London: Colburn, 1830), p. 285.

[138]*Ibid.*, p. 327.

[139]Thomas Chandler Haliburton, *Historical and Statistical Account of Nova Scotia* (Halifax: Howe, 1829; reprinted Belleville, Ont.: Mika, 1973), I, 63.

[140]Joseph Howe, *Western and Eastern Rambles: Travel Sketches of Nova Scotia*, ed. M. G. Parks (Toronto: University of Toronto, 1973), p. 117.

[141]William Dunlop, *Tiger Dunlop's Upper Canada*, New Canadian Library, No. 5 (Toronto: McClelland & Stewart, 1967), pp. 94–5.

[142]Magrath, *Authentic Letters*, p. 287.

[143]Anon, *The Backwoods of Canada: Letters from the Wife of an Emigrant Officer*, (London: Knight, 1836), p. 159.

IX

Reprehension and Regulation 1845-1867

Not Worth a Dam

In 1846, a settlement was concluded in the boundary dispute between British Columbia and Oregon, with the result that the lower Columbia River basin, which was the principal area of contention, was yielded to the United States of America. A story was circulated among the British inhabitants of the West Coast at that time that Great Britain had given up her claim to the district because the salmon of the Columbia River could not be angled. Tradition states that a brother of Sir Robert Peel, the British prime minister, was serving in the naval establishment at Victoria at that time and had repeatedly fly-fished the Columbia River, but without success. Being thus continually frustrated, he was reported to have written to the prime minister that the salmon on the coast were too uneducated to take a fly, and that therefore, "there was no use making a fuss about the country for it wasn't worth a ----."[1] There are no records to suggest that the Atlantic salmon — on this continent at least — played a similar role in the loss or gain of national territory; in the North Atlantic colonies, that distinction was held by the cod, which for centuries figured prominently in the conflicts between France and Britain.

There is no doubt, however, that interest in salmon was increasing after 1840; from the middle of that decade, the species was referred to and considered more frequently in the proceedings of state and colonial legislatures and in international agreements on trade and privilege. One reason for this increased interest was that it was now obvious to certain individuals that salmon numbers were diminishing in many areas, and were scarce or absent in several regions where formerly they had been found in considerable abundance. Even in the normally productive Miramichi and Chaleur Bay regions, salmon were declining noticeably. Although commercial export of the species had been increasing in the British coastal colonies since the mid-1820s, the increase was being achieved at the cost of a rapid reduction in spawning stock, and the point would eventually be reached where there would not be enough adult stock escaping to maintain productive population levels.

In the 1840s, frequent reports were also made concerning the destruction of vast numbers of both juvenile and adult salmon on the spawning grounds and below the ever-increasing number of milldams being constructed on the rivers; these dams were also barring salmon from their normal freshwater haunts, thus reducing the rearing area formerly available. Netting was reported to be utterly unrestricted throughout the geographical range of the species, with nets often stretching entirely across rivers and estuaries. Some individuals pointed out that such unrestricted and irresponsible actions could not long continue without serious consequences to the future of the fishery.

Such dire warnings were well founded, for one salmon fishery after another failed in the mid-1840s: export records show that shipments from Newfoundland steadily declined between 1842 and 1846, dropping by 46 percent over the period; New Brunswick exports fell by 28 percent between 1844 and 1848; and in Nova Scotia, the customs house records for 1848 indicate that the province — for the first time — was importing more barrels of salmon than it was exporting.[2] Although one may question the use of export figures as a true indicator of fish abundance or scarcity — particularly during the 1846–51 period, when a general economic depression affected the commerce of the British colonies — other sources indicate that any decline illustrated in the export trade figures only slightly magnified what was actually happening to the resource itself.[3]

The wholesale destruction of salmon and the subsequent catch decline was being described by commercial fishermen, anglers, fishery overseers, and others in poignant terms, and even the casual observer could see that the fisheries in Upper Canada and southern New England were, by 1850, things of the past. Throughout the 1850s, the only region that appeared to sustain a salmon fishery in relatively undiminished proportions was Labrador, but it was predicted that even that remote area would soon be depleted of its stock, because of the rapacious fishing activity that was seasonally carried out and expanded.

Whatever cause or combination of causes had had the most deleterious impact on the fishery was the subject of much discussion in its day, but the result of the impact was clear. In commenting about the old story of apprentices in England becoming piqued at having to eat salmon more than twice a week, Richard Nettle stated that by 1857,

Seldom can either master or man get a nibble, much less a bite! The vile practice of fishing at all seasons and by all appliances, has driven the noble, tho' dogged fish from the shores, and the result has been, the destruction of a greater portion of the fisheries and the rise in the price of Salmon, of at least one thousand per cent.[4]

Stock decline was not the only reason why an increased interest was shown in the species during the 1850s and 1860s, because many individuals still believed — as did their ancestors — that the resource was inexhaustible and only at one of the low points of a recurring cycle. Indirectly, it was the general advancement in commercial, social, technological, and political environments at this time that directed more attention to the salmon.

Commercially, the opportunities for trade were increasing, particularly after 1851. This was largely brought about by trade reciprocity with the United States and by new developments in transportation, since most of eastern North America was crossing the threshold of a great railway construction and shipbuilding era by 1845. New techniques for preserving fish had also been developed, and the shipment of salmon packed in ice and in vacuum-sealed tins was rapidly replacing the pickled-salmon trade. Advances in the development of better fishing gear and new fishing methods also resulted in the capacity to catch more fish with less effort. Apart from this, changing cultural and social forces created a new breed of fisherman — the sportsman — and during this period, the influence of the angler was becoming an important factor in the future of the salmon.

Political independence was also evolving in the British colonies during the 1840s, and this was a condition reflected in the fishery by an increase in colonial-inspired legislation. Nova Scotia and New Brunswick achieved responsible government in 1848, the Canadas in 1849, and Newfoundland in 1855. The new form of government meant that the governors and their respective councils became more attuned to the wants and attitudes of the people, which in turn allowed the colonies to flex their legislative muscles, and hopefully to provide more apt regulation for the fishery. With this new sense of responsibility, the various legislative assemblies began to examine in detail the many phases of colonial industry; with regard to the inland and sea fisheries, they launched investigations to determine their potential and to discover the extent to which they could be improved and developed.

New Brunswick was the first to engage upon such a study, in 1846, followed shortly afterwards by Lower Canada. The findings of the official investigators basically substantiated what had already been rumored or suspected: the fishery was in a deplorable state. The investigations further revealed that there had been little attention paid to the regulations previously enacted — a rather obvious conclusion, considering the absurdity, if not the antiquity, of some of the statutes; fishermen and settlers alike knew no law of season and fished indiscriminately. The studies also revealed that many rivers in which salmon formerly abounded were now completely devoid of the species as a result of overfishing and obstruction by dams. The investigators expressed the need for fisheries protection, and this was attempted to a considerable extent by various legislative actions during the 1850s and early 1860s.

Regulation, management, and supervision of the resource, however, was a monumental task for the fledgling civil authorities. Inability to enforce the new laws and the general failure of the population to abide by them resulted in a continued depression in salmon stocks until the time of Confederation. Throughout this period, a handful of men like Moses Perley of New Brunswick, William Chearnley of Nova Scotia, and Richard Nettle of Quebec, continued to campaign for a full appreciation and understanding of the resource potential under sound management; these men continued to lay the foundation of the protective policies adopted from time to time by the colonial and, later, the national administrations.

Control over the sea fishery was particularly difficult and practically impossible. This segment of the fishery was the responsibility of Great Britain, who exercised management principally — and ineffectually — through the operations of the Admiralty. The mother country's lack of interest in this regard disturbed the colonies, and they repeatedly made representations for more protection in the sea fishery, chiefly from encroachments by American fishing vessels. Britain's apparent apathy toward the North Atlantic fishery was well reflected by the Treaty of 1818, which had given American fishermen coastal fishing rights in some areas and provided for an ineffectual three-mile limit in others: this boundary was still flagrantly abused by the Americans, and for all practical purposes, the coast as well as the deep-sea fishery was in Yankee hands.

British apathy was, to a certain extent, matched by a seeming colonial inactivity in the industry. Lorenzo Sabine, a noted American historian and commentator of the day, remarked that:

No American visits Nova Scotia without being amazed at the apathy which prevails amongst the people, and without calculating the advantage they enjoy, but will not improve. Almost every sheet of water swarms with cod, pollock, salmon, mackerel, herring, alewives....[5]

Obviously, the Americans recognized the great potential of the fishery, even if the British colonials did not. Thomas Chandler Haliburton's outspoken Yankee friend, Sam Slick, described the situation in somewhat more colorful language:

They [Nova Scotians] do nothing in these parts but eat, drink, smoke, sleep, ride about, lounge in taverns... and they are in the midst of fisheries... all sorts of fisheries too, River fisheries of shad, salmon, gasperouse [sic] and herring.... O dear! it beats all; and they don't do nothin' with 'em but leave 'em to us.[6]

What Sabine judged to be apathy, and what Sam Slick interpreted as laziness, was to a large degree brought on by frustration and the inability to compete with the energy and force of American fishermen. Liberally interpreting the Convention of 1818, Americans were descending upon all the harbors and bays of British America from the St. Croix to Labrador, under the pretexts of obtaining shelter or water or drying their catch — and setting their nets in the process. The acts of encroachment became so frequent in some regions that local fishermen were forced to adopt a passive attitude or suffer the consequences.

One might add, however, that the interpretation of the 3-mile limit was open to question by both nationalities, particularly where it applied to Chaleur Bay and the Bay of Fundy: did it follow the indentations of the coast or extend from headland to headland? There is evidence also that some groups of British colonial fishermen benefitted considerably from American encroachment: when New Englanders could not effectively fish a certain area themselves, they frequently entered into arrangements with local fishermen; in Passamaquoddy Bay, for example, a large number of weirs were leased to Americans.[7] This was a profitable, easy, and guaranteed way for fishermen to dispose of their catch. New Brunswickers, however, appeared to accept the American presence more freely than Nova Scotians.

Generally, the colonies protested to the home government about these treaty infractions and about the growing number of confrontations in the fisheries between Americans and British subjects. Action from Great Britain was slow, however, and by 1851, Nova Scotia had taken it upon herself to provide two protection vessels, while New Brunswick had launched one for the same purpose. A few years later, Nova Scotia's fisheries protection fleet numbered four, New Brunswick had two, and Canada and Prince Edward Island had one apiece. This small force, however, did not intimidate the United States; Daniel Webster, the American Secretary of State, wrote that

it is not to be expected that the United States will submit their rights to be adjudicated upon by the petty tribunal of the provinces; or that we shall allow our vessels to be seized on by constables or other petty officers, or condemned by the Municipal Courts of Quebec and Newfoundland, New Brunswick or Canada.[8]

Great Britain ultimately held the colonial reins and wished to avoid any open conflict in the fishery. She finally attempted to placate her colonies by entering upon negotiations with the Americans to settle the problem of fishing rights, using the dispute as one of the main bargaining points in the Treaty of Reciprocity formulated in 1854. By this treaty, the 3-mile limit was abolished, and the Americans were given the right to fish anywhere along the British colonial coast for all species except shellfish, salmon, shad, and other river fish. In exchange, British colonial fishermen were allowed free trade with the American market and the right to fish in American waters. There were mixed feelings about this arrangement in the colonies. The principal of free trade was acknowledged as a good thing, but since the fishery off the coast of the eastern United States was of little value, the provision allowing British subjects to fish there could hardly be considered a fair exchange for the benefits which the Americans would derive from fishing east of the St. Croix River. There was also considerable doubt as to whether colonial fishermen could compete successfully in the American market. As it turned out, however, both the Americans and the British benefitted greatly by this arrangement, which was in effect from 1854 to 1865.[9]

The magnetic effect of the open American market immediately fostered an increased exploitation of the salmon resource; each colonial fisherman took what he could when he could, resulting in little chance for the already-declining stocks to revive. Despite the treaty terms the Americans, moreover, were also reaping a vast harvest of salmon in the British colonies, particularly on the northern shores of the Gulf of St. Lawrence. By the late 1860s, the resource was down to its lowest level in history and had ceased to be an important segment of the general fishery in many communities and regions. When Reciprocity expired in 1865, the terms of the 1818 Convention were reinstituted, and the old animosities between American and British fishermen flared up once again. History was being repeated, and the attitude of the British government toward the United States was best expressed, perhaps, in the following confidential orders issued to Vice Admiral Sir James Hope respecting fisheries protection:

> It is therefore, at present, the wish of Her Majesty's Government neither to concede, nor for the present, to enforce any rights in this respect, which are in their nature open to any serious questions and that American Fisheries should not be interfered with unless they are found within three miles of a line drawn across the mouth of a bay or creek which is less than ten geographical miles in width.[10]

New Brunswick

During the mid-1840s, the New Brunswick government was greatly interested and involved in the various proposals relating to railroad construction within the colony, particularly the Grand Trunk scheme, which was intended to connect Halifax with Quebec City. Such a prospect was favorably considered in official circles, due to its great potential for intercolonial trade; figuratively speaking, it could unfreeze the Gulf of St. Lawrence ports and allow commerce to continue for a full twelve months of the year.[11]

The fisheries of the province were much neglected at this time, and it was thought that the advent of the railway might help to revitalize the industry. When a survey of the proposed line was authorized in 1846, Moses Perley was requested, as the most suitable resident observer, "to ascertain what encouragement the proposed Trunk line, or its Branches, would give to the fisheries, and the facilities for prosecuting them in the Gulf of St. Lawrence."[12]

Perley was indeed the man best suited for the scope of this assignment. Born at Maugerville in 1804, and a direct descendant of Israel Perley, who had founded that community in 1761, Moses Perley spent his childhood

summers hunting, fishing, and trading with the Indians along the Saint John River. He later studied law and was admitted to the bar in 1830. Sometime around 1840, he was appointed commissioner of Indian affairs, an office which he filled both judiciously and capably. In 1843, he was named provincial emigrant agent, another appointment to which he brought characteristic vigor and imagination. His versatility, wide-ranging interests, and familiarity with the natural resources of New Brunswick made him an obvious choice for various special government projects, and so it was that he was called upon to report on the feasibility and implications of the Grand Trunk scheme with respect to the fisheries.[13]

Perley presented his exhaustive report to the Legislature in March 1849. Among his observations were numerous astute comments regarding the provincial salmon fisheries. He pointed out, with respect to the salmon resource, that the prodigious quantities which had once frequented eastern New Brunswick rivers had now greatly diminished. This decline he attributed to several obvious factors: a complete disregard for the limits of the fishing season; the multitudinous man-made obstructions on the streams; and the generally destructive fishing methods then employed — sweep nets, drift nets, and spears. His conclusion was that "The preservation and maintenance of the salmon fisheries of New Brunswick generally, is a subject well worthy of earnest attention."[14]

The members of the New Brunswick Legislature read Perley's report with considerable interest and concern, with the result that he was next asked to carry out a further survey of the shore and river fisheries of the Gulf of St. Lawrence, with the specific purpose of ascertaining what legislative action should be undertaken to improve them. Such a rapid call to action was quite unusual in the 1840s, and that such an undertaking was, in fact, continued was in no small way due to the energy of the governor, Sir Edmund Walker Head, who had been appointed to office midway through Perley's first investigation.

Head was a most unusual governor, in that he possessed a genuine desire to increase the prosperity of the inhabitants by doing all in his power to create a strong agricultural and piscatorial economic base for the province. He also possessed more than a passing interest in salmon, for he experienced great delight and satisfaction in angling.[15] Head's specific instructions to Perley for this second mission stated that "The destruction of fish in rivers, and the injury to the salmon fishery by mill dams, by illegal modes of fishing and by the destruction of salmon out of season, will form an important branch of enquiry."[16]

After carrying out this work and completing his report in 1850, Perley was again directed to carry out a similar investigation in the Bay of Fundy area: this he completed in 1851. During his 5 years investigating the fishery, he traveled some 900 miles, over 500 of them by canoe. The mass of information that Perley collected during these investigations gave a comprehensive picture of the New Brunswick fishery of his day, and provided the foundation for a series of publications which he prepared, beginning in 1849. These studies, which were widely distributed, publicized the resource, and indicated the great potential which at that time was only nominally realized along the province's coastline. As a supplement to his general reports, he also published, in 1852, the first comprehensive list of fish species to be found in the fresh and salt waters of eastern Canada. Perley's work ranks, even yet, as among the foremost and most detailed of its type into this branch of New Brunswick's economic life.

Basically, Perley concluded from his studies that there was great neglect and inactivity in the colonial sea fisheries, with the reverse being true in the river fishery; the latter, in fact, was being overrun with activity and was abominably abused almost everywhere. He stated that every encouragement should be given to the inhabitants to take advantage of their rich offshore resources, in order to lessen the pressure on the inland fishery; he also emphasized that immediate action was necessary to regulate and manage the river fishery more effectively before total destruction ensued.

It will be remembered that when New Brunswick became a colony in 1784, general laws for fisheries regulation were enacted, and the responsibility for enforcement was delegated to the county Sessions Courts. Although some local administrations made attempts to exercise this responsibility, their efforts were generally ineffectual, and little time or effort was lavished on policing the statutes; 77 years of disregarded and latent laws could not be considered anything but disgraceful. Drift netting was illegal, but still carried out; spearing was illegal, but still carried out; and fishways were required, but few were ever built — in fact, of the 845 milldams that existed in New Brunswick in 1851, not one possessed an effective fishpass.[17]

Perley's principal recommendations with respect to the salmon fishery were thus that

A 'close time' should be established, during which salmon should not be taken in any way. The taking of 'grilse' or small salmon under a certain weight should be restricted, and their sale prohibited. Spearing should be disallowed, and the regulations for this fishing for salmon should be as uniform from country to country as possible.[18]

In addition, Perley recommended that all salmon nets should be assessed, and the fee applied to the payment of overseers. He also presented the idea that all fisheries operating from Crown land should be leased, and advocated the introduction of a better fish inspection system.

Perley's views of the fishery and how it should be regulated would undoubtedly have resulted in his being tarred and feathered in many fishing communities around New Brunswick, but to the legislators and the governor, his detailed and comprehensive studies provided clear enough proof that what he said was not to be taken lightly: the evidence was massed in his favor.

After considering his 1849 report, the fisheries committee of the Legislature fully supported his recommendations and set about to formulate a revised set of statutes to conserve a resource which, for all practical purposes, had been "rediscovered." In the legislators' opinion, "the full and uninterrupted enjoyment of the fisheries on the coasts of this province, forms an incalculable source of wealth and is of inestimable value to the people of New Brunswick."[19]

New regulations were enacted in 1851; they were intended for the sea and river fisheries in general, with some clauses specifically respecting salmon. For example, the salmon laws for all counties in the province were made uniform. A season of April 1 to August 31 was imposed, and a fine of 10 shillings was levied on each fish captured outside this season. A weekend closure was applied, from sunset on Saturday to sunrise on Monday; spearing during the closed season was forbidden; the appointment of two wardens per county was authorized; fishing leases were to be issued for waters adjacent to ungranted land; man-made obstructions (i.e. milldams) were required to possess fishways; pollution of streams was forbidden; and angling was permitted to September 16.[20]

Unfortunately for the province, both Perley and Governor Head soon went on to greater things: Head to the governor-generalship of Canada, and Perley to appointment in 1855, as a fishery commissioner to enforce the Reciprocity Treaty. In this capacity, Perley regularly traveled outside the province; part of his responsibility lay in determining the Atlantic coastal limits within which British subjects had the sole right to fish. While engaged in this inspection work off the coast of Labrador in August 1862, he was taken ill, died on board ship, and was buried at Forteau.

New Brunswick continued to formulate regulations concerning the general fishery from time to time after 1851, the last legislation before Confederation being passed on April 20, 1863.[21] Although it was generally admitted that the laws were well devised and appropriate for the resource, the civil authorities responsible for their application were still generally unwilling or unable to enforce them, with the result that the fishing populace blatantly abused the rules, or found means by which they could be circumvented.

With particular regard to the latter, there were two rather common examples by which this was openly but legally accomplished. In one instance, the legislators established means by which some provincial revenue might be derived from the salmon fishery by including a section in the Act of 1863, placing a tax on all nets over 49 fathoms in length: a tax of $0.50 was applied to 50-fathom nets, and 1 cent was added for each fathom in excess of this standard. To avoid the tax, many fishermen shortened their nets to less than 50 fathoms, fished two small ones instead of one long one, and began to construct tails and pounds on the outer ends of the nets to increase the effective mesh area, without extending their actual length beyond the outer edge of the stand. In another instance, "killock nets" — nets secured with cumbersome killock anchors — were not required to be brailed or taken up during the weekly closed time; this, of course, resulted in a trend toward the use of such nets. Since the law also neglected to specifically state that killock nets had to be taken up after the close of the salmon season, therefore they were commonly left in the water under the pretext of being set for bass or some other species still in season.[22]

That the new statutes had failed to regulate the old problems is clearly evident in the comment of one contemporary observer:

> All the rivers in New Brunswick are very much damaged by over netting, both in the tideway, along the coast, and also in fresh water. At first, it appears a miracle how any salmon can manage to pass the labyrinth of nets, set with hardly any restriction; for although there are very fair fishery laws, they are but seldom enforced. The fish wardens for the most part are useless, their appointments sinecures, and mere political jobs....[23]

The word "useless" appears frequently in the literature of the day with regard to fisheries officers; even W. H. Venning, who later became New Brunswick's chief fisheries inspector, admitted that "The mode that has hitherto obtained of appointing Fishery Wardens and Overseers of the Fisheries has been so loose and careless that in most instances these officers have been quite useless."[24]

In the wardens' defence, it should be said that their office was an almost impossible one to occupy with any degree of efficiency. Months sometimes passed after their appointments before they knew what was required of them; as late as 1866, only two officers in the province possessed copies of the 1851 Fisheries Act which they were appointed to uphold. It was also evident that the justice handed out in the courts made a mockery of what effort the officers did expend in the course of their duty.[25] Each overseer also had a ridiculously large territory to police, considering the transportation and communication facilities of the age. Two men had been appointed in each county; this meant that in Saint John County, each man was responsible for only about 300 square miles, while in Northumberland County, a phenomenal 2400 square miles was assigned to each officer. More adequate arrangements were eventually made by appointing additional wardens and by redefining the important fishing areas. In 1864, 12 districts were set up for purposes of improving the protection and management of the fishery. There were still gaps in the arrangement, however, and even on the eve of Confederation, some districts had only two wardens, while others had one or occasionally none.[26]

An additional problem was that in many cases, the wardens were generally neither popular nor respected; they were undoubtedly well aware that their efforts did little to improve the fishery or to encourage changes in the numerous unlawful aspects of its operation — they were, indeed, useless, and the law was impotent. For that matter, by the end of the pre-Confederation period in New Brunswick, the legal system as it applied to the fisheries was no more effectual than at the time when the first legislation of the province was formulated.

CHALEUR BAY

The reported export of salmon from the Restigouche fishery — the river fishery above Campbellton — was 565 barrels (113 000 lb pickled) in 1845. Exports had been generally increasing since 1839, reaching a peak of 766 barrels (153 000 lb pickled) in 1846.[27] These increased exports, however, could not be construed to imply a productive fishery, for the phenomenal catches of former years were still well remembered. Moses Perley visited the Restigouche in 1848, when catches were again falling off; 643 barrels had been exported in 1847, but this had dropped to 381 barrels a year later.[28] The decline led Perley to comment that "for a long period... no river in North America (except perhaps the Columbia) yielded so large a supply of salmon as the Restigouche. But its character, in this respect, is fast passing away; the numbers have fearfully diminished of late years."[29]

Low salmon runs and catches were reported for the Restigouche fishery throughout the 1850s and 1860s. The returns of 1861, for example, show that only 220 barrels were exported.[30] One man who had come to the Restigouche for some sport fishing in 1862 remarked that "We were much surprised and disappointed by the paucity of salmon on our way up, and when we reached the forks only succeeded in killing two, after several days fishing. We therefore came to the conclusion that the river as regards salmon was a myth."[31]

Not only was the number of fish declining, but the average weights of commercially caught salmon were also decreasing. In the 1830s, it was not uncommon for 11 fish to fill a 200-pound barrel; in the early 1840s, an average of 15 fish filled a barrel; and in 1848, it was said that no fewer than 17 were required. Perley concluded that the average weight of the general run in 1849 was even smaller,[32] and such a trend indicates both a declining population and a removal of the higher age classes from the available stock.

There were three basic fishing methods utilized in the area during this period. John Mowat, overseer on the Canadian side of the river, reported that a great portion of the yield was taken in estuary nets; in addition, a considerable number were caught with the spear, and a few by drift or sweep netting.[33] Estuary nets were the mainstay of the fishery and could be found among the islands above Campbellton, at the head of tide, and along the main stream to the mouth of the Patapedia River. These nets were apparently set for as long as open water permitted, and from the descriptions available, their frequency of occurrence might be compared to the teeth of a comb. The greatest concentration was among the islands of the lower river, where they were occasionally set to extend from shore to shore; freshets and lumbering activity, however, from time to time disrupted this practice, but the effect on the fish runs into the Restigouche was still pronounced. Even at the time of Confederation, Venning reported that "The extent of netting among the numerous islands and shoals at the head of tide is so excessive that the passage of fish is seriously impeded."[34] These estuary nets had always been viewed as the devices responsible for the continued depression of the once famous Restigouche fishery. Another writer reported that "this method of lawless capture had reduced the annual supply of fish to a minimum."[35]

Drift netting, although illegal, was also carried out on the lower 80 miles of the main river; further upstream, where drifting became impractical, the spear took over, and large parties of Indians and groups of white settlers ventured to the spawning grounds of the Kedgwick, Upsalquitch, Patapedia, and the main river each season, returning with canoe loads of adult fish. This method of capture was so intense that Alexander Monro stated, "the fish is speared and chased on the spawning grounds to such an extent that their existence is threatened."[36]

Apart from overfishing, there was another factor which continued to abet the destruction of salmon, particularly on the Restigouche and its tributaries — lumbering activities. Although many areas were still free of dams[37] and the selective cutting system of the lumberman did not completely devastate the watershed, the annual spring stream drives had the effect of scouring the spawning beds and destroying the ova and fry. In addition, the rivers were highways for supplying woodsmen's upriver camps, and teams of horses hauling scows and barges trod through the shallows, pulling their loads over some of the best rearing gravel on the river.

It is difficult to understand why effective governmental measures were not applied to the Restigouche fishery to correct the decline that had continued for so many years. Even actively applying the existing laws might have accomplished much in remedying the problem; were not the Chaleur salmon formerly one of the prime economic factors in the area's prosperity, and did they thus not deserve this attention? Government, however, remained generally inactive in remedying the situation, and considerable local apathy also prevailed.

It was generally accepted de facto that lumbering economically superseded fishing in the Chaleur region. Furthermore, there was a basic incompatibility in the laws of the two political units — New Brunswick and Quebec — which shared the regional fishery. In 1848, the County of Bonaventure, Quebec, had regulated the fishery along the Chaleur Bay shore, the Cascapédia and the north bank of the Restigouche, imposing an 1845 regulation which simply stated that drift netting was disallowed, that nets below the islands were not to exceed 150 fathoms, and that nets in the river could not extend more than two-thirds across the width of the channel.[38] New Brunswick statutes of the same period were considerably more stringent,[39] and obviously, New Brunswick fishermen were not going to obey these regulations when their counterparts on the Quebec side were less restricted; it was much easier and more convenient for both groups to ignore the laws altogether.

The situation was compounded by the fact that New Brunswick made no effort to appoint an overseer for some time, and even in 1867, only one man was responsible for stopping illegalities on the New Brunswick side of the river.[40] Even when the overseer did his rounds, it was evident that his efforts often left something to be desired, as witnessed by an observer in 1862:

I met an Indian while on the Restigouche, who had been hired by the warden of the river, to take him up in a canoe on his one annual inspection, which I suppose he required to enable him to satisfy his conscience, on pocketing his salary, some £40 per annum. The individual in question called at the houses of the different owners of nets, and after informing them of their legal length, without inspecting the same, finished up by asking for a salmon. Having made about twenty such visits, not forgetting the salmon, he returned home and drew his salary. Some of the wardens are proprietors of nets, and do not trouble their heads how they are set, provided they catch fish.[41]

The bay fishery in Restigouche County was little attended until the late 1850s. Monro erroneously reported early in the decade that there were no fishing establishments on the coast and that the inhabitants merely took enough salmon for their own immediate use.[42] Nonetheless, 35–45 stands existed along the New Brunswick shore at that time; between the mouth of the river and Dalhousie, for example, 11 net stands could be found until 1866,[43] after which the number increased considerably. Perley mentioned that one of the stands at Bon Ami Rocks yielded 26 barrels (8200 lb fresh) in 1849,[44] and catches like this apparently encouraged an expansion of the fishery around the bay. This expansion, however, was relatively slow, for only a slight increase in the number of berths was witnessed between Perley's visit in 1849 and P. Miller's investigation in 1867.[45] The nets used in the bay fishery were different from those used in the river, and were constructed to form a trap or pound at one end. Generally, they were fixed into position by the use of pickets, but on the rocky shores seaward from Dalhousie, they were devised as floating traps. These devices were referred to as float, wing, hook, or gill nets, and were the only style of trap used in the Chaleur region prior to Confederation.[46]

Upon leaving the Restigouche and continuing down the bay, there were concentrations of nets in the Charlo and Jacquet River areas. Salmon runs into the Charlo River had greatly diminished by Perley's time, and a milldam, which totally stopped migration, was erected across the stream a short time after his visit. A dam was in existence on the Benjamin River in 1849, but salmon were known to ascend the sluiceway during high water; specimens were still taken in the pool below the structure in the 1860s by the Indian with his spear and the white settler with his sweep net. In the 1840s, one individual had counted 100 salmon ascending the sluice in one day; the fish, he stated, averaged 8 pounds.[47]

The Jacquet River was still unobstructed in 1849, and consequently was reported to be the best salmon river between the Restigouche and the Nepisiguit. The river, however, was heavily fished, forming one leg of a poaching circuit which started on the lower Restigouche, extended up the Upsalquitch, from there over the watershed divide to the upper reaches of the Jacquet, and down to the shore. Despite the illegal depredations which took place on this circuit, the Jacquet continued to sustain good fall runs of fish.[48]

Next to the Restigouche, the Nepisiguit fishery was the best on the New Brunswick side of Chaleur Bay, with catches and exports ranging between one-quarter and one-half those of the former. The same declining trend, however, was witnessed here, exports dropping from 216 barrels in 1846 to 156 barrels in 1848.[49] In the 1860s, however, the fishery appeared to sustain itself much better than that of the Restigouche, which may have been due to the fact that a greater reliance had been placed on the coastal fishery than on that of the river.

Salmon fishing stands in the Nepisiguit region could be found from the Restigouche County line to New Bandon, or Janeville, and Salmon Beach. Monro reported in the early 1850s that "The salmon fishery at Janeville... can hardly be surpassed;"[50] large numbers were being packed in tins and sent to United States and British markets at this time. By 1867, there were at least four firms in the region canning salmon from the 45 licensed fishing stands of Nepisiguit Bay, and forwarding their produce via the Shediac–St. Andrews railway to the United States.[51]

The Nepisiguit fishery was subjected, however, to the same problems which plagued the Restigouche: laws were ignored and abused, and poaching was rampant. Perley noted that the Nepisiguit River was illegally fished in every possible way from the head of tide to Grand Falls; he was so shocked by the abuse which he personally witnessed that he wrote to the clerk of the peace at Bathurst in 1849, requesting that immediate action be taken. The county Sessions Court forthwith dispatched a posse upriver, returning with 12 dozen salmon — but no poachers. The court, however, assured Perley that

> The authorities here, have always been alive to the necessity of preserving the salmon fisheries in the Nepisiguit; but from want of funds, and perhaps defects in the law, their rules and regulations are either openly violated, or secretly evaded.[52]

The regulations alluded to had been fairly well devised and were passed by the July 1848 Sessions Court sitting: all net fishing had to cease on July 31; no nets could be set in Bathurst Harbour; upriver nets must be set from the shore; mesh size could be no smaller than 5.5 inches; all nets had to be marked with the owner's name; and no salmon could be speared above the head of tide on the Middle, Tetagouche, or Nepisiguit rivers.[53] Regardless of the regulations, however, the situation did not improve, and Campbell Hardy reported in 1855, for example, that netting, although outlawed in the fresh water of the river, was still carried on to a "frightful" extent.[54] Abuse of the laws perhaps reached a height in an incident which, although unsupported, supposedly took place in the tideway of the Nepisiguit around 1860:

> Several years ago while I was in New Brunswick, a proprietor of a net at Bathurst was prosecuted by the warden for having a mesh of an illegal size. The delinquent wrote to a friend of his then a member of the Legislative Assembly of New Brunswick, and representative of his county. The Honourable Member managed to get the law altered, so as to make the net of a legal mesh, not only this, but he made the law retrospective, in the meantime staying further proceedings.[55]

Salmon protection on the Nepisiguit improved somewhat in the late 1860s, due to the efforts of fisheries overseer James Hickson, John Ferguson, and a collection of ardent anglers. Hickson was reported to be "imbued with a fish-preserving spirit that amounts almost to a passion," and he left no stone — or poacher — unturned to protect the species. Ferguson, a business baron in northern New Brunswick, was said to be the only mill owner in the province who recognized the worth of the salmon by taking it upon himself to build and maintain a fishpass in his dam on the Tetagouche River. Ferguson, along with J. Dewolf Spurr, who had secured a sport fishing lease on the Nepisiguit, was also directly responsible for placing a warden on the river to assist in curbing any illegal activities.[56]

Sport fishing on the river was well established by 1849, when Perley reported salmon anglers, noting that Grand Falls was one of the best fly-fishing spots, although many good pools existed between that point and salt water. In 1853, Campbell Hardy told of one old semihermit who had entrenched himself at Pabineau Falls, 7 miles from Bathurst, and who had established a reputation as the Izaak Walton of the Nepisiguit. It was stated that salmon taken in the river at this time averaged from 8 to 12 pounds each, but the occasional 18-pound fish was captured as well. With the growth of sport fishing, some of the local inhabitants made their reputations as guides, and of these individuals, Hardy wrote:

> Certainly these men were the best hands at working a canoe that I ever seen [sic], and though when not observed, they were very much given to spearing salmon on the sly, are the best possible, and in fact indispensable guides to the sportsman of the Nepisiguit.[57]

In the Caraquet, Miscou, and Shippegan areas, cod and herring were the principal mainstay of the Jersey firm, Robin and Co., and the local Acadian inhabitants. Occasional catches of salmon were made, however, in the mackerel and herring nets — five barrels, for example, were reported shipped from Caraquet once in the 1840s. There was also occasional speculation that salmon fishing off Miscou Island might have promise, if some devotion were given to the task. As an experiment, Andrew Wilson, a Scottish immigrant, placed a salmon net off the island in 1848; 12 specimens were taken, the largest weighing 18 pounds. No concentrated effort, however, was subsequently made to take advantage of the runs which migrated past these islands.[58]

Further north, one of the major fishing stations, or rooms, on the Quebec side of Chaleur Bay was at Paspébiac, where the firm of Robin and Co. was in chief control. As with their operation on Miscou Island, the company was principally engaged in the cod fishery, with much of the dry product being shipped to the Mediterranean and South America. There was some salmon fishing at Gaspé and other points along the northern shore of Chaleur Bay but, as in New Brunswick, salmon interest was focused on the Restigouche River.[59]

Miramichi

Salmon exports from the Miramichi region began to increase slightly in the 1830s and appeared to have reached a peak in 1842, when 2295 barrels (723 000 lb fresh) were exported. Between 1843 and 1845, exports were again declining, however, and in 1849, only 1000 barrels were shipped; in 1853 it was estimated that the yield amounted to only 396 barrels of pickled salmon, with an additional 162 500 pounds being preserved otherwise.[60] Although such records are not absolute indicators of the state of the fishery, it is apparent that in this case they did reflect the actual situation on the Miramichi, for Perley noted in 1849 that the catch of salmon, bass and gaspereau had diminished considerably from former years.

These low yield levels continued, and in 1855, Monro stated that the abundance of salmon in the Miramichi was largely becoming a matter of history: "very few, comparatively speaking, are now taken at all." Exports were down to 400 barrels (126 000 lb fresh) a year by this time,[61] although one must also consider the amount caught and consumed locally. A recovery was somewhat evidenced in 1861, when the census implied that the yield was close to 400 000 pounds for all of Northumberland County. Nevertheless, a downward trend predominated, and in 1867 it was reported that fewer salmon reached the spawning grounds of the Miramichi than at anytime in the past.[62]

At the time of his investigations in the late 1840s, Moses Perley observed that the fishery regulations of the Miramichi were outdated, little change having been made to them since 1799; despite some alterations in 1845, the statutes remained inadequate, and Perley recommended that immediate remedial action be taken. A large part of the problem, however lay not in the inadequacy of the law, but in the belief that the fish were there to be taken, and that no one had the right to tell the local inhabitants where, when, and how to take them. As noted previously, the few overseers had their hands tied: they were outnumbered, had little support, were basically frustrated colonial servants, were receiving little remuneration for their trouble — and some were even out-of-pocket as a result of transportation expenses.

Perley's report showed that although the legal salmon fishing period was between April 1 and August 31, no season was actually being observed. Nets were sealing off entire river channels from bank to bank, and one man reported that they were placed at such frequent intervals between the harbor and the head of tide that it was a wonder that any fish escaped to reach the spawning grounds. It was believed by certain individuals at this time that the only reason some salmon did manage to enter the Miramichi was because of the clear passage that had to be made available through the fishing gear for timber ships to reach Newcastle. On the Miramichi, many modes of fishing were employed, and new ones developed. No consideration was being given to the fact that grilse and black salmon were being captured and marketed; black salmon, in fact, sold for as much as 15 pence each. The timber trade also operated against the species: stream driving, dam building, letting sawdust into the streams, and replacing the small, water-powered mills with large steam operations were all constant hazards to stock survival.[63]

With all these problems and/or irregularities to choose from, the scapegoat and most commonly recognized cause for the depression in the upriver salmon catch was instead acknowledged to be the Portage and Fox islands fishing operations. Almost every fisherman and overseer on the Miramichi not directly involved in the Portage and Fox islands fisheries condemned them as the most destructive operation on the coast, and for more than a quarter of a century, they served to attract attention away from the other abuses that were being perpetrated in the bay and river fishery.

The island operations dated from about 1843, when William Fraser constructed several buildings on Portage Island, at the mouth of Miramichi Bay, and began canning salmon in hermetically sealed tins. He obtained the fish from local berth-holders at three pence a pound, and packed the produce in 2-pound tins; the success of this enterprise was reported 3 years later.

> Near Tabusintac, at Portage Island... a large fishing establishment... during the last three years has been extensively engaged in putting up lobsters and salmon in tin cases, hermetically sealed for foreign markets; and last season there were put up and shipped no fewer than 13 000 cases each containing two pounds of salmon or the best of three or four lobsters.[64]

In 1849, the station on Portage Island was reported to have packed 22 000 pounds of salmon in this manner,[65] and 4 years later, it was reported that "The quantity of salmon put up this year on Partridge [sic] Island is something almost fabulous."[66] This "fabulous" amount was some 162 500 pounds,[67] but by this time, other canning establishments were beginning to operate locally, so Monro's figure may include the production from more than one cannery.

It is interesting to note that these firms depended largely on the fruits of an illegal fishery, for the legislation of 1799 contained an article that strictly forbade a salmon fishery from being carried out on either Fox or Portage Island.[68] Apparently this regulation had always been ignored, for in former years the French-speaking settlers who resided on the islands also claimed the right to the fishery by a minute of council — which, somehow, no one could locate. These settlers either fished or leased the privilege to fish off the islands, and when Fraser conveniently situated his canning business on Portage Island, the future of the fishing population there seemed assured. A short time later, another cannery, owned by Alexander Loudon, was placed on Fox Island.[69] An army officer who visited the latter location in the late 1840s stated that any number of 12–18-pound salmon could be purchased from the local fishermen at two shillings each,[70] which is an implied, if not quantitative, example of the magnitude and value of the island's resource.

About 1863, the provincial government violated its own 1799 legislation by superseding the real or imaginary fishing claims of the settlers and placing the entire Portage Island fishery up for auction. A firm owned by George Letson won the bid, but when a threat of litigation ensued over his proposed establishment on the island, the former claimants were allowed to reoccupy their old stands.[71]

In 1864, the island canneries were exporting more than 400 000 pounds of salmon to the United States and United Kingdom markets,[72] but in the following year, the future of the fishery was somewhat in question when Portage Island was granted to the Admiralty; the island protected Miramichi Bay and the approaches to the river, and thus was strategically important. The only change that took place, however, was that the right to lease fishing stands now fell to the Admiralty rather than to the local fishermen. Apparently the fishermen did not protest too strongly and were willing to pay the small fee required for the right to continue fishing their respective stands. The fees, in fact, were used for the betterment of the area, insofar as the money went to support two Presbyterian clergymen on the mainland and the two schools at Burnt Church.[73]

Approximately 30 fishing stands were in operation on the islands in 1867. Many of the nets were almost 300 fathoms long, and none were less than 50; combined, almost 7 miles of nets existed on these two islands alone — a formidable network through which the salmon had to pass. Besides these set nets, which also contained hooks or tails, numerous swing or pivot nets were employed in the offshore, shoal waters. Swing nets were relatively new innovations, appearing around 1840 as a useful method for capturing mackerel and herring, being anchored at one end with a killock, while the other end swung freely with the tide; they were also found to be particularly good salmon catchers, and consequently, their numbers were increasing each season. An extra advantage in employing the killock net was that it was exempt from the regulation relating to closed time, and could be fished throughout the weekend.[74]

Other noted fishing regions around Miramichi Bay were Escuminac, Baie du Vin, Nappan Bay, Burnt Church, Neguac, and Oak Point; in all these areas, approximately 75 stands were in operation each year between 1850 and 1870. On the north shore of Miramichi Bay, the fishery was especially productive between Burnt Church and Oak Point; with the introduction of swing nets off the islands in Miramichi Bay, however, the Oak Point fishery in particular declined noticeably from season to season. From Sheldrake Island to the confluence of the Northwest and Southwest branches of the river, set nets also studded the shore at all convenient fishing points.[75]

In 1849, James Price described the bay and lower river fishery in some detail, noting that:

> In the bay and below the confluence of the tide, salmon are taken partly by set nets, which are not permitted by law to extend beyond a certain portion of the river and estuary; and partly by seining, and drift nets or sweep nets as they are technically termed, which, while suffered for the purposes of the herring and gaspereau fisheries, cannot be restrained from taking salmon and grilse at the same time.[76]

Price also mentioned that set nets were frequently formed into pounds at one end and that similar nets were being employed in the river fishery as well. In 1855, Campbell Hardy described the pound nets:

> These nets are attached to stakes driven into the bed of the river, and stretch out from shore for nearly a hundred yards. At the furthest from the shore, the net curves backwards, so that the salmon, after cautiously swimming alongside in hopes of discovering an egress, becomes baffled when he arrives at the end and strikes the net.[77]

Some fishermen who fished the ordinary gill or bar net on the northwest branch of the river were also in the habit of placing a hook or tail on the outer end. This tail was generally 5–10 fathoms long and anchored with a killock. It was reported that fishermen who owned such devices were prone to lift their killock at night and extend their bar net in a straight line in order to fish more of the channel — and to evade the regulation which stipulated that nets which extended for more than 50 fathoms into the river were subject to a higher tax. On the Northwest Miramichi and its tributaries, approximately 70 of these and other set nets were being used by 1865, including 19 on the freshwater reaches of the main stream, 5 on the Little Southwest branch, and 3 on the Sevogle.[78]

Net fishing on the Southwest Miramichi River was carried out all the way from Beaubears Island to Boiestown, with the largest concentration being on the lower river, below the mouth of the Renous; concentrations of stake nets could also be found at Astle, at the mouth of the Cains, and about 6 miles below Boiestown at Price's Island. Some of these nets were frequently observed sealing off the entire width of the river. In these freshwater sections of the Miramichi, the net competed with other devices; seining the pools and drifting were still regular pursuits — the mouth of the Renous being one traditional spot for the sweep net — and the spear still reigned supreme in the rapids and on the spawning beds.[79]

James Price, who had credited set nets with the ruination of the salmon fishery, took the opposite tack when it came to describing salmon spearing. He took exception to the Act of 1845 and the continuing legislation that outlawed this mode of capture, and claimed that such laws were a severe burden to the upriver settlers, to whom spearing was the only method of capturing salmon — nets not being suitable in shallow water.[80] Since most of the local river people looked upon taking salmon as a right and spearing as a reasonable recourse to that right, the spear continued to hang blatantly outside the woodshed when not in use, and the locals continued to compete with groups of other individuals who came to the upper river from as far away as Chatham and Fredericton on illegal spearing expeditions.

Many traditional and seasonally used "poaching roads" connected the western half of the province with the Miramichi: from Bristol, on the Saint John River, the road through Glassville to Juniper was an easy route to the Northwest Branch of the Southwest Miramichi, while the Nashwaak–Miramichi portage witnessed the passage of nets, canoes and spears in one direction, and salmon in the other.[81] One contemporary report related that as many as 100 canoes were engaged in one night's illegal fishing on the spawning grounds of the upper Southwest Miramichi. Participants in this activity often drove each other forcibly from the best areas, and with a man being able to take 80 fish a night, poaching was well worth the effort; the long arm of the law appeared not to stretch very far on the Miramichi.[82]

The declining fishery which Perley had reported emphasized the need for better regulations. In 1850, a motion was made in the Legislature to consolidate and amend the fishery laws of the Miramichi, but the plans made to have Perley continue his investigations throughout the province stayed the motion, on the grounds that a complete set of revised statutes would be considered for the province when Perley had completed these investigations.[83] Concurrent with the subsequent passing of new laws in 1851 was the formation of the Miramichi Fishing Society, which was officially founded in 1852. The principal object of the society, as declared in its second report to the Legislature, was

> to promote the extension of the river and gulf fisheries, to improve the modes of catching, curing, barreling and inspecting fish, to procure and publish information respecting the fisheries in other countries, and in every other judicious way to foster and encourage this branch of trade.[84]

For a number of years the society submitted annual reports to Fredericton, which were subsequently published in the *Journals* of the House. Among their activities was a "Salmon Festival," which took place at Chatham on August 14, 1860. At this exhibition, the products of the Miramichi fishery were displayed and the following prizes were given: £2 for the best two barrels of #1 salmon; fifteen shillings for the best one dozen smoked salmon; £2 for the best 48-pound box of hermetically sealed cans of preserved salmon; and £2 for the best 31-pound sample of spiced salmon.[85] The existence of this society helped to create a conservation presence in the Miramichi fishery and added some weight to the application of the laws in that section of the province; it was partly due to their efforts that the salmon resource managed to show some local improvement in the 1860s.

RICHIBUCTO AND SHEDIAC

Salmon fishing had traditionally been carried out only for local needs along the Gulf of St. Lawrence shore between Escuminac and Cape Tormentine; south of Kouchibouguac Bay, these local needs had been satisfied with such proficiency that by the time Moses Perley visited the area, the salmon runs had been practically eliminated. Furthermore, the fishery of this region had been carried out without official regulation: since men had first inhabited the area, no local statutes regarding salmon were ever placed on the books.

Dams had barred both the Shediac and Scoudouc rivers for several years, and Perley stated that in 1846,

> a run of salmon, apparently the last of their race, entered the Shediac and Scadouc [sic] Rivers, and ascended nearly to the dam on each. It was reported that on a Sabbath day, many persons were engaged in destroying these fish... with spears, scythes, pitchforks and such other offensive weapons as came to hand; apparently the destruction was complete, as little has since been heard of salmon in these rivers.[86]

A dam constructed on the Cocagne River in the 1830s had pealed the death knell of the salmon in that stream, and by 1845, only the occasional fish was reported in its waters. The few specimens that still annually visited the Buctouche River were unmercifully slaughtered, and it too was devoid of any run by 1850. The Richibucto had not had any substantial runs since the Powell operations had existed, while in the Kouchibouguac, a dam had facilitated the total elimination of salmon from that stream. The only fishery left, and one which was quite lucrative for the time, was along Kouchibouguac Bay. Nets set off the beaches in June and July were apparently taking advantage of the salmon on their migration route to the Miramichi and, perhaps, to Chaleur Bay; between 1843 and 1847, annual exports from this fishery at Richibucto were reported to be anywhere from 61 to 137 barrels. Perley reported that 200 barrels was the yield in 1849, and the census of 1861 showed a phenomenal yield of approximately 250 000 pounds.[87]

UPPER BAY OF FUNDY

Between the mouth of the Saint John River and the Petitcodiac estuary, no regular commercial fishing base or singularly important fishing station existed, although most of the inhabitants along the shore fished at the mouths of the streams, where they erected weirs and nets to meet their own needs. The salmon captured along this coastline were generally small, and local fishermen referred to them as "fiddlers."[88] Monro stated in 1855 that great value was placed on the salmon fishery by these people,[89] but repeated seasonal exploitation of these relatively small rivers, plus the erection of mill-dams, was greatly reducing annual benefits throughout the late 1850s and 1860s.

Salmon had not entered the Mispec River since the early 1820s because of a milldam constructed at that time, although it was once reported that the Mispec was a great spawning and nursery area for the species, the fish even ascending to Loch Lomond and its feeder brooks: an old resident of the area, a Mr. Trafton, reported that he had known salmon as plentiful in the stream as "flies in the summer"; unfortunately, unlike flies, the Mispec salmon had no wings.[90] Black River, Emerson Creek, and Gardner Creek were also deserted by the mid-1860s, due to the erection of dams, but at Tynemouth Creek, salmon managed to persist to a certain extent.

A rather unique trip-weir had been in operation at the mouth of this latter creek for many years, and took a considerable quantity of both salmon and herring: by the use of a barrier net, which stretched entirely across the estuary, and by using a hinged sill and capstans, the weir was made to lie prostrate during the incoming tide; as the tide receded, the weir was hoisted to the upright position, enclosing all species on the shoreward side. This device became inoperative in the early 1850s, but salmon were still taken in a net that was set completely across the river's mouth. Later, two dams were erected on the creek, the second of which was located about 1.5 miles upriver; although salmon sometimes navigated past the first dam, they could not go further than the second, above which their principal spawning grounds existed.[91]

Weirs of the more conventional type were also taking small quantities of salmon in the Quaco (St. Martins) area, but lumbering operations at Big Salmon River had removed any chance of the species entering that stream. Perley commented in 1851 that

> Just where the river makes its final leap into the sea, there is a solid dam from bank to bank, upon which there are two double sawmills; a quarter of a mile above, there is another dam of similar character, upon which there is one single sawmill. In neither of these dams is there any fishway, and fish are therefore wholly excluded from the river.... The settlers here said, that before the dams were built across Salmon River, the fishing was excellent and persons came from all parts to catch salmon there. One man had caught as many salmon there during a single season, as sold for £90 [i.e. 7200 lb]; and during another season, fifty years since, Wright and Tufts caught 40 barrels [12 600 lb fresh] while some others who fished in company, caught 20 barrels [6300 lb fresh] more — now not a single salmon is caught in the river.[92]

Further east, the Little Salmon River was also dammed, and fish could not ascend. The same situation prevailed at Goose Creek and Goose River; in the former, salmon had been reported in considerable numbers prior to dam construction in 1838. By 1867, the species were still barred from ascending any of these streams, although at least in the basin of Goose River, they could still be seen occasionally. The Point Wolfe River was also dammed, as was the Upper Salmon River, otherwise known as the Alma River. Salmon managed to pass the dam on the latter stream, but they were fortunate if they could escape the spear fishermen who kept watchful eyes at the head of the mill pond. Just before Confederation, the Alma was reported to be free of any serious obstructions, since the dam there was in disrepair; that this small stream continued to support freshwater fish at that time was shown by the report that one thousand salmon were taken with spears and nets in the upper reaches of the river in 1867.[93]

Family weirs also existed along this coastline; one at Alma, for example, was owned by fourteen local residents, and an old photograph shows salmon lying in it.[94] The weir at the mouth of Goose River captured seven barrels of salmon (2205 lb fresh) in 1850, and in 1849, nearly 500 fish were reported taken in a Point Wolfe weir.[95] It appears likely that at least 20 000 pounds of salmon were taken annually between Cape Enragé and Mispec in the 1850s and 1860s. As for the Petitcodiac, great numbers of salmon had previously frequented both it and its tributaries, although their numbers began to decline about 1830, likely because of weirs, set nets, and local overfishing.

Few people were concerned with salmon preservation along this rugged south coast of the province, but at least one inclination toward conservation was reported in the mid-1850s: Gideon Vernon, who owned the dam and weir at Point Wolfe, had attempted each year to place a few breeding fish into the headpond of his mill, by carrying live fish from the weir over the dam in barrels of water. When Vernon was approached in later years about the possibility of placing a fishway in this dam, he willingly agreed, and expressed that it could probably be accomplished at a trifling cost; the fishway was built in 1871, and in October of that year the first natural run to the river occurred in more than 20 years.[96] The Point Wolfe subsequently had the reputation of being the best salmon stream on the coast.

SAINT JOHN RIVER

Of the Saint John River at mid-century, Charles Lanman wrote: "The river abounds with salmon and shad, and the former though rather small, may be taken by the angler on the principal tributaries… and the common modes of taking them are with the spear and drift net." Lanman later contradicted himself by saying that the salmon in 1848 were "not sufficiently abundant… to form an important article of trade";[97] other contemporary reports indicate, however, that this comment is suspect, although a slight depression in commercial activity may have been evident at this time.

It appears that the Saint John region fishery did not suffer the marked declines similar to those evidenced in the Gulf of St. Lawrence stocks during this same period. This situation may have been partly due to compensating yields from the expanding drift-net fishery. Although a later depression did occur in the fishery, it corresponded more closely with the fluctuating pattern of catches evidenced historically on the Atlantic coast of Nova Scotia, where the low point in commercial productivity has traditionally occurred some years later or earlier than in the Gulf of St. Lawrence.

Another visitor to Saint John in 1849 had the following comment to make about the city's fishery:

The city has a very extensive commerce, and is very largely engaged in the fisheries and the timber trade. The fisheries are a source of considerable wealth and employ many of the inhabitants. The stranger can see scores and hundreds of fishing smacks and boats approach the wharves when they come sufficiently near to be seen for the fog which obscures them till within a few rods of the landing, all of which are always loaded with the finest fishes.[98]

Perhaps some of the smacks which the gentleman described were those engaged in the harbour drift-net fishery for salmon, a practice which, although contrary to provincial law, was pursued with great vigor, with the assent of the city Corporation. Although drifting was chiefly carried out at night, it was not for reasons of blinding the eyes of those charged with policing the provincial statute, for Saint John men did not hesitate to drift, either during the day or on the Sabbath — a day when all fishing was forbidden. The nets used by these small boats were generally 200 fathoms long and 40 meshes deep, and it frequently required great skill to navigate this equipment through the shipping in the harbor. Perhaps the fog was too thick for our visitor to see the other basic fishing units locally used: weirs, made of 2.75 inch mesh nets, hung on ribbands and timber pickets, and supplemented with leaders running out from high-water mark to the circular pond at the low-water mark; they were also frequently referred to as fykes.[99]

The system of selling weir and fixed-net berths by lottery was still being carried out in the 1850s, under much criticism by the bona fide fishermen, who were not always able to secure the stand which they wanted. Eighty to one hundred lots were leased annually in the lottery; and in the early 1850s, they were being purchased from the winners of the draw for anything from a few shillings to £40, £50, or even £100.[100] The lottery, in keeping with other Saint John fishing activities, was contrary to provincial law, but it remained in operation until 1862. After that date, the contentious system was abolished by a civic bylaw and replaced by an open auction, which took place each year on the first Tuesday in January. Successful bidders were allowed to construct weirs or erect fixed salmon nets on their lots on both the east and west side of the harbor; it is interesting to note that the annual auction was lucrative enough in 1860s, that the monies gathered from the sale of the east side lots went to build a new city hall.[101]

The harbor fishery had increased in importance since the 1830s, and the expanding American market provided a ready outlet. In 1850, the total harbor fishery for shad, salmon and gaspereau was valued at £20 000, and it was estimated that 32 000 salmon were taken, 17 150, or 55 percent of which found their way to the United States.[102] In that year alone, 15 tons of salmon and lobster were shipped in ice to Eastport, Maine, where the U.S. Treat Company was packing its fish in tins. Fishermen were locally obtaining five shillings per fish for their catch, large or small, but on the United States market the price was double.[103] Exports were down in 1851, due to a depression in the fishery which continued for a few years; but by 1861, the annual yield in the harbor had risen to around 30 000 fish, and in 1864, it had reached 40 000 fish, a large percentage of which was packed in ice and again exported to the United States.[104]

By this latter date, fishermen were selling their catch by the pound, a 12-pound salmon now bringing them six shillings.[105] Between 1845 and 1867, it is estimated that the annual yield of salmon from the harbor fluctuated between 250 000 and 500 000 pounds.[106] During the latter half of this period, reputable sources reported that as many as 1500 salmon had been taken in one tide by drift nets alone between Musquash and the Partridge Island beacon.[107]

Drift netting was expanding rapidly along the coast to Charlotte County in the early 1860s, and by 1867 Venning reported: "If the nets I have this season seen drifting at one time in the bay, had been stretched in a line, they would have extended to Digby."[108] This westward expansion of the fishery in the 1860s and the establishment of salmon-fishing communities such as Piserinco (Lorneville) was in contrast to what had been reported of the region in 1850, for at that time it was stated that "From Point Lepreau to Saint John Harbour there are no regular fishing establishments."[109]

Many of the tributaries to the Saint John, particularly those below Fredericton, still possessed considerable runs of salmon in the early 1860s, although they were unmercifully exploited with the spear. There were some rivers, however, in which the situation was becoming desperate. In 1853, it was noted that "dams erected across the river have produced this change. The few salmon that now appear in the Oromocto, Nashwaak, Meduxnekeag, Mispec, Great Salmon River, Emerson, Gardner, and Goose Creek is attributed to the same cause."[110] Salmon were reported to be abundant in the Kennebecasis — at least to Sussex Vale — and in the Hammond River to Titus' Mill, twelve miles from Darlings Island.[111] At French Village they were continuously taken by about 1000 souls who "pretend farming but are chiefly engaged in hunting and fishing."[112] The Kennebecasis was one of the more densely populated river valleys in southern New Brunswick and, in consequence, severe inroads were being made on annual fish

runs; the almost continuous series of pools and shallows which existed for the 50 miles between Hampton and Goshen provided excellent ground for the spearsman.

The Nerepis River remained free from obstruction for many years and flowed through wild and uninhabited country. At the junction of this river with the Saint John, the salmon fishery was recognized as second to none, with between 1500 and 2000 fish being taken annually.[113] It was once reported that salmon were frequently netted in the vicinity of Britain's Point as late as November, with the product going to Boston packed in ice.[114] The returns for 1861 showed 2150 salmon being taken in Kings County,[115] the largest percentage of which undoubtedly came from the Morrisdale-Nerepis-Westfield area.

The Salmon and Gaspereau rivers at the head of Grand Lake had both been dammed prior to 1840, but the structure on the former was breached in 1843, and by 1850, salmon were once again reported as frequenting the stream in considerable numbers, continuing to do so until after Confederation. By 1860, however, the streams of Queens County had generally deteriorated, and salmon fishing reverted to an activity of little consequence; only 65 fish appeared on the local returns in 1861.[116]

The principal salmon stream in York County — if not on the entire Saint John River — was the Nashwaak, which had been famous ever since the importance of the various tributary streams was first considered. The entire watercourse of this tributary, however, was subject to disruption and development after 1851 by the New Brunswick and Nova Scotia Land Company, a consortium of land and timber speculators that had secured control over some 500 000 acres of property between the Saint John and Miramichi rivers in 1834.[117] The dam erected at Milltown by 1850[118] was far too prominent a structure not to receive the attention of the New Brunswick Legislature, which sat almost directly across the Saint John River from the Nashwaak's confluence. Only the occasional salmon succeeded in passing up the dam's sluiceway, and the government was compelled to attempt to enforce the Fishery Act provision which pertained to fishways. Even the governor, Arthur Hamilton Gordon, used his direct influence to have the regulations complied with, but to no avail; such was the apparent power of the lumber barons of the day. The damage caused by the Milltown dam was compounded when the Land Company opened up the headwaters of the Nashwaak by building the settlement of Stanley; as a result, the small numbers of salmon which managed to pass the dam at one end of the river were unmercifully killed on the spawning grounds at the other. Although the activities of the New Brunswick and Nova Scotia Land Company greatly interfered with tributary salmon runs in York County, 25 000 pounds were still taken in 1861 from the main Saint John River flowing through the region.[119]

Most of the Saint John tributaries above Fredericton were obstructed by dams before 1845, making the streams only fractionally accessible to salmon. They could still be seen, however, at the base of the mighty Grand Falls, as noted by one writer in 1855: "I was told by the settlers at the Falls, that they had often seen salmon making vigorous attempts on the boiling Basin below the grand pitch, to struggle with the tremendous cataract."[120]

A moderately sized tributary, the Salmon River, entered the basin of the Saint John a few miles below Grand Falls. This stream was formerly the resort of "immense numbers of salmon," but throughout the 1850s and 1860s, they were gradually diminished by drift netting. Only 788 fish were reported taken in 1861 in all of Victoria County, where formerly there were many thousands captured.[121] After 1850, salmon were rarely seen on the main Saint John River above the mouth of the Aroostook.[122] Netboy reported that salmon once ascended the latter for more than 100 miles, before the building of the Tinker Dam in the early years of the 20th century.[123] One of the more important Aroostook tributaries was the Big Machias River, frequented by prolific numbers of salmon until it was dammed around 1844. Venning assumed that the series of falls and rapids located where the Tinker Dam is now situated was an obstruction to salmon in the 1860s; it may have been in times of low water, but in any case this gorge, with its falls and rapids, was a region where salmon were swept out with nets in considerable numbers.[124]

The Rivière de Chute and the Monquart and Shikatehawk rivers were not particularly recognized as salmon streams, but the Big and Little Presqu'ile were two tributaries of the Saint John River upon which salmon were traditionally speared by the early settlers. The Becaguimec River was obstructed by a mill dam, as were the more important Meduxnekeag and Eel rivers, where dams and gristmills were located a few hundred yards from their mouths. The Shogomoc River was also dammed.[125]

Another great salmon tributary of the upper Saint John system, the Tobique River, was dammed in the 1830s at Red Rapids, some 11 miles from its mouth. By the mid-1840s, however, the dam had been cut away and salmon again increased in numbers. The river remained open for many years after, and since the upper waters were not frequented by settlers to any great extent, the Tobique largely reverted to its natural state until after Confederation, except for the fishing activities of the band of Indians who had their principal settlement at the river's mouth. Gesner reported that the Tobique abounded in salmon during the middle and late 1840s. He had known a single spearsman to fill 12 barrels with salmon near the river's mouth in 1842.[126]

In 1866, a man named Mackwirth Shore attempted to settle along the upper Tobique, canoeing a consider-able distance upriver and noting the salmon that were abundant on the rapids; it was October, and spawning time for the fish. He also recorded that some of the salmon were maimed with spear marks, evidence that the Indians pursued the species to the headwaters, as Venning noted a year later. Shore's attempt at homesteading on the upper Tobique did not, to say the least, progress well, mainly because he could procure little sustenance except fish. Although he managed to construct a cabin, his food supplies quickly dwindled and, by the end of November, he was "beginning to look very hard at the squirrels." When his tobacco ran out and he was forced to substitute it with willow bark, he decided to quit the country and return to Saint John, which he said "was notorious for the beauty of its women." Little did he realize that in a few years, the salmon on the Tobique would lure many fly-fishing sportsmen away from these same attractions of the metropolitan city.[127]

Nova Scotia

Like New Brunswick, Nova Scotia was delinquent in managing its sea and inland fisheries in the mid-1840s. Some old statutes were in the colonial records, but they were repeatedly evaded and their enforcement was neglected; no practical, central control, therefore, existed in the fishery. The Quarter Sessions of the various counties, in whose hands rested responsibiliity for the local fisheries, continued from time to time to enact regulations; like the provincial statutes, such local laws were generally inadequate and ignored. Interest in, and knowledge of, the fishery was principally confined to those Nova Scotians who were actually engaged in the operation itself, and their concern was largely of a parochial nature. It was not uncommon to find a Bluenoser who was engaged in a specific fishery, but who knew or cared little about what similar resources existed in the next county. It was, in fact, common for Nova Scotian saltwater men to know more about the Labrador fisheries than about those carried on in the harbors adjacent to their home port, for it was in Labrador and the northern Gulf of St. Lawrence that many of them were fishing in the 1840s and 1850s. Considering the provincial fishery in 1850, one Haligonian wrote:

I think there is scarcely a man in the province who has a correct idea of the present value of our fisheries; and I am sure, that few can conceive to what extent they are capable of being carried, under sound and judicious legislation and management.[128]

If no one in the province could recognize the potential value of the fisheries, it generally followed that they cared little for how the industry was carried on or for the preservation of some species and the economic development of others. With respect to salmon, although the species was increasing in value on the home and foreign market, it also appeared to be following certain other species into extinction, due to the fact that it was fished by any method, in any place, at any season, and in any numbers; in addition, it was being barred from access to many natal waters. In an 1848 description of Nova Scotia, Sir John Harvey commented:

> Salmon are found in most of the rivers which they ascend to deposit their spawn. The salmon fisheries of this province, at its first settlement were very productive, as may be judged by the fact that 1000 barrels were drawn from the Liverpool [Mersey] River in one season....The erection of grist and saw mills upon the streams, had in many instances, destroyed, and in all has greatly limited this fishery. Salmon are still caught in quantities upon the coast, for the supply of the home or United States market, and many of the rivers still attract the angler, and furnish to the Indians and poorer settlers, by whom salmon are speared, a portion of subsistence. But it is difficult to protect the River Fisheries, from the number of proprietors of lands along the banks, who can seldom agree in local regulations for their management, and by whom general laws are so easily evaded.[129]

By the early 1850s, however, a change in attitude was discernible. Moses Perley's reports on the New Brunswick fishery were being widely circulated and read throughout the colonies, and Nova Scotians were particularly interested in his comments concerning the Bay of Fundy fishery, since they had witnessed declines in their own resources in that area. Perley's work pointed out some of the reasons for concern, as well as recommendations for improvement. This growing provincial interest was again reflected by the fact that the government had, by 1850, received a number of petitions complaining of abuses in the fishery, particularly those relating to the obstruction of rivers by milldams. When one considers the long list of mills recorded in the 1851 census — mills which, for the most part, required a head of water provided by a dam — it is quite impossible to imagine why anadromous fish had not forsaken the province's streams a decade earlier.[130]

Subsequently, an act was passed authorizing the County Sessions Courts to make regulations for inclusion in a legislative enactment which would be applicable to the whole province. To investigate the need for new regulations and to review and make recommendations in this regard, a Fisheries Committee of the Provincial Legislature was formed. In 1851, the committee made its report to the Assembly; it recommended several provisions respecting the salmon fishery, including a closed season from July 30 to November 1, and a fishway law which made it compulsory for millowners to provide fish passage in their dams between April and November. The committee also called attention to the imperfect way in which fish inspectors reported their annual returns, pointing out that the task was "very carelessly discharged"; finally, a brief report was given on recent developments in fish culture in Europe, which implied that such practices might be considered for application in Nova Scotia.[131]

The Legislature was attentive to the committee's report, and in the 1853 session passed a law encompassing several of the committee's recommendations. Firstly, the capture of salmon in inland waters between June 30 and March 1 was forbidden.[132] Another clause stipulated that fishpasses would be required in milldams, and provisions were also made for the appointment of river wardens to police the act in each county at a salary of £25 per annum. The Legislature followed up these regulations by sending out a circular letter to the county wardens in 1854 to determine if the new regulations had had any effect. Apparently they had not, for in Halifax County alone, only 5 of the enumerated rivers were not obstructed to fish passage.

At this time, the Legislature became acquainted with Captain William Chearnley, an ardent sports fisherman who had known many of the rivers in the province since the 1830s, and who was a firm advocate of fisheries management. He was well versed in the ways of salmon and was instrumental in forming, in 1853, a Halifax group known as the Provincial Association for the Protection of Inland Fisheries and Game of Nova Scotia, otherwise known as the Fisheries Protection Society. This group exercised a strong influence on government and informed the general public of the need for fisheries protection. The society concentrated its efforts on the rehabilitation of the province's streams, and to this cause devoted both manpower and money. The association also published papers on fisheries matters, and in Halifax County, where its strength was greatest, the society paid a certain number of overseers to enforce the fishery laws — laws which the society helped to create, but which the Legislature was somewhat delinquent in enforcing.[133]

Chearnley was elected the association's first president. He was also appointed supervisor of the inland fisheries of Halifax County, but his influence apparently exceeded these bounds since, like Perley in New Brunswick, his opinions were sought with regard to fisheries protection throughout the colony. His reports to the Legislature gave descriptions of many provincial rivers completely obstructed by dams. On this somewhat scanty basis alone, it might be concluded that anadromous fish production must have been severely reduced from its original potential, perhaps by as much as 70 or 80 percent. Chearnley was alarmed to find to what extent small-mesh nets and other devices were being used to catch both juvenile and adult salmon; he also discovered that entire stream widths were being sealed off by nets and weirs to capture every fish that entered fresh water. The sawdust, slabs and other refuse from mill operations covered the stream beds, and sometimes piles of mill waste which reached 20 feet in height were found in the rivers.[134]

Unfortunately, the initial steps taken by the Legislature in 1853 to manage the fishery more effectively were not followed by the persistence required to effect a recognizable improvement in most regions of the province, and a falling off of the salmon continued. In 1854, the Fisheries Committee reported that the salmon yield was at its lowest value since the advent of the timber trade in the early 1800s,[135] and a general report on the salmon fishery in British North America at this time said of Nova Scotia that "The salmon has entirely disappeared from some parts of the colony and has ceased to be plentiful in all of the rivers and streams."[136]

When pursuing the promotional literature extant on the resources of the colony at this time, one receives the distinct impression that a prosperous salmon fishery existed; for example:

> The salmon, the common trout, and the salmon trout (*Salmo trutta*), are plentiful in nearly all the streams, and afford fine sport to the angler; and the fishes of the former species are so numerous and so fine a quality as to be of some importance as an article of commerce.[137]

These glowing reports, however, were written to sing the praises of the colony to prospective immigrants and tourists; such descriptions, however, were hardly credible to those already settled in the region. The export records also served to create a similarly misleading impression of the salmon resource. An examination of the statistical records presented by Lorenzo Sabine for the years 1845 to 1850, for example, indicates that, on the average, close to 2 million pounds of salmon were exported from the province annually.[138] It is known, however, that large proportions of these totals included catches made by Nova Scotians in Newfoundland and Labrador, or imported from other colonies and trans-shipped through the colony to external markets; these imports, for example, amounted to 50 percent of the total export in 1845, 78 percent in 1846, and 61 percent in 1847.[139]

The average export of locally captured salmon can be calculated at approximately 1 million pounds. If one adds to this the amount captured and consumed locally, the total catch in Nova Scotia during this period would probably range between 1 and 1.5 million pounds annually. By today's standard, this hardly represents a depletion of the stocks, but the state of things in the 1850s was compared to the past, and to the people of that period the state of the fishery looked grim. From the 1851 returns for the various counties, it is apparent that salmon were disappearing from many regions of mainland Nova Scotia, in a decline that appeared to be creeping along the Atlantic coast from west to east. The best fishery was now concentrated in the eastern third of the province, where the coastal fishery was the mainstay; just over 45 percent of the total provincial catch came from Antigonish and Guysborough counties, and another

third from the island of Cape Breton. Since figures are incomplete for the period from 1852 to 1855, we can only assume that the verbal reports of a continued decline would be reflected in the statistical records; data for the period from 1856 to Confederation tend to show that a downward trend was still prevalent.[140]

In 1858, the province discontinued paying county wardens, and turned over the entire responsibility for the river fisheries to the various counties. Between that date and 1863, there is scarcely a note in the *Journals* of the House of Assembly relating to the provincial fisheries. Responsibility for this state of affairs, however, cannot be laid entirely on the government. This was a period of rapid colonial development and commercial growth, when the Reciprocity Treaty was encouraging Nova Scotians to reap benefits while they could. Almost 40 percent of colonial profit came from the fishery, and exploitation of the resource was inevitable. Furthermore, many developments such as schools, roads, navigational aids, etc., demanded support from the colony's meager revenues; because of the administrative overload, any responsibility that could be delegated to the counties was quickly handed to them. Again, the fisheries were to suffer.[141]

The financial conditions of the counties then were even worse than those of the province, and as a result, there was little financial support available for fisheries protection on a local basis. Those wardens who were appointed were either remiss in their duties or frustrated by the magnitude of their task; they were frequently not paid for their work, and on rare occasions they exercised their duty at their own expense. In many areas, the owners of milldams — which were generally believed to be the worst detriment to the river fisheries — were the magistrates themselves, so little improvement could be expected in that quarter. The laws in general were ignored by all.[142]

Examples of fish stock destruction at this time are frequent. Moses Perley, for example, while visiting the Margaree River in 1860, in his capacity as fishery commissioner for the British government, reported that the ineffectual protection afforded to the southwest branch of the river by the local warden was such that the officer, instead of being paid for his work, should be jailed. On the LaHave, it was said that one enterprising farmer had, at the end of a mill flume, placed eel pots "in which barrels of young salmon [smolts] were destroyed and given to the pigs."[143] Conditions were deplorable in many other areas, and total destruction of the salmon appeared to be a prime objective for Nova Scotians: as one writer reported, "The spirit of wanton extermination is rife; and it has been well remarked, it really seems as though the man would be loudly applauded who was discovered to have killed the last salmon."[144]

These frequent accounts of the complete disregard for the fishery and its laws could not go on indefinitely without further attention being given by the Legislature. In 1864, the season was unusually dry, and many streams and rivers in the province possessed very low water levels. Such conditions were particularly bad for salmon, and many were taken in pools and at the foot of un-navigable falls and runs. Because of certain representations from concerned individuals, with respect to these and other abuses, a Law Amendments Committee was established by the Legislature; its mandate was to examine the river fisheries and recommend changes in the existing statutes. The Hon. A. G. Archibald, chairman of the committee, subsequently reported on various cases of "criminal neglect" and urged the "most energetic means" for restoration and protection.[145]

The recommendations were acted upon by vigorous legislation in 1865: a commercial salmon-fishing season was established, which extended from March 1 to July 31 in all waters west of Halifax, and from March 1 to August 15 in the Bay of Fundy and to the east of Halifax; a $40 fine was imposed for fishing outside these seasons. A weekend closure was also legislated, bag nets were outlawed in any river, harbor, or within one mile of any river, and netting and spearing of salmon in any freshwater segment of a river was made illegal. Nets were allowed to be set only on one side of a river estuary and were restricted to one-third the width of the river channel and to one-eighth mile from the base of any dam. In addition, millowners were required to construct fishpass facilities in their dams according to a specific pattern.[146]

The Fisheries Protection Society had long advocated this need for fishways and, in fact, had submitted a general design which was accepted by the Legislature as the one to be used in all such man-made obstructions. The statutes described the required construction as follows:

> Such fish-ladder shall have a slope of not more than one foot in seven; shall have an opening of not less than three feet in width at the top of the dam and shall be so placed that there shall at all times be at least one foot in depth of water over the mouth thereof; the bottom of such ladder to be water-tight and to be covered with stone, and at every six feet, pieces of wood or stone to be fastened at right angles to the sides thereof, and to be secured to each side alternately, so as to make the current of water flow from side to side, — the openings to be not less than one foot in width, and the pieces of wood or stone so jutting out from the sides to be not less than two feet in height; the lower end of such fish-ladder to be secured to the bottom of the main channel of the river or otherwise shall be conformable to the model of the fish-ladder now deposited in the office of the Provincial Secretary.[147]

There were problems with the new legislation immediately. The law which compelled the construction of fish ladders throughout the province, for example, received much criticism, some of it coming from the Fisheries Protection Society itself. The general belief was that the fishway design could not be applied universally throughout the province and that a complete study of fishway types under varying conditions and in other regions of the world would have to be undertaken to establish the most effective devices for any particular situation. The fishway legislation was, therefore, repealed in 1866 for all areas outside Halifax County except the Clyde River, where it was intended to test the success of the particular fishway design.[148]

The remaining stipulations of the 1865 act were also open to immediate abuse. It was ludicrous to believe that all estuarial fishermen were going to fish only on one side of the river, while such a deeply-imbedded technique as spear fishing would be more difficult to break than the tobacco habit — attitudes and actions cannot be changed as abruptly as legislation. Perhaps the impracticability of the regulations was anticipated, for the Legislature virtually nailed the lid on the statute's efficiency by making the county Sessions again responsible for appointing river wardens and enforcing the regulations; as one observer stated, "there the matter ended... whether or not the Warden did his duty they never troubled their heads to enquire."[149]

The Nova Scotian fishery, therefore, remained in an unrestricted state right up to the time of Confederation; the acknowledged causes of the great destruction of the resource were milldams without fishways, spearing on the spawning grounds, and illegal netting in all places where nets could be set. Writing about the state of the fishery in 1867, Frederick Vieth remarked that fishermen still knew no distinction of season, and that the appointed county inspectors were negligent in their duty; the county magistrates, furthermore, permitted laws to be violated before their very eyes.[150] The wave of legislative interest which was witnessed within the province in the 1850s and early 1860s had subsided, and "the condition of our rivers at the present time [1867] is in many places as deplorable as it was described in 1854."[151] The final word was voiced by the Legislature's Fishery Committee in 1867, when it reported that:

> notwithstanding the successive legislation of many years on this important subject, the wanton and unwise destruction of the various kinds of fish frequenting the rivers of this Province, has hitherto been but little or none checked.[152]

CAPE BRETON

In 1865, a warden in Inverness County reported that

> The only valuable river fishery is the Margaree where a large quantity of alewives are taken and salmon and trout are abundant...there are [a] few salmon and trout taken at Mabou, but the number is limited, about 20 barrels of the former are exported annually.[153]

Records indicate that the total yield from Inverness County was in the range of 60 000 pounds in 1851 and 46 000 pounds in 1861.[154] An increasing number of salmon were being taken outside the river areas, although the Margaree was still accounting for a large portion of the catch.

The Margaree was undoubtedly the best known river along the coast at this time; reports indicate that it was becoming a favorite resort for the angler, but it was also reported to be heavily poached.[155] Its fame as a salmon stream was surpassed only by its reputation as a gaspereau fishing area, the fish spawning in great numbers in Lake Ainslie. Both salmon and gaspereau stocks were declining in the 1850s, principally due to the unrestricted use of weirs; when Perley visited the river in 1860, he remarked of the latter that:

> In general, these fish traps, when in use, appear to have fully occupied one-half the river, and now that the water is low, several exended across the whole channel, obligating my party to cut away portions in order to get through with the canoes. The number of these fish traps was so great as to induce me to believe that, besides being fished in a most improper and unfair manner, the river was greatly overfished.[156]

These weirs were basically designed for gaspereau, and although a county regulation stipulated that there could be no upstream mouth in which the spawners could be caught while returning to the sea, both upstream and downstream traps were common.

The early salmon fishery which had developed at St. Ann's was still being carried out in the 1850s and 1860s, principally by settlers of the area for local consumption only. The main salmon rivers were the Baddeck and Middle rivers, although the Rev. R. J. Uniacke reported that the rivers to the north of Sydney also produced salmon in great numbers.[157] The story of depletion here was similar to the rest of the province; in the late 1860s, a Baddeck resident wrote that salmon were becoming extinct in the local streams, "in consequence of their being caught when coming up the rivers to spawn [with] spears and nets being mostly used for their capture."[158]

The principal area for salmon fishing in Cape Breton County was the Mira River and its two main tributaries, the Salmon and Gaspereau rivers. As with Victoria County, salmon were used mainly for local consumption, with very little being exported. Great activity was concentrated on the Mira system during the salmon runs, with flakes erected for curing fish on the spot. A report from the area in the 1860s mentioned that gaspereau had been almost exterminated by the unrestricted use of nets; the salmon run was also greatly reduced for similar reasons.[159]

The salmon fishery of Richmond County was valuable at this time only to local settlers, but many were engaged in the pursuit, particularly in the areas of the Grand and Inhabitants rivers.[160]

GUYSBOROUGH COUNTY

In 1845, Guysborough County was recognized as the foremost salmon-producing area in Nova Scotia, and this distinction was apparently maintained well past the period of Confederation. The 1851 and 1861 census returns showed that the region accounted for at least 36 percent of the province's annual salmon yield.[161] Although the coastal fishery of Chedabucto Bay helped the county to maintain this record, the gem of the river fishery was the St. Mary's, of which it was written that:

> Perhaps in the whole of the Lower Provinces there does not exist so charming a river as this is. It is of great extent, and its main stream is supplied by waters from two magnificent flows, known as the East and West branches. The scenery along its margins is of great grandure, and the graceful manner in which it winds through the vast extent of agricultural and natural meadow land, fully entitle it to be called 'The beautiful St. Mary's.'[162]

Its "fisheries were second to none," but even at this time there was doubt as to how long the St. Mary's could maintain its record. Lumbering was rapidly superseding fishing as the county's principal activity; consequently, stream driving and milldams were beginning to threaten the runs, while areas of the watersheds which had hitherto been relatively free from exploitation were now invaded by lumbermen, so that soon it was said: "the lumbermen vie with the Indians in skill in their nightly spearing expeditions."[163]

By 1867, it was reported that the St. Mary's fishery was uttering its "last gasp" because of the lumber industry and the unrestricted practices of local fishermen.[164] Although there were no dams on the main river, it was reported that

> fully 200 nets of all lengths, and fixed in every spare place, were set in the tideway... But no pen could EXAGGERATE the number of them [nets] placed about its inland or fresh waters. These may be seen of all kinds, some directly across or overlapping each other; others, fixtures, (stake nets) and the margins of the lake on East River [Glenelg Lake] literally abound in these engines of destruction....The whole population are up and doing....Here is a river that any country in the world would be proud of, unobstructed, it is true, but so illegally overnetted and so disturbed by constant spearing, that it is a perfect miracle a single salmon has the good fortune to escape to its spawning grounds.[165]

Miracles, apparently, were common in Nova Scotia at this time, for although the same concentrated destruction was taking place throughout the province, salmon nevertheless continued to reappear each season in spite of the war waged on their numbers.

The city of Halifax was reputed to have one of the best fish markets in the world during the 1840s and 1850s.[166] As far as salmon were concerned, this market was principally supplied by the fishery carried out at Ferguson, Herring and Portuguese coves, between Halifax and Sambro. The market was so popular that it was open 7 days a week, much to the chagrin of the local clergy:

The fish market is open from 6 to 9 o'clock a.m. Last Sabbath, between 7 and 8 o'clock, there were twenty-six stalls with Fish, nine boats afloat, and four on the slip; one hundred and twenty-four persons purchased fish between 7 and 8 o'clock.[167]

Halifax was also the chief exporting center of the province, and customs house accounts for 1851 show that 340 tierces and 6412 barrels of salmon (approximately 1 384 400 lb pickled) left the province from this town. Very little actually came from the vicinity or even from the province; indeed, we are told by P. S. Hamilton that the largest portion of fish caught within the province was usually not cured at all, but was sent to the various markets in the fresh state.[168] This would suggest that the cured (barrels) product was in fact captured outside home waters.

The rivers and brooks around Halifax provided a ready source of salmon until the 1850s, at which time many streams became so obstructed that a Fisheries Protection Society was formed to try and improve the situation. As noted previously, this group was principally interested in Halifax County, but their activities carried influence throughout the province. By the mid-1860s, membership exceeded 100, but although they continued to advertise the terrible disregard that was rampant in the fisheries and continued to pay wardens in Halifax County, their progress was, in general, slow. In the 1840s, for example, salmon were to be found in substantial numbers on the Sackville River, north of Halifax. One Bedford resident had angled 19 in one day in 1848, his smallest specimen weighing 18 pounds. Commercial salmon fishermen were also fishing Bedford Basin at this time; but after a dam was built about 6 miles upstream from the Sackville River's mouth in the 1850s, salmon runs decreased to the point where neither the angler nor the commercial fisherman found it worthwhile to fish in the area. The Fisheries Protection Society tried to rehabilitate the Sackville River at the time of Confederation by having a warden put on the river and by spending one hundred dollars to place a fishway in the dam. An increase in netting abuses, however, curtailed any direct improvement.[169]

To the eastward of Halifax, Little Salmon River, draining Lake Major, was reported to be an excellent salmon, trout, and gaspereau stream prior to, possibly,

1825. A dam, however, ruined this reputation until 1865, at which time a heavy freshet swept away the barrier, and salmon were reported to be again returning. Big Salmon River, or Salmon River, Lawrencetown, had not been a salmon stream since the mid-1840s, due to a number of dams that had been placed along its course. The Chezzetcook, although not dammed, showed little promise: "Snares of this description, of every conceivable size of mesh, are much used at this place, capturing all fish that attempt to seek the inland waters. Salmon were once very common to this river."[170] Petpeswick Stream was another brook completely closed to anadromous runs by a dam at the head of tide.

The Musquodoboit — the River of Plenty — was reported to be abounding in salmon in 1847; one angler at that time was said to have taken seven salmon each day for a week, a total catch that could hardly be surpassed by the seasonal take of all anglers on the river in recent years. The river was still a noted angling stream in 1864, but by 1868, Frederick Vieth reported that the salmon being caught were chiefly taken in commercial nets set in the harbor. Another noted angling stream was the Charles, or Ship Harbour River, which had also been a traditional Indian fishing location. Although a dam existed on this river, it was equipped with a fishpass that appeared to function sufficiently — or occasionally enough — to keep the salmon run viable until the middle 1860s, when Vieth reported that

The mill site of this river has, however, since then fallen into other hands, and the fish pass alluded to is replaced by one I have mentioned as useless. Will it be believed that lately below this dam, a magistrate in that locality was seen encouraging some Indians to spear all the salmon that they could see, and purchasing the fish from them for a trifle, to take direct to Halifax, to retail at an enormous profit.[171]

The Salmon River at Jeddore had been obstructed with a dam at its mouth for many years, and the Tangier River was reported to be "shamefully overnetted." The situation on the rivers at Sheet Harbour was just as bad: on the East River Sheet Harbour, a fishway had been placed in the principal dam in 1862, but because of the dam's considerable height and the fishway's poor design, salmon could not ascend. By 1868, it was reported that only about one-fiftieth of the salmon were being taken in the Sheet Harbour area as compared to former years:

Mill dams and bag nets have done their deadly work too well, and almost ruined these once far-famed streams. Salmon River (running into Beaver Harbour), [Port Dufferin], Quoddy, Ecum Secum and Liscomb, each flowing into its own bay, are all either so totally obstructed by mill dams, or so unfairly netted in every way, that their fisheries must of necessity shortly be remembered only as that which has been, but no longer exists.[172]

To the west of Halifax, most rivers flowing into St. Margaret's Bay, such as the Indian, Northeast, East and Hosier, were reported to be free of obstructions in 1866. The exception was Ingram River, where the owners of a mill had been opposed to any effort to have a fishpass constructed; by 1868, however, an "apology of a fishway" had been built, through which fish could pass only during high water.[173] Spearing and illegal netting appeared to be a tradition on the river. Indian River was providing good angling in 1866; about 3 miles from its mouth, there was a large dam through which the Fisheries Protection Society had built a fishpass, and the Society had also provided a warden for this river.[174] The Hosier River was an especially good, small, salmon stream, as was Nine Mile Stream, reputed to be one of the prettiest in Nova Scotia. The latter had its source in the lakes near Hammonds Plains, and entered the sea at Shad Bay; an officer on this river in 1864 reported that "I saw stretched across the tideway upwards of eight nets and seines, which prevented even the smallest fish from escaping."[175] Unfortunately, those streams which had free access in 1866 were all obstructed by dams in 1868.

SOUTHWESTERN NOVA SCOTIA

The once-productive rivers of Lunenburg County had also declined steadily during the 1850s and 1860s. The Petite Rivière, for example, was so severely netted each year at the harbor that one observer noted: "it would be quite impossible for the smallest of living things in the water to pass the obstructions."[176] Salmon were also scarce in the LaHave River due to illegal netting and the great barriers required for mill operation. All around Mahone Bay, illegal trap nets of great size were employed. The Mush-a-mush was also totally obstructed. The only river not obstructed by milldams at this time was the Gold, which thus enjoyed great popularity as an angling stream; netting in the harbor, however, was extreme, with fully 100 nets being employed annually.[177]

In a letter written to the Legislature's Fisheries Committee in 1854, Patrick Gough stated that salmon entered Queens County rivers from the last of April to the last of July, spawning in October, and that the run on the Medway was 2 weeks earlier than on the Mersey. With his letter, Gough also submitted a proposed fishway design to be used in the province.[178] His submission was prompted in part by the knowledge that the salmon fishery of the county as a whole was considered of so little importance in 1850, that no returns were shown on the reports for that year. In 1861, however, the recorder saw fit to note the county's salmon catch as six barrels plus 186 smoked fish, probably no more than 4000 pounds total.[179]

The excellent salmon fishery of the Mersey River was almost nonexistent by 1850. A milldam had been constructed at the head of tide, and several more about it, all completely obstructing the passage of fish.[180] The few salmon returning to the base of the dam each year were speared and served on the tables of local residents. It was said that those who obstructed the Mersey or Liverpool River in such a way were individuals who perhaps should have set an example in conservation of the species: "One is or was a Member of the Legislative Council, and another a Magistrate and formerly a Member of the House of Assembly."[181]

The Medway River was also barred to the ascent of salmon by dams until the mid-1860s, when they became disused and breached; fish were reported to be returning by 1867, but numerous dams were again erected or repaired, all without fishways. Apparently, salmon occasionally managed to overcome these structures by ascending the log sluices, and enough fish generally made it through to the spawning grounds to sustain a small population.[182]

Little can be said of the salmon fishery in western Nova Scotia between 1845 and 1867, other than that it rapidly declined with the erection of sawmills on the various streams, and was only nominally carried out by 1867. It is estimated that probably no more than 1000 salmon were taken seasonally in Yarmouth and Shelburne counties combined, immediately prior to Confederation, these being taken in estuarial nets and probably comprising runs making for the Bay of Fundy.

All the former salmon rivers in Shelburne County — the Clyde, Shelburne, Roseway, Sable, Jordan, Tigney, and Barrington — were blocked with dams by the mid-1860s, and the situation would not improve until after Confederation. Salmon formerly entered the Tusket River in great numbers, but by 1867 it was believed that estuarial weirs and traps along the lower river had largely eliminated them. By 1869, the 20 estuarial weirs were catching only an average of 100 pounds of salmon each, and the traps and dip nets of the river took only 370 pounds in total.[183]

BAY OF FUNDY

The small rivers of Digby and Annapolis counties were also somewhat obstructed by milldams during the 1840s, 1850s, and 1860s, but small numbers of salmon were still recorded ascending such streams as the Chegoggin, Salmon, Meteghan, Grosses Coques, Bear, Moose, and Lequille rivers in 1868. The Salmon and Moose rivers were formerly two of the best small salmon streams in this corner of the province, but their stock had been virtually depleted by dam obstructions. The Lequille was reported to be heavily poached, as were other sections of the Annapolis River; salmon still achieved the headwaters of the Annapolis, however, since it was reported that approximately 3000 pounds were taken illegally from the river in Kings County in 1869. The Round Hill River was free of obstructions and remained one of the principal spawning and nursery areas on the system. Further up the watershed, the Nictaux River also remained a prime rearing region.

Throughout the upper Bay of Fundy and its tributary rivers, salmon were taken in small numbers throughout the period. Along the coast, weirs continued to be used, particularly between Morden and Scots Bay. It was reported in 1868 that considerable numbers of salmon continued to be taken in Minas Basin, particularly in the Economy River; these fish, however, rarely averaged more than 4 pounds apiece. Salmon continued to ascend the Gaspereau River, where they provided some sport for local anglers, and they were still prevalent in the Cornwallis River, even ascending Kentville Brook. They were also found in the Avon River and its tributaries.

Spearing seems to have been the most prevalent method of taking the species in this region of the Minas Basin; a few weirs were operated with some success, and although a considerable amount of shad drift netting was undertaken, the nets were not strong enough to catch and hold the salmon. There were no hindrances to the runs on the Shubenacadie and Stewiacke rivers until the upper regions of the former stream were reached. The fish were then kept from entering their former spawning grounds in the tributaries to Grand Lake by the locks on the Shubenacadie Canal; the worst obstruction was at Horne's Lock, where the salmon were said to be unmercifully netted and speared each season.[184]

NORTHUMBERLAND STRAIT

Of the Northumberland Strait region of Nova Scotia, it was reported in 1868 that "The fisheries of these rivers are of little extent, being allowed to decline as the country has become settled."[185] River Philip was the one exception.

In the eastern end of Pictou County and in Antigonish County, the shore fishery for salmon was an important economic fact throughout the period. Great quantities of fish, some weighing 35 or 40 pounds, were caught in large diamond traps along the beaches during June and July, and a salmon-canning business also developed in the 1860s.[186]

Prince Edward Island

In 1845, Prince Edward Island had already achieved the reputation of being the "fish and chip" colony of America. Potato exports had grown so rapidly, for example, that local markets were overlooked, and an act had to be passed by the Legislature in 1846, limiting their

export for a short period of time.[187] A new interest in the colonial fisheries potential spread like a contagion throughout much of British North America after Perley published his reports on the New Brunswick fishery, and Prince Edward Island was not excluded from at least a temporary attack of concern in this regard. Efforts were made by the government in 1851 to encourage the cod and mackerel industry and in the following year, an act was passed to regulate the alewife and salmon fishery.[188]

The 1852 statute was the first legislation passed since 1780 to deal in any way with the salmon fishery; such consideration was long overdue, for the species had already disappeared from many of the island's streams because of the unrestricted use of the spear and the net. Salmon normally ran into the island's freshwater streams late in the year,[189] and due to the nature of the streams themselves — relatively small, shallow and readily accessible to human observation — the fish were speared en masse by groups of local inhabitants, who could easily empty a stream of its entire run in a few nights of leisurely fall fishing. Article V of the new regulations forbade this practice between October 1 and March 1. Sweep netting, seining and all other methods of salmon fishing were also forbidden in all bays, rivers, creeks, ponds, and streams between the dates previously mentioned, and a fine not exceeding £5 was to be levied on any offender; Indians were the sole exception.[190]

An important aspect of this act was the provision for the appointment of overseers to enforce the regulations and to forward statistical returns on the fish production of the island. Such overseers were to be nominated for the job through a petition signed by at least 20 persons, and their salary was set at £5 per annum. Continuing its interest in the salmon fishery, the Legislature voted the grand sum of £15, apparently the salary for three overseers, for use in the protection of salmon in 1855. Finding this expenditure inadequate, however, the allotment was increased to £25 in the following year.[191]

Although the first statistical returns for the island's fish production and export were made in 1856, salmon went unnoted until the following year, when ten barrels were reported exported from Charlottetown for the United States market, and were valued at £30, or 3.5 pence per pound.[192] Although exports of salmon appeared regularly on the statistical returns after 1857, it is virtually impossible to obtain an exact picture of the extent of these exports in terms of the number of salmon they represented; entries in the records were made in barrels, boxes, cases, packages, tierces, and pounds, the conversion of which is uncertain in many cases. The only indication of the quantity shipped is gained from the monetary value of the exports. In examining these figures, the total value between 1857 and 1867 was £6,746.12s.8d.; since the value of pickled salmon averaged approximately ten pence per pound during this period, an export of 161 942 pounds is implied — or approximately 15 000 pounds annually. The highest export year was 1865, when an estimated 23 000 pounds left the colony.[193]

Besides these exports, salmon were also fished for local consumption, especially in the streams on the north side of the island, such as the Winter River, where as many as 200 fish were known on one occasion to have been taken directly from the spawning beds. Salmon fishing was also carried out at Tignish, Cascumpeque Bay, Kildare, Tracadie, Greenwich, Newfrage, and Savage Harbour, but as in past times, they were never so plentiful as in St. Peter's Bay and the Morelle River. Again in 1860, the Legislature found it expedient to further restrict the fishery by forbidding the catching, selling, or purchasing of salmon between September 1 and April 1; and although spearing was still legal, the lack of fish in the rivers during the open season was deemed enough to discourage that tool. A ban was also imposed on Sunday fishing. The regulations remained in force for 10 years, but because spearing was still carried out, the legislation did little to perpetuate salmon stocks in Prince Edward Island's rivers.[194]

Lower Canada

In 1849, an incident took place in Lower Canada which was a prelude to events which were to affect significantly the future management of Atlantic salmon on the entire continent. In that year, an influential Quebec City brewer, a Mr. Boswell, purchased the fishing rights of the upper Jacques Cartier River to save it from the rapacious commercial fishing activity of Louis Dery, who dip-netted salmon at the 10-foot falls near Dery's Bridge. The brewer had developed a scheme to capture salmon near the spawning time, artificially breed them, and deposit the eggs in large numbers in the waters of his lease.

At this time, however, the downstream sections of the Jacques Cartier were heavily fished by sportsmen, commercial fishermen, and poachers; Boswell realized that if his fish were ever to return to his part of the stream, he would have to secure some kind of control over the other fishing operations on the river. He petitioned the Legislature, asking for protection for his enterprise, but was turned down. Very little information about the art of pisciculture had yet made its way across the Atlantic, and even if it had, the Legislature would probably have decided that salmon were still plentiful enough in Canada in 1850 not to require any artificial assistance in multiplying their numbers, particularly when the effort was aimed at profiting private speculators. Boswell was forced to abandon his plans, and soon relinquished his title to the fishery. He was not entirely discouraged, however, and wrote to his brother, a Dublin attorney, explaining his ideas in the science of fish culture. Around 1852, this brother purchased a stream in Ireland which

was barren of salmon and, through the manipulation of some spawning stock, reseeded his section of the stream with fish; in a few years, the returns from his efforts were remarkable, and in 1856 he sold his fishery for £9,000.[195]

The salmon fishery was in a relatively healthy state in Lower Canada during the mid-1840s and early 1850s; fish weighing from 16 to 18 pounds were apparently not uncommon, and could be purchased for as little as 2 shillings each.[196] Salmon, however, could not continue to survive the increasing degree of exploitation which was taking place each year without some loss in future strength and even the threat of extermination.

The Jacques Cartier River provides a good example of the trends occurring in many streams during this period. In 1829, the river abounded in salmon, and prior to 1845 it was reported that fish in the thousands ran into the river. By the time of Boswell's purchase, the catch was down to a few hundred salmon a year, and by 1860, down to a few dozen. Commercial fishing was carried out in 1850 only on the lower 10 miles of stream, the upper limit of which was terminated by the previously mentioned falls, over which salmon could pass, but only with some difficulty; the falls, in addition to being the site of Dery's fishery, were also a rendezvous for sport anglers from Quebec City. Charles Langevin, whose country home backed on the Jacques Cartier River at Dery's Bridge, maintained a close watch on the stream's salmon resource between 1850 and 1856, and he noted a decline from 410 fish caught in 1850, to only 185 in 1856.[197] After almost ten years of depression, however, the Jacques Cartier began to improve, largely due to the efforts of the Quebec Fish and Game Club, which took an active interest in this river. Members of the club were eager to conserve stock for their own angling purposes, and the presence of members on any river normally made that stream unhealthy for poachers — but secure for the salmon. By 1867, the Jacques Cartier was again furnishing good sport.[198]

Proceeding easterly along the south shore of the St. Lawrence, one could encounter salmon fisheries at various locations all the way to the tip of Gaspé. The fishery, however, was declining, and one individual wrote that "The streams emptying into the St. Lawrence from the south, are not worth mentioning as salmon rivers, having been ruined by mill dams, except those that empty into Gaspé Basin."[199] Only a few ports were involved in the export trade; from Gaspé, for example, 275 and 290 barrels of salmon were shipped in 1848 and 1849, respectively.[200]

On a provincial scale, however, the fishery of the upper St. Lawrence was relatively unimportant; the territory of consequence — the place where the action was — was that extensive coastline from the mouth of the Saguenay River to Blanc Sablon, for here the salmon fisheries were being developed and expanded at a rapid rate. One of the principal reasons for this was the Hudson's Bay Company's serious entry into the fishery. Salmon were not foreign to the company; although we generally think of it as a great fur-trading institution, the English-based firm was always looking for profitable ventures by exploiting anything, whether it was duck quills or whales. Fishing was a regular pursuit at many of the company's posts, engaged in originally to meet the food requirements of employees and their dog teams. In the early part of the century, a Pacific salmon fishery had developed at the company post of Fort Langley, on the Fraser River in British Columbia, and barreled salmon were shipped as rations to the interior fur-trade forts; by 1850, pickled fish were being shipped from Fort Langley to Hawaii at $15 per barrel. It was thus only a matter of time before the company looked to its eastern posts for new profit potential.[201]

As has already been noted, the Hudson's Bay Company was well entrenched along this coastline of Quebec, for purposes of fur trading and for pursuing the local cod and whale fisheries. Quite naturally, the company's interest extended to salmon, although initially the species was not actively exploited. An example of the company's operations at this time, with respect to salmon, is given in the writings of R. M. Ballantyne, a company man and an author who enticed many Old Country boys into the firm's employ by his adventurous and colorful writings concerning the great North American wilderness. In his book entitled *Hudson Bay*, Ballantyne described an 1846 visit to the company's salmon fishery at Moisie River, where between 80 and 90 tierces of salmon were cured annually:

> In about four hours we arrived at the mouth of the Moisie where the first fishery is established. Here we found that our men had caught and salted a good many salmon, some of which had just come from the nets, and lay on the grass, plump and glittering in the pristine freshness.…We had one put in the kettle immediately.…The salmon had only commenced to ascend the river that day, and were being taken by fifties at a haul in the nets. The fishery was attended by three men, who kept seven or eight nets constantly in the water, which gave them enough of employment — two of them attending to the nets, while the third split, salted and packed the fish in large vats.[202]

At this time, the Moisie River was regarded as providing the most outstanding salmon fishery on the coast. When Ballantyne visited the area in 1846, there were only a few Hudson's Bay Company men fishing there; by the early 1850s, however, additional leases had been made to other concerns interested in the region, and much greater activity resulted.[203]

The Hudson's Bay Company's plunge into the Labrador salmon fishery on a truly commercial basis was first recommended by the white-bearded man whom we see in the famed photograph, driving the last spike into the Canadian Pacific Railroad. In 1843, Donald Smith was placed in charge of the HBC post at Mingan. Perhaps out of gratitude, he sent the company's governor, George Simpson, a gift of "Labrador Salmon and Cranberries." It was when Smith was transferred to Esquimaux Bay in 1848 that he began to develop the company's Labrador salmon fishery, with Simpson's blessing.

Smith recognized that Labrador salmon had always secured a good and steady price in Europe, particularly in the London markets. Since the fur business was largely idle during the late spring and early summer, Smith convinced his superiors that the company's employees could be well occupied during this time — and obtain considerable profit — in the salmon fishery. Receiving the permission he required, Smith worked diligently to build up a company fishery, often getting involved directly in the physical activities associated with the enterprise.[204]

Company fishing operations soon spread or expanded all along the coast from the mouth of the Saguenay River to northern Labrador. Besides continuing operations at their former stations and at the King's Posts, which they had inherited from the North West Company in 1821, the Hudson's Bay Company extended its operations on a seasonal basis to many uninhabited river mouths. For this purpose, the company established a fleet of small schooners to fish, supply the shore establishments, and collect produce from the posts.[205]

By the late 1840s, the company's salmon-fishing operations had grown tremendously, perhaps to the extent that more than 500 000 pounds were taken annually by all their operations in the northern gulf.[206] A statistical report of 1848 listed the total salmon exports from "Quebec city, Gaspé town and New Carlisle" as 70 tierces and 28 barrels, approximately 26 000 pounds.[207] Obviously, these figures in no way suggest the true situation of the Lower Canadian salmon fishery of this period, since they make no mention of the Labrador product whatever. Not only was the Hudson's Bay Company reaping a profitable harvest from the north shore of the Gulf of St. Lawrence in the late 1840s, but other interests from the United States and Nova Scotia were also securing vast harvests at the mouths of coastal streams.[208] Stocks were being rapidly depleted by 1850, and in 1853 a report on the fishery stated that many of the formerly good fishing stations had had to be abandoned: "streams that half a century ago offered sufficient for domestic consumption, and thousands of barrels for export, now yield only hundreds of barrels, and the quantity is rapidly diminishing."[209]

So rampant, unchecked, and destructive did the fishery become that legislation was finally considered. It was at this time that Sir Edmund Head arrived in Quebec as governor of Canada, a post that he held from 1854 to 1861. He was intent upon repeating the actions that he had initiated in the New Brunswick fisheries while governor of that colony immediately prior to his present posting. To investigate the fisheries of Lower Canada, Head enlisted the help of Richard Nettle, a well-known local angling enthusiast and advocate for fisheries reform. Nettle was a native of Devonshire, England, where he was no stranger to the salmon, spending a fair amount of his spare time clutching a fly rod. He emigrated to Canada around 1842, and the sight of Quebec's productive salmon streams enhanced his enthusiasm for angling. To meet Canadian conditions, he developed his own fishing fly, which became popular with other anglers and which was later named after him. Nettle's initial knowledge of the fishery and his subsequent investigations provided a framework for legislative action.[210]

On 30 May 1855, the Legislative Assembly of the combined provinces of Upper and Lower Canada passed an act to regulate the fishery. The season was set to extend from February 1 to September 30; the use of stake or barrier nets was outlawed; and the minimum salmon-net mesh size was established at 2 inches in diameter. Although spearing was still legal, a torch light was no longer allowed.[211] It is difficult, however, to see how the law was effective. It was unlikely that salmon fishing in the major areas, restriction or no restriction, could be carried out before February 1 or after September 30; even if the weather did not curb the fishermen, the economics of the operation would. Furthermore, any salmon which could not be caught in a net smaller than 2 inches would not be worth retaining anyway. The only real sacrifice was to throw away the torch while spearing. Even the fine of £2.10s. was little inducement not to break the law. Before passage of this salmon act, it was noted that "Every person fished when, where, and how he chose; and the principal rivers were in the hands of the Hudson's Bay Company, whose agents were continually embroiled in dispute and strife with other fishermen."[212] There was little reason to see why this would change.

The disputes and strife arose primarily because there was no consistent policy in effect concerning fishing rights. Some companies, or fishermen, for example, secured fishing leases from agents of the various seigneuries, while the Hudson's Bay Company retained its fishing rights as part of its general trading leases at the King's Posts and elsewhere. There were many areas, also, where the right to the fishery was assumed on a "first come, first served" basis, and where seasonal occupation depended more on might than right.

Realizing the problems that still existed in the colony's fisheries, Joseph Couchon, Commissioner of Crown Lands, stated in his 1857 annual report that:

> The products of the Salmon Fisheries of Lower Canada have been steadily decreasing. The total number of barrels of salmon taken on all the coasts of Canada in the Lower St. Lawrence and the Gulf, including the Canadian Coast of Labrador, during the year 1856 did not exceed 2500 barrels. The decrease in this branch of the fisheries has been very great. To give a striking instance, the River St. Paul, on the Coast of Labrador, which at one time yielded fourteen hundred barrels of salmon in a single year, now yields only ninety barrels. It is evident that if measures be not taken of a more effective nature than any that have hitherto been adopted for its protection, this valuable branch of the fishery will come to an end.[213]

In this same year, Couchon drafted legislation which, when enacted, went some distance toward rectifying the inequalities which existed. Firstly, the government was empowered to reenter into direct control of all valuable rivers in the colony. When this was accomplished, a system of "lease and license" was established, and all fishermen had to secure permits, initially through the Crown Lands Office, to engage in the salmon fishery. The legislation also required that a separate branch of the latter office be established as responsible for the fisheries, and as a result, the Fisheries Branch came into being on June 10, 1857; its mandate was fisheries protection and management in the united colonies of Upper and Lower Canada. Finally, the fishery was divided further into sport and commercial segments, relating directly to fresh and salt water, respectively.[214]

Even after the system of licensing was established, it was still possible for certain commercial lessees to hold vast areas under their control. A Mr. Corbet, for example, held the rights to all the Anticosti Island fisheries; according to James Richardson, who was conducting a geological survey of the island in 1856, Corbet's operations were confined entirely to the taking of salmon and salmon-trout at various locations. Extant records show that catches of 500 and 600 salmon per tide were made in seines and set nets at the mouths of some rivers on Anticosti.[215]

By the late 1850s and early 1860s, the system of leasing fisheries was deemed not only successful in limiting illegalities and discouraging severe stock depredations, but also profitable to the colonial coffers; this was particularly true for the sport fishery. The original leasing policy in angling had been for the Crown Lands Office to grant a license either for some specifically named river, or carte blanche for any or all rivers not previously let; the license was good for one season. This policy was later modified to cover leases up to 5 years and the value of such a lease ranged anywhere from $250 to $2,000 for the 5-year period, or from $50 to $400 per year. The cost of the leases was to help pay for the overseers who were appointed, but it eventually more than paid for the salaries of all individuals in the Fisheries Branch.[216]

A serious issue over which the government had little control — and to which administrative officials seemingly showed little concern — was the perennial problem of American incursion into the north shore fishery. Their increasing presence led to local incidents of harassment and bickering, and to a general lack of order which was described in the early 1840s by one disgruntled observer as follows:

> Indeed, for some years back, the fisheries have been so crowded thereabouts as to seriously annoy each other, and endless quarrels are going on. So far there has been no blood spilt, but, if government does not soon interfere and enforce some regulations, there is no saying what may happen in a country where the total absence of every mark of authority has bred a contempt for government and laws — where violence is the best title, and audace [audacity?] confers most right.[217]

By 1856, no improvement was discernible; in that year, the Rev. William Agar Adamson presented to the Canadian Institute a paper entitled "The Decrease, Restoration and Preservation of Salmon in Canada," in which he noted some alarming occurrences in the salmon fishery:

> For the last two or three years schooners from the United States have regularly arrived, in the salmon season, at the Bay of Seven Islands, their crews well armed, and have set their nets in the river Moisie, in despite of the officers of the H.B.C. Similar circumstances have occurred at other fishing stations in the tributaries of the St. Lawrence;....The river Bersinies [Betsiamites] has this year been altogether in the hands of a speculating and rapacious American, who employed the spear of the Indian to furnish him with mutilated salmon, several boxes of which he brought to this city [Quebec], in the month of September, when they were out of season, unfit for food and flavorless, having previously glutted the markets of Portland, Boston and New York with more palatable fish....I see no better method [of regulation] than the employment, during the summer months, of one or two armed steamers of light draught of water, such as are used for a similar purpose on the east coast of Denmark.[218]

The only visible evidence of government control and influence on the vast northern coast was, for many years, the dozen or so lighthouses scattered along this desolate shore; these were visited annually by a supply ship sent out from Trinity House at Quebec. In 1850, however, seemingly in anticipation of Adamson's proposal, Lower Canada purchased the vessel *Doris* in England and commissioned her for fisheries protection duties in the Gulf of St. Lawrence. The *Doris* was a wooden, seagoing paddle steamer, and apparently performed little better than a floating barrel, since she was rather squat in appearance and inadequately powered. She was said to be completely inappropriate for the job. Her captain, Pierre Fortin, was appointed stipendiary magistrate for the north coast and was the chief administrator of law and order in the sea and river fisheries of the Gulf. He was untiring in showing Canada's presence on the fishing grounds, despite the problems inherent in the *Doris*, and soon convinced the government to replace this unendearing vessel with another which was more

suitable to the task. Fortin and his new, beautiful, and more efficient schooner, *La Canadienne*, continued in the fisheries protection service until Confederation, and the captain later became known as *Le Roi du Golfe*.[219]

Apart from whatever encroachments the Americans were making, the Hudson's Bay Company still had the largest interest in the north shore fishery; by 1857, they held the greatest number of licenses, and were carrying on regular seasonal fishing operations at many of the following locations: Esquimaux [St.-Paul], Natashquan, Mingan, St.-Jean, Trout, Moisie, Ste.-Marguerite, Pentecôte, Trinité, Godbout, Manitou, St.-Augustin, Manicouagin, Outardes, Papinachois, Betsiamites, Blanches, Portneuf, Escoumains, Grandes and Petites-Bergeronnes, Misissiquinak [Mistassini], and St. Pancras [Baie Comeau].[220]

Many individuals blamed the firm for its apparent unchecked and wasteful activity in the fishery, but others such as Nettle saw the Hudson's Bay Company as the only safeguard to the existence of salmon against the depredations of the Americans and other rapacious, speculating firms.[221] The company thus found itself the more or less unwilling protector and guardian of the fishery for a government that had the power to grant — or refuse to grant — the necessary licenses.

Richard Nettle, who was appointed Superintendent of Fisheries for Lower Canada in 1857,[222] was not altogether pleased with the legislation that he had helped to formulate. He was particularly disappointed in the fact that the bill introduced to the House in 1856, which would provide fishways in milldams, had never passed third reading. The continued decline in salmon stocks, the American encroachment, and the lack of proper regulatory measures all rankled with Nettle, who began his duties as Superintendent with intentions to improve the Gulf fisheries. He divided the coast into five districts: Ste.-Anne River to St.-Charles River; St.-Charles River to Murray Bay; Murray Bay to Saguenay River; Saguenay River and tributaries; Saguenay River to Blanc Sablon; and placed an officer in charge of each. He also employed *La Canadienne* in vigorous patrol work on the north coast to support the newly appointed officers.[223]

Apart from these measures, Nettle also grasped at an idea which might solve the problem of stock depletion for all time — artificial propagation. Boswell had tried to restock the Jacques Cartier River in the late 1840s with ripe female salmon. Nettle had visited him on occasion and was impressed with the possibilities. Nettle was obviously aware of the contemporary European successes in the field of artificial fish culture, and in addition, he may have known of the efforts of Drs. Garlick and Ackley, who successfully bred speckled trout artificially in Ohio in 1855 and 1856.[224] Apart from living in times more suited to the acceptance of the idea of artificial propagation, Nettle had several other things in his favor when he asked the government's permission to attempt some experiments in fish culture: he was generally acknowledged to be the foremost authority on the fisheries of Lower Canada, he was a civil servant, and he was a friend of the governor.

After receiving permission, Nettle began to construct a small hatching house on the banks of the St.-Charles River, near Quebec City. From the river he obtained a water supply, which was directed into a group of lead-lined or zinc-lined wooden spawning boxes in the hatching house. Trout eggs were collected from the Jacques Cartier River, and approximately 8000 were distributed in the gravel beds of the spawning boxes. The resulting fry hatch from this "ovarium" was fed on pulverized, hard-boiled liver and small worms through 1858; they were reported to have attained the length of 3 inches by the fall, and were described as being almost as broad as they were long. In 1858, Nettle supplied his hatching trays with another 8000 eggs taken from two pairs of salmon also obtained in the Jacques Cartier River. Seventy percent of the eggs hatched and became young fish. Nettle therefore became the first individual in North America to raise salmon eggs to the swimming-fry stage, and the first fish-culturist in Canada. Unfortunately, although his operation was carried through into the 1860s, it was finally abandoned as being impractical.[225]

Upper Canada

By 1846, there was strong evidence to suggest that salmon stocks frequenting the streams of the upper St. Lawrence watershed were considerably less abundant than formerly: between 1846 and 1850, for example, when the use of gill nets was increasing in the waters of Lake Ontario, the yields of salmon decreased notably with each succeeding season. It is difficult, however, to obtain an unbroken history of the resource decline at this time, since little narrative material and very little documentation of a statistical nature is available until the time of Confederation, at which date the salmon fishery was practically a thing of the past.[226]

Extant comments on the Lake Ontario fisheries, however, indicate that salmon declined at a very rapid rate, beginning in the late 1830s; by 1840, noticeably fewer fish were being taken in the southwestern regions of the lake. By 1846, most of the streams west of Oswego, New York, and Oshawa, Ontario, were no longer considered productive areas. There were, however, exceptions: John McCuaig, who later became Superintendent of Fisheries for Upper Canada, reported that 300 000 salmon were taken at Port Credit in 1856;[227] so incredible is this figure, however, that it must be viewed with suspicion, since in this same year, the Rev. William Adamson stated:

I have myself, within a few years, taken the true *Salmo Salar* in Lake Ontario, near Kingston, and many persons in Toronto know that they are taken annually at the mouths of the Credit, the Humber and at Bond Head, in the months of May and June, which is earlier than they are generally killed below Quebec.... At the present moment, with the exception of a few in the Jacques Cartier, there is not one to be found in any river between the Falls of Niagara and the city of Quebec.[228]

The truth of the situation in 1856 lies somewhere between the two extremes represented by the views of McCuaig and Adamson. Official reports on the Upper Canadian fisheries appeared at least as early as 1859, but since little mention was made of salmon in them, it must be assumed that the species was relatively unimportant by this time, and thus scarce. Commercial and angling seasons were still in effect, however, extending from March 1 to August 1 and from March 1 to September 1, respectively.[229]

By 1865, the fishery on the American side of Lake Ontario was considered to be on the verge of extinction. Since 1860, for example, the Oswego River run had been reduced to stragglers, and at Port Ontario, the catch was only a fraction of its former magnitude.[230] The extent of the Canadian salmon fishery was just as bad; a report of 1866 stated that:

[The] Salmon fresh from the sea is found in Lake Ontario, and is taken with the gill-net at the Humber mouth, and occasionally even at the *Ultima Thule* of the bar of Hamilton Bay, as well as at Bond Head and the mouths of the Credit and Trent (to the extent in all of between one and two hundred fish in the course of the season).[231]

In the following year, it was noted that the Trent River salmon no longer existed. Other commercial fisheries, however, were reaching a degree of prominence in the colony, and a series of statutes were brought forward in 1864 to regulate this activity, principal of which was an inspection act, as well as legislation prohibiting the buying of fish out of season and using drugs and lime to catch fish.[232]

Just as in Lower Canada, conservation was now entering the thoughts of certain individuals in Upper Canada. There were suggestions afoot in 1864 that certain salmon streams in Ontario should be set apart specifically and solely for natural propagation purposes, the Moira and Credit at first being recommended as the most desirable in this regard.[233] In 1865, Samuel Wilmot, a man destined to become the guiding force in Canadian fish culture over the next 30 years, recommended that the government set aside areas in which artificial propagation could be undertaken. As evidence of the practicality of such an undertaking, Wilmot described experiments which he had conducted in his own basement where, by using water from a nearby stream, he had raised fish from eggs in trays.

In 1866, Wilmot was successful in his government representations; by an order-in-council, Newcastle, or

Wilmot's Creek, was reserved for the natural and artificial propagation of salmon under Wilmot's supervision. Wilmot's Creek was once a noted salmon stream, in which upwards of a thousand fish could be counted at spawning time. They were taken unmercifully with the spear, and were frequently an article of trade with the city of Rochester in the United States. Unrestricted fishing had reduced the salmon run to extremely low levels by the time Wilmot managed to preserve the watercourse.

Regardless of the questionable chance of obtaining enough spawning stock from the creek, Wilmot set out to build a small holding pond on the river bank, over which he erected a fairly substantial 15' × 36' building, which he referred to as the "reception house." A dam was built upstream from this structure to supply water to a reception pond that contained a wire trap. By late fall, he had managed to contain 15 male and female spawners in his reception house. His project, however, met with a severe setback when, as he was about to artificially spawn this collected stock, the reception house was broken into and 11 of the fish were taken. However, he managed to spawn successfully the remaining four fish, from which he obtained 15 000 ova.

Transferring these eggs to hatching boxes in the basement of his home, he maintained them throughout the winter without significant losses. His supply of spring water fluctuated only between 40 and 44° F, and a large portion of his eggs hatched in 70 days. These fry eventually reached the parr stage and were released into their native stream, with the exception of a few that were kept for study. Some of these fish smoltified in 1868. His success at producing fry from the artificial spawning process resulted in his pursuing the venture again in the fall of 1867, this time with increased financial help from the government. Further problems arose; although he had managed to collect 25 breeding fish and obtained over 50 000 ova from them, he discovered that many of the eggs were immature and did not fertilize properly. Nonetheless, a considerable number successfully hatched and were released into the creek. Under the direction of Wilmot and with the support of the new Dominion government, artificial fish culture was to grow rapidly in Canada and become the example for the rest of North America.[234]

Newfoundland and Labrador

In the five years prior to 1844, exports of salmon from Newfoundland and that section of Labrador administered by Newfoundland were calculated to be in the range of 5000 tierces annually; by 1849, the combined exports of both territories had risen to over 6000 tierces each season, a figure representing over 2.75 million pounds of round, fresh salmon.[235] Even these phenomenal figures may have been low estimates for the period, for in 1852 one unspecified station alone on the Labrador coast was reported to have taken 1200 tierces.[236]

The 1850s were prosperous times for Newfoundland. The colony finally achieved responsible government in 1855, and this gave her the opportunity to have a more active role in directing her own progress and industry. Newfoundland administrators took particular pride in the fact that they had defeated the Convention of 1857, between France and Britain, which would have allowed certain French fishing and occupation privileges in Newfoundland and Labrador that had not previously been granted in the Treaty of 1783. The 1783 treaty, for example, had forbidden the establishment of permanent stations on the French Shore and had allowed both nations to fish there concurrently. All parties ignored these provisions, and for those Newfoundlanders who chose to establish on the French Shore, their position was somewhat precarious. In various instances, resident French fishermen refused to allow Newfoundlanders to fish; they were also accused of extracting from the resident British planters along the western coast of Newfoundland half the salmon the latter caught in the rivers, as payment, on the plea that the French actually possessed exclusive rights to the streams. Prior to 1857, Great Britain had maintained the sole right to negotiate with France concerning the latter country's shore fishing rights in Newfoundland. In 1857, however, objections and representations from the colony regarding the newly signed Convention, resulted in Britain nullifying the agreement and conceding control in the matter to the Newfoundland Assembly. Final say concerning the French Shore was now in the hands of Newfoundlanders, and they began to enact regulations that would effectively curb French encroachment and expansion in the colony.[237]

The fishery ran Newfoundland; even the Assembly could not sit during the fishing season because of the number of members directly involved in the industry.[238] At this time, the fishery was also changing in several ways. It had been customary in the past for the salmon fishery to be concentrated around the mouths of various rivers and streams, but now the coastal fishery was beginning to grow; around Trinity Bay, for example, it was reported that "The salmon are caught on the open coast far from rivers or estuaries; those frequenting our brooks are small and worthless, are never interfered with, except a stray one may be taken by a trout fisher."[239] In addition to this new fishing trend, more men from the west and northeast coasts were venturing to Labrador, where new fishing stations rapidly grew up and became permanent, taking the place of the previous ship fishery system, whereby bays and harbors were visited only periodically during the season. This new development was seen by the authorities as a desirable trend, since it tended to make fisheries protection easier, and it also helped to ease the strain on local salmon stocks:

Persons who have fixed establishments for salmon fishery, are of course too mindful of their interests to net the rivers across, or not to observe the close season; but it is those who arriving first at a stream, take possession and determine to make the most of it, regardless of the future.[240]

Prowse mentioned that the general fishery of Newfoundland was marked with prosperity in the late 1850s, but began to suffer a protracted decline at the beginning of the next decade. In 1860, for example, there was a partial failure in the fishery, and in 1862 the resource was even more severely disrupted as a result of adverse weather. Fish catches were low, and by 1864 the fishery was on the brink of total failure. Many operations were reduced to such an extent that the island's economy was almost destitute. During these dark days in Newfoundland's economic history, many people forsook the island, and other would-be colonists were advised to shun its shores. The general fishery was not to improve until 1867, the year of the "Great Fishery."[241]

The salmon resource somewhat paralleled the trend in the general industry, although a less severe or long-lasting disruption appears to have occurred. Between 1857 and 1861, for example, average annual exports of salmon from the colony were calculated at approximately the equivalent of two million pounds, largely due to increased Labrador catches. In 1864, however, catches dropped to levels which had occurred only twice since 1837. A slight increase was apparent in 1865, and former average levels were again reached in 1867, with an unparalleled salmon fishery in 1869.[242]

If conditions on the island of Newfoundland at times slipped toward the depths of desperation and destitution, the coast of Labrador was a frontier perpetually subjected to hard times, particularly for the lower classes. One of many examples underlining the sorry state of the region was an incident related in 1848 by the captain of HMS *Alarm*, who was responsible for investigating and settling contentious matters on the Labrador shore that year:

[Another] case was brought before me by a man named Chas. Dickes, a planter resident of Grand Point, 3 miles west of Blanc Sablon, and a settler of 24 years, who upon hearing a Man of War was in Forteau, walked across the country to lay a charge against a stronger party for having torn up his seal and salmon nets, as he asserted they prevented his own catch being so great as it otherwise would be. The poor man was thus deprived of his season's profit and probably his winter subsistence.[243]

Examination of contemporary documents shows as well that the many minor and major conflicts along the Labrador coast were well lubricated with liquid spirits, which the captains of the trading vessels found were welcomed in every port. Organized government and religion were still sadly lacking from the region, but

when the Lord Bishop of the Church of England in Newfoundland visited the coast in 1848, he cautiously commented that "Nearly all the settled inhabitants are or profess to be, or at least profess a desire to be members of the Church of England."[244] Add to these situations the mixed backgrounds of those involved in the Labrador enterprise — French, American, Newfoundlander, Canadian, and British — and it is not surprising that a constant state of turmoil and strife was prevalent.

The salmon fishery of Labrador was fully developed by 1845, and good profits were being made by many of the trading firms from outside the region, if not by the "live here's" themselves.[245] The principal unit of the Labrador salmon fishing gear used at this time was aptly described by Lambert DeBoileau, who became involved in the industry in 1861:

The mode of catching these [salmon] is with a "fleet" of three nets, which are fastened to each other so as to form a pourd [pound]; the fish in striking the first and even the second of these may not be meshed but he cannot escape the third, as when once there, it is impossible for it to retrace its swim. The mode of curing salmon is less difficult than that of curing codfish. After being caught, it is merely cut down the back, cleaned, and put into puncheons, and salted and repacked into smaller casks for shipment.[246]

At this time, salmon were caught along the shores of the Strait of Belle Isle and even off Belle Isle itself. Henley Harbour, Indian Harbour, Square Island, Thomas Bay, and Groswater Bay were all noted locations, and Labrador salmon were selling for 40 cents each. One of the most important southerly stations was at Pinware River, a stream reported to be always abounding with the species. This station became the exclusive privilege of one family around 1857, and remained in their hands for over 50 years. Even in the most northerly posts of the colony, such as Nain, the Moravian Mission was helping to defray its expenses there by engaging in a small salmon export trade.[247]

The Hudson's Bay Company, which was so active in the Quebec section of Labrador, was also developing a wide interest in the area of Labrador administered by Newfoundland. Esquimaux Bay (Hamilton Inlet) was the headquarters of the company's trader in Labrador, Donald Smith, who had been appointed to that position in 1852. As in Quebec, many local interests were jealous of the company's influence and critical of their operations, particularly with respect to the fishery. The well-established fishing and trading firm of Hunt and Henley was particularly vocal, and protested as early as 1859 about the destructive tactics used by the HBC in the fishery. Hunt and Henley operated at Esquimaux Bay, as well as at Sandwich Bay, and fervent rivalry took place between the two firms, each trying to out-commercialize the other. By 1860, Hunt and Henley appeared to have the upper hand over the larger firm, for they had begun a guarded experiment with the process of putting up salmon in tins for export.[248] Secrets were not long kept in the realm of cutthroat commercialism, however, and Donald Smith soon discovered that canning showed considerable promise; he reported his opinions to the company's board of directors in a letter of July 22, 1863, and it did not take the HBC long to follow the example set by its competitor:

> I would beg to bring to the notice of the Board, a new branch of the business, which, from the minute inquiries I have made, I feel convinced would be attended with considerable profit, and for carrying on which one of our stations in Esquimous [sic] Bay is well adapted. I refer to preserving salmon fresh in tins. The business has been carried on by Messrs. Hunt and Henley for several years back, and that it has been amply remunerative may be inferred by the fact that this season they have entered much more largely into it, intending to preserve not less than 50,000 pounds. But we are not left to conjecture on the subject, for their agent, Mr. Goodrich, who from some cause, probably owing to some recent changes in the conduct of their business, is at present more than usually communicative, assures me that it is by far the most profitable part of the business.[249]

In 1866, the Hudson's Bay Company reopened its Fort Chimo post in the Ungava region; due to the interest in salmon which had filtered north from the Labrador district headquarters and the office of Donald Smith, a salmon fishery was immediately considered. In the journals of the Fort Chimo post for 1867, reference was made to the company's salmon fishery at Munroe's Cove; the first season, however, was far from successful, as the following excerpt from the post manager's report proves: "did not do so well as I expected in fishing and hunting having only 500 of the former [salmon]."[250] In successive years, however, the Chimo post prospered; this was said to be largely due to the regular yearly visits of the company's steamship, the *Labrador*, which carried away whale oil, furs, and salted salmon, thus eliminating the difficult supply problems that had plagued the establishment in earlier years.[251]

As on the island of Newfoundland, and for the same reasons, salmon fishing in Labrador was about to suffer a temporary decline. The return was reported to be only 1208 tierces during the adverse 1862 season. In 1863, the return almost doubled, but in 1864 it dropped to 500 tierces and in 1865 to 87 tierces. Although these figures are suspect for several reasons, there is little doubt that 1864 and 1865 were poor years in Labrador, particularly southward of Sandwich Bay;[252] even the Indian Harbour fishery, at the mouth of Hamilton Inlet, was pronounced abortive in 1864, and one report suggested that the entire Hamilton Inlet fishery produced only 200 tierces, when usually five times that much was taken.[253]

Low catches prevailed again in 1865, except in Esquimaux Bay, where the Hudson's Bay Company reported 1657 tierces taken. The poor catches there the previous year were probably instrumental in encouraging the Hunt and Henley firm to sell their operation to the Hudson's Bay Company and move their principal operation to Sandwich Bay. Even at this latter location, however, they were not as successful as during the year previous, taking only 450 tierces instead of 1200.[254]

Other areas south of Sandwich Bay also proved a failure when compared with former years. A member of the Slade family, who controlled the salmon fishery of both the Lewis and Hawke rivers, abandoned the former altogether in 1865, and took only 3 tierces of salmon in the latter.[255] Further evidence of the poor fishery comes from a description of St. Francis Harbour, made by a visitor in the fall of 1864: "This is a small hole amongst the rocks with a merchant's establishment and a salmon fishery attached. They are now catching about 50 a day, and complain that they are doing very ill. They have caught as many as 800 in a day."[256]

Again as on the main island of Newfoundland, the Labrador fishery had recovered considerably by 1867, to the extent that no better year had been known. In the outports, it was called the year of the "Great Fishery," and this was in spite of a severe gale which set back the Labrador fishery for several weeks.[257]

New England

By 1846, New England's salmon fishery was well advanced in its decay, as has already been outlined in the previous chapter. Except for the fishery on the Penobscot River, the American salmon industry was practically defunct as a viable commercial enterprise in home waters. Each year, expanding American markets were increasingly dependent on imports of salmon from British North American sources. According to federal records, these imports had grown from 0.75 million pounds a year in 1832 to 1.25 million pounds in 1843; by 1848, imports were recorded at 2.25 million pounds, with the demand still growing.[258]

William Herbert's book on fish and fishing, published in 1849, stated that "Although salmon ranged as far south along the eastern seaboard as Connecticut, the Kennebec is now the limit of its range."[259] Herbert credited this loss to the extensive use of stake nets throughout the species' former American range. The original southern limit of the salmon had therefore been reduced by about 1000 miles of indented coastline, or 25 000 square miles of watershed. From all indications, Maine — the salmon's only remaining stronghold in the United States — would also be devoid of the species in short order. The recently built Augusta Dam on the Kennebec River, for example, limited salmon to a spawning area of only one-half mile of stream immediately below the dam; after 1850, fish stocks began to decline until around 1860, when it was thought that they were close to extinction.

This decline was reflected in an examination of the catch records of John Brown of Bowdoinham, a man who had salmon-fished the Kennebec at the same location for 35 years. Brown had captured an average of 42.5 salmon annually in his commercial net in the 6 years prior to 1845. Between 1845 and 1849, his average catch was 14 fish a year. In 1850, he caught only 5 fish; and in the years 1855, 1857, and 1858, only one specimen was captured each season.[260]

With the opening of the Saint Croix wilderness, stories were told of a small variety of salmon inhabiting the upper lakes of the watershed. One of the first individuals to officially record the existence of these salmon was A. C. Hamlin, who reported in 1849, "I learned from the hunters that the great lakes which supplied the Saint Croix River abounded with little salmon, whose boldness and activity delighted the few sportsmen who had ventured to penetrate the lonely forests in which the fishing places are situated."[261] Many individuals asserted that these small salmon had made their appearance in the region only in recent times, being no less than the sea-run variety which had become land-locked and stunted because of the erection of barrier dams on the system. The Indians, however, identified this small salmon in their traditions and said that it had always been present in many of the lakes, not only of the St. Croix system, but also of other waterways to the west; they also reported that both the sea-run and landlocked fish had always been speared at the outlet of Sebago Lake.[262]

Declines in fish abundance during the late 1850s had inspired a few individuals to attempt some rehabilitative solutions. In 1853, Theodatus Garlick and Prof. H. A. Ackley, two distinguished surgeons from Cleveland, Ohio, collected speckled trout at Sault Ste. Marie and at Port Stanley, in Ontario, and transferred them to a series of ponds constructed in a ravine on Dr. Ackley's property. By raising trout to adulthood, they managed to prove that artificial fish propagation was a viable pursuit in the New World. Their prize brood female, called "Norad Queen," repeatedly produced ova and became so familiar with the artificial life imposed upon her that she became "as tame as a tame chicken." Norad Queen and her male counterpart, "Triton," were the pride of the two doctors, and were displayed to visitors at every opportunity.

After Garlick and Ackley's work became publicized in the Cleveland Academy of Natural Science and in the *Ohio Farmer*, a cleric by the name of the Rev. John Backman made it known that the Garlick and Ackley experiments were not the first efforts in the field of pisciculture to be carried out in the United States. Backman claimed to have artificially propagated fish as early as 1804, but there were too many peculiarities in his declaration to establish a valid claim. He eventually discredited himself entirely and ruined his chance to become known as America's first fish culturist, by claiming to have hatched young fry from dried perch eggs.[263]

Garlick and Ackley continued their experiments through to 1857, and a considerable interest was aroused in all states of the Union by their efforts. A man who began trout culture in August 1864, but who later graduated to salmon, was Seth Green of Livingston County, New York. He subsequently became the United States' first noted salmon culturist.[264] These early American efforts at pisciculture were generally superceded in importance, however, by Samuel Wilmot's success with salmon propagation in Ontario, as discussed previously.

Angling

Charles Hallock, who began a long career as an enthusiastic angler in the mid-1840s, wrote that "Fly fishing was in its infancy then. It was an art scarcely known in America and but little practiced in England. The progressive school of old Izaak and Kit North had few graduates with honor."[265] That fly-fishing was little practiced in Britain at this time was largely due to the demands of the sport; although salmon anglers could be found in almost any corner of the kingdom, their numbers were limited because of the one principal requirement necessary for the prosecution of the sport — leisure time. In the 1840s, this was not a commodity enjoyed by the majority of Britons. Angling, therefore, was not a pleasure of the masses, but the diversion of those endowed with either material wealth or social status.

For those fortunate enough to partake of the sport, Scotland in particular was the college and training ground for the salmon fisherman; and more graduates were being turned out each year after passing their finals on the Tweed, Tay, Thorso, and the twenty or so other choice Scottish rivers. Among these graduates were officers of the British military, who were to become the vanguard of those practicing the art in the British American colonies.

Salmon angling in America, however, was slow to take root and grow; although social differences were again part of the reason for this slow development, there were several other factors which discouraged the sport and kept it lagging behind its European counterpart. The isolation and remoteness of many North American salmon rivers were not, surprisingly, the prime factors in discouraging the angler; instead, it was the belief that the American salmon were too uneducated to take a fly.[266]

As already noted, Magrath mentioned in 1833 that the salmon of Lake Ontario were so well fed that they were rarely known to be taken with the rod, and as late as 1855, it was thought a waste of time to angle the Saint John River.[267] Even when the Miramichi and Nepisiguit rivers were finally acknowledged as supplying some sport to the angler, the Restigouche was shunned for its nonproductive notoriety; one angler even went so far as to say that the value of the river with regard to salmon was a myth.[268] So poor was the general reputation of angling that even those gentlemen sportsmen whom Hallock described as "trained to legitimate work" in America, initially traveled to Scotland to angle their salmon.[269]

Although a few gentlemen adventurers and military men considered it part of the game to confront the tangled underbrush, the hordes of mosquitoes and the gangs of unruly poachers, in order to cast a line on some unspoiled colonial river, the truly devout and more affluent angler still believed that North America could hardly be expected to provide the proper environment, social or otherwise, for the cultured and serious fisherman.

Apart from this, to the industrious inhabitants of the colonies and the states, the so-called "art" of fly-fishing was a waste of both time and money. Richard Dashwood noted of the inhabitants of the Atlantic colonies that: "These people can never understand one's going to any trouble and expense for mere sport — the almighty dollar is always uppermost in their minds."[270] To the majority of these colonists, imbued with the Protestant work ethic, it was inconceivable that an individual would spend a lot of time and money to capture a few salmon by the ridiculous method of angling, when thousands could be captured in a short time by using a spear or a length of net — and at considerably less personal inconvenience.

Despite these curbing influences, increasing numbers of tourists and gentlemen from Europe and the United States were visiting British North American salmon streams during the middle and late 1850s, with the result that some of the more adventurous local inhabitants were gradually attracted to the sport — although they were frequently cautioned against becoming too involved: "hunting and fishing, like gambling, are very alluring, and should therefore not be indulged in by any, especially by the poorer classes, to a greater exent than they can afford."[271] Many colonials still felt that angling was a device of the devil, to lure people away from a Christian life, and to at least one Nova Scotian clergyman, the sport was classed as one of the many "sins and sorrows" to be found among certain segments of the population.[272]

By 1860, the attraction of the sport was definitely spreading, and after this date, salmon angling rapidly became one of the chief sporting attractions in North America. This rise in general popularity was largely brought about by the writings of men such as Charles Lanman, William H. Herbert (Frank Forrester), and Campbell Hardy, and by the group of eager pupils whom they influenced. Books such as *Days and Nights of Salmon Fishing* (1843) by William Scrope; *An Angler in Canada, Nova Scotia and the United States* (1848) by Lanman; *Frank Forrester's Fish and Fishing of the United States and British Provinces of North America* (1849); and *Sporting Adventures in the New World* (1855)

by Hardy, publicized the great pleasures to be found in angling the wild, beautiful and bountiful streams of the eastern colonies, and forcefully presented the axiom that fly-fishing was "all ethereal, vitalizing, elevating. There is nothing grovelling in fly-fishing — nothing gross or demoralizing."[273]

Campbell Hardy, an officer of the Royal Artillery, called New Brunswick "the headquarters of the fly fisherman," and cited the Nepisiguit, Restigouche, and Miramichi as those rivers affording the angler particular satisfaction. Hardy first angled in the Miramichi in 1852, and noted that "Notwithstanding the shallowness of the water, from the unprecedented drought which occurred in that summer, excellent sport was obtained on it, and on its tributary the Sevogle." The main river at Boiestown was undoubtedly the most popular area, since it could be approached with relative ease from either Chatham or Fredericton. Hardy also angled the Nepisiguit in 1852, apparently with considerable success, for upon his departure from Bathurst for Halifax, he wrote: "Our salted fish — more than two-thirds of one hundred and ninety salmon which had been captured during our twelve days' sojourn on the Nepisiguit — was to follow us by the stage."[274]

Soon, people from all over North America, parts of Europe, and even native New Brunswickers, were discovering that the province was a paradise for the salmon angler, and possessed unbounded potential. Moses Perley, writing in the mid-1850s, noted that:

Fly-fishing for salmon, in Nova Scotia and New Brunswick, increases annually, as the various rivers become known, and the proper localities and seasons are ascertained....it is believed, that there are many rivers, especially in the northern part of New Brunswick, yet untried, which if visited by experienced sportsmen, not afraid of rough work at the onset, would afford good sport, and heavy fish during the whole of every season.[275]

The eagerness that these devotees displayed toward their adopted sport in New Brunswick is no better illustrated than in the writings of a British army officer who came to the colony with his fly rod in the early 1860s. Richard Lewis Dashwood arrived at his posting to the Saint John garrison in February 1862, and "Having shaken down into barracks, I began to make enquiries as to the commencement of the fishing season." It was not until 1 July, however, that he traveled by railway coach to Shediac, by steamer to Dalhousie, and by canoe to the forks of the Restigouche, to cast his fly on his first North American salmon water. For several reasons, however, his venture was almost a total failure, for Dashwood succeeded in taking only two fish after several days of fishing.

Such considerable effort for so little reward could not possibly discourage an angler who was also a commissioned officer in the army — and a Britisher as well.

Hearing of the renowned Margaree River in Cape Breton, Dashwood set about to plan his next fishing venture. Unfortunately, circumstances were still not in his favor. After an arduous voyage by water, he erected his fishing camp beside a Margaree salmon pool, which was invaded by a group of poachers who emptied it of fish before Dashwood's very eyes. This was only one of a series of incidents that raised Dashwood's military hackels, and made him rashly condemn the Margaree as the most heavily poached river on the continent: "I cared less for the Margaree than any river I have ever visited in North America. It was too civilized, and you were apt to have your camp surrounded, especially on Sundays by a crowd of loafers and gaping natives." Dashwood, in fact, classed all Cape Bretoners as "very ignorant and rather lawless." It was probably fortunate for him that he had not published these views before he left the island.[276]

Regardless of Dashwood's condemnation of the Margaree, that river was one of the most popular salmon angling streams in Nova Scotia at this time. Success seemed almost assured, despite the poachers: "One sportsman from Sydney killed with his rod last summer [1864] as many as thirty salmon of the finest description in a very short time."[277] Indeed, from the early 1860s, the governor of the colony and the admiral of the fleet made seasonal visits to the Margaree, and many other distinguished anglers from the United States and Great Britain followed suit.[278]

On mainland Nova Scotia, the Gold River continued its popularity. Even some of the Indians in that locality were forsaking the spear for the artificial fly; John Penall, a Micmac who lived near Gold River Bridge, and who was a respected forest and fishing guide, was said to be the most expert fly-fisherman in the province.[279] The LaHave River also provided "splendid" sport, as did the Mill, or Medway, although the latter was somewhat "bothered by sawdust."[280] Along the Eastern Shore, the St. Mary's and Indian rivers remained popular, as were the "Musquedoboit [sic] and the runs between the Ship Harbour Lakes."[281] Actually, the angler in Nova Scotia had no difficulty whatever at this time in locating areas to fish for trout and salmon: "There is hardly a stream and never a lake...in all the myriad lakes of this country where fish do not abound. Where there is so great an abundance it seems invidious to make a choice of any particular lake or river...."[282]

As elsewhere, few Nova Scotians took up the sport, but townspeople could more readily afford the time to engage in such "idle" activity. Haligonians seemed particularly susceptible to this "disease;" certain of the garrison officers took their sport so seriously that they were flailing the waters west of Halifax as early as March, and it was not unthought of to start the salmon angling season on the Medway River in January.[283] So noticeably did the angling citizens of Halifax pursue their sport on Sundays and holidays that their activities

raised the eyebrows of certain religious elements in the city. In a "Statement of Sabbath Desecrations in and around Halifax," published in 1862, it was noted that:

> On Sabbath, the 11th of this month, there were not less than forty individuals seen angling on the lakes on the St. Margaret's Bay Road, thirty of whom had left Halifax that morning with their fishing-rods. A considerable number left town, with their rods, in other directions.[284]

Prelude to the Future

On July 1, 1867, the British North America Act created the Dominion of Canada by federating the old colonies of Upper and Lower Canada, Nova Scotia and New Brunswick. Section 91 of the new act assigned to the federal parliament authority over the "Sea Coast and Inland Fisheries"; and a Department of Marine Fisheries, with a separate Fisheries Branch, was created. Peter Mitchell, a native of Newcastle, New Brunswick, premier of the province in 1866, and one of the Fathers of Confederation, was appointed minister of the new department; and he set about to assemble his organization immediately, recruiting staff and initiating investigations into all aspects of the fisheries of the individual provinces. This latter action was meant to provide him with the background necessary to orientate the department toward the needs of the fishery as a whole and to prepare for fisheries regulation and protection.

Receiving a number of comprehensive reports from the rather hurried investigations of men such as Peter Miller and William Venning in New Brunswick, Thomas Knight and H. W. Johnstone in Nova Scotia, and Pierre Fortin in Quebec, Mitchell was prepared by early 1868 to implement fishery legislation and place his mandate on a fully operational footing. On May 22, 1868, "An Act for Regulating the Fishery and the Protection of Fisheries" received royal assent; and by the time the Fisheries Branch celebrated its first birthday (July 1, 1868), its infrastructure was well established and its operation active; it had expended a total of $32,887.49 and generated a revenue of $19,536.51.

Among other provisions, Canada's first fishery act created a staff of fishery officers and wardens, established fishing seasons, weekly closed times, pollution control measures, and regulations respecting types of fishing gear and their use; a fishing lease and license system was established for both the sport and commercial fishery, and fishway legislation was implemented for milldams. With respect to the salmon fishery specifically, the following points were included in the act:
- kelt ("foul or unclean") fishing was disallowed.
- the taking of fry, parr, smolts and salmon of less than three pounds was prohibited.
- the destruction, taking, or selling of salmon roe were prohibited except under permit.
- no fishing was allowed in tributaries frequented by

spawning salmon.

- the minimum size of salmon nets was set at 5 inches, extended measure.
- the distance between salmon nets could not be less than 250 yards.
- free passage of fish must be allowed in the main channel of a river, with no net extending more than two-thirds across the width of a stream.
- fishways could not be used as commercial fishing devices.

Throughout the initial years of the department's existence, a number of measures were implemented under the Fisheries Act which appeared to impact significantly upon the fishery resource; one such measure was the setting aside of a number of streams from commercial and sport exploitation to allow increased natural production. Coupled with this was the establishment of a series of fish culture stations; between 1868 and 1888, eight such hatcheries were constructed (Newcastle, Ontario, 1868; Miramichi, New Brunswick, and Restigouche, Quebec, 1873; Gaspe and Tadoussac, Quebec, 1874; Bedford, Nova Scotia and Sandwich, Ontario, 1875; and Grand Falls, New Brunswick, 1880); all stations except that at Sandwich were concerned principally with artificial salmon culture.

Along with these measures, concerted efforts of the department at establishing fishways and providing policing and enforcement of the fishery laws through its staff of officers was seen to have improved the salmon resource significantly in the first decade of the nation's existence, particularly in New Brunswick and Nova Scotia where yields in the salmon fishery increased approximately twofold and threefold, respectively between 1867 and 1874. The gains were temporary, however, and the resource again began to decline. For example, fishery officer James Hickson reported of the Chaleur Bay fishery in 1883:

> "The steady decline in the catch of salmon on our coast indicates the end of this fishery at no distant day."[285]

Apparently the familiar story of the salmon's ultimate destiny was once again evident; and although advances were made from time to time in resource management, new problems arose in the 20th century to complicate and succeed the old — new problems caused by activities identified or envisaged by such words or phrases as clearcutting, pulp mills, domestic and industrial pollution, hydroelectric development, mining, drift netting, forest spraying, highseas fishery, and acid rain. The intensity and acceleration of these new problems more than offset the conservation efforts that were initiated to counteract them, and the general overall trend for the salmon was one of decline to the present.

At the time that Hickson made his comment about Chaleur Bay, for example, the catch for the area approximated 0.5 million pounds,[286] and had fallen to that level from a high of almost 2 million pounds reported in the early 1800s. By today's standards, however, 500 000 pounds would hardly represent a poor catch for the region; in 1971, for example, only 119 000 pounds were taken in Chaleur Bay, with only 342 000 pounds being caught in all the Maritime Provinces combined.[287] Studies in 1971 showed that the numbers of fish available for spawning purposes was at an all-time low in the Maritimes, and that for a number of years the juvenile populations in the streams had also declined significantly. These observations led the Federal government to impose a commercial salmon fishing ban in New Brunswick in 1972, which continued for 5 years; since then, continued low levels of salmon resulted in a number of additional fishing restrictions in all salmon fishing provinces. Although Hickson's "no distant day" has been delayed in its arrival, his prophesy appears to be nearing fulfillment.

On the other hand, perhaps a reconsideration of the chapters in the salmon's history will reveal why there is still encouragement for the future of the species. For despite the predominantly exploitive and destructive picture sketched, there are certain elements in the salmon's history that reject Hickson's prophesy. One statement that emerges from history is that the salmon is an extremely resiliant creature, reappearing again and again despite what seem to be wholesale attempts to eliminate it entirely. Another fact which emerges is that the species has always been economically important; regardless of the careless way in which it has been exploited, it has remained a valuable though apparently limited renewable resource.

By extension, the salmon has played an intrinsic and interwoven role in the history of the Atlantic seaboard in North America. To follow the story of the species is to grasp, in its essentials, the ebb and flow of colonial history, for *Salmo salar* has traditionally affected virtually all facets of that complicated progression of names, dates, and events: trade, settlement, exploration, international relations, culture, territorial expansion, recreation, scientific investigation, and even religion. In a direct way, it kept the Indian and the settler alive, provided innumerable fishermen with a livelihood, supplied governments with natural resource wealth, and sustained the sportsman in recreation.

These values have not gone unnoticed. Most recently, for example, it has been recognized that salmon, like the birds in the mine, provide one of the best indicators of our environmental condition:

> Fish are a part of our early warning system that helps to warn us of how badly we are fouling our environment. The time has come to assert the principle that where aquatic life thrives, the community dependant on that water supply can also survive.[288]

At present, the importance of *Salmo salar* is being recognized with increased attention, assisted by an enhanced social and environmental concern. When meshed with the better means, technical ability, and expertise now available to solve both old and new problems in the fishery, the future of the species could be more promising today than at any time in the past. We must act on this promise, for we cannot afford to lose the salmon.

NOTES

[1]Quoted in George M. Grant, *Ocean to Ocean* (Toronto: Campbell, 1873; reprinted Toronto: Coles, 1970), p. 310.

[2]Lorenzo Sabine, *The Principal Fisheries of the American Seas* (Washington: Armstrong, 1853), p. 91.

[3]D. C. Masters, *Reciprocity, 1846–1911*, Historical Booklet No. 12 (Ottawa: Canadian Historical Association, 1969), p. 3, notes that the depression of 1846–51 was brought about by the repeal of the Corn Laws, which had given preferential treatment to colonial produce entering Great Britain. Exports of timber and fish suffered less from the revocation of these laws than did other articles of trade. This would suggest, therefore, that the declines in salmon export were affected more by stock scarcity than lack of markets.

[4]Richard Nettle, *The Salmon Fisheries of the St. Lawrence* (Montreal: Lovell, 1857), p. 7.

[5]Sabine, *Principal Fisheries*, p. 63.

[6]Quoted in *Ibid.*, p. 64.

[7]Abraham Gesner, *New Brunswick with Notes for Emigrants* (London: Simonds and Ward, 1847), pp. 283–284.

[8]Quoted in Charles B. Elliott, *The United States and the Northeastern Fisheries* (Minneapolis: University of Minnesota, 1887), p. 72.

[9]Masters, *Reciprocity*, p. 9: "The export of fish from the colonies, chiefly the Maritimes, doubled between 1853 and 1860 to reach the value of $1,700,000." Thomas F. Knight, *Report on the Fisheries of Nova Scotia* (Halifax: Grant, 1867), p. 14, quotes the following: "The fishermen in this locality [Guysborough County] have, since the commencement of the Reciprocity Treaty, say for the past ten years, made more money than during any ten years previous."

[10]Confidential Orders and Instructions to Vice Admiral Sir James Hope respecting Protection of Fisheries in British North America, 1866, Public Archives of Prince Edward Island.

[11]James Hannay, *History of New Brunswick* (Saint John: Bowes, 1909), I, 121–122.

[12]Moses Perley, *The Sea and River Fisheries of New Brunswick* (Fredericton: Simpson, 1852), Appendix 1, p. 229.

[13]W. A. Spray, "Perley, Moses Henry," in *Dictionary of Canadian Biography* (Toronto: University of Toronto Press, 1976), IX, 628–631.

[14]Perley, *Fisheries of New Brunswick*, p. 17.

[15]W. S. MacNutt, *The Atlantic Provinces* (Toronto: McClelland & Stewart, 1972), p. 235. Nettle, *The Salmon Fisheries*, pp. 3, 39; Major W. Ross King, *The Sportsman and Naturalist in Canada* (London: Huest and Blackett, 1866; reprinted Toronto: Coles, 1974), p. 248.

[16]Perley, *Fisheries of New Brunswick*, p. 299.

[17]Alexander Monro, *New Brunswick, With a Brief Outline of Nova Scotia and Prince Edward Island* (Halifax: Nugent, 1855), pp. 236–237. "Mr. W. H. Venning's Report," in *Reports of the Fisheries, etc., of the Dominion of Canada* (Ottawa: Hunter Rose, 1868), p. 20, notes that in 1867, Ferguson's mill dam on the Little River, Bathurst, was the only structure in the province to have a sufficient fishpass.

[18]Perley, *Fisheries of New Brunswick*, p. 28.

[19]Quoted in Monro, *New Brunswick*, p. 83.

[20]*Statutes of New Brunswick* (1851), 14 Vic., cap. 31.

[21]"Venning's Report," p. 10. W. S. MacNutt, *New Brunswick: A History, 1784–1867* (Toronto: Macmillan, 1963), p. 406, notes that during the session of 1863, the Legislature also adopted a policy of renting fishing stations; a total of £770 was realized from the auction of these first commercial stands.

[22]"Mr. P. Miller's Report," in *Reports of the Fisheries, etc., of the Dominion of Canada (in 1867)* (Ottawa: Hunter Rose, 1868), p. 15. "Venning's Report," p. 8.

[23]Richard Lewis Dashwood, *Chiploquorgan, or Life by the Camp Fire* (London: Simpkin, Marshall, 1872), p. 31.

[24]"Venning's Report," p. 21.

[25]*Ibid.*

[26]*Journals of the House of Assembly of New Brunswick* (1864), Appendix 2, pp. 1–2. The districts were, as follows: Island of Grand Manan; Campobello Island and Charlotte County; Saint John River, mouth to Prince William; Saint John River, Prince William upward; Miramichi River, eastward of Middle Island; Miramichi River, Middle Island to Beaubears Island; Southwest Miramichi River, Beaubears Island to Boiestown; Southwest Miramichi River, Boiestown to source; Nepisiguit River to Northumberland–Gloucester boundary; Nepisiguit River; Northumberland–Gloucester boundary to Morrisy Rock; and Restigouche River.

[27]Perley, *Fisheries of New Brunswick*, p. 17.

[28]*Ibid.*

[29]*Ibid.*, pp. 75–76.

[30]*Census of the Province of New Brunswick, 1861* (Saint John: Day, 1862), p. 152.

[31]Dashwood, *Chiploquorgan*, pp. 17–18.

[32]Perley, *Fisheries of New Brunswick*, pp. 75–76.

[33]John Mowat, *Chaleur Bay* (n.p.: privately printed, ca. 1889), p. 4.

[34]"Report of W. H. Venning," in *Annual Report* of the Department of Marine and Fisheries (1868), Appendix 3, p. 21.

[35]*Scoto-Canadiensis*, "Salmon Fishing on the Restigouche," in the *Maritime Monthly*, II (6) (December, 1873), 542–543.

[36]Monro, *New Brunswick*, p. 191.

[37]*Ibid.*: "sawmills are comparatively few in this county, and the passage of fish up the rivers is less interrupted than elsewhere."

[38]Perley, *Fisheries of New Brunswick*, Appendix 8, pp. 236–237.

[39]*New Brunswick Statutes*, 3 William IV, cap. 37.

[40]"Miller's Report," p. 1.

[41]Dashwood, *Chiploquorgan*, pp. 31–32.

[42]Monro, *New Brunswick*, p. 191. MacNutt, *New Brunswick*, p. 334, quotes Governor Head as brooding over the neglect in the fisheries: "I have seen the whole bay of Chaleur abounding as it does in fish with scarcely a boat upon its surface."

[43]"Miller's Report," pp. 5–6; Mowat, *Chaleur Bay*, p. 4.

[44]Perley, *Fisheries of New Brunswick*, p. 77.

[45]"Miller's Report," pp. 5–6.

[46]"Salmon Fisheries of the Bay Des Chaleur," in *Annual Report* of the Department of Marine and Fisheries (1888), Appendix 7, Drawing No. 1.

[47]Perley, *Fisheries of New Brunswick*, p. 75.

[48]"Miller's Report," p. 4.

[49]Perley, *Fisheries of New Brunswick*, p. 17.

[50]Monro, *New Brunswick*, p. 197.

[51]"Miller's Report," pp. 7–10. Margaret Hunter, *Pioneer Settlers of the Bay Chaleur* (Sackville: Tribune, 1978), p. 30, notes that by 1862, two Boston firms, Messrs. Levy and Samuel and Messrs. Underwood and Company, were exporting upwards of 90 000 cases of preserved salmon yearly, and were employing local settlers to catch the fish.

[52]Perley, *Fisheries of New Brunswick*, pp. 73–74.

[53]*Ibid.*, Appendix 7, pp. 234–235.

[54]Campbell Hardy, *Sporting Adventures in the New World* (London: Hurst and Blackett, 1855), p. 112.

[55]Dashwood, *Chiploquorgan*, p. 32.

[56]"Miller's Report," pp. 8–9.

[57]Hardy, *Sporting Adventures*, pp. 82, 98.

[58]Perley, *Fisheries of New Brunswick*, pp. 17, 35.

[59]*Ibid.*, pp. 48, 52.

[60]*Ibid.*, p. 17, gives the following export figures for the Miramichi: 1841, 1614 barrels; 1842, 2295 barrels; 1843, 1093 barrels; 1844, 1616 barrels; 1845, 1836 barrels; 1846, 146 barrels; 1847, 1513 barrels; 1848, 1571 barrels.

[61]Monro, *New Brunswick*, pp. 207–208.

[62]"Venning's Report," p. 2.

[63]Perley, *Fisheries of New Brunswick*, pp. 61, 62, 70. Black salmon are "spent" or spawned out fish that have remained in freshwater over the winter. No lover of fresh, bright fish would ever eat one, but they were often the first salmon encountered in the spring, and were thus utilized since nothing else was available at that time.

[64]Richard George Augustus Levigne, *Echoes from the Backwoods* (London: Colburn, 1846), I, 35, notes that the Davidson firm operated this station around 1843. It may be that both Davidson and Fraser were connected with the same operation, Fraser being Davidson's agent on the island. Perley, *Fisheries of New Brunswick*, p. 27, notes that by 1848, this establishment was under the charge of George Letson.

[65]Perley, *Fisheries of New Brunswick*, p. 28.

[66]M. Perley to Charles Lyman, (1853) in New Brunswick Scrapbook No. 2, pp. 180–185, New Brunswick Museum Archives.

[67]Monro, *New Brunswick*, p. 208.

[68]*New Brunswick Statutes*, 39 Geo. III, cap. 5.

[69]"Miller's Report," p. 19.

[70]Burrows Willcoks Arthur Sleigh, *Pine Forests and Hacmatack Clearings* (second edition; London: Bentley, 1853), pp. 90–91.

[71]"Miller's Report," p. 14.

[72]Henry Youle Hind, *Eighty Years Progress in British North America* (Toronto: Stebbins, 1863), p. 580.

[73]"Miller's Report," p. 14.

[74]*Ibid.*, pp. 14, 22.

[75]*Ibid.*, pp. 14–15.

[76]James Price to Moses Perley, 8 October 1849, cited in Perley, *Fisheries of New Brunswick*, pp. 66–67.

[77]Hardy, *Sporting Adventures*, p. 118.

[78]"Miller's Report," pp. 18–19.

[79]"Venning's Report," p. 3.

[80]Perley, *Fisheries of New Brunswick*, pp. 67–68.

[81]"Venning's Report," p. 1.

[82]Perley, *Fisheries of New Brunswick*, p. 62. "Venning's Report," pp. 1–2.

[83]*New Brunswick Journals* (1850), p. 72. Perley, *Fisheries of New Brunswick*, p. 291.

[84]Quoted in Monro, *New Brunswick*, pp. 207–208.

[85]"Miramichi Fishing Society Report," in *New Brunswick Journals* (1860), Appendix 9, p. 3.

[86]Perley, *Fisheries of New Brunswick*, p. 81.

[87]*Ibid.*, p. 55; *New Brunswick Census* (1861), p. 152.

[88]Perley, *Fisheries of New Brunswick*, p. 142.

[89]Monro, *New Brunswick*, p. 133.

[90]"Venning's Report," p. 20.

[91]Perley, *Fisheries of New Brunswick*, p. 137.

[92]*Ibid.*, pp. 138–139.

[93]*Ibid.*, pp. 140, 142. "Venning's Report," p. 18.

[94]"Venning's Report," p. 18. Photograph in possession of Audley Haslem, Alma, N.B.

[95]Perley, *Fisheries of New Brunswick*, pp. 140–141.

[96]*Ibid.*, p. 141. "Venning's Report," p. 18. *Annual Report* of the Department of Marine and Fisheries (1871), Appendix N, pp. 117–118.

[97]Charles Lanman, *An Angler in Canada, Nova Scotia and the United States* (London: Bentley, 1848), pp. 267–268. Lanman republished this book in 1856, with some alterations.

[98]J. C. Myers, *Sketches on a Tour through the Northern and Eastern States, The Canadas and Nova Scotia* (Harrisonburg, Virginia: Wartmann, 1849), p. 280.

[99]Perley, *Fisheries of New Brunswick*, pp. 128–133.

[100]*Ibid.*, p. 129. W. O. Raymond, "The Fishery Quarrel," in *The New Brunswick Magazine*, III, 2 (1899), 69, notes that the largest sum paid was around $400.

[101]Raymond, "The Fishery Quarrel," p. 69. "Venning's Report," p. 10.

[102]Perley, *Fisheries of New Brunswick*, p. 140. Considering the total value of fish exports, and the price and quantity of salmon, then the latter would represent about forty per cent of the total export value.

[103]*Ibid.*, pp. 120–121, 131.

[104]Charles Lanman, *Adventures in the Wilds of the United States and British American Provinces* (Philadelphia: Moore, 1856), II, 14.

[105]Hind, *Eighty Years Progress*, p. 580.

[106]Lanman, *Adventures in the Wilds*, II, 14.

[107]"Venning's Report," pp. 10–11.

[108]*Ibid.*, p. 10. This comment would imply the existence of between one hundred and 150 drift-net boats, since the distance between Saint John and Digby is approximately 45 miles (40 000 fathoms), and drift-net boats used between 250 and 400 fathoms of net each.

[109]Perley, *Fisheries of New Brunswick*, p. 127.

[110]Sabine, *Principal Fisheries*, pp. 88–89.

[111]Perley, *Fisheries of New Brunswick*, pp. 133–134.

[112]Lanman, *An Angler in Canada*, pp. 268–269.

[113]Perley, *Fisheries of New Brunswick*, p. 154.

[114]"Venning's Report," p. 9.

[115]*New Brunswick Census* (1861), p. 152.

[116]Perley, *Fisheries of New Brunswick*, p. 154; "Venning's Report," pp. 8–9. *New Brunswick Census* (1861), p. 152.

[117]Monro, *New Brunswick*, p. 6.

[118]Perley, *Fisheries of New Brunswick*, p. 135.

[119]"Venning's Report," p. 7.

[120]Hardy, *Sporting Adventures*, p. 110.

[121]"Venning's Report," p. 5.

[122]*New Brunswick Census* (1861), p. 152.

[123]Anthony Netboy, *The Atlantic Salmon, A Vanishing Species?* (London: Faber, 1968), p. 327.

[124]Leonard Hutchins, "Will Salmon Return to the Aroostook?" in *The Country Times* (Aroostook County, Maine), 13–14 May 1972, p. 10. "Venning's Report," p. 5.

[125]"Venning's Report," pp. 5–6.

[126]Gesner, *New Brunswick*, p. 79. Perley, *Fisheries of New Brunswick*, p. 135.

[127]Mackwirth Shore, *Two Months on the Tobique, New Brunswick: An Emigrant's Journal, 1851* (London: Smith, Elder, 1866), pp. 42, 100, 133–134, 143.

[128]Hon. John E. Fairbanks to Moses Perley, Nov. 18, 1850, cited in Perley, *Fisheries of New Brunswick*, p. 246.

[129]Sir John Harvey, "Description of Nova Scotia in 1848," in *Report* of the Public Archives of Nova Scotia (1947), pp. 28–29.

[130]Perley's reports were in such demand that the New Brunswick government authorized a second printing of all three in 1852. "Fisheries Committee Report," in *Journals of the House of Assembly of Nova Scotia* (1851–52), Appendix 75, p. 366. Harvey, "Description of Nova Scotia," p. 28. Monro, *New Brunswick*, p. 313: "There were 10 steam mills, 237 tanneries, 398 grist mills, and 1,153 saw mills, making a total of 1,798 for the entire province."

[131]"Fisheries Committee Report," p. 336.

[132]*Statutes of Nova Scotia*, 16 Vic., cap. 17. Thomas F. Knight, *The River Fisheries of Nova Scotia* (Halifax: Grant, 1867), p. 31. This provision, (the early season), although known to have been abused, helped to perpetuate the exploitation of early-run salmon stock — the run which was always of particular interest to the inhabitants because it represented the first fruits of the fishery after a winter of eating from the pickle barrel. This early season fishery may ultimately have had much to do with the present-day scarcity of early-run salmon in many Nova Scotian rivers.

[133]Knight, *River Fisheries*, pp. 32, 38–39. "Fisheries Committee Report," in *Nova Scotia Journals* (1854), Appendix 64, pp. 294–297.

[134]Knight, *River Fisheries*, pp. 38–39.

[135]"Fisheries Committee Report" (1854), Appendix 64, p. 299.

[136]Sabine, *Principal Fisheries*, p. 88.

[137]P. S. Hamilton, *Nova Scotia Considered as a Field for Emigration* (London: Weale, 1858), p. 58.

[138]Sabine, *Principal Fisheries*, p. 91.

[139]*Ibid*.

[140]Hamilton, *Nova Scotia*, p. 62. "Trade and Commerce Reports," in *Nova Scotia Journals* (1856–1861), passim.

[141]Knight, *River Fisheries*, pp. 13, 35. *Nova Scotia Journals* (1856), Appendix 86, pp. 287, 290, 291 show that total Nova Scotian exports were valued at £247,668 in 1854, and £1,472,215 in 1855; fish products amounted to 39.8 per cent and 38.9 per cent of these totals, respectively.

[142]Knight, *River Fisheries*, pp. 3, 25, 71. "Mr. Johnson's Report," in *Reports of the Fisheries, etc., of the Dominion of Canada (in 1867)*, p. 8.

[143]Knight, *River Fisheries*, pp. 32, 36–37.

[144]Hardy, *Sporting Adventures*, pp. 238–239.

[145]Quoted in Knight, *River Fisheries*, pp. 6, 37.

[146]*Ibid.*, p. 40.

[147]Quoted in *Ibid.*, pp. 43–44. The stone bottom in the fishway was apparently thought necessary in order that the salmon would recognize that the natural stream bed was being traversed.

[148]*Nova Scotia Journals* (1866), Appendix 56, p. 1.

[149]Frederick H. D. Vieth, *A Brief Report on the Conditions of the Principal Rivers on the South Coast of Nova Scotia* (Halifax: Compton, 1868), pp. iii–iv.

[150]*Ibid.*, p. 17.

[151]Knight, *River Fisheries*, p. 9.

[152]"Report of the Fisheries Committee," in *Nova Scotia Journals* (1867), Appendix 33, p. 1.

[153]Quoted in Richard John Uniacke, *Sketches of Cape Breton and Other Papers Relating to Cape Breton Island*, ed. C. Bruce Fergusson (Halifax: Public Archives, 1958), p. 161. Twenty barrels suggests a yield of some 6300 pounds of round, fresh salmon from the Mabou area.

[154]E. M. MacDonald, *Census of Nova Scotia, 1860–1* (Halifax, 1862), p. 254.

[155]Dashwood, *Chiploquorgan*, pp. 75–76.

[156]Quoted in Knight, *River Fisheries*, p. 36.

[157]Uniacke, *Sketches of Cape Breton*, p. 65.

[158]Quoted in Knight, *River Fisheries*, p. 25.

[159]Information obtained from Donald Holmes, former Chief, Conservation and Protection Branch, Environment Canada, Maritimes Region. Knight, *River Fisheries*, pp. 24–25.

[160]Knight, *River Fisheries*, p. 24; *Annual Report* of the Department of Marine and Fisheries (1869), pp. 96–98.

[161]MacDonald, *Census of Nova Scotia, 1860-1*, p. 254, notes that the 1851 returns showed 601 barrels of salmon from Guysborough County, out of a total of 1669 barrels for the entire province; in 1861, 829 barrels, out of a total of 2481, came from the county.

[162]Vieth, *Principal Rivers*, p. 14.

[163]Hardy, *Sporting Adventures*, p. 238.

[164]Vieth, *Principal Rivers*, p. 14.

[165]*Ibid.*, pp. 14–15.

[166]Francis Duncan, *Our Garrisons in the West* (London: Chapman and Hall, 1864), p. 35.

[167]James D. Gordon, *Halifax: Its Sins and Sorrows* (Halifax: Conference, 1862; reprinted Halifax: Friends of the Old Town Clock, n.d.), p. 11.

[168]Monro, *New Brunswick*, p. 324. These figures, including shad, may be in error. *Nova Scotia Journals* (1851–52), Appendix 30, p. 270, shows that 5741 barrels and 238 boxes of salmon were shipped from Halifax in 1851. Hamilton, *Nova Scotia*, p. 63.

[169]Vieth, *Principal Rivers*, pp. iii, 10. Knight, *River Fisheries*, pp. 38–39, 68–69.

[170]Vieth, *Principal Rivers*, pp. 10–12, 69.

[171]*Ibid.*, p. 13.

[172]*Ibid.*, p. 14.

[173]Knight, *River Fisheries*, p. 68. "Johnston's Report," p. 3.

[174]Knight, *River Fisheries*, p. 68.

[175]Quoted in Vieth, *Principal Rivers*, p. 10.

[176]*Ibid.*, p. 6.

177Ibid., pp. 6–8.

178Nova Scotia Journals, (1854), Appendix 64, p. 300.

179MacDonald, Census of Nova Scotia, 1860-1, p. 24.

180Vieth, Principal Fisheries, p. 5.

181"Johnston's Report," p. 2.

182Vieth, Principal Fisheries, p. 5.

183All information on western Nova Scotia is found in Knight, River Fisheries, pp. 20–21, and in Annual Report of the Department of Marine and Fisheries (1869), App. 12, pp. 87–89.

184See Knight, River Fisheries, pp. 20–21; Annual Report of the Department of Marine and Fisheries (1869) App. 12, pp. 81–86; and Vieth, Principal Fisheries, p. 22.

185Knight, River Fisheries, pp. 25–26.

186See Annual Report of the Department of Marine and Fisheries (1869) App. 13, p. 103; and App. 12, p. 96[95].

187See Statutes of Prince Edward Island, 1846.

188Prince Edward Island Statutes, 14 Vic. C[21], 15 Vic., C. 42.

189Parliamentary Reporter, (P.E.I.), March 25, 1869, pp. 108–109.

190Prince Edward Island Statutes, 15 Vic. C. 42.

191Ibid., 18 Vic. C. 29; 19 Vic. C. 4.

192"Export Returns," in Prince Edward Island Journals (1856–1857).

193Ibid., (1857–1867).

194Parliamentary Reporter, March 25, 1869, p. 108. Prince Edward Island Statutes, 23 Vic. C. 22.

195Nettle, Salmon Fisheries, pp. 78–79.

196Sleigh, Pine Forests, p. 399.

197Nettle, Salmon Fisheries, pp. 69, 70.

198The Canadian Handbook and Tourist Guide (Montreal: Longmore, 1867; reprinted Toronto: Coles, 1971), p. 86.

199Ibid., pp. 45–46.

200Perley, Fisheries of New Brunswick, p. 84.

201Douglas Leechman, "Commodityes besides Furrs," in The Beaver, Spring 1974, 46, 50–51.

202Robert Michael Ballantyne, Hudson Bay (fourth edition; London: Nelson, 1846), pp. 90, 191.

203Ibid., p. 190. Edward Weeks, The Moisie Salmon Club (Barre, Massachusetts: Barre, 1971), pp. 12–13, suggests that 80 000 to 100 000 salmon would be a moderate guess for the numbers ascending the river in the mid-1850s. Apart from the commercial fishery, the Moisie was also an angler's river, with two leases being held: one by a group from Boston, and the other by Captain James Strachan of Toronto.

204Beckles Willson, The Life of Lord Strathcona and Mount Royal (London: Cassell, 1915), p. 130; W. L. Morton, "Donald A. Smith and Governor George Simpson," in The Beaver, Autumn 1978, 4–9. During this period, he was known as "Labrador Smith."

205Nettle, Salmon Fisheries, pp. 24, 25.

206Ballantyne, Hudson Bay, p. 190, notes that the Moisie station alone sometimes accounted for 80–90 tierces (33 000–37 000 lb). With at least 24 fishing stations in operation, 500 000 pounds might appear to be a conservative estimate of the company's annual salmon catch.

207Sabine, Principal Fisheries, p. 89. In another section of Sabine's book (p. 76) 3667 barrels are reported exported in 1848. This was the presumed export from Chaleur Bay.

208Nettle, Salmon Fisheries, pp. 26–27.

209Sabine, Principal Fisheries, p. 88.

210See Public Archives of Canada Inventory, Manuscript Group II, Colonial Office Papers (Ottawa: Queens Printer, 1961) p. 69. See also King, The Sportsman in Canada, p. 265.

211Nettle, Salmon Fisheries, pp. 125–126.

212King, The Sportsman in Canada, pp. 248–249.

213Quoted in E. D. T. Chambers, The Fisheries of the Province of Quebec (Quebec: Department of Colonization, Mines and Fisheries, 1912), I, 162.

214King, The Sportsman in Canada, p. 249; Chambers, Fisheries of Quebec, p. 159. The Fisheries Branch was established by 20 Vic. C. 21.

215"Report of James Richardson," in Geographical Survey of Canada Progress Report, 1855-1856 (Ottawa: Government Printing Office, 1857), p. 204. Nettle, Salmon Fisheries, p. 25.

216King, The Sportsman in Canada, pp. 248, 261–262.

217Chambers, Fisheries of Quebec, p. 136.

218William Agar Adamson, "The Decrease, Restoration and Preservation of Salmon in Canada," in Canadian Journal of Science, Literature and History, VII, (Toronto: The Canadian Institute, 1856), 6–7.

219Annual Report of the Department of Marine and Fisheries (1868), p. 2. Thomas E. Appleton, Usque ad Mare (Ottawa: Department of Transport, 1968), pp. 15–16, notes that the Doris was 142 feet long, with a beam of 21 feet and a draft of 13 feet; her tonnage was registered at 223. She was sold in 1855, and was wrecked the following year in the Strait of Belle Isle.

220Nettle, Salmon Fisheries, p. 28. The Hudson's Bay Company first leased the King's Posts and the seigneury of Mingan in 1832. Ibid., p. 30, notes that the company in 1857 valued its salmon at five shillings each, and that the total value of the catch by the company in that year was £37,500. This would convert to a catch of 150 000 salmon, undoubtedly representing more than 1 million pounds.

221Ibid., pp. 110–111; Weeks, Moisie Salmon Club, p. 14. F. Gray Griswold, Fish Facts and Fancies (New York: Scribner's, 1926), p. 75, quotes Napoleon Comeau, fishery guardian on the Godbout River for 50 years, as crediting the Hudson's Bay Company with indirectly preserving the salmon fishery, but for another reason: "One of the worst enemies of the salmon is, in my opinion, the trout. Trout were unmercifully netted and seined during the period the Hudson's Bay Company had the monopoly of our northern rivers, and to this fact, perhaps we can ascribe the continued supply of salmon in spite of the excessive netting."

222Chambers, Fisheries of Quebec, p. 160.

223Nettle, Salmon Fisheries, pp. 29–30. King, The Sportsman in Canada, pp. 249, 266. Appleton, Usque ad Mare, p. 16.

224Theodatus Garlick, A Treatise on the Artificial Propagation of Certain Kinds of Fish (Cleveland: Brown, 1857), pp. 7–16.

225J. A. Rodd, "Sketch of the Development of Fish Culture in Canada," in Journal of the American Fisheries Society, Vol. 54 (Washington: The American Fisheries Society, 1924), 148–149. Chambers, Fisheries of Quebec, pp. 168–174.

226Sherwood Fox, "The Literature of Salmo salar in Lake Ontario and Tributary Streams," in Proceedings and Transactions of the Royal Society of Canada, Third series, XXIV (1930), 50.

227"Special Appendix Reports," in *Annual Report* of the Department of Marine and Fisheries (1903), p. xi; King, *The Sportsman in Canada*, pp. 247–248.

228William Agar Adamson, "The Decrease, Restoration and Preservation of Salmon in Canada", *Canadian Journal of Science, Literature and History*, Vol. VII (Toronto: The Canadian Institute, 1856) pp. 2–3.

229King, *The Sportsman in Canada*, pp. 260–261.

230G. Browne Goode, ed., *The Fisheries and Fishing Industries of the United States* (Washington: U.S. Commission of Fish and Fisheries, 1884), I, 473.

231King, *The Sportsman in Canada*, p. 258.

232*The Canadian Handbook and Tourist Guide*, p. 129. Also see *Consolidated Statutes of Upper Canada, 1864*, pp. 625–628, 708–712.

233King, *The Sportsman in Canada*, p. 259.

234Rodd, "Development of Fish Culture," pp. 149–152.

235D. W. Prowse, *A History of Newfoundland* (London: Macmillan, 1895; reprinted Belleville, Ont.: Mika, 1972), p. 710.

236"Report of Commander Arthur A. Cochrane," in *Journals of the House of Assembly of Newfoundland* (1853), p. 130.

237Prowse, *Newfoundland*, pp. 474, 476. Harold A. Innis, *The Cod Fisheries* (Toronto: University of Toronto, 1954), pp. 396–397.

238William Menzies Whitelaw, *The Maritimes and Canada Before Confederation* (Toronto: Oxford University Press, 1966), p. 30.

239"Fisheries Committee Report," in *Newfoundland Journals* (1862), p. 446. This comment was made during the period when the colonies of Nova Scotia and New Brunswick were complaining of severe declines in their salmon fishery; could it have been possible, even in the 1850s and 1860s, that the declines witnessed in these latter colonies may have been caused in part by the interception of Acadian salmon runs by the developing Newfoundland coastal fishery?

240"Commander Cochrane's Report," p. 130.

241Prowse, *Newfoundland*, pp. 484, 491–492, 496; P. B. Waite, *The Life and Times of Confederation: 1864–1867* (Toronto: University of Toronto Press, 1965), p. 162.

242See respective "Exports" tables in *Journals* of the House of Assembly (Newfoundland) for the years 1857 to 1868.

243Report of the Captain, H.M. Sloop *Alarm*, October 1848, in Colonial Office Supplementary Documents, I, Miscellaneous Papers, Vol. 18, "Fisheries, 1712–1852, Public Archives of Canada.

244CO Supplementary Documents, I Miscellaneous Papers, Vol. 18, "Fisheries 1712–1852", (1848), Public Archives of Canada.

245P. W. Browne, *Where the Fishers Go* (New York: Cochrane, 1909), p. 78: "It is a well known fact that some of the large business firms in Nova Scotia owe their beginnings to the trade carried on in the Straits of Belle Isle."

246Lambert DeBoileau, *Labrador Life*, ed. Thomas F. Bredin (Toronto: Ryerson, 1969), p. 16.

247*Newfoundland Journals* (1853), p. 130. Browne, *Fishers*, pp. 95, 224. Alpheus Spring Packard, *The Labrador Coast* (New York: Hodges, 1891), p. 154.

248Willson, *Life of Lord Strathcona*, pp. 130, 166–167. See also, "Report of B. Sweetland on the Labrador Fishery in 1865," in *Newfoundland Journals* (1866), p. 530.

249Quoted in Willson, *Life of Lord Strathcona*, pp. 166–167.

250Quoted in Shirlee A. Smith, "Fort Chimo 100 Years Ago," in *The Beaver*, Winter 1967, 26.

251K. G. Davies, *Northern Quebec and Labrador Journals and Correspondence, 1819–1835* (London: Hudson's Bay Company Record Society, 1963), p. lxxviii.

252Prowse, *Newfoundland*, pp. 491-492. See also W. G. Gosling, *Labrador: Its Discovery, Exploration and Development* (London: Alston Rivers, 1910), p. 476. There is reason to believe that Gosling — and others — failed occasionally, if not consistently, to report on the salmon caught by the Hudson's Bay Company and the Hunt and Henley firm in Hamilton Inlet (Esquimaux Bay) and Sandwich Bay; see Gosling's own remark about 1200 tierces of salmon being taken in Sandwich Bay in 1864 (possibly 1863), and the remark about 1657 tierces being taken by the Hudson's Bay Company in Esquimaux Bay in 1865, in "Sweetland's Report," *Newfoundland Journals* (1866), p. 530.

253Packard, *Labrador Coast*, pp. 216, 399.

254"Sweetland's Report," in *Newfoundland Journals* (1866), p. 530. Willson, *The Life of Lord Strathcona*, pp. 166–167. Gosling, *Labrador*, p. 419.

255"Sweetland's Report," p. 530.

256J. F. Campbell, *A Short American Tramp in the Fall of 1864* (Edinburgh: Edmonston and Douglass, 1865), p. 70.

257Prowse, *Newfoundland*, p. 496.

258Perley, *Fisheries of New Brunswick*, p. 238.

259William Henry Herbert, *Frank Forrester's Fish and Fishing of the United States and British Provinces in North America* (London: Bentley, 1849), pp. 62–63.

260C. G. Aitkens, "The River Fisheries of Maine," in Goode, *Fisheries and Fishing Industries*, I, 717–719.

261A. C. Hamlin, "On The Salmon in Maine," p. 3.

262*Ibid.*, p. 15; also Goode, p. 47, and Hallock, *Fishing Tourist*, pp. 101–102.

263Garlick, *Artificial Propagation*, pp. 7–8, 133, 136–37.

264Knight, *River Fisheries*, pp. 51–52.

265Charles Hallock, *The Fishing Tourist*, (New York: Harper, 1873), p. 17.

266George M. Grant, *Ocean to Ocean* (Toronto: Campbell, 1873; reprinted Toronto: Coles, 1970), p. 310.

267Campbell Hardy, *Sporting Adventures in the New World* (London: Hurst and Blackett, 1855), p. 109.

268Richard Lewis Dashwood, *Chiploquorgan or Life by the Camp Fire* (London: Simpkin, Marshall, 1872), pp. 17–18.

269Charles Hallock, *The Salmon Fisher* (New York: Harris, 1890), pp. 42, 67.

270Dashwood, *Chiploquorgan*, pp. 26–27.

271Alexander Monro, *New Brunswick, with a Brief Outline of Nova Scotia and Prince Edward Island* (Halifax: Nugent, 1855), p. 96.

272James D. Gordon, *Halifax: Its Sins and Sorrows* (Halifax: Conference, 1862; reprinted Halifax: Friends of the Old Town Clock, n.d.), p. 11.

273Hallock, *The Fishing Tourist*, p. 21; he also noted here that "Fly-fishing gives more varied play and greater exercise to the muscles; it bestows a keener excitement; it intensifies the perceptive facilities; it requires nicer judgement than bait-fishing, quicker and more delicate manipulation, and greater promptness in emergencies; it is more humanizing in its influences; it is beautiful in its associations, and poetic in the fancies it begets."

[274]Hardy, *Sporting Adventures*, pp. 101, 106, 108–109.

[275]Richard Nettle, *The Salmon Fisheries of the St. Lawrence* (Montreal: Lovell, 1857), p. 123.

[276]Dashwood, *Chiploquorgan*, pp. 4, 75–77.

[277]*Sketches of Cape Breton and other Papers Relating to Cape Breton Island*, ed. C. Bruce Fergusson, (Halifax, Public Archives of Nova Scotia, 1958), p. 65.

[278]Ibid.

[279]MacEachern and MacDonald, "The Salmon Fishery of Nova Scotia," p. 46.

[280]Dashwood, *Chiploquorgan*, p. 73.

[281]Duncan, *Our Garrisons*, p. 75. Nettle, *Salmon Fisheries of the St. Lawrence*, p. 123. MacEachern and MacDonald, "The Salmon Fishery of Nova Scotia," p. 46. Frederick H. D. Vieth, *Recollections of the Crimean Campaign* (Montreal: Lovell, 1907), p. 214, notes that the Liscomb River was also angled at this time by William Chearnley, who was reported to have constructed a rather unique and more or less permanent fishing camp on the river.

[282]Duncan, *Our Garrisons*, p. 95.

[283]*Annual Report* of the Department of Marine and Fisheries (1876), Supplement 4, p. 197. See also Dashwood, *Chiploquorgan*, p. 72, and Hallock, *The Fishing Tourist*, p. 34.

[284]Gordon, *Sins and Sorrows*, p. 11.

[285]Quoted in *Annual Report* of the Department of Marine and Fisheries (1883), Supplement 2, p. 72.

[286]*Ibid.*, pp. 82, 116: 491 780 pounds of salmon, fresh weight. The figures taken for this calculation are those listed for Restigouche and Gloucester counties in New Brunswick, and for Bonaventure County in Quebec, excepting the figures for the communities of Shippegan, Grand Anse, Pokemouche and Tracadie, for which the origin of the catch is possibly south of Chaleur Bay. For information and comment on the landings of salmon in Chaleur Bay ca. 1800, see John Stewart, *An Account of Prince Edward Island in the Gulph of St. Lawrence, North America* (London: Winchester, 1806), p. 299, and Patrick Campbell, *Travells in America*, ed. H. H. Langton (Toronto: Champlain Society, 1937), pp. 66, 75.

[287]C. E. Wykes and R. W. Dunfield, *1971 Atlantic Salmon Commercial Catch Statistics, Maritimes Region* (Halifax: Resource Development Branch, 1972), p. 24, notes that in 1971, the Bonaventure County, Quebec, salmon catch was 66 843 pounds, and only 52 387 pounds were taken in the New Brunswick portion of Chaleur Bay in the same year.

[288]Excerpted from a speech given by C. P. Ruggles, Chief, Resource Development Branch, Department of Fisheries and Forestry, to the Amherst Rotary Club, Amherst, N.S., 8, June 1970.

Appendix A

Historical Methods of Packing Salmon

Throughout the preceding study, references have often been made to the amounts of salmon captured in, or reported from specific fisheries in eastern North America. These quantities were frequently expressed historically in tierces, barrels, half-barrels, kitts, casks, cases, boxes, hermetically sealed tins, packages, smoked or fresh salmon, or in pounds. Some of these terms are archaic in the modern fishing vocabulary, and are either of little value or, at least, somewhat mystifying to the reader who is unfamiliar with their historical meaning or quantitative significance. It has been considered beneficial, therefore, to convert these terms to a common quantitative denominator which could be recognized and understood by those who desired a more complete appreciation of the data.

In light of modern requirements for yield statistics in fisheries management, one of the more common and most valuable units of measurement is the live weight of fish. This live weight is sometimes referred to as round, fresh weight, and represents the weight of a freshly caught fish, before cleaning, processing, or preserving. This live weight criterion, therefore, has been chosen to represent the historical data whenever weight conversions have been made in this study. The following discourse describes, in some detail, the steps taken in the conversion process to establish live-weight standards.

Most of the historical statistical data on salmon catch and export were expressed in various measures of volume: for example, in barrels, the barrel being originally statuted as a volumetric unit. Because of this, two considerations have to be entertained when converting historical volumetric units to fresh-weight bases. First, the weight capacity of each type of container listed in the historical records must be determined. This weight capacity was usually a legislated standard, and can thus be frequently ascertained by examining the statutes of the various colonies, states, or countries involved in the fishery. Second, since container weights were usually given in processed weights (e.g. pounds pickled, smoked, or cleaned), the relationships of the various processed weights to the live weights must also be calculated. This is done by examining traditional fish curing and preserving techniques of the period, to determine the weight-loss factors as a result of processing.

Statistical records show that prior to the beginning of the 20th century, salmon for the export trade was usually preserved in the salted state and packed into various sizes of barrels. Barrel sizes, as already noted, were regulated by law to contain a certain volume. In the fish trade, however, it was the practice to class these containers by the weight of the produce contained therein; thus the weights and measures statutes which refer to fish containers specify weight–volume relationships. The standard fish barrel, for example, was to contain 200 pounds of pickled fish, and was to be specifically termed a fish barrel. Barrellike containers of sizes larger or smaller than the standard fish barrel went by other names.[1] The following list gives the various names applied to the barrel in the fish trade, along with the standard or regulated weights of the product contained therein:

tun	1600 pounds
butt	800 pounds
puncheon	600 pounds
hogshead	400 pounds
tierce	300 pounds
barrel	200 pounds
half barrel ("third" of a tierce)	100 pounds
quarter barrel (firkin)	50 pounds
kitt (kit)	25 pounds

The tun, butt, puncheon, and hogshead were rarely used in the salmon export trade, although at times they were employed in the curing process. The half barrel was also termed a third, as its weight was one-third that of a tierce. All of the listed containers were shaped like a barrel, with the exception of the kitt, which resembled the bottom half of a cone.[2] In actuality, all these container weights usually varied plus or minus 10 percent from the regulated weight, as a result of inconsistencies in curing or packaging, and most records indicate that underweight was more common. Occasionally, nonspecific terms such as package, cask, and keg appear in the statistical records, and are either synonymous with unidentified specific containers, or collectively represent unit groupings.

Two other containers mentioned in the statistical records are the box and the case. When discussing smoked or canned salmon, both terms refer to rectangular, wooden containers which held fish in multiples of 12 pounds, with 24-, 48-, and 84-pound units being the most common. With respect to tinned salmon, individual 1- or 2-pound cans were packed, usually 12 or 24 to a case.

When considering the entire operation of the salmon fishery in North America in earlier days, the catching of fish was only the first, and perhaps the easiest segment of the operation. Although salmon were often taken only for immediate consumption, more frequently the fishery was called upon either to provide for a personal future store of food, or to provide a commodity for commercial sale and profit. In these cases, the fish had to be kept in some way to make them suitable for long-term storage. Proper and effective preservation of the catch, therefore, was an extremely important aspect of the fishery.

(a) *Salt Curing*. There were several traditional methods of preserving fish in historical times: Indians were familiar with drying, cooking, and pulverizing fish flesh, and northern tribes also kept fish by using nature's natural seasonal refrigerator — winter. Although there is some evidence that certain native tribes may have used natural salt to preserve meat and fish, the great age of salt curing began in North America with the European cod fishery.

Mather Byles DesBrisay, in his book on Lunenburg County, remarked:

> William Buckles was a Zealand Holland fisherman, and in 1386 he discovered that salt would 'keep' fish to that degree that they could be packed for export. In that year he salted herrings and packed them in barrels.[3]

Salt pickling was thus the principal means of preserving salmon during the early years of the fishery. So important and universal was this method that the volume of the salmon catch was more often governed by the availability of salt than the availability of fish. With the advent of other methods of preservation in the mid-1800s, the pickled-salmon trade declined, and pickling was only undertaken by local inhabitants who wished to store a few barrels of fish for winter consumption. Newfoundland was the only North American colony to continue to export a large portion of its annual catch in the pickled state well into the 20th century, the other Atlantic colonies ceasing this trade by 1900.[4]

Although there are several methods of salt curing fish, the most satisfactory and accepted for fatty species such as salmon was by pickling. The diary of Lambert DeBoileau, 1861, described this simple procedure in Labrador, as follows: "The mode of curing salmon is less difficult than that of curing codfish. After being caught, it is merely cut down the back, cleaned, and put into puncheons, and salted and repacked into small casks for shipment."[5]

The method which DeBoileau described had long been employed universally in the salmon fishery. Other reports indicate that after the salmon were split and gutted, they were thoroughly cleaned and placed in layers in large, dry, tight containers, such as the puncheon, with salt distributed between each layer of fish. This sandwich of salmon and salt — known as the press pile — resulted in the removal of water from the flesh of the fish, which water then combined with the salt to form a brine or pickle. Through osmosis, there was a partial replacement of water in the tissues of the fish with salt, and thus the salmon was "pickled in its own juice" and preserved.

After approximately two weeks' curing in this manner, the fish were taken from the press pile, cleaned of surface salt and pickle, and weighed into the appropriate measures for the containers into which they were being packed. The following Nova Scotian statute of 1864 describes the repacking process in some detail:

> the fish shall be carefully sorted and classed according to their respective numbers and qualities. Each cask shall contain fish of the same kind and quality, properly packed in separate layers, and on every layer of fish so packed in the cask, a sufficient quantity of suitable salt shall be regularly placed, the quantity to be not less than half a bushel for a barrel, and in like proportion for other packages at the direction of the inspector. After the cask shall have properly packed and headed it shall be filled with clean pickle, sufficiently strong to float the fish of the kind packed.[6]

This procedure was followed more or less universally in the British North American colonies and was dictated by statute law.

When the pickling process was complete in the press pile, the salmon had been reduced to an average 63.5 percent of their original fresh, round weight. In other words, a barrel of 200 pounds of pickled fish would be equivalent to approximately 315 pounds of round, fresh salmon. This is an average figure, the variation in loss depending on inconsistencies in the pickling process, the size and condition of the fish, and the skill with which the cleaning process was completed. The fish packing firm of Ward Little, Halifax, for example, required 1000 pounds of fresh salmon to produce 600 pounds pickled, and the standard conversion used by Federal fisheries inspectors is 150 pounds fresh to 100 pounds pickled.[7]

Some records refer to spiced, soused, or soaked salmon being shipped in barrels to various markets. These products were generally variations of the normal pickling process, in which the pickling time was shortened, the salt cure was less potent, or the flavor was enhanced with spices.[8]

(b) *Smoking*. The palatable qualities of smoked salmon have been appreciated by epicurean eaters of fish since the earliest times, and since the mid-1700s, smoked salmon has appeared on the import/export records of North America. The smoked-fish trade never matched that of pickled fish in volume, but in some regions, it may have accounted for as much as one-third of the salmon export trade.[9] The business of smoking salmon for commercial export reached its peak in the 1830s and then declined, but remained a noticeable segment of the trade, particularly in Nova Scotia and New Brunswick, until the First World War. In New England, however, it had declined to insignificance before 1850.[10]

In Atkins' history of the Maine fisheries, the method of smoking salmon was described in the following way:

> the salmon were prepared by first splitting, removing the backbone, but leaving the head on, and salting for two or three days, according to the size of the fish. When sufficiently salted they are washed off, spread by applying thin braces of cedar or spruce across the back, and then hung up in the highest part of a little domestic smokehouse. Constant exposure to smoke for two or three days completed the process.[11]

Commercial smokehouses, of course, were larger than the "little domestic" ones; in Nova Scotia, the average size of the former was reported to be about 30 feet square, with a high roof probably in excess of fifteen feet. Rock maple (*Acer saccharium*) was considered the best wood for smoking, but beech and oak were also adequate. Sometimes the twigs or fruit of the juniper bush and rosemary or wild peppermint were used to impart additional flavor to the flesh. The fish were kept well away from the fire and heat, but the two or three days mentioned by Atkins for smoking were probably too short a period for a good commercial cure; slow smoking with a slight fire produced the best results.[12]

Fisheries inspection records show that it took between 150 and 175 pounds of round, fresh salmon to produce 100 pounds of the smoked produce, depending on the size and condition of the fish. In smoking, the desired weight loss was about 10 percent from the fresh, gutted state.[13]

(c) *Canning*. In the late 1700s, various societies and government agencies in Britain and France set aside prize money for anyone who could develop a better method of preserving foodstuffs. This was prompted principally by a desire to provide the armies and navies of these countries with better provisioning. In 1806, a young Paris chef, Nicholas Appert, demonstrated a new and successful method of preserving fruits and vegetables. His procedure was to fill wide-mouthed bottles with fruit, and to set the jars brim high in water, which was kept boiling for six hours; the jars were then sealed with layers of wax and cork, while they remained in boiling water for some time. To protect from breakage, preserves were eventually put up in cans made from tinned sheets of heavy-gauge wrought iron.[14]

In 1819, knowledge of the canning process was brought to America by two Englishmen, Ezra Daggett and Thomas Kansett, who started canning operations in Boston; it was not until 1839, however, that salmon were first preserved in sealed tins in North America, this development beginning in Saint John, New Brunswick.[15] During the early 1840s, one of the more important canning operations on the east coast was that of the Treat Company, which operated at Allen's Island, between Eastport and Lubec, Maine. They canned a variety of products, including green peas, Indian corn, lobsters, and salmon, the latter being procured from Saint John Harbour. It was these Maine interests who were responsible for initiating the Pacific Coast salmon-canning industry in 1864.[16]

By 1845, salmon canning was also started at Portage Island in Miramichi Bay, where as early as 1849, 22 000 pounds were put up in "hermetically sealed tins." Before Confederation, it was said that as many as 400 000 pounds of salmon were processed at this station in one season.[17] The canning process spread rapidly to all eastern Canadian regions; by the 1860s the Hunt and Henley firm in Labrador was canning salmon, and their immediate competitors, the Hudson's Bay Company, also entered the business several years later under the keen supervision of Lord Strathcona.[18] At the peak of the tinned salmon business in eastern Canada (1873–1875), over 2.25 million pounds were preserved in that fashion each year.

Although the canning industry on the east coast prospered until the mid-1870s, it was soon overshadowed by the industry in British Columbia; the great volumes of canned salmon which were eventually produced in this latter region relegated the Atlantic produce to a minor place in the American export trade, and made the eastern enterprise uneconomical.[19] In the Maritimes, however, small volumes of salmon were still being tinned for local markets after 1900.

In the canning process itself, the salmon were cleaned, the tail, head, and fins were removed, and the flesh was thoroughly washed and sometimes scraped with a knife, though the scales were not removed. The fish were then cut in sections, the length of which corresponded with the height of the can, and the sections were placed inside the tin. The lid was then soldered on, and the containers were placed in water to see if the tins were tightly sealed. They were then boiled in natural salt water or water containing calcium chloride, higher temperatures being achieved by the addition of salt to the water. After being boiled for an hour and a quarter or an hour and a half, the cans were removed from the water and vented by punching a small hole in the top of the tin; the air being expelled, the hole was then soldered closed and the tin was thus hermetically sealed. The tin was again boiled for another hour and a quarter, since if cooking was completed before the tins were vented, the internal pressure buildup would be sufficient to burst the can. The containers were afterward tested by being tapped on the lid with a nail; if the tin was not sealed properly, a distinct tinny sound would be emitted, and the tin had to be resoldered.[20] Various records show that it took an average of 84 pounds of round, fresh salmon to produce 48 pounds of salmon pack; this represented a weight loss of 43 percent.[21]

(d) *Fresh, Packed in Ice.* Although man had long employed the system of preserving some of his perishable foodstuffs in ice, he not always possessed the means of obtaining ice when he needed it, and therefore had to store it in this way only during the winter months. In 1780, a Scotsman developed the technique of preserving salmon in ice as a commercial export operation,[22] and quantities of the fish were transported after that time in crushed ice or snow, principally during the cooler months. But it was not until considerable advances had been made in transportation in the mid-1840s, and the subsequent development of ice boxes and insulated containers in the 1850s, that the fresh, packed-in-ice salmon trade grew significantly.

Writing of the Saint John salmon fishery in 1847, Moses Perley said: "Since the establishment of regular steamers from the Port of Saint John to Boston, large quantities of fresh salmon, packed in ice, have been exported, and the commodity has greatly increased in value."[23] A year later, Sabine reported: "It will be seen that the exportation of cured salmon from New Brunswick ceased entirely in 1848 — the whole catch, not required for local consumption, having been packed in ice and shipped fresh."[24] Although not strictly true with respect to the entire New Brunswick catch being shipped in ice, Sabine's comment does stress the fact that this fresh-fish trade did quickly surpass all other methods of salmon export. Only a small number of fish were exported fresh in 1845, but by 1850 as many as 400 000 pounds a year left Saint John alone in that state, and by 1860 this figure reached 0.5 million pounds. The fact that fresh salmon could leave Saint John and be on the tables of New Yorkers, Philadelphians, and Bostonians in 3 days did much to encourage the trade.[25]

Further advances were made in the 1860s, when mechanical and chemical refrigeration assisted the icing techniques already in use. Just before Confederation, Samuel Wilmot, Canada's chief fish culturist, reported on a new method being employed in Quebec: during the winter, a fishing firm on the Moisie River put up large quantities of ice and snow in sawdust sheds there, and when sufficient salmon were taken in season, they were packed in the ice and transported to Quebec City, where they were "put into a freezing room, where by an admixture of ice and salt, placed within zinc plates, the temperature was reduced to many degrees below the freezing point; they soon became frozen and may be kept in this state for many months."[26]

Salmon were generally gutted and cleaned before freezing and usually immediately after being caught, for it was found that the flesh quickly deteriorated in quality — even when packed in ice — if left in the round state. Heading, gutting, and cleaning subjected the fish to a weight loss of between 20 and 25 percent.[27]

The frozen-fish trade became very popular, and much experimentation took place with respect to new, quick-freezing techniques. The Piper firm of Alliston Point, Bathurst, was freezing salmon in 1868 by using "chemical agencies" and then packing the fish immediately in ice for export. It was reported that "The owner of the establishment seemed to throw a shroud of mystery over the manipulations connected with his process, and strangers whose curiosity tempted them to visit it will find their reception a freezing one."[28]

Piper's frozen salmon were shipped to Saint John via Shediac and the recently opened European and North American Railroad which operated between Shediac and Saint John; from Saint John, they departed by steamer for Boston.[29] By 1881, iced or frozen salmon were being shipped regularly to the Boston market from April to August,

the earliest coming from the Kennebec and Penobscot, and the latest from Labrador Coast via Quebec and Montreal on the Intercolonial Railway. They were packed in large wooden boxes from 200 to 300 pounds, and during the last part of the season, are frozen in large numbers for preservation until the next season's catch is obtained.[30]

There was still a limit, however, to how far away the fresh product could be shipped. Exports to western Canada and Europe still had to be in the pickled, smoked, or canned state, although in 1879, a Gaspé fishery officer reported

that a representative of French firms, one Mr. Lemesurier, visited the coasts of Gaspé and Bay des Chaleurs for the purpose of making contracts with fishermen and purchasing their salmon fresh. It is Mr. Lemesurier's intention to ship fish to France in a fast sailing steamer, so that they may arrive there as fresh as possible...owing to a peculiar mode of preservation which they [French firms] have invented.[31]

It is believed that Mr. Lemesurier's plans came to naught. By the turn of the century, further attempts had been made to ship the frozen product to Great Britain, but the practice did not meet with commercial success.[32] In 1908, however, Mr. E. Gibb of Aberdeen, Scotland, attempted an innovative way of supplying his native country with fresh North American fish: he brought over a large steamer equipped with water tanks, in which freshly caught, live fish were placed. There is no evidence, however, that this floating fish tank provided the success which was intended.[33]

FOOTNOTES

[1]George Selby Howard, ed., *The New Royal Cyclopaedia and Encyclopedia* (London: Hogg, 1760), p. 1334.

[2]Charles L. Cutting, *Fish Saving: A History of Fish Processing from Ancient to Modern Times* (London: Leonard Hill, 1955), p. 88.

[3]Mather Byles DesBrisay, *History of the County of Lunenburg* (Toronto: Briggs, 1895; reprinted Belleville, Ont.: Mika, 1972), p. 469.

[4]See statistical tables in *Annual Reports* of the Department of Marine and Fisheries, 1868 to 1920.

[5]Lambert DeBoileau, *Labrador Life*, ed. Thomas F. Bredin (Toronto: Ryerson, 1969), p. 16.

[6]*Statutes of Nova Scotia*, 27 Vic., Cap. 85.

[7]Figures obtained in communication with the Ward Little Company, Halifax. Weight conversion information obtained from the Inspection Branch, Department of Fisheries and the Environment, Halifax.

[8]Moses Perley, *The Sea and River Fisheries of New Brunswick* (Fredericton: Simpson, 1852), p. 162.

[9]C. G. Atkins, "The River Fisheries of Maine," in G. Browne Goode, ed., *The Fisheries and Fishing Industries of the United States* (Washington: U.S. Commission of Fish and Fisheries, 1884), Vol. 1, p. 91.

[10]See the yield records in the appendices to *Annual Reports* of the Department of Marine and Fisheries for the years 1868 onward. Atkins, "River Fisheries," p. 683.

[11]Atkins, "River Fisheries," p. 683.

[12]Perley, *Fisheries of New Brunswick*, pp. 161–162.

[13]Weight conversion information obtained from the Inspection Branch, Department of Fisheries and the Environment, Halifax. See also, G. H. O. Burgess and others, ed., *Fish Handling and Processing* (Edinburgh: Her Majesty's Stationery Office, 1965), p. 97.

[14]F. Huntly Woodcock and W. R. Lewis, *Canned Foods and the Canning Industry* (London: Pitman, 1938), pp. 2–3, 5.

[15]*Ibid.*, p. 5. Cicely Lyons, *Salmon, Our Heritage* (Vancouver: Mitchell, 1969), p. 140.

[16]Lyons, *Salmon*, pp. 140–141. Perley, *Fisheries of New Brunswick*, p. 121. Allen's Island is now known as Treat Island.

[17]Perley, *Fisheries of New Brunswick*, pp. 27–28. Richard George Augustus Levigne, *Echoes from the Backwoods* (London: Colburn, 1846), I, 35, noted that "13,000 cases (cans) each containing two pounds of salmon or the best of three or four lobsters" were put up at Portage Island in 1845. Henry Youle Hind, *Eighty Years Progress in British North America* (Toronto: Stebbins, 1863), p. 583.

[18]Beckles Willson, *The Life of Lord Strathcona and Mount Royal* (London: Cassell, 1915), pp. 166–167.

[19]*Ibid.*, p. 130, and the statistical records for canned salmon in B.C. and the Maritime Provinces, found in the *Annual Reports* of the Department of Marine and Fisheries, 1870–1900.

[20]David Stair Jordan and Charles H. Gilbert, "The Salmon Fishing and Canning Interests of the Pacific Coast," in Goode, *Fisheries and Fishing Industries*, p. 747.

[21]See note 13.

[22]Alex Russel, *The Salmon* (Edinburgh: Edmonston and Douglas, 1864), p. 4.

[23]Perley, *Fisheries of New Brunswick*, p. 17.

[24]Lorenzo Sabine, *The Principal Fisheries of the American Seas* (Washington: Armstrong, 1853), p. 89.

[25]Charles Lanman, *Adventures in the Wilds of the United States and British American Provinces* (Philadelphia: Moore, 1856), II, 14, noted that the average take from the harbor between 1845 and 1848 was around 35 000 salmon. Perley, *Fisheries of New Brunswick*, pp. 17, 25.

[26]"Report of S. Wilmot," in *Annual Report* of the Department of Marine and Fisheries (1869), Appendix 15, p. 106.

[27]Burgess, *Fish Handling*, pp. 145–146. See also note 13.

[28]"Mr. Miller's Report," In *Reports of the Fisheries, etc., of the Dominion of Canada (in 1867)* (Ottawa: Hunter Rose, 1868), p. 8.

[29]*Ibid.*

[30]Goode, *Fisheries and Fishing Industries*, p. 194.

[31]"Reports of the Fishery Officers, 1878," in *Dominion Sessional Papers*, Series 3, XII, 4 (1879), Appendix 1, p. 78.

[32]P. W. Browne, *Where the Fishers Go* (New York: Cochrane, 1909), p. 58.

[33]Wilfred T. Grenfell, *Labrador: The Country and the People* (New York: Macmillan, 1922), p. 339.

Appendix B

Salmon Catch/Export Statistics

TABLE 1.   Exports of salmon, New Brunswick, 1789–1819.

Year	Tierces		Barrels	Packages	Smoked	Boxes
				Number of		
1789[a]	3 000					
1806[b]	4 000					
1808[c]	35		185.5	2 467	1 452	44
1809[d]			1 647		5 632	2 876
1810[e]			369.5	1 784	5 259	
1811[f]			706	989	343	25
1813[g]	5 000	to	2 000			
1814[h]	2 000					
1819[i]			362			

[a]Miramichi exports, ca. 1789; Patrick Campbell, *Travels in America*, p. 66.
[b]Chaleur Bay exports, ca. 1806; John Stewart, *An Account of Prince Edward Island in the Gulph of St. Lawrence, North America*, p. 299.
[c]Miramichi (35 tierces and 74 barrels), and Saint John exports, Public Archives of Canada (PAC), "Colonial Office Papers" (CO-193).
[d]Saint John exports; James Hannay, *History of New Brunswick*, (11), p. 312.
[e]Miramichi (93 tierces) and Saint John exports; PAC CO-193.
[f]St. Andrews (10 kitts, included under "boxes") and Saint John exports; PAC, CO-193.
[g]Range of annual exports in northern New Brunswick until ca. 1814 was between 2000 barrels and 5000 tierces; Robert Clooney, *A Compendious History of the Northern Part of the Province of New Brunswick and the District of Gaspé in Lower Canada*, pp. 171–172.
[h]Provincial export; Abraham Gesner, *New Brunswick with Notes for Emigrants*, p. 270.
[i]Saint John exports; *Journal of the House of Assembly*, New Brunswick, 1847, Appendix, p. cxlvii.

TABLE 2.   Exports of salmon, New Brunswick, 1820–1848.[a]

Year	Barrels	Kitts	Smoked
		Number of	
1820	372		
1821	836		
1822		2 271	548
1823			6 861
1824		3 662	6 961
1825			380
1827	504	2 692	2 655
1828	295	1 725	2 531
1829	1 189	2 721	5 795
1830	1 776	2 635	5 350
1831	1 199	2 597	4 812
1832	692	2 947	4 897
1833	652	2 151	3 708
1834	160	1 965	4 596
1835	1 363	5 278	9 476
1836	902	4 650	6 964
1837	1 843	1 120	6 073
1838	930	8 261	
1839	1 400	5 600	10 201
1840	1 804	2 276	1 059
1841	1 825	2 653	4 853
1842	2 879	1 232	1 858
1843	2 155	855	900
1844	2 479	6 419	406
1845	2 621	1 261	80
1846	1 311	1 529	20
1847	2 426	170	2 243
1848	2 175		5 460

[a]Figures for the period 1820 to 1829 inclusive are from the *Journal of the House of Assembly*, New Brunswick, 1847, Appendix, p. cxlvii (exports from Saint John, 1820-1825) and Appendix, p. clix (exports from the province, 1827-1829). Figures for the period from 1830 to 1848 inclusive are from Lorenzo Sabine, *The Principal Fisheries of the American Seas*, p. 91.

TABLE 3.   Yield in the salmon fishery, New Brunswick, 1850–1867.

Year	Number of					
	Salmon	Tins	Barrels	Smoked	Cases	Pounds
1850	23 000[a]	(400 000)[b]				
1851	4 437[c]					
1852	35 000[d]					
1853	35 000[d]	162 500[e]	396[e]			
1854	35 000[d]					
1860	50 000[f]					
1861[g]	72 118	143 111	767	84		
1862[h]				138 509	9 987[i]	
1863			833	7 659	9 439[i]	
1864	11 567	47 382	629	38 957		
1865	17 826	14 997		6 535		
1867[j]		388 000	136			405 400

[a]Exported in the fresh state; Lorenzo Sabine, *The Principal Fisheries of the American Seas*, p. 91.

[b]Tins (pounds) preserved in the Miramichi region, ca. 1850: H. Y. Hind, *Eighty Years Progress in British North America*, p. 583.

[c]Number of salmon exported from St. John; *Journal of the House of Assembly*, New Brunswick, 1852.

[d]Average catch at Saint John, 1852-1854; Charles Lanman, *Adventures in the Wilds of the United States and British American Provinces*, (11), p. 14.

[e]Gulf Region catch; Hind, p. 583.

[f]*Journal of the House of Assembly*, Newfoundland, 1860.

[g]Salmon production; George Day, Census of the Province of New Brunswick, p. 152.

[h]Export figures for the period from 1862 to 1865 inclusive are from the respective *Journal[s] of the House of Assembly*, New Brunswick.

[i]Suspected cases of tinned salmon.

[j]Production from the northern Gulf shore of the province only; *Reports on the Fisheries, Etc. of the Dominion of Canada*, 1868, "Mr. Miller's Report", pp. 1–23.

TABLE 4. Exports of salmon, Newfoundland, 1721–1845.

Year	Number of tierces	Year	Number of tierces	Year	Number of tierces
1721	530[a]	1778	924	1817	2 858
1739	1 000[b]	1784	725	1818	1 663
1743	1 000[b]	1785	2 341	1819	2 125
1746[c]	1 613	1786	2 596	1820	1 808
1748	2 450	1787	3 865	1821	1 916
1749	1 802	1788	3 736	1822	2 650
1750	1 255	1789	2 327	1823	2 257
1751	867	1790	2 990	1824[e]	2 546
1752	1 741	1791	3 585	1825	3 127
1753	847	1792	4 598	1826	3 204
1754	1 320	1793	3 202	1827	2 889
1755	950	1794	5 614	1828	2 330.5
1757	4 848	1795	3 588	1829	2 795
1758	1 520	1797	2 465	1829[f]	3 865
1759	2 310	1800	1 797	1830	4 322
1760	1 850	1801	1 688	1831	3 710
1763[d]	694	1803	3 709	1832	3 302.5
1764	2 320	1804	3 739	1833	2 901
1765	1 172	1805	1 916	1834[g]	2 625
1766	1 119	1806	2 040	1835	2 477
1767	1 006	1807	3 469	1836	2 130
1768	40 386	1808	3 272	1837	2 262
1769	919	1809	4 064	1838	4 408
1770	649	1810	5 747	1839	2 922
1771	1 258	1811	2 694	1840	3 396
1772	734	1812	3 831	1841	3 642
1773	3 543	1813	3 737	1842	4 715
1774	3 501	1814	3 425	1843	4 058
1775	4 366	1815	2 752	1844	3 753
1776	2 307	1816	2 659	1845	3 545

[a]Dictionary of Canadian Biography, (11), ed. David Hayne, p. 609.
[b]Harold Innes, The Cod Fisheries, pp. 148–149.
[c]Figures for the years 1746 to 1760, 1770 to 1803, 1820 to 1823, 1825 to 1829, and 1830 to 1833 inclusive are from the Public Archives of Canada (PAC), "Colonial Office Papers" (CO-194).
[d]Figures for the years 1763 to 1769, 1804 to 1819, 1838, 1839 and 1842 inclusive are from D. W. Prowse, A History of Newfoundland, pp. 694, 697, 710.
[e]George R. Young, The British North American Colonies, p. 147.
[f]Montgomery R. Martin, History of Nova Scotia, p. 313.
[g]Figures for the years 1834 to 1837 inclusive are from the respective Journal[s] of the House of Assembly, Newfoundland.
[h]Figures for the years 1840 to 1841 and 1843 to 1845 inclusive are from the respective Newfoundland "Blue Book[s] of Statistics."

TABLE 5. Exports of salmon, Newfoundland, 1846–1867.

Year		Number of		
	Tierces	Barrels	Packages	cwt.
1846[a]		5 201		
1847		4 917		
1848		3 822		
1849		5 911		
1850	1 933	1 700		
1851[b]	2 956	1 613	18[d]	
1852	2 899	765		
1853	2 840	1 626	1 387	
1854	2 601	602	167	
1855	2 481	647	176	
1856	1 216	1 156	190	
1857	2 486	815	46	
1858	2 726		109	
1859	3 716		29	
1860[c]	3 963			51
1861	2 924			
1862	4 227			14
1863	3 179	1 767		46
1864	1 765	1 257		11.5
1865	2 418	1 598		103
1866	2 917	977	873[d]	
1867	2 472	1 867	516[d]	

[a]Figures for the years 1846 to 1850 inclusive are from the respective Newfoundland "Blue Book[s] of Statistics."
[b]Figures for the years 1851 to 1859 inclusive are from the *Journal of the House of Assembly*.
[c]Figures for the years 1860 to 1867 inclusive are from the respective *Journal[s] of the House of Assembly*, Newfoundland.
[d]Number of cases canned.

TABLE 6. Exports of salmon, Nova Scotia, 1761–1850.

Year	Number of				
	Barrels	Tierces	Halves	Kitts	Others
1761[a]	34	30			
1762	127				
1763	56	35			23[b]
1764	76	30			44[b]
1765		49			315[c]
1785[d]	2 850				
1806[e]	675				
1807[e]	871				
1816[f]	70				
1831	1				64[g]
1839	1 114			2 278	
1840	357[h]				
1841	1 818	81	27	957	1 343[i]
1842	2 059	48	114	1 446	209[i]
1843	4 588			849	
1844[j]	5 187	357	215	862	853[k]
1845	7 814	203	336	779	320[l]
1846	6 118				
1847	5 125	376	923	331	396[m]
1848	2 011	49		2 718	
1849	5 055				
1850[n]	6 573	803	1		

[a]Figures for the years 1761 to 1765 and 1831 to 1843 inclusive are from the Public Archives of Canada (PAC), "Colonial Office Papers" (CO-221), "Shipping Returns, Port of Halifax."
[b]"Casks."
[c]Ten "kegs", 5 "firkins", and 30 "smoked" [boxes].
[d]Lorenzo Sabine, *The Principal Fisheries of the American Seas*, p. 91.
[e]Montgomery Martin, *History of Nova Scotia*, p. 62. Values are exclusive of Cape Breton.
[f]Richard Brown. *A History of the Island of Cape Breton*, p. 433. The figure is for Cape Breton only.
[g]"Cases."
[h]Partial record represents only that portion exported to Great Britain.
[i]"Thirds."
[j]Figures for the years 1844 to 1849 are from the respective *Journal[s] of the House of Assembly*, Nova Scotia.
[k]414 "thirds," 71 "boxes", and 368 "fish."
[l]224 "thirds," and 91 "boxes."
[m]325 "thirds," and 71 "boxes."
[n]*Journal of the House of Assembly*, Nova Scotia, 1851, "Return of pickled fish inspected."

TABLE 7. Return of picked salmon inspected and estimated total dollar value of salmon exports, Nova Scotia, 1851–1859.

| Year | Return:[a] Number of | | | Estimated $ value of salmon exports[b] |
	Tierces	Barrels	Halves	
1851		817		59,735[c]
1852		1 270	1	52,815[d]
1853				91,845[e]
1854	69	3 276	45	67,645[f]
1855	61	3 273	137	94,985[g]
1856	59	2 759.5	52	70,440[h]
1857	77	1 633	26.5	56,450[i]
1858		3 088	49	58,770[j]
1859		4 212	35	78,265[k]

[a]Values are from the respective *Journal[s] of the House of Assembly*, Nova Scotia.
[b]Values for the years 1853 to 1856 inclusive are derived from Thomas Knight, *Report on the Fisheries of Nova Scotia*, p. 30. The 1857 value is from the *Nova Scotia Trade and Commerce Report*, 1858. All other values are from the respective *Journal[s] of the House of Assembly*, Nova Scotia.
[c]Salmon exports actually reported to value £11,947.
[d]Salmon and shad exports valued at £10,723, 1% of which is estimated to be shad.
[e]Salmon and shad exports valued at $98,035, 6% of which is estimated to be shad.
[f]Salmon and shad exports valued at $80,285, 16% of which is estimated to be shad.
[g]Salmon and shad exports valued at $103,420, 8% of which is estimated to be shad.
[h]Salmon and shad exports valued at $82,945, 15% of which is estimated to be shad.
[i]Salmon exports actually valued at £11,290.
[j]Salmon exports actually valued at £11,754.
[k]Salmon exports actually valued at £15,653.

TABLE 8. Exports of salmon and trout, Nova Scotia, 1860–1866.

Year	$ Value of salmon and trout exports[a]
1860	96,184
1861	65,118
1862	49,640
1863	69,499
1864	63,826
1865	62,177
1866	61,263

[a]Values are from Thomas Knight, *Report on the Fisheries of Nova Scotia*, p. 30. Trout exports at this time are not expected to exceed 5% of the total value shown. Landed value of salmon was approximately $10 per barrel, and the market value ranged from $13 to $15 per barrel of 200 pounds.

TABLE 9. Exports of salmon, Labrador, 1767–1867.

Year	Number of tierces	Year	Number of tierces
1767[a]	45	1812	2 069
1772[b]	140	1813	2 129
1773	265	1820	417
1774	865	1825	1 124
1775	1 414	1827[e]	750
1776	1 032	1828	600
1779[c]	890	1829	2 200
1782	80	1830	935
1784[d]	762	1831[f]	2 430
1785	676	1860[g]	1 080
1786	665	1861	1 061
1792	138	1862	1 208
1804	600	1863	2 172
1805	554	1864	514[h]
1806	420	1865[i]	1 657
1810	1 480	1866	846
1811	1 270	1867[j]	600

[a]Values for the years 1767, 1804 to 1825, 1829, and 1866 are from W.G. Gosling, *Labrador: Its Discovery, Exploration and Development*, pp. 476, 478.
[b]Values for the years 1772 to 1776 inclusive are from respective *Privy Council Papers*, No's 841: 2019 to 851: 2026.
[c]Values for the years 1779, 1782, and 1786 are from Wilfred Grenfell, *Labrador: The Country and the People*, p. 336.
[d]Values for the years 1784, 1785, and 1792 are from the Public Archives of Canada, "Colonial Office Papers" (CO Sup. I, Misc. 18).
[e]Values for the years 1827, 1828, and 1830 are from the Provincial Archives of Newfoundland, "Boundary Dispute Documents."
[f]Lorenzo Sabine, *The Principal Fisheries of the American Seas*, p. 78.
[g]Values for the years 1860 to 1864 inclusive are from the *Journal of the House of Assembly*, Newfoundland, 1866.
[h]Does not include 51 000 pounds packed in tins in 1864.
[i]*Privy Council Papers*, 410: 1288.
[j]*Journal of the House of Assembly*, Newfoundland, 1868. Value does not include an unspecified amount packed in tins.

TABLE 10. Exports of salmon, Prince Edward Island, 1857–1867.[a]

Year	Number of				
	Barrels	Pounds	Boxes	Packages	Cases
1857	10				
1859		300			
1861			86		
1862				20	
1863	17		712		
1864	2.5			737	
1865			328	877	11
1866	8			1360	
1867	86		8		

[a]Values are from the respective *Journal[s] of the House of Assembly*, Prince Edward Island.

TABLE 11. Exports of salmon, Quebec, 1783–1813.

Year	Number of		
	Barrels	Tierces	Smoked
1783[a]			304
1784		1 000[b]	221[c]
1786		1 100	253
1797[d]	1 500		
1803[e]	197	610	
1804[f]	264	597	
1807[g]	215		
1808	1 958		
1809	1 666		
1810	893		
1811	3 266.5		
1812	2 161.5		
1813	2 152		

[a]Values for the years 1783 and 1786 are from Lorenzo Sabine, *The Principal Fisheries of the American Seas*, p. 76.
[b]Estimated annual production from Gaspé and Chaleur Bay, E.D.T. Chambers, *The Fisheries of the Province of Quebec* (1), p. 114.
[c]Sabine, p. 76.
[d]Exports from the North Shore (Mingan); James F. More, *The History of Queens County*, p. 81.
[e]Average Canadian export, 1801-1805; Hugh Gray, *Letters from Canada*, p. 171.
[f]*Royal Gazette*, St. John, N.B. (newspaper), January 14, 1805.
[g]Values for the years from 1807 to 1813 inclusive are from Public Archives of Canada (PAC), ''Colonial Office Papers'' (CO-47).

TABLE 12.   Exports of salmon, Quebec, 1820–1867.

Year	Number of				
	Barrels	Tierces	Halves	Kitts	Others
1820[a]	254	166	36		2[b]
1821[c]	62				
1822	547	590			
1823	592	418			
1825	401	416			
1826	673	242		18	
1827	469	435	56	20	1[d]
1828	460	434			
1829	268	478	79	5	2[d]
1830	133	272	135	99	
1831	385	201	77		
1832[e]	2 962				
1833	53	184	20		
1834	200	205		310	
1835	240	286	41		2[b]
1836	137	141	124		
1837	341	256	88		
1838	1 618				
1839	16	60	62		4[f]
1843	858				
1848	3 667				
1849		290			
1856	2 500				
1857[g]	1 200				
1859[h]	250				
1860	320				
1864[i]	760				
1865	16				1 591[j]
1866	656				
1867[k]	4 768.5				

[a]Values for the years 1820, 1822–1823, 1826–1827, 1829–1831, 1833–1837, 1839, and 1849 inclusive are from Public Archives of Canada, Colonial Office Papers (CO-47).
[b]"kegs."
[c]Values for the years 1821, 1825, 1828, and 1856 are from E.D.T. Chambers, *The Fisheries of the Province of Quebec* (1), pp. 121, 134 and 152.
[d]"puncheons."
[e]Values for the years 1832, 1838, 1843, and 1848 are from Lorenzo Sabine, *The Principal Fisheries of the American Seas*, p. 76.
[f]"finkins."
[g]Harold Innes, *The Cod Fisheries*, p. 358.
[h]Values for the years 1859 and 1860 are from Edward Weeks, *The Moisie Salmon Club*, p. 13, and represent the catch for the Moisie region.
[i]Values for the years 1864 to 1866 inclusive are from the respective *Journals of the House of Assembly*, Nova Scotia, and represent the amount of export to Nova Scotia only.
[j]"boxes."
[k]*Annual Report of the Department of Marine and Fisheries*, 1868, Appendix 7, p. 95.

Bibliography

I. PUBLISHED WORKS

Acadiensis, ed., David Russell Jack, Vol. 1, No. 1, Saint John (New Brunswick), 1901.

Acts of the General Assembly of His Majesty's Province of New Brunswick. 1824, Queens Printer (George K. Lurgin) Fredericton, 1824.

Adams, A. Leith. Field and Forest Rambles. Henry S. King and Co., London, 1873.

Aiton, Grace. The Story of Sussex and Vicinity. Kings County Historical Society (New Brunswick), 1967.

Akins, T. B. History of Halifax City. facsimile edition, Mika Studio, Belleville (Ontario), 1975; originally published by the Nova Scotia Historical Society, Halifax, 1895.

Annual Report. 1973. Environment Canada, Fisheries and Marine Service, Resource Development Branch, Maritimes Region, Halifax, 1974.

Annual Report. 1971. Environment Canada, Fisheries and Marine Service, Resource Development Branch, Newfoundland Region, St. John's, 1972.

Annual Report of the Commissioner of Fisheries, Game and Forests. New York, 1895.

Annual Report[s] of the Department of Marine and Fisheries. Department of Marine and Fisheries, Ottawa, 1868 to 1913.

Annual Report[s] of the Department of Naval Service. Department of Naval Service, Ottawa, 1914 to 1918.

Annual Report of the Geological Survey of Canada. Series 2, Vol. 8, Geological Survey of Canada, Ottawa, 1895.

Appleton, Thomas E. Usque Ad Mare. Department of Transport, Ottawa, 1968.

Arbuckle, Doreen Menzies. The north west Miramichi, Westboro Printers Ltd., Ottawa, 1978.

Arctic. (Bulletin of the Arctic Institute of North America), Vol. II, No. 2, Arctic Institute of North America, Montreal, 1958.

Arsenault, Bona. History of the Acadiens. Éditions Lemeác, Ottawa, 1978.

Atkin, Ronald. Maintain the right. MacMillan Company of Canada, Ltd., Toronto, 1958.

Atlantic Salmon Association Centennial Award Fund. lecture series, Atlantic Salmon Association, Montreal, nd.

Atlantic salmon commercial catch statistics, Maritimes region. Individual issues for the years from 1967 to 1976, compiled by C. E. Wykes (1967 to 1969), C. E. Wykes and R. W. Dunfield (1970, 1971), and R. W. Dunfield (1972 to 1976); Environment Canada, Fisheries and Marine Service, Maritimes Region, Halifax, 1968 to 1977.

Atlantic Salmon Journal, The. The Atlantic Salmon Association, Montreal, issues for the years 1964 through 1975.

Atlantic Salmon Sport Catch Statistics, Maritimes area. Individual issues for the years from 1970 to 1976, compiled by R. W. Dunfield, Environment Canada, Fisheries and Marine Service, Maritimes Region, Halifax, 1971 to 1977.

Backwoods of Canada, The. (Letters from the wife of an emigrant officer). Charles Knight, London, 1836.

Baldwin, R. M. and J. Baldwin. The Baldwins and the great experiment. Longmans Canada Ltd., Don Mills (Ontario), 1969.

Ballan, William. The importance and advantage of Cape Breton, truly stated and impartially considered. John and Paul Knopton, London, 1746.

Ballantyne, Robert Michael. Hudson Bay. 4th edition, Thomas Nelson and Sons, London, 1846.

Bardach, John. Downstream. Grosset and Dunlop, New York, 1964.

Bas Saint-Laurent Gaspésie (tour guide). Gouvernement du Québec, Ministère du Tourisme, de la Chasse et de la pêche, Québec, 1972.

Baxter, James Phinney, ed. Documentary history of the State of Maine. Vol. 11, 23. Collections of the Maine Historical Society, 2nd series, Portland, 1908 and 1916.

Beaver, The. (magazine) ed. Malvina Bolis, The Hudson's Bay Company, Winnipeg. Issues between 1970 and 1978.

Berriman, A. E. Historical metrology: a new analysis of the archaeological and historical evidence relating to weights and measures. 1964. Originally published in 1953.

Biggar, H. P., ed. The precursors of Jacques Cartier, 1497-1534. Publications of the Canadian Archives, No. 5, Government Printing Bureau, Ottawa, 1911.

The voyage of Jacques Cartier. Publications of the Public Archives of Canada, No. 11. Ottawa, 1925.

Bingay, James. A history of Canada. Thomas Nelson and Sons, Toronto, 1947.

Blakely, Phillis R., and John N. Grant, ed. Eleven exiles. Dunburn Press Limited, Toronto, 1982.

Blakey, Robert. Angling, or how to angle and where to go. George Routledge and Sons, London, nd.

Blanc, M., P. Banarescu, J. L. Gaudet, and J. C. Hureau. European inland water fish: a multilingual catalogue. Fishery News, London, 1971.

Blond, Georges. The great migration of animals. Collier Books, New York, 1962.

Bock, Philip K. The Micmac indians of Restigouche. (Bulletin 213), National Museum of Canada, Ottawa, 1966.

Bolger, Francis, W. P., ed. Canada's smallest province. The Prince Edward Island Centennial Commission. 1973.

Bonnycastle, Sir Richard Henry. Newfoundland in 1842. Henry Colburn, London, 1842.

Book of knowledge. ed., E. V. McLaughlin. 20 Vol., The Grolier Society, New York, 1944.

Bouchette, Joseph. The British dominions in North America. Longman, London, 1832.

A topographical dictionary of the Province of lower Canada. Longman, Rees, Brown, Green and Longman, London, 1832.

Brown, George S. Yarmouth, Nova Scotia: a sequel to Campbell's history. Rand Avery, Boston, 1888.

Brown, George W. Building the Canadian Nation. J. M. Dent and Sons (Canada) Limited, Toronto, 1849.

Brown, Richard. A history of the Island of Cape Breton. Sampson Low, London, 1869.

Browne, George Waldo. The St. Lawrence River. Weathervane Books, New York, 1905.

Browne, P. W. Where the fishers go. Cochrane Publishing Company, New York, 1909.

Buckingham, James S. Canada, Nova Scotia, New Brunswick and the other British provinces in North America. Fisher, Son and Co., London, 1843.

Bulletin of the Natural History Society of New Brunswick.

No. 13, Natural History Society of New Brunswick, Saint John, 1896.

Bulletin of the New York Public Library. February, 1931, New York Public Library, New York, 1931.

Bulletin of the Public Archives of Nova Scotia. No. 16, Public Archives of Nova Scotia, Halifax, 1961.

Burgess, G. H. O., C. L. Cutting, J. A. Lovern, and J. J. Waterman, ed. Fish handling and processing. Her Majesty's Stationery Office, Edinburgh, 1965.

Burnaby, Rev. Andrew. Travells through the middle settlements in North America...1759–1760. 2nd edition, Cornell University Press, Ithaca (New York), 1968.

Burwash, Dorothy. English merchant shipping, 1460–1540. University of Toronto Press, 1969.

Butler, William Francis. The wild north land. Facsimile edition, Hurtig Publishers, Edmonton (Alberta), 1968; originally published in 1873.

Calderwood, W. L., Salmon hatching and salmon migration (The Buckland Lectures for 1930). Edward Arnold and Co., London, 1931.

Calnek, W. A. History of the county of Annapolis. Facsimile edition, Mika Studio, Belleville, Ontario, 1972; originally published by William Briggs, Toronto, 1897.

Campbell, D., and R. A. MacLean. Beyond the Atlantic Roar. (The Carleton Library, #78), McClelland and Stewart Ltd., Toronto, 1974).

Campbell, J. F. A short American tramp in the fall of 1864. Edmonston and Douglass, Edinburgh, 1865.

Campbell, Patrick. Travells in America. ed., H. H. Langton, Champlain Society, Toronto, 1937.

Canada's first city. Lingley Printing Co. Ltd., Saint John, N.B., 1962.

Canadian Archives report[s]. Kings Printer, Ottawa. Issues from 1900 to 1910.

Canadian Fish Culturist, The. Queen's Printer, Ottawa. Issues from 1957 to 1962.

Canadian Handbook and Tourist Guide, The. Facsimile edition, Coles Publishing Company, Toronto, 1971; originally published by Longmore and Co., Montreal, 1867.

Canadian Illustrated News, The. Vol. 2, No. 23. (October 24, 1863) G. E. Desbarats, ed., Montreal, 1863.

Canadian Journal of Science, Literature and History. New series, Vol. VII, The Canadian Institute, Toronto, 1856.

Carrington, Richard. Mermaids and mastodons. Arrow Books Ltd., London, 1960.

Cartwright, George. A journal of transactions and events during a residence of nearly sixteen years on the coast of Labrador. 3 Vol., Allin and Ridge, Newark, 1792.

⎯⎯⎯ Captain George Cartwright and his Labrador Journal, 1770-1786. ed., C. W. Townsend, D. Estes and Company, Boston, 1911.

Cattermole, William. Emigration: the advantages of emigration to Canada. Facsimile edition, Coles Publishing Company, Toronto, 1970; originally published by Simpkin and Marshall, London, 1831.

Carver, J. Travels through the interior parts of North America in the years 1766, 1767 and 1768. Facsimile edition, Coles Publishing Company, Toronto, 1974; originally published by J. Walter and S. Crowder, London, 1778.

Census of Nova Scotia, 1860-1. ed., E. M. MacDonald, Halifax, 1862.

Census of the Province of New Brunswick, 1861. George Day, printer, Saint John, 1862.

A century of colonial painting (catalogue #N.G. 31-1964-3), The National Gallery of Canada, Ottawa, 1964.

Chambers Encyclopedia. New edition, Georges Newnes, London, 1950.

Chambers, Captain Ernest J. The Canadian marine. Canadian Marine and Fisheries History Publisher, Toronto, 1905.

Chambers, E. T. D. The Ouananiche and its Canadian environment. Harper and Brothers, New York, 1896.

⎯⎯⎯ The fisheries of the Province of Quebec, Part 1. Department of Colonization, Mines and Fisheries, Quebec, 1912.

Champlain, Samuel de. The voyages and explorations of Samuel de Champlain. 2 Vol., ed., Edward Gaylord Bourne, The Courier Press Limited, Toronto, 1911.

Chase, George, W., The history of Haverhill. Haverhill (Massachusetts), 1861.

Chaytor, Alfred H. Letters to a salmon fisher's son. John Murray, London, 1910.

Clark, Andrew Hill. Acadia: the geography of early Nova Scotia to 1760. University of Wisconsin Press, Madison, 1968.

Clarke, George Frederick. Someone before us. Brunswick Press, Fredericton, 1968.

Clarke, John M. The Gaspé. Yale University Press, New Haven. 1935.

Clooney, Robert. A compendious history of the northern part of the Province of New Brunswick and the District of Gaspé in Lower Canada. Joseph Howe, Halifax, 1832.

A collection of the Acts passed in the Parliament of Great Britain particularly applying to the Province of Upper Canada and of such ordinances of the late Province of Quebec as have force of law therein. York, 1818.

Collections of the Massachusetts Historical Society. The Massachusetts Historical Society, Boston, selected volumes published between 1794 and 1870.

Collections of the New Brunswick Historical Society. The New Brunswick Historical Society, Saint John, selected volumes published between 1894 and 1971.

Collections of the Nova Scotia Historical Society. The Nova Scotia Historical Society, Halifax, selected volumes published between 1879 and 1978.

Collie, Michael. New Brunswick. The MacMillan Company of Canada Limited, Toronto, 1974.

Comeau, Napoleon A. Life and sport on the North Shore. Telegraph Printing Company, Quebec, 1923.

Consolidated Statutes of Upper Canada. 1864.

County Times, The (newspaper). Aroostook County, Maine, May 13–14, 1972.

Crowell, Edwin. A history of Barrington Township. Facsimile edition, Mika Studio, Belleville (Ontario), 1973; originally published in Yarmouth, N.S., 1923.

Cunningham, Robert, and John B. Prince. Tamped clay and saltmarsh hay. Brunswick Press, Fredericton, 1976.

Cutting, Charles L., Fish saving: A history of fish processing from ancient to modern times, Leonard Hill, London, 1955.

Cutting, R. E., and R. W. Gray, "Biological Conservation Subcommittee Report," Atlantic salmon review task force. Appendix B, Department of Fisheries and Oceans, Halifax, 1979.

Dalhousie Review. Vol. 31, Review Publishing Company, Halifax, 1951.

Dashwood, Richard Lewis. Chiploquorgan or life by the camp fire. Simpkin, Marshall, London, 1872.

Davidson, W. H. William Davidson: 1740–1790. The North Shore Leader, Newcastle (New Brunswick), 1947.

Davies, K. G., ed. Northern Quebec and Labrador Journals and correspondence, 1819–1835. Hudson's Bay Company Record Society, London, 1963.

Davis, Harold A. An international community on the St. Croix (1604–1930), Maine Studies No. 64, University of Maine, Orono, 1974.

Dawson, Samuel Edward. Stanford's compendium of geography and travel. Vol. I (Canada and Newfoundland), Edward Stanford, London, 1897.

DeBoileau, Lambert. Labrador life. Ed., Thomas F. Bredin, The Ryerson Press, Toronto, 1969.

Dennis, Clara. Cape Breton over. The Ryerson Press, Toronto, 1942.

Denys, Nicholas. The description and natural history of the coasts of North America (Acadia). Trans. and ed. by William Francis Ganong, The Champlain Society, Toronto, 1908.

DesBrisay, Mather Byles. History of County of Lunenburg. Facsimile edition, Mika Studio, Belleville, 1972; originally published by William Briggs, Toronto, 1895.

de Villebon, Joseph Robiniou. Acadia at the end of the Seventeenth Century. Ed., John Clarence Webster (New Brunswick Museum Monographic Series No. 1), The Tribune Press, Sackville (New Brunswick), 1934.

Dictionary of Canadian Biography. Gen. ed., Francess Halpenny. 6 Vol., University of Toronto Press, Toronto, 1966–1983.

Dièreville, Sieur de. A relation of a voyage to Port Royal in Acadia or New France. Ed., J. C. Webster, The Champlain Society, Toronto, 1933.

Dionne, N. E. Champlain. ("The Makers of Canada" series, Vol. 1) Morang and Company Ltd., Toronto, 1906.

Dinsdale, Tim. The Leviathans. Revised edition, Futura Publications Limited, London, 1976.

Dominion Sessional Paper, 18. Kings Printer, Ottawa, 1905.

Douville, Raymond, and Jacques Donat Casanova. Daily life in early Canada. Trans., Carola Congreve, MacMillan Company, New York, 1968.

Downey, Fairfax. Louisbourg: key to a continent. Prentice Hall, Inc., New Jersey, 1965.

Duncan, Francis. Our garrisons in the west. Chapman and Hall, London, 1864.

Duncanson, John V. Falmouth: a New England Township in Nova Scotia, 1760–1965. n.p., Windsor, Nova Scotia, 1965.

Dunlop, William. Tiger Dunlop's Upper Canada. (New Canadian Library edition, No. 5), McClelland and Stewart, Toronto, 1967.

Dymond, John R. Family Salmonidae. Reprinted from Fishes of the Western North Atlantic. I(3), ed., John Tee-Van (Memoir of the Sears Foundation for Marine Research), Yale University Press, New Haven, 1963.

Eaton, A. W. H. History of Kings County (Nova Scotia), The Salem Press, Salem, 1910.

Eccles, W. J. The ordeal of New France. (Radio script; History of Canada, part 2), Canadian Broadcasting Corporation, Toronto, 1969.

Elliott, Charles B. The United States and the Northeastern fisheries. The University of Minnesota, Minneapolis, 1887.

Environment needs you, The. (Brochure #En. 21-572) Information Canada, Ottawa, 1972.

Farmers Almanack, The. 1825 edition, ed., C. H. Belcher, Halifax, 1825.

Fisher, Peter. History of New Brunswick. New Brunswick Historical Society, Saint John, 1921; reprinted from the original published by Chubb and Sons, Saint John, 1825.

Forest and outdoors. (magazine), February 1954.

Benjamin Franklin: his life, ed., D. H. Montgomery, Ginn and Company, Boston, 1906.

Funk and Wagnalls new encyclopedia. 1973 edition, 27 Vol., Funk and Wagnalls Inc., New York, 1973.

New standard dictionary of the English language. Funk and Wagnalls Inc., New York, 1946.

Ganong, William Francis. Ste. Croix (Dochet) Island. Monographic Series 3, New Brunswick Museum, Saint John, 1945.

The history of Miscou and Shippegan. Historical Studies #5, New Brunswick Museum, Globe Printing, Saint John, 1946.

Garlic Theodatus. A treatise on the artificial propagation of certain kinds of fish. Tho. Brown, Cleveland (Ohio), 1857.

Gathorne-Hardy, A. F. The salmon. (Fur, Feather and Fin Series), Longmans, Green and Co., New York, 1898.

Gazette. Saint John (New Brunswick), 1798 to 1805.

Geographical Survey of Canada progress report, 1855–1856. Government Printing Office, Ottawa, 1857.

Gesner, Abraham. New Brunswick with notes for emigrants. Simonds and Ward, London, 1847.

Goode, G. Browne, ed., The fisheries and fishing industries of the United States. 5 Vol., U.S. Commission of Fish and Fisheries, Washington, 1884–1887.

Gordon, James D. Halifax: its sins and sorrows. Friends of the Old Town Clock, Halifax, nd.; originally published by Conference Job Printing Office, Halifax, 1862.

Gosling, W. G. Labrador: its discovery, exploration and development. Alston Rivers Ltd., London, 1910.

Gourlay, Robert. Statistical account of Upper Canada. 3 Vol., Simpkin and Marshall, London, 1822.

Grant, George M. Ocean to ocean. Facsimile edition, Coles Publishing Company, Toronto, 1970; originally published by James Campbell and Son, Toronto, 1873.

Grant, John N. The development of Sherbrooke Village to 1880. The Nova Scotia Museum, Halifax, 1972.

Gray, Hugh. Letters from Canada. Facsimile edition, Coles Publishing Company, Toronto, 1971; originally published by Longman, Hurst, Ries and Orme, London, 1809.

Grenfell, Wilfred T. Labrador: the country and the people. MacMillan Co. Ltd., New York, 1922.

Griswold, F. Gray. Fish facts and fancies. Charles Scribner's Sons, New York, 1926.

Gross, Robert A. The minutemen and their world. Hill and Wang, New York, 1976.

Gubbins, Joseph. Gubbin's New Brunswick Journals. 1811 and 1813, ed., Howard Temperley, Kings Landing Corporation, Fredericton, 1980.

Guillet, Edwin C. Early life in Upper Canada. The Ontario Publishing Company, Toronto, 1933.

Haklyut, Richard. The principal navigations of the English Nation. Everyman's Library edition, Vol. 5 and 6, J. M. Dent and Sons, London, 1962.

Haliburton, Thomas C. The clockmaker. McClelland and Stewart Ltd., Toronto, 1958.

Historical and statistical account of Nova Scotia. 2 Vol., Facsimile edition, Mika Studio, Belleville (Ontario), 1973; originally published by Joseph Howe, Halifax, 1829.

Hallock, Charles, The fishing tourist. Harper and Brothers, New York, 1873.

The salmon fisher. The Harris Publishing Company, New York, 1890.

Hamilton, P. S. Nova Scotia considered as a field for emigration. John Weale, London, 1858.

Hamilton, W. D. and W. A. Spray. Source material relating to the New Brunswick Indian. Hamray Books, Fredericton, 1977.

Hand Book of Indians of Canada. (Sessional Paper #21A), Geographical Board of Canada, Ottawa, 1913.

Hanlon, Joseph H. Handbook of Package Engineering. McGraw-Hill Book Company, New York, 1971.

Hannay, James. History of New Brunswick. 2 Vol., John A. Bowes, Saint John, 1909.

Hardy, Campbell. Sporting adventures in the New World. Hurst and Blackett, London, 1855.

Forest life in Acadia. Chapman and Hall, London, 1869.

Harpers Magazine. No. 214 (March, 1868), Harper and Brothers, New York, 1868.

Harvey, D. C. The French regime in Prince Edward Island. Yale University Press, New Haven, 1926.

Harvey, D. C., ed. Journeys to the Island of St. John. The MacMillan Company of Canada Limited, Toronto, 1955.

Hatton, Joseph. Newfoundland: the oldest British Colony. Chapman and Hall, London, 1883.

Hay, G. U. A history of New Brunswick. W. Gage and Co. Ltd., Toronto, 1903.

Head, C. Grant. Eighteenth Century Newfoundland. The Carleton Library No. 99, McClelland and Stewart Limited, Toronto, 1976.

Hennepin, Louis. A new discovery of a vast country in America. Facsimile edition, Coles Publishing Co., Ltd., Toronto, 1974; originally published in 1698.

Herbert, William Henry. Frank Forresters fish and fishing in the United States and British Provinces in North America. Richard Bentley, London, 1849.

Heriot, George. Travels through the Canadas. Facsimile edition, M. G. Hurtig Ltd., Edmonton, 1971.

Hewes, Gordon W. Aboriginal use of fishery resources in northwestern North America. Unpublished thesis, University of California Library, 1947.

Hickling, C. F., The farming of fish. Pergamon Press, London, 1968.

Higginson, Francis. New England's plantation. Reprinted in "Tracts and Other Papers", Vol. 1, ed., Peter Force, Washington, 1836; originally published in London, 1630.

Hind, H. Y. et al. Eighty years progress in British North America. L. Stebbins, Toronto, 1863.

Hoffman, Bernard, G. Cabot to Cartier: sources for historical ethnography of northeastern North America. University of Toronto Press, Toronto, 1961.

Holbrook, Stewart H. The American lumberjack. Collier Books, New York, 1962.

Hollingsworth, S. The present state of Nova Scotia with a brief account of Canada and the British Islands on the coast of North America. William Creech, Edinburgh, 1787.

Howard, George Selby. The new Royal Cyclopaedia and Encyclopedia. A. Hogg, London, 1788.

Howe, Joseph. Western and eastern rambles: travel sketches of Nova Scotia. Ed., M. G. Parks, University of Toronto Press, Toronto, 1973.

Howison, John. Sketches of Upper Canada. Facsimile edition, Coles Publishing Company, Toronto, 1970; originally published by Oliver and Boyd, Edinburgh, 1821.

Howley, James P. The Beothucks or Red Indians. Facsimile edition, Coles Publishing Company, Toronto, 1974; originally published by Cambridge University Press, 1915.

Hubbard, R. W., ed. Thomas Davies, 1737–1812. National Gallery, Ottawa, 1972.

Humphreys, John. Plaisance. Publications in History #3, National Museum of Canada, Ottawa, 1970.

Hunter, Margaret. Pioneer settlers of the Bay Chaleur. The Tribune Press Ltd., Sackville, N.B., 1978.

The Inland Fisheries and Game Protection Society. Halifax County, Nova Scotia, MacNab and Shaffer, Halifax, 1865.

Innis, Harold A. Select documents in Canadian economic history, 1497–1783. University of Toronto Press, Toronto, 1929.

The cod fisheries. University of Toronto Press, Toronto, 1954.

International Atlantic Salmon Symposium, 1972. (Special Publication Series, Vol. 4, No. 1), The International Atlantica Salmon Foundation, The Atlantic Salmon Research Trust, New York and St. Andrews, 1973.

International Wildlife Encyclopedia, The. Vol. 1, ed., Dr. Maurice Burton and Robert Burton, Marshall Cavendish Corporation, New York, 1969.

Jameson, [Anna]. Winter studies and summer rambles in Canada. 3 Vol., facsimile edition, Coles Publishing Company, Toronto, 1972; originally published by Saunders and Otley, London, 1838.

Jeffreys, Thomas. A natural and civil history of the French Dominions in North and South America. T. Jeffreys, London, 1761.

Jensen, Albert A. A brief history of the New England offshore fisheries. (Fishery Leaflet 594), U.S. Bureau of Commercial Fisheries, Washington, 1967.

Jesuit relations and allied documents. 73 Vol., ed., Reuben G. Thwaites, Vol. 28, 30, 31, 32, 43, Cleveland, 1896–1901.

Johnson, Samuel. A Dictionary of the English Language. J. F. and C. Rivington, London (6th edition), 1785; (9th edition), 1790.

Johnstone, Ken. The vanishing harvest. The Montreal Star (1968) Ltd., Montreal, 1972.

Jost, A. C. Guysborough sketches and essays. Kentville Publishing Company, Kentville, 1950.

Journal of the American Fisheries Society. Vol. 54, The American Fisheries Society, Washington, 1924.

Journal[s] of The House of Assembly of New Brunswick. Volumes for the years 1784 to 1867.

Journal[s] of The House of Assembly (Newfoundland). Volumes for the years 1853 to 1866.

Journal[s] of The House of Assembly (Nova Scotia). Volumes for the years 1839 to 1867.

Journal[s] of The House of Assembly (Prince Edward Island). Volumes for the years 1856 and 1857.

Journals of The House of Representatives of Massachusetts. Massachusetts Historical Society reprints, Vol. 16, Massachusetts Historical Society, Boston, 1935.

Kane, Paul. Wanderings of an artist. Facsimile edition, Hurtig Publisher, Edmonton, 1968; originally published by Longman, Brown, Green, Longmans and Roberts, 1859.

Kaulback, Ruth E., Historic saga of Leheve (La Have). Halifax, 1970.

Keller, Werner. The Bible as history. Bantam Books, New York, 1974.

Kerr, William Hastings. The fishery question: or American rights in Canadian Waters. Daniel Rose, Montreal, 1868.

King, Major W. Ross. The sportsman and naturalist in Canada. Facsimile edition, Coles Publishing Company, Toronto, 1974; originally published by Hurst and Blackett, London, 1866.

Knight, Thomas F. Report on the fisheries of Nova Scotia. A. Grant, Halifax, 1867.

    The river fisheries of Nova Scotia. A. Grant, Halifax, 1867.

Knox, John. The Journals of Captain John Knox. 3 Vol., the Champlain Society, Toronto, 1914.

    The siege of Quebec. Ed., Brian Connell, Pendragon House, Mississauga, 1980.

Lack, David. The natural regulation of animal numbers. Clarendon Press, Oxford, 1970.

Lanctot, Gustave, A history of Canada. 2 Vol., Clarke, Irwin and Company Limited, Toronto, 1964.

Lanman, Charles. An angler in Canada, Nova Scotia and the United States. Richard Bentley, London, 1848.

    Adventures in the wilds of the United States and British American Provinces. 2 Vol., John W. Moore, Philadelphia, 1856.

Laws of New Brunswick. 2 Vol., Kings Printer, Fredericton, 1824.

Lawson, Mrs. William. History of the townships of Dartmouth, Preston and Lawrencetown. Facsimile edition, Mika Studio, Belleville (Ontario), 1972; originally published by Morton and Co., Halifax, 1893.

LeDanois, Edward, Fishes of the world. Countryman Press, Woodstock (Vermont), nd.

Leggett, Robert. Ottawa waterway. University of Toronto Press, Toronto, 1975.

Lehnes, Ernst and Johanna Lehnes. How they saw the New World. Tudor Publishing, New York, 1966.

Lescarbot, Marc. The history of New France. 3 Vol., ed., W. L. Grant, The Champlain Society, Toronto, 1914.

Levigne, Richard George Augustus. Echoes from the backwoods. Henry Colburn, London, 1846.

Lounsbury, Ralph Greenlee. The British fishery at Newfoundland, 1634–1763. Archon Books, Hampden (Connecticut), 1969.

Lyons, Cicely. Salmon, our heritage. Mitchell Press Ltd., Vancouver, 1969.

MacBeath, George, and Dorothy Chamberlin. New Brunswick: the story of our province. W. J. Gage Limited, Toronto, 1965.

MacDonald, J. W. History of Antigonish County (1876). ed., R. A. MacLean, Formac Limited, Antigonish, N.S., 1975.

MacKay, Donald. Anticosti: the untamed island. McGraw-Hill Ryerson Limited, Toronto, 1979.

MacKay, Douglas. The Honorable Company. Revised edition, McClelland and Stewart Limited, Toronto, 1966.

MacKay, R. A., ed. Newfoundland: economic, diplomatic and strategic studies. Oxford University Press, Toronto, 1946.

MacKinnon, D. A. and A. B. Warburton. Past and present in Prince Edward Island. Charlottetown, 1905.

MacMechan, Archibald. Sagas of the sea, J. M. Dent and Sons Ltd., London, 1923.

MacNutt, W. S. New Brunswick: a history, 1784–1867. MacMillan of Canada, Toronto, 1963.

    The Atlantic Provinces. McClelland and Stewart, Toronto, 1972.

MacTaggart, John. Three years in Canada. 2 Vol., Henry Colburn, London, 1829.

Magrath, T. W. Authentic letters from Upper Canada: with an account of Canada field sports. Dublin, 1833.

Mann, John. Travels in North America. Reprint by Sainte Anne's Point Press, Fredericton, 1978; originally published by Andrew Young, Glasgow, 1824.

Maritime Monthly, The. Vol. II, No. 6, (December, 1873), J & A McMillan, Saint John (New Brunswick), 1873.

Marsden, Joshua. The narrative of a mission to Nova Scotia, New Brunswick and the Somers Islands..., J. Kershaw, London, 1827.

Martin, R. Montgomery. History of Nova Scotia. Whittaker and Co., London, 1837.

Masson, L. R., ed. Les Bourgeois de la Compagnie du nord-ouest. De L'imprimerie Générale A Coté et Cie, Quebec, 1890.

Masters, D. C., Reciprocity, 1846–1911. Historical Booklet No. 12, The Canadian Historical Association, Ottawa, 1969.

McDougall, John Lorne. History of Inverness County. Facsimile edition, Mika Studio, Belleville (Ontario), 1972; originally published in Truro, N.S., 1922.

McGregor, J. Historical and descriptive sketches of the maritime colonies of British America. Andrew Picken and Son, Liverpool, 1828.

McLennan, J. S., Louisbourg from its foundation to its fall, 1713–1758. MacMillan and Co. Ltd., London, 1918.

McLeod, Robert. In the Acadian land. Bradlee Whidden, Boston, 1899.

McLoughlin, E. V., ed. Book of knowledge. 1944 edition, 10 Vol., The Grolier Society, New York, 1944.

McFarlan, Richard. River and brook fisheries. Reporter's Office, Fredericton, 1847.

Miller, John C. The first frontier — life in Colonial America. Laurel Edition, Dell Publishing Co., Inc., New York, 1974.

Miller, Thomas. Historical and genealogical record of the first settlers of Colchester County. Facsimile edition, Mika Studio, Belleville, 1972; originally published by A.W. MacKinlay, Halifax, 1873.

Mills, Derek. Salmon and trout: a resource, its ecology, conservation and management. Oliver and Boyd, Edinburgh, 1971.

Milner, W. C. The Basin of Minas. reprinted from *The Acadian*, Wolfville nd., manuscript at Public Archives of Nova Scotia, Halifax.

Monro, Alexander. New Brunswick, with a brief outline of Nova Scotia and Prince Edward Island. Richard Nugent, Halifax, 1855.

Moorsom, William Scarth. Letters from Nova Scotia. Henry Colburn, London, 1830.

More, James F. The history of Queens County (Nova Scotia). Facsimile edition, Mika Studio, Belleville, 1972; originally published by Nova Scotia Printing Company, Halifax, 1873.

Morison, Samuel Eliot. The European discovery of America.

Morse, William Inglis, ed. Acadiensia Nova, 1598–1779: new and unpublished documents and other data relating to Acadia. 2 Vol., Bernard Quaritch Ltd., London, 1935.

Morton, Thomas. New English Canaan. London, 1632: Reprinted in *Tracts and Other Papers*, Peter Force, ed., Vol. 2, Washington, 1838.

Mowat, Farley. West Viking. Little, Brown and Company, Boston, 1965.

Mowat, John. Chaleur Bay, n.p., n.d., privately printed by the author ca. 1889.

Murdock, Beamish. A history of Nova Scotia or Acadia, 3 Vol., James Barnes, Halifax, 1895.

Murphy, J. M. The Londonderry heirs. Black Printing Co. Ltd., Middleton (Nova Scotia), 1976.

Murray, A. R. and T. J. Harman. A preliminary consideration of the factors affecting the productivity of Newfoundland streams. (Technical Report No. 130), Fisheries Research Board of Canada, St. John's, 1969.

Myers, J. C. Sketches on a tour through the northern and eastern states, the Canadas and Nova Scotia, J. H. Wartmann and brothers, Harrisonburg (Virginia), 1849.

National Geographic. Vol. 142, No. 3 (September, 1972), The National Geographic Society, Washington, 1972.

The native peoples of Atlantic Canada. The Carleton Library No. 72, ed., H. F. McGee, McClelland and Stewart Limited, Toronto, 1974.

Native trees of Canada. Bulletin No. 61, 5th edition, Department of Northern Affairs and Natural Resources, Ottawa, 1956.

Nature/Science Annual. 1975 edition, Time-Life Books, New York, 1974.

Neary, Peter, and Patrick O'Flaherty. ed., By great waters. University of Toronto Press, Toronto, 1974.

Needham, Walter. Grandfather's book of everyday things. Paperback Library Inc., New York, 1966.

Netboy, Anthony. The Atlantic salmon, a vanishing species? Faber and Faber, London, 1968.

The salmon, their fight for survival. Houghton Mifflin Co., Boston, 1974.

Salmon: the world's most harassed fish. André Deutsch, London, 1980.

Nettle, Richard. The salmon fisheries of the St. Lawrence. John Lovell, Montreal, 1857.

New Brunswick Magazine, The. Vol. 3, No. 2 (August, 1899), ed., K. W. Reynolds, Saint John (New Brunswick), 1899.

A new and complete Dictionary of Arts and Sciences. Vol. 3, W. Owen, London, 1763–1764.

A new English Dictionary based on historic principals. 8 Vol., ed., James Augustus Henry Murray, The Clarendon Press, Oxford, 1888–1928.

Newfoundland and Labrador Fishing Guide. Newfoundland and Labrador Tourist Development Division, Department of Economic Development, St. John's, 1970.

North. (magazine), Department of Indian Affairs and Northern Development, Ottawa, issues from September, 1968 to April, 1971.

Nova Scotia Tour Book. 1971 edition, Nova Scotia Travel Bureau, Department of Trade and Industry, Halifax, 1971.

Occasional papers in archaeology and history. No. 1, Department of Indian Affairs and Northern Development, Ottawa, 1970.

Oldmixon, John. The British Empire in America. 2 Vol., London, 1708.

Oliphant, Edward. The history of North America and its United States. J. Johnstone, Edinburgh, 1800.

Ommanney, F. D. The fishes. Life/Nature Library, Time-Life Books, New York, 1963.

O'Neill, Paul. The oldest city: the story of St. John's, Newfoundland. Press Porcepic, Erin (Ontario), 1975.

Owen, Charles Boidman. An epitome of history, statistics, etc., of Nova Scotia. English and Blackada, Halifax, 1842.

Owens, Captain William. Narrative of American voyages and travels of Captain William Owens, R.N. ed., Victor Hugo Paltsils, New York Public Library, New York, 1942.

Packard, Alpheus Spring. The Labrador Coast. Hodges, New York, 1891.

Palmer, C. H. The salmon rivers of Newfoundland. Farrington Printing Co., Boston, 1928.

Parkman, Francis. The conspiracy of Pontiac. 10th edition, Collier-MacMillan Ltd., London, 1966.

A half century of conflict. 3rd edition, Collier-MacMillan Ltd., London, 1966.

Parsons, John W. History of salmon in the Great Lakes, 1850–1970. (Technical Paper No. 68), United States Department of the Interior, Fish and Wildlife Service, Bureau of Sport Fisheries and Wildlife, Government Printing Office, Washington, 1973.

Past and present of Prince Edward Island. ed., D. A. MacKinnon and A. B. Warburton, Charlottetown, 1905.

Patterson, George. A history of the County of Pictou, Nova Scotia. Facsimile edition, Mika Studio, Belleville, 1972; originally published by Davison Brothers, Montreal, 1877.

Patterson, R. H. Physical characteristics of Atlantic Salmon spawning gravel in some New Brunswick streams. (Technical Report No. 785), Department of the Environment, Fisheries and Marine Service, Biological Station, St. Andrews, 1978.

Patterson, R. M. Far pastures. Gray's Publishing Ltd., Sidney, B.C. 1973.

Findlay's River. MacMillan of Canada, Toronto, 1968.

Pearson, John C., ed. The fish and fisheries of colonial North America. Department of the Interior, U.S. Fish and Wildlife Service, Washington, 1972.

Pedley, Rev. Charles. A history of Newfoundland. Longmans, Green, London, 1863.

Pennsylvania Magazine of History and Bibliography. Vol. 59, Historical Society of Pennsylvania, 1935.

Peopling of Newfoundland, The. ed., John J. Mannion, (Social and Economic Papers, 8, Institute of Social and Economic Research, Memorial University of Newfoundland) University of Toronto Press, Toronto, 1977.

Perkins, Simeon. The diary of Simeon Perkins. 1 Vol., ed., Harold Innis, The Champlain Society, Toronto, 1948.

Perley, Moses. The sea and river fisheries of New Brunswick. J. Simpson, Fredericton, 1852.

Peters, Samuel A. General history of Connecticut…, C. D. Appleton and Co., New York, 1877.

Pohl, Frederick. Prince Henry Sinclair: his expedition to the New World in 1398, Clarkson N. Potter Inc., New York, 1974.

Polar Secrets. Ed., Seon Manley and Gogo Lewis, Doubleday and Company Inc., New York, 1968.

Porter, T. R., L. G. Riche, and G. R. Traverse. Catalogue of rivers in insular Newfoundland. 4 Vol. (A, B, C, D), (Data Record Series No. NEW/D-74-9), Environment Canada, Fisheries and Marine Service, Newfoundland Region, 1974.

Port au Choix National Historic Park. (Brochure #QS-T034-000-BB-A2), Department of Indian and Northern Affairs, Ottawa, nd.

Pote, Captain William, Jr. The Journal of Captain William Pote Jr., during his captivity in the French and Indian War, 1745–1747, 2 Vol., New York, 1896.

Power, G. The salmon of Ungava Bay, (Technical Paper No. 22, October, 1969), Arctic Institute of North America, Montreal, 1969.

Prebble, John. Culloden. Penguin Books Ltd., Harmondsworthy, 1977.

Prenties, Samuel Walter. Ensign Prenties' narrative. ed., G. G. Campbell, McGraw-Hill Ryerson, Toronto, 1968.

Proceedings and Transactions of the Royal Society of Canada. 3rd series, Vol. 24, Section 2, Royal Society of Canada, Ottawa, 1930.

Prowse, D. W. A history of Newfoundland. Facsimile edition, Mika Studio, Belleville, 1972; originally published by MacMillan and Co., London, 1895.

Pugh, Ellen. Brave his soul. Dodd, Mead and Company, New York, 1970.

Quick Canadian Facts. 23rd edition, ed., C. J. Harris, Thorn Press, Toronto. 1967.

Raddall, Thomas H. Halifax, warden of the North. McClelland and Stewart, Toronto, 1971.

Rankin, Duncan Joseph. History of Antigonish county. Facsimile edition, Mika Studio, Belleville, 1972.

Rawlyk, George A. Yankees at Louisbourg. (University of Maine Studies, 2nd series, No. 85), University of Maine Press, Orono, 1967.

    Nova Scotia's Massachusetts. McGill-Queens University Press, Montreal, 1973.

Rayburn, Alan. Geographical names of New Brunswick. (Toponymy Study, No. 2), Canadian Permanent Committee on Geographical Names, Department of Energy, Mines and Resources, Ottawa, 1975.

Raymond, William O. The river St. John, 2nd edition, The Tribune Press, Sackville (New Brunswick), 1950.

Reeves, John. History of the Government of the Island of Newfoundland. Facsimile edition, Johnson Reprint Corporation, New York, 1967; originally published in London, 1793.

Report on the Dominion Government expedition to the northern waters and Arctic Archipelago of the D.G.S. "Arctic" in 1910. Department of Marine and Fisheries, Ottawa, 1911.

Report of the Royal Commission investigating the fisheries of the Maritime Provinces and the Magdalen Islands. Kings Printer, Ottawa, 1928.

Report of the United States Commission of fish and fisheries. (1873–4 and 1874–5). United States Commission of Fish and Fisheries, Government Printing Office, Washington, 1876.

Reports of the Fisheries, etc., of the Dominion of Canada (in 1867). (Senate Report), Hunter Rose and Company, Ottawa, 1868.

Reports of the Nova Scotia Archives. Volumes for the years from 1933 to 1947. These reports may be found in the *Journals of the House of Assembly (Nova Scotia)* for the respective years, or in collected volumes published by the Nova Scotia Archives, 2 Vol.

Rostlund, Erhard. Freshwater fish and fishing in native North America. (University of California Publications in Geography, Vol. 9), University of California Press, Berkeley and Los Angeles, 1952.

Rowan, John J. The emigrant and sportsman in Canada. Facsimile edition, Coles Publishing Company, Toronto, 1972; originally published by Edward Stanford, London, 1876.

Russel, Alex. The salmon. Edmonston and Douglas, Edinburgh, 1864.

Sabine, Lorenzo. The principal fisheries of the American seas. Robert Armstrong, Washington, 1853.

Sage, Dean. The Restigouche and its salmon fishing. D. Douglas, Edinburgh, 1888.

Salmon and Trout Magazine, The. Number 46 (January, 1927), Fishmonger's Hall, London, 1927.

Schwartz, William, ed. Voices for the wilderness. Ballantine Books, New York, 1969.

Scott, Genio C. Fishing in American waters. Harper and Brothers, New York, 1875.

Scott, W. B., Freshwater fishes of eastern Canada. 2nd edition, University of Toronto Press, London, 1954.

Shore, Mackwith. Two months on the Tobique, New Brunswick: an emigrant's Journal, 1851. Smith, Elder, London, 1866.

Simcoe, Mrs. John Graves. The diary of Mrs. John Graves Simcoe. ed., J. Ross Robertson. Facsimile edition, Coles Publishing Company, Toronto, 1973; originally published by William Briggs, Toronto, 1911.

Sleigh, Burrows Willcoks Arthur. Pine forests and Hacmatack clearings. 2nd edition, Richard Bentley, London, 1853.

Sollows, G. C., J. A. Dalziel, J. E. Cheeseman, G. H. Huxter, and H. V. E. Smith. Preliminary survey of the rivers and commercial fishery of northern Labrador. II (Manuscript report 54-1), Resource Development Branch, Department of Fisheries, Halifax, 1954.

Sporting Magazine. 1843 edition, Pittman, London, 1843.

Sports Illustrated. (magazine), Sports Illustrated, Philadelphia, issue for May 25, 1970.

Statutes at large, 1758–1804. (a consolidation of the Acts of the House of Assembly of Nova Scotia to the year 1804).

Statutes of Upper Canada to the Time of the Union. Vol. 1 (Public Acts), Queens Printer, Toronto, 1841.

Stewart, John. An account of Prince Edward Island in the Gulph of St. Lawrence, North America. W. Winchester and Son, London, 1806.

Stewart's Quarterly. Vol. 1, No. 2, Saint John (New Brunswick), 1867.

St. John, Charles. Sketches of the wild sports and natural history of the Highlands. London, 1878.

Storer, D. H. A synopsis of the fishes of North America. Facsimile edition, A. Asher and Co., B. V. Amsterdam, 1972; originally published in 1846.

Talbot, Edward Allen. Five years residence in the Canadas..., 2 Vol., Longman, London, 1824.

Talman, James J. Basic documents in Canadian history. D. van Nostrand Company Inc., Princeton (New Jersey), 1959.

Tolson, Elsie Churchill. The Captain, the Colonel and me. The Tribune Press Limited, Sackville, New Brunswick, 1979.

Townsend, C. W. Along the Labrador coast. D. Estes, Boston, 1907.

Transactions of the Nova Scotia Institute of Natural Science. Nova Scotia Institute of Natural Science, selected volumes published between 1865 and 1866.

Trench, Charles Chenevix. A history of angling. Follett Publishing Company, Chicago, 1974.

Trueman, Stuart. The ordeal of John Gyles. McClelland and Stewart Ltd., Toronto, 1966.

Trumbell, Benjamin. A complete history of Connecticut. Vol. 1, New Haven, 1818.

Uniacke, Richard John. Uniacke's sketches of Cape Breton and other papers relating to Cape Breton Island. (P.A.N.S., Nova Scotia Series), ed., C. Bruce Fergusson, Public Archives of Nova Scotia, Halifax, 1958.

Vieth, Frederick, H. D. A brief report on the conditions of the principal rivers on the south coast of Nova Scotia. Compton and Co., Halifax, 1868.

 Report upon the conditions of the rivers in Nova Scotia (1881–1883). MacLean, Roger and Co., Ottawa, 1884.

 Recollections of the Crimean Campaign.... John Lovell and Son Ltd., Montreal, 1907.

Wadden, R. N. Department of Fisheries of Canada, 1867–1967. Department of Fisheries, Ottawa, 1967; reprinted from the *Annual Review* of the Fisheries Council of Canada (1967), Ottawa, 1967.

Waite, P. B. The life and times of Confederation: 1864–1867. University of Toronto Press, Toronto, 1965.

Wallis, Wilson D., and Ruth Sawtell Wallis. The Micmac Indians of Eastern Canada. University of Minnesota Press, Minneapolis, 1955.

 The Malecite Indians of New Brunswick. (Department of Northern Affairs and Natural Resources Anthropological Series No. 40, Bulletin 18), Queens Printer, Ottawa, 1957.

Walton, Izaak. The compleat angler. Weathervane Books, New York, 1975.

Warburton, Alexander Bannerman. A history of Prince Edward Island. Barnes and Co., Saint John, 1923.

Waterman, Charles, F. Fishing in America. Holt, Rinehart and Winston, New York, 1975.

Webster, J. Clarence. An historical guide to New Brunswick. Revised edition, New Brunswick Government Bureau of Information and Tourist Travel, 1947.

Webster's Third New International Dictionary. ed., Philip Babcock Gove, G. C. Merriman Co., Springfield (Mass.), 1971.

Weeden, William B. Economic and social history of New England. 1620–1789. 2 Vol., Hillary House Publishers Ltd., New York, 1963. A reprint of the 1890 edition.

Weeks, Edward. The Moisie Salmon Club. Barre Publishers, Barre (Massachusetts), 1971.

Wells, Henry P. The American salmon fisherman. Harper and Brothers, New York, 1886.

West, John. The substance of a journal. L. B. Seeley and Son, London, 1827.

Whitelaw, William Menzies. The Maritimes and Canada before Confederation. Oxford University Press, Toronto, 1966.

Wild rivers: Newfoundland and Labrador. Parks Canada, Ottawa, 1977.

Willson, Beckles. Nova Scotia: the province that has been passed by. Constable and Co. Ltd., London, 1911.

 The life of Lord Strathcona and Mount Royal. Cassell, London, 1915.

Wilson, Isaiah. The geography and history of the County of Digby. Halloway Bros., Halifax, 1900.

Witchell, Nicholas. The Loch Ness Story. Penguin Books Ltd., Middlesex (England), 1975.

Wolff, Lee. The Atlantic salmon. Barnes, New York, 1958.

Woodbine Angling Yearbook. (1973 edition), ed., Colin Graham, The Queen Ann Press, London, 1973.

Woodcock, F. Huntly, and W. R. Lewis. Canned foods and the canning industry. Sir Isaac Pitman and Son Ltd., London, 1938.

Wooding, F. H. Canada's Atlantic salmon. (2nd edition), Queens Printer, Ottawa, 1956.

Wright, Esther Clark. The Miramichi. The Tribune Press, Sackville (New Brunswick), 1944.

 The Loyalists of New Brunswick. n.p., Fredericton, 1955.

 The Saint John River and its tributaries. n.p., 1966. People and places I: New Brunswick. Lancelot Press, Windsor (Nova Scotia), 1973.

Wynn Graeme. Timber colony. University of Toronto Press, Toronto, 1981.

Yankee. (magazine), Yankee Inc., Dublin (Vermont), June, 1972.

Young, George R. The British North American Colonies: Letters to the Honorable E. G. S. Stanley, M.P., J. Ridgway and Sons, London, 1934.

Zimmerly, David William. Cain's land revisited. Institute of Social and Economic Research, Memorial University, St. John's, 1975.

II. LIBRARIES AND ARCHIVES

Cambridge Military Library, Halifax, N.S.

Cape Breton Regional Library, Sydney, N.S.

Chaleur Bay Museum, Dalhousie, N.B.
  -Plan of the Town of Dalhousie, 1820
  -Grant to Peter Bonamy, 1788

Desbrisay Museum, Bridgewater, N.S.

Department of Fisheries and Oceans, Maritimes Regional Library, Halifax, N.S.
  -Annual Reports of the Department of Marine and Fisheries

Halifax Memorial Library, Halifax, N.S.

Harriet Irving Memorial Library, Fredericton, N.B.

Izaak Walton Killam Library, Halifax, N.S.
  -Collections of the Massachusetts Historical Society
  -Sporting Magazine

Margaree Salmon Museum, North East Margaree, N.S.

Nova Scotia Legislative Library, Halifax, N.S.
  -Nova Scotia Statute Books
  -Statutes at Large, 1758–1804
  -Journals of the House of Assembly, N.S.
  -Journals of the House of Assembly, Nfld.

New Brunswick Legislative Library, Fredericton, N.B.
  -New Brunswick Statute Books
  -Journals of the House of Assembly, N.B.
  -Census of the Province of New Brunswick, 1861

New Brunswick Museum Archives, Saint John, N.B.
  -Naval Office Records
  -New Brunswick Scrapbook No. 2
  -Jarvis Papers
  -Hazen Papers
  -Gazette

Public Archives of Canada, Ottawa, Ontario
  -Colonial Office Papers
  -Consolidated Laws of Newfoundland, 1892
  -Public Archives of Canada Inventory
  -Maps and Photographs

Public Archives of Nova Scotia, Halifax, N.S.

Public Archives of New Brunswick, Fredericton, N.B.

Public Archives of Prince Edward Island, Charlottetown, P.E.I.
  -Prince Edward Island Statute Books
  -Journals of the House of Assembly of Prince Edward Island
  -The Parliamentary Reporter

St. Francis Xavier University Library, Antigonish, N.S.

Yarmouth Library, Yarmouth, N.S.

III. UNPUBLISHED MANUSCRIPTS AND REPORTS

DeWolfe, Gordon. Economic History of the Saint John Basin

Dunfield, R. W. Nova Scotia Stream Inventory

IV. MISCELLANEOUS

Fisheries Research Board Translation Series, No. 2016, Fisheries Research Board, St. Andrews

CBC Television News, April 13, 1975

W-5 (C.T.V.), April 13, 1975

Letter of G. Paterson, Mount Allison University, to Director General, Dept. of Fisheries and Oceans, Maritimes Region (Letter #10417), March 16, 1979.

V. MAPS   (Specific maps and charts not published in previously mentioned biographical material)

Atlantic Salmon Rivers of New England, International Atlantic Salmon Foundation, New York, 1979
Map of Eastern Part of New France or Canada, Jacques Bellin, 1755, Reprinted by Penn Prints, New York, 1968.
Plan of the River Chibenacadie, 1754, Public Archives of Canada (map section), Ottawa
A Sketch of the River Exploits, 1768, Public Archives of Canada (map section), Ottawa
Plan of the Town of Dalhousie, 1820, Chaleur Area Museum, Dalhousie, N.B.
George Sproules Map of the Scoodic Shore, 1802, Public Archives of Canada (map section), Ottawa